HISTORY OF NATIONS.

DEATH OF SOCRATES

HISTORY OF GREECE

BY

GEORGE GROTE, Esq.

VOL. IX.

REPRINTED FROM THE LONDON EDITION.

THE BRADLEY COMPANY, PUBLISHERS.
NEW YORK

CONTENTS.

VOL. IX.

PART II.

CONTINUATION OF HISTORICAL GREECE.

CHAPTER LXIX.

CYRUS THE YOUNGER AND THE TEN THOUSAND GREEKS.

CHAPTER LXX.

RETREAT OF THE TEN THOUSAND GREEKS.

CHAPTER LXXI

PROCEEDINGS OF THE TEN THOUSAND GREEKS, FROM THE TIME THAT THEY REACHED TRAPEZUS, TO THEIR JUNCTION WITH THE LACEDÆMONIAN ARMY IN ASIA MINOR.

Greek cities on the Euxine — Sinôpê with her colonies Kerasus, Kotyôra, and Trapezus. — Indigenous inhabitants — their relations with the Greek colonists. — Feelings of the Greeks on the Euxine when the Ten Thousand descended among them. — Uncertainty and danger of what they might do. — Plans of the army — Cheirisophus is sent to Byzantium to procure vessels for transporting them. — Regulations for the army proposed by Xenophon during his absence. — Adopted by the army — their intense repugnance to farther marching. — Measures for procuring transports. Marauding expeditions for supplies, against the Colchians and the Drilæ. — The army leave Trapezus, and march westward along the coast to Kerasus. — Acts of disorder and outrage committed by various soldiers near Kerasus. — March to Kotyôra — hostilities with the Mosynœki. — Long halt at Kotyôra — remonstrance from the Sinopians. — Speech of Hekatonymus of Sinôpê to the army — reply of Xenophon — Success of the reply — good understanding established with Sinôpê. —

CHAPTER LXXII.

GREECE UNDER THE LACEDÆMONIAN EMPIRE.

Sequel of Grecian affairs generally — resumed. — Spartan empire — how and when it commenced. — Oppression and suffering of Athens under the Thirty. — Alteration of Grecian feeling towards Athens — the Thirty are put down and the democracy restored. — The Knights or Horsemen, the richest proprietors at Athens, were the great supporters of the Thirty in their tyranny. — The state of Athens, under the Thirty, is a sample of that which occurred in a large number of other Grecian cities, at the commencement of the Spartan empire. — Great power of Lysander — he establishes in most of the cities Dekarchies, along with a Spartan harmost. — Intimidation exercised everywhere by Lysander in favor of his own partisans. — Oppressive action of these Dekarchies. — In some

CHAPTER LXXIII.

AGESILAUS KING OF SPARTA. — THE CORINTHIAN WAR.

Triumphant position of Sparta at the close of the war — introduction of a large sum of gold and silver by Lysander — opposed by some of the Ephors. — The introduction of money was only one among a large train of corrupting circumstances which then became operative on Sparta. — Contrast between Sparta in 432 B. C., and Sparta after 404 B. C. — Increase of peculation, inequality, and discontent at Sparta. — Testimonies of Isokrates and Xenophon to the change of character and habits at Sparta. — Power of Lysander — his arrogance and ambitious projects — flattery lavished upon him by sophists and poets. — Real position of the kings at Sparta. — His intrigues to make himself king at Sparta — he tries in vain to move the oracles in his favor — scheme laid for the production of sacred documents, as yet lying hidden, by a son of Apollo. — His aim at the kingship fails — nevertheless he still retains prodigious influence at Sparta. — Death of Agis, king of Sparta — doubt as to the legitimacy of his son Leotychides. Agesilaus, seconded by Lysandes, aspires to the throne. — Character of Agesilaus. — Conflicting pretensions of Agesilaus and Leotychides. — Objection taken against Agesilaus on the ground of his lameness,— oracle produced by Diopeithes — eluded by the interpretation of Lysander. — Agesilaus is preferred as king — suspicions which always remained attached to Lysander's interpretation. — Popular conduct of Agesilaus — he conciliates the ephors — his great influence at Sparta — his energy, combined with unscrupulous partisanship. — Dangerous conspiracy at Sparta — terror-striking sacrifices. — Character and position of the chief conspirator Kinadon — state of parties at Sparta — increasing number of malcontents. — Police of the ephors — information laid before them. — Wide-spread discontent reckoned upon by the conspirators. — Alarm of the ephors — their manœuvres for apprehending Kinadon privately. — Kinadon is seized, interrogated, and executed — his accomplices are arrested, and the conspiracy broken up. — Dangerous discontent indicated at Sparta. — Proceedings of Derkyllidas and Pharnabazus in Asia. — Persian preparations for reviving the maritime war against Sparta — renewed activity of Konon. — Agesilaus is sent with a land-force to Asia, accompanied by Lysander. — Large plans of Agesilaus, for conquest in the interior of Asia.—General willingness of the Spartan allies to serve in the expedition, but refusal from Thebes, Corinth, and Athens. — Agesilaus compares himself with Agamemnon — goes to sacrifice at Aulis — is contemptuously hindered by the Thebans. — Arrival of Agesilaus at Ephesus — he concludes a fresh armistice with Tissaphernes. — Arrogant behavior and overweening ascendency of Lysander — offensive to the army and to Agesilaus. — Agesilaus hum

CONTENTS.

CHAPTER LXXIV.

FROM THE BATTLE OF KNIDUS TO THE REBUILDING OF THE LONG
WALLS OF ATHENS.

War in Central Greece against Sparta — called the Corinthian war. — Relations of Sparta with the neighboring states and with her allies after the
accession of Agesilaus. Discontent among the allies. — Great power of
Sparta, stretching even to Northern Greece — state of Herakleia. —
Growing disposition in Greece to hostility against Sparta, when she becomes engaged in the war against Persia. — The satrap Tithraustes sends
an envoy with money into Greece, to light up war against Sparta — his
success at Thebes, Corinth, and Argos. — The Persian money did not
create hostility against Sparta, but merely brought out hostile tendencies
pre-existing. Philo-Laconian sentiment of Xenophon. — War between
Sparta and Thebes — the Bœotian war. — Active operations of Sparta
against Bœotia — Lysander is sent to act from Herakleia on the northward — Pausanias conducts an army from Peloponnesus. — The Thebans
apply to Athens for aid — remarkable proof of the altered sentiment in

CHAPTER LXXV

FROM THE REBUILDING OF THE LONG WALLS OF ATHENS TO THE PEACE OF ANTALKIDAS.

Large plans of Konon — organization of a mercenary force at Corinth. —
Naval conflicts of the Corinthians and Lacedæmonians, in the Corinthian
Gulf. — Land-warfare — the Lacedæmonians established at Sikyon — the
anti-Spartan allies occupying the lines of Corinth from sea to sea. — Sufferings of the Corinthians from the war being carried on in their territory. Many Corinthian proprietors become averse to the war. — Growth
and manifestation of the philo-Laconian party in Corinth. Oligarchical
form of the government left open nothing but an appeal to force. — The
Corinthian government forestall the conspiracy by a *coup d'état.* — Numerous persons of the philo-Laconian party are banished ; nevertheless
Pasimêlus the leader is spared, and remains at Corinth. — Intimate
political union and consolidation between Corinth and Argos. — Pasimêlus admits the Lacedæmonians within the Long Walls of Corinth. Battle within those walls. — The Lacedæmonians are victorious — severe loss
of the Argeians. — The Lacedæmonians pull down a portion of the Long
Walls between Corinth and Lechæum, so as to open a free passage across.
They capture Krommyon and Sidus. — Effective warfare carried on
by the light troops under Iphikrates at Corinth — Military genius and
improvements of Iphikrates. — The Athenians restore the Long Walls
between Corinth and Lechæum — expedition of the Spartan king Agesilaus, who, in concert with Teleutias, retakes the Long Walls and
captures Lechæum. — Alarm of Athens and Thebes at the capture of the
Long Walls of Corinth. Propositions sent to Sparta to solicit peace —
The discussions come to no result. — Advantages derived by the Corinthians from possession of Peiræum. At the instigation of the exiles, Agesilaus marches forth with an army to attack it. — Isthmian festival —
Agesilaus disturbs the celebration. The Corinthian exiles, under his protection, celebrate it ; then, when he is gone, the Corinthians from the city
perform the ceremony over again. — Agesilaus attacks Peiræum, which
he captures, together with the Heræum, many prisoners, and much booty.
— Triumphant position of Agesilaus. Danger of Corinth. The Thebans
send fresh envoys to solicit peace — contemptuously treated by Agesilaus.
— Sudden arrival of bad news, which spoils the triumph. — Destruction
of a Lacedæmonian mora by the light troops under Iphikrates. — Daring
and well-planned manœuvres of Iphikrates. — Few of the mora escape to
Lechæum. — The Lacedæmonians bury the bodies of the slain, under
truce asked and obtained. Trophy erected by Iphikrates. — Great effect
produced upon the Grecian mind by this event. Peculiar feelings of Spartans ; pride of the relatives of the slain. — Mortification of Agesilaus —
he marches up to the walls of Corinth and defies Iphikrates — he then
goes back humiliated to Sparta. — Success of Iphikrates — he retakes

HISTORY OF GREECE.

PART II.

CHAPTER LXIX.

CYRUS THE YOUNGER AND THE TEN THOUSAND GREEKS.

IN my last volume, I brought down the History of Grecian affairs to the close of the Peloponnesian war, including a description of the permanent loss of imperial power, the severe temporary oppression, the enfranchisement and renewed democracy, which marked the lot of defeated Athens. The defeat of that once powerful city, accomplished by the Spartan confederacy, — with large pecuniary aid from the young Persian prince Cyrus, satrap of most of the Ionian seaboard, — left Sparta mistress, for the time, of the Grecian world. Lysander, her victorious admiral, employed his vast temporary power for the purpose of setting up, in most of the cities, Dekarchies or ruling Councils of Ten, composed of his own partisans; with a Lacedæmonian Harmost and garrison to enforce their oligarchical rule. Before I proceed, however, to recount, as well as it can be made out, the unexpected calamities thus brought upon the Grecian world, with their eventual consequences, — it will be convenient to introduce here the narrative of the Ten Thousand Greeks, with their march into the heart of the Persian empire and their still more celebrated Retreat. This incident, lying apart from the main stream of Grecian affairs, would form an item, strictly speaking, in Persian history rather than in Grecian. But its effects on the Greek mind, and upon the future course of Grecian affairs, were numerous and important;

while as an illustration of Hellenic character and competence measured against that of the contemporary Asiatics, it stands preeminent and full of instruction.

This march from Sardis up to the neighborhood of Babylon, conducted by Cyrus the younger and undertaken for the purpose of placing him on the Persian throne in the room of his elder brother Artaxerxes Mnemon, — was commenced about March or April in the year 401 b. c.   It was about six months afterwards, in the month of September or October of the same year, that the battle of Kunaxa was fought, in which, though the Greeks were victorious, Cyrus himself lost his life.   They were then obliged to commence their retreat, which occupied about one year, and ultimately brought them across the Bosphorus of Thrace to Byzantium, in October or November, 400 b. c.

The death of king Darius Nothus, father both of Artaxerxes and Cyrus, occurred about the beginning of 404 b. c., a short time after the entire ruin of the force of Athens at Ægospotami.   His reign of nineteen years, with that of his father Artaxerxes Longimanus which lasted nearly forty years, fill up almost all the interval from the death of Xerxes in 465 b. c.   The close of the reigns both of Xerxes and of his son Artaxerxes had indeed been marked by those phenomena of conspiracy, assassination, fratricide, and family tragedy, so common in the transmission of an Oriental sceptre.   Xerxes was assassinated by the chief officer of the palace, named Artabanus, — who had received from him at a banquet the order to execute his eldest son Darius, but had not fulfilled it. Artabanus, laying the blame of the assassination upon Darius, prevailed upon Artaxerxes to avenge it by slaying the latter; he then attempted the life of Artaxerxes himself, but failed, and was himself killed, after carrying on the government a few months. Artaxerxes Longimanus, after reigning about forty years, left the sceptre to his son Xerxes the second, who was slain after a few months by his brother Sogdianus; who again was put to death after seven months, by a third brother Darius Nothus mentioned above.[1]

---

[1] See Diodor. xi, 69; xii, 64–71; Ktesias, Persica, c. 29–45; Aristotel. Polit. v, 14, 8.   This last passage of Aristotle is not very clear.   Compare Justin, x, 1.

For the chronology of these Persian kings, see a valuable Appendix i Mr. Fynes Clinton's Fasti Hellenici, App. 18, vol. ii, p. 313–316.

The wars between the Persian empire, and Athens as the head of the confederacy of Delos (477–449 B. C.), have been already related in one of my earlier volumes. But the internal history of the Persian empire during these reigns is scarcely at all known to us; except a formidable revolt of the satrap Megabyzus, obscurely noticed in the Fragments of Ktesias.[1] About 414 B. C. the Egyptians revolted. Their native prince Amyrtæus maintained his independence, — though probably in a part only, and not the whole, of that country,[2] — and was succeeded by a native Egyptian dynasty for the space of sixty years. A revolt of the Medes, which took place in 408 B. C., was put down by Darius, and subsequently a like revolt of the Kadusians.[3] The peace concluded in 449 B. C., between Athens and the Persian empire, continued without open violation, until the ruinous catastrophe which befel the former near Syracuse, in 413 B. C. Yet there had been various communications and envoys from Sparta to the Persian court, endeavoring to procure aid from the Great King during the early years of the war; communications so confused and contradictory, that Arta xerxes (in a letter addressed to the Spartans, in 425 B. C., and carried by his envoy Artaphernes who was captured by the Athenians), complained of being unable to understand what they meant, — no two Spartans telling the same story.[4] It appears that Pissuthnes, satrap of Sardis, revolted from the Persian king, shortly after this period, and that Tissaphernes was sent by the Great King to suppress this revolt; in which having succeeded, by bribing the Grecian commander of the satrap's mercenary troops, he was rewarded by the possession of the satrapy.[5] We find Tissa-

---

[1] Ktesias, Persica, c. 38–40.

[2] See the Appendix of Mr. Fynes Clinton, mentioned in the preceding note, p. 317.

There were some Egyptian troops in the army of Artaxerxes at the battle of Kunaxa; on the other hand, there were other Egyptians in a state of pronounced revolt. Compare two passages of Xenophon's Anabasis, i, 8, 9; ii, 5, 13; Diodor. xiii, 46; and the Dissertation of F. Ley, Fata et Conditio Ægypti sub imperio Persarum, p. 20–56 (Cologne, 1830).

[3] Xen. Hellen. i, 2, 19; ii, 1, 13.

[4] Thucyd. iv, 50. πολλῶν γὰρ ἐλθόντων πρεσβέων οὐδένα ταὐτὰ λέγειν.

This incompetence, or duplicity, on the part of the Spartan envoys, helps to explain the facility with which Alkibiades duped them at Athens (Thucyd. v. 45). See above, in this History, Vol. VII. ch. lv. p. 47

[5] Ktesias, Persic. c. 52.

phernes satrap in the year 413 B. C., commencing operations
jointly with the Spartans, for detaching the Asiatic allies from
Athens, after her reverses in Sicily; and employing the Spartans
successfully against Amorges, the revolted son of Pissuthnes, who
occupied the strong maritime town of Iasus.[1]

The increased vigor of Persian operations against Athens, after
Cyrus, the younger son of Darius Nothus, came down to the Ionic
coast in 407 B. C., has been recounted in my preceding volume;
together with the complete prostration of Athenian power, accomplished during the ensuing three years.   Residing at Sardis and
placed in active coöperation with Greeks, this ambitious and energetic young prince soon became penetrated with their superior
military and political efficiency, as compared with the native Asiatics.   For the abilities and character of Lysander, the Peloponnesian admiral, he contracted so much admiration, that, when
summoned to court during the last illness of his father Darius in
405 B. C., he even confided to that officer the whole of his tribute
and treasure, to be administered in furtherance of the war;[2] which
during his absence was brought to a victorious close.

Cyrus, born after the accession of his father to the throne, was
not more than eighteen years of age when first sent down to Sardis
(in 407 B. C.) as satrap of Lydia, Phrygia, and Kappadokia, and
as commander of that Persian military division which mustered at
the plain of Kastôlus; a command not including the Ionic Greeks
on the seaboard, who were under the satrapy of Tissaphernes.[3]
We cannot place much confidence in the account which Xenophon
gives of his education; that he had been brought up with his
brother and many noble Persian youths in the royal palace, —
under the strictest discipline and restraint, enforcing modest habits,
with the reciprocal duties of obedience and command, upon all of
them, and upon him with peculiar success.[4]   It is contradicted by
all the realities which we read about the Persian court, and is a
patch of Grecian rather than of Oriental sentiment, better suited
to the romance of the Cyropædia that to the history of the Anabasis.   But in the Persian accomplishments of horsemanship

---

Thucyd. viii, 28.   See Vol. VII, ch. lxi, p. 389 of this History.

Xen Hellen. ii, 1, 14.   Compare Xen. Œconom. iv, 20.

Xen. Anab. i, 1, 2; i, 9, 7; Xen. Hellen. i, 4, 3.

Xen Anab. i, 9, 3–5.   Compare Cyropædia, i, 2, 4–6; viii, 1, 16, etc.

mastery of the bow and of the javelin, bravery in the field, daring as well as endurance in hunting wild beasts, and power of drinking much wine without being intoxicated, — Cyrus stood preëminent; and especially so when compared with his elder brother Artaxerxes, who was at least unwarlike, if not lazy and timid.[1]   And although the peculiar virtue of the Hellenic citizen, — competence for alternate command and obedience, — formed no part of the character of Cyrus, yet it appears that Hellenic affairs and ideas became early impressed upon his mind; insomuch that on first coming down to Sardis as satrap, he brought down with him strong interest for the Peloponnesian cause, and strenuous antipathy to that ancient enemy by whom the Persian arms had been so signally humbled and repressed.   How zealously he coöperated with Lysander and the Peloponnesians in putting down Athens, has been shown in my last preceding volume.[2]

An energetic and ambitious youth like Cyrus, having once learnt from personal experience to appreciate the Greeks, was not slow in divining the value of such auxiliaries as instruments of power to himself.   To coöperate effectively in the war, it was necessary that he should act to a certain extent upon Grecian ideas, and conciliate the good will of the Ionic Greeks; so that he came to combine the imperious and unsparing despotism of a Persian prince, with something of the regularity and system belonging to a Grecian administrator.   Though younger than Artaxerxes, he seems to have calculated from the first upon succeeding to the Persian crown at the death of his father.   So undetermined was the law of succession in the Persian royal family, and so constant the dispute and fratricide on each vacancy of the throne, that such ambitious schemes would appear feasible to a young man of much less ardor than Cyrus.   Moreover he was the favorite son of queen Parysatis,[3] who greatly preferred him to his elder brother Artaxerxes.   He was born after the accession of Darius to the throne, while Artaxerxes had been born prior to that event; and, as this latter consideration had been employed seventy years earlier by

---

[1] Plutarch, Artaxerx. c. 2–6; Xen. Anab. *ut sup.*

[2] See Vol. VIII. ch. lxiv, p. 135.

[3] Darius had had thirteen children by Parysatis; but all except Artaxerxes and Cyrus died young. Ktesias asserts that he heard this statement from Parysatis herself (Ktesias, Persica, c. 49).

queen Atossa[1] in determining her husband Darius son of Hystaspes
to declare (even during his lifetime) her son Xerxes as his intended successor, to the exclusion of an elder son by a different
wife, and born before his accession, — so Cyrus, perhaps, anticipated the like effective preference to himself from the solicitations
of Parysatis. Probably his hopes were farther inflamed by the
fact that he bore the name of the great founder of the monarchy;
whose memory every Persian reverenced. How completely he
reckoned on becoming king, is shown by a cruel act performed
about the early part of 405 B. C. It was required as a part of
Persian etiquette that every man who came into the presence of
the king should immerse his hands in certain pockets or large
sleeves, which rendered them for the moment inapplicable to
active use; but such deference was shown to no one except the
king. Two first cousins of Cyrus, — sons of Hieramenês, (seemingly one of the satraps or high Persian dignitaries in Asia Minor), by a sister of Darius, — appeared in his presence without
thus concealing their hands;[2] upon which Cyrus ordered them both
to be put to death. The father and mother preferred bitter complaints of this atrocity to Darius; who was induced to send for
Cyrus to visit him in Media, on the ground, not at all fictitious,
that his own health was rapidly declining.

If Cyrus expected to succeed to the crown, it was important
that he should be on the spot when his father died. He accordingly went up from Sardis to Media, along with his body guard of
three hundred Greeks, under the Arcadian Xenias; who were so
highly remunerated for this distant march, that the rate of pay was
long celebrated.[3] He also took with him Tissaphernes as an ostensible friend; though there seems to have been a real enmity between them. Not long after his arrival, Darius died; but without
complying with the request of Parysatis that he should declare in

---

[1] Herodot. vii, 4.   [2] Xen. Hellen. ii, 1, 8, 9; Thucyd. viii, 58.

Compare Xen. Cyropæd. viii. 8, 10; and Lucian, Navigium seu Vota, c
30, vol. iii, p. 267, ed. Hemsterhuys with Du Soul's note.

It is remarkable that, in this passage of the Hellenica, either Xenophon
or the copyist, makes the mistake of calling Xerxes (instead of Artaxerxes)
father of Darius. Some of the editors, without any authority from MSS.
wish to alter the text from Ξέρξου to Ἀρταξέρξου.

[3] Xen. Anab. i, 4, 12.

favor of Cyrus as his successor. Accordingly Artaxerxes, being proclaimed king, went to Pasargadæ, the religious capital of the Persians, to perform the customary solemnities. Thus disappointed, Cyrus was farther accused by Tissaphernes of conspiring the death of his brother; who caused him to be seized, and was even on the point of putting him to death, when the all-powerful intercession of Parysatis saved his life.[1] He was sent down to his former satrapy at Sardis, whither he returned with insupportable feelings of anger and wounded pride, and with a determin..u resolution to leave nothing untried for the purpose of dethroning his brother. This statement, given to us by Xenophon, represents doubtless the story of Cyrus and his friends, current among the Cyreian army. But if we look at the probabilities of the case, we shall be led to suspect that the charge of Tissaphernes may well have been true, and the conspiracy of the disappointed Cyrus against his brother, a reality instead of a fiction.[2]

The moment when Cyrus returned to Sardis was highly favorable to his plans and preparations. The long war had just been concluded by the capture of Athens and the extinction of her power. Many Greeks, after having acquired military tastes and habits, were now thrown out of employment; many others were driven into exile, by the establishment of the Lysandrian Dekarchies throughout all the cities at once. Hence competent recruits, for a well-paid service like that of Cyrus, were now unusually abundant. Having already a certain number of Greek mercenaries, distributed throughout the various garrisons in his satrapy, he directed the officers in command to strengthen their garrisons by as many additional Peloponnesian soldiers as they could obtain. His pretext was, — first, defence against Tissaphernes, with whom, since the denunciation by the latter, he was at open war, — next, protection of the Ionic cities on the seaboard, who had been hitherto comprised under the government of Tissaphernes, but had now revolted of their own accord, since the enmity of Cyrus against him had been declared. Miletus alone had been prevented from executing this resolution, for Tissaphernes, reinforcing his garrison in that place, had adopted violent measures of repression, killing or banishing several of the leading men.

Xen. Anab. i, 1, 4.   [2] So it is presented by Justin, v, 11.

Cyrus, receiving these exiled Milesians with every demonstration
of sympathy, immediately got together both an army and a fleet.
under the Egyptian Tamos,[1] to besiege Miletus by land and sea.
He at the same time transmitted to court the regular tribute due
from these maritime cities, and attempted, through the interest of
his mother Parysatis, to procure that they should be transferred
from Tissaphernes to himself. Hence the Great King was deluded
into a belief that the new levies of Cyrus were only intended for
private war between him and Tissaphernes; an event not uncommon between two neighboring satraps. Nor was it displeasing to
the court that a suspected prince should be thus occupied at a distance.[2]

Besides the army thus collected around Miletus, Cyrus found
means to keep other troops within his call, though at a dis
tance and unsuspected. A Lacedæmonian officer named Klearchus, of considerable military ability and experience, presented
himself as an exile at Sardis. He appears to have been banished, (as far as we can judge amidst contradictory statements,)
for gross abuse of authority, and extreme tyranny, as Lacedæmonian Harmost at Byzantium, and even for having tried to
maintain himself in that place after the Ephors had formally dismissed him. The known efficiency, and restless warlike appetite
of Klearchus,[3] procured for him the confidence of Cyrus, who gave
him the large sum of ten thousand Darics, (about £7600), which
he employed in levying an army of mercenary Greeks for the
defence of the Grecian cities in the Chersonese against the Thracian tribes in their neighborhood; thus maintaining the troops until

---

[1] Xen. Anab. i, 1, 6; i, 4, 2.

[2] Xen. Anab. i, 1, 7, 8, ὥστε οὐδὲν ἤχθετο (the king) αὐτῶν πολεμούντων.

[3] Xen. Anab. i, 1, 9; ii, 6, 3. The statements here contained do not
agree with Diodor. xiv, 12; while both of them differ from Isokrates (Orat
viii, De Pace, s. 121; Or. xii, Panath. s. 111), and Plutarch, Artaxerxes.
c. 6.

I follow partially the narrative of Diodorus, so far as to suppose that the
tyranny which he mentions was committed by Klearchus as Harmost of
Byzantium. We know that there was a Lacedæmonian Harmost in that
town, named as soon as the town was taken, by Lysander, after the battle of
Ægospotami (Xen. Hellen. ii, 2, 2) This was towards the end of 405 B. C.
We know farther, from the Anabasis, that Kleander was Harmost there w
400 B. C. Klearchus may have been Harmost there in 404 B C.

they were required by Cyrus. Again, Aristippus and Menon, — Thessalians of the great family of the Aleuadæ at Larissa, who had maintained their tie of personal hospitality with the Persian royal family ever since the time of Xerxes, and were now in connection with Cyrus,[1] — received from him funds to maintain a force of two thousand mercenaries for their political purposes in Thessaly, subject to his call whenever he should require them. Other Greeks, too, who had probably contracted similar ties of hospitality with Cyrus by service during the late war, — Proxenus, a Bœotian ; Agias and Sophænetus, Arcadians ; Sokrates, an Achæan, etc., — were also empowered by him to collect mercenary soldiers. His pretended objects were, partly the siege of Miletus ; partly an ostensible expedition against the Pisidians, — warlike and predatory mountaineers who did much mischief from their fastnesses in the south-east of Asia Minor.

Besides these unavowed Grecian levies, Cyrus sent envoys to the Lacedæmonians to invoke their aid, in requital for the strenuous manner in which he had seconded their operations against Athens, — and received a favorable answer. He farther got together a considerable native force, taking great pains to conciliate friends as well as to inspire confidence. " He was straightforward and just, like a candidate for command," — to use the expression of Herodotus respecting the Median Dëiokês ;[2] maintaining order and security throughout his satrapy, and punishing evil doers in great numbers, with the utmost extremity of rigor ; of which the public roads exhibited abundant living testimony, in the persons of mutilated men, deprived of their hands, feet, or eyesight.[3] But he was also exact in rewarding faithful service,

---

[1] Xen. Anab. i, 1, 10 ; Herodot. vii, 6 ; ix, 1 ; Plato, Menon, c. 1, p. 70, c. 11, p. 78 C.

[2] Herodot. i. 96. 'Ο δὲ (Dëiokês) οἷα μνεώμενος ἀρχὴν, ἰθύς τε καὶ δίκαιος ἦν.

Xenoph. Hellen. iii, 1, 1 ; Diodor. xiv, 19.

[3] Xen. Anab. 1, 9, 8. Πολλάκις δ᾽ ἰδεῖν ἦν ἀνὰ τὰς στειβομένας ὁδούς, καὶ ποδῶν καὶ χειρῶν καὶ ὀφθαλμῶν στερουμένους ἀνθρώπους.

For other samples of mutilation inflicted by Persians, not merely on malefactors, but on prisoners by wholesale, see Quintus Curtius, v. 5, 6. Alexander the Great was approaching near to Persepolis, " quum miserabile agmen, inter pauca fortunæ exempla memorandum, regi occurrit. Captivi erant Græci ad quatuor millia ferè, quos Persæ vario suppliciorum modo

both civil and military. He not only made various expeditions
against the hostile Mysians and Pisidians, but was forward in
exposing his own person, and munificent, rewarding the zeal of all
soldiers who distinguished themselves. He attached men to his
person both by a winning demeanor and by seasonable gifts. As
it was the uniform custom, (and is still the custom in the East),
for every one who approached Cyrus to come with a present in
his hand,[1] so he usually gave away again these presents as marks
of distinction to others. Hence he not only acquired the attachment of all in his own service, but also of those Persians whom
Artaxerxes sent down on various pretences for the purpose of
observing his motions. Of these emissaries from Susa, some were
even sent to obstruct and enfeeble him. It was under such orders
that a Persian named Orontes, governor of Sardis, acted, in levying open war against Cyrus ; who twice subdued him, and twice
pardoned him, on solemn assurance of fidelity for the future.[2] In
all agreements, even with avowed enemies, Cyrus kept faith ex
actly ; so that his word was trusted by every one.

Of such virtues, (rare in an Oriental ruler, either ancient or

---

affecerunt. Alios pedibus, quosdam manibus auribusque, amputatis, inus-
tisque barbararum literarum notis, in longum sui ludibrium reservaverant,"
etc. Compare Diodorus, xvii, 69 ; and the prodigious tales of cruelty recounted in Herodot. ix, 112 ; Ktesias, Persic. c. 54–59 ; Plutarch, Artaxerx.
c. 14, 16, 17.

It is not unworthy of remark, that while there was nothing in which the
Persian rulers displayed greater invention than in exaggerating bodily suf-
'ering upon a malefactor or an enemy, — at Athens, whenever any man
was put to death by public sentence, the execution took place within the
prison by administering a cup of hemlock, without even public exposure.
It was the minimum of pain, as well as the minimum of indignity ; as any
one may see who reads the account of the death of Sokrates, given by Plato
at the end of the Phædon.

It is certain, that, on the whole, the public sentiment in England is more
humane now than it was in that day at Athens. Yet an Athenian public
could not have borne the sight of a citizen publicly hanged or beheaded in
the market-place. Much less could they have borne the sight of the prolonged tortures inflicted on Damiens at Paris in 1757 (a fair parallel to the
Persian σκάφευσις described in Plutarch, Artaxerx. c. 16), in the presence
of an immense crowd of spectators when every window commanding a
view of the Place de Grève was let at a high pr.ce, and filled by the best
company in Paris.

[1] Xen. Anab. i, 9, 13.   [2] Xen. Anab. i, 6, 6.

modern.) — and of such secret preparations, — Cyrus sought to reap the fruits at the beginning of 401 B. C. Xenias, his general at home, brought together all the garrisons, leaving a bare sufficiency for defence of the towns. Klearchus, Menon, and the other Greek generals were recalled, and the siege of Miletus was relinquished; so that there was concentrated at Sardis a body of seven thousand seven hundred Grecian hoplites, with five hundred light armed.[1] Others afterwards joined on the march, and there was, besides, a native army of about one hundred thousand men. With such means Cyrus set forth, (March or April, 401 B. C.), from Sardis. His real purpose was kept secret; his ostensible purpose, as proclaimed and understood by every one except himself and Klearchus, was to conquer and root out the Pisidian mountaineers. A joint Lacedæmonian and Persian fleet, under the Lacedæmonian admiral Samius, at the same time coasted round the south of Asia Minor, in order to lend coöperation from the sea-side.[2] This Lacedæmonian coöperation passed for a private levy effected by Cyrus himself; for the ephors would not formally avow hostility against the Great King.[3]

The body of Greeks, immortalized under the name of the Ten Thousand, who were thus preparing to plunge into so many unexpected perils, — though embarking on a foreign mercenary service, were by no means outcasts, or even men of extreme poverty. They were for the most part persons of established position, and not a few even opulent. Half of them were Acadians or Achæans.

Such was the reputation of Cyrus for honorable and munificent dealing, that many young men of good family had run away from their fathers and mothers; others of mature age had been tempted to leave their wives and children; and there were even some who had embarked their own money in advance of outfit for other poorer men, as well as for themselves.[4] All calculated on a year's

---

[1] Xen. Anab. i, 2, 2–3   [2] Xen. Hellen. iii, 1, 1.   [3] Diodor. xiv, 21.

[4] Xen. Anab. vi, 4, 8. Τῶν γὰρ στρατιωτῶν οἱ πλεῖστοι ἦσαν οὐ σπάνει βίου ἐκπεπλευκότες ἐπὶ ταύτην τὴν μισθοφορὰν, ἀλλὰ τὴν Κύρου ἀρετὴν ἀκούοντες, οἱ μὲν καὶ ἄνδρας ἄγοντες, οἱ δὲ καὶ προσανελωκότες χρήματα, καὶ τούτων ἕτεροι ἀποδεδρακότες πατέρας καὶ μητέρας, οἱ δὲ καὶ τέκνα καταλιπόντες, ὡς χρήματα αὐτοῖς κτησάμενοι ἥξοντες πάλιν, ἀκούοντες καὶ τοὺς ἄλλους τοὺς παρὰ Κύρῳ πολλὰ καὶ ἀγαθὰ πράττειν. Τοιοῦτοι οὖν ὄντες, ἐπόθουν εἰς τὴν Ἑγγάδα σώζεσθαι. Compare v. 10, 10.

campaign in Pisidia; which might perhaps be hard, but would certainly be lucrative, and would enable them to return with a well-furnished purse. So the Greek commanders at Sardis all confidently assured them; extolling, with the emphasis and eloquence suitable to recruiting officers, both the liberality of Cyrus[1] and the abundant promise of all men of enterprise.

Among others, the Bœotian Proxenus wrote to his friend Xenophon, at Athens, pressing him strongly to come to Sardis, and offering to present him to Cyrus, whom he, (Proxenus,) considered as a better friend to him than his own country;[2]" a striking evidence of the manner in which such foreign mercenary service overlaid Grecian patriotism, which we shall recognize more and more as we advance forward. This able and accomplished Athenian, — entitled to respectful gratitude, not indeed from Athens his country, but from the Cyreian army and the intellectual world generally, — was one of the class of Knights or Horsemen, and is said to have served in that capacity at the battle of Delium.[3] Of his previous life we know little or nothing, except that he was an attached friend and diligent hearer of Sokrates; the memorials of whose conversation we chiefly derive from his pen, as we also derive the narrative of the Cyreian march. In my last preceding chapter on Sokrates, I have made ample use of the Memorabilia of Xenophon; and I am now about to draw from his Anabasis (a model of perspicuous and interesting narrative) the account of the adventures of the Cyreian army, which we are fortunate in knowing from so authentic a source.

---

[1] Compare similar praises of Ptolemy Philadelphus, in order to attract Greek mercenaries from Sicily to Egypt (Theokrit. xiv, 50–59).

[2] Xen. Anab. iii, 1, 4. Ὑπισχνεῖτο δὲ αὐτῷ (Proxenus to Xenophon) εἰ ἔλθοι, φίλον Κύρῳ ποιήσειν· ὃν αὐτὸς ἔφη κρείττωἑαυτῷ νομίζειν τῆς πατρίδος.

[3] Strabo, ix, p. 403. The story that Sokrates carried off Xenophon, wounded and thrown from his horse, on his shoulders, and thus saved his life, — seems too doubtful to enter into the narrative.

Among the proofs that Xenophon was among the Horsemen or Ἱππεῖς of Athens, we may remark, not only his own strong interest, and great skill in horsemanship, in the cavalry service and the duties of its commander, and in all that relates to horses, as manifested in his published works, — but also the fact, that his son Gryllus served afterwards among the Athenian horsemen at the combat of cavalry which preceded the great battle of Mantineia (Diogen Laërt. ii, 54).

On receiving the invitation from Proxenus, Xenophon felt much inclined to comply.   To a member of that class of Knights, which three years before had been the mainstay of the atrocities of the Thirty, (how far he was personally concerned, we cannot say,) it is probable that residence in Athens was in those times not peculiarly agreeable to him.   He asked the opinion of Sokrates ; who, apprehensive lest service under Cyrus, the bitter enemy of Athens, might expose him to unpopularity with his countrymen, recommended an application to the Delphian oracle.   Thither Xenophon went ; but in truth he had already made up his mind beforehand. So that instead of asking, " whether he ought to go or refuse, — he simply put the question, " To which of the gods must I sacrifice, in order to obtain safety and success in a journey which I am now meditating ? "   The reply of the oracle, — indicating Zeus Basileus as the god to whom sacrifice was proper, — was brought back by Xenophon ; upon which Sokrates, though displeased that the question had not been fairly put as to the whole project, nevertheless advised, since an answer had now been given, that it should be literally obeyed.   Accordingly Xenophon, having offered the sacrifices prescribed, took his departure first to Ephesus and thence to Sardis, where he found the army about to set forth. Proxenus presented him to Cyrus, who entreated him earnestly to take service, promising to dismiss him as soon as the campaign against the Pisidians should be finished.[1]   He was thus induced to stay, yet only as a volunteer or friend of Proxenus, without accepting any special post in the army, either as officer or soldier. There is no reason to believe that his service under Cyrus had actually the effect apprehended by Sokrates, of rendering him unpopular at Athens.   For though he was afterwards banished, this sentence was not passed against him until after the battle of Korôneia in 394 B. C., where he was in arms as a conspicuous officer under Agesilaus, against his own countrymen and their Theban allies, — nor need we look farther back for the grounds of the sentence.

Though Artaxerxes, entertaining general suspicions of his brother's ambitious views, had sent down various persons to watch him, yet Cyrus had contrived to gain or neutralize these spies, and

---

[1] Xen. Anab. iii, 1, 4–9 ; v. 9, 22–24.

had masked his preparations so skilfully, that no intimation was conveyed to Susa until the march was about to commence. It was only then that Tissaphernes, seeing the siege of Miletus relinquished, and the vast force mustering at Sardis, divined that something more was meant than the mere conquest of Pisidian freebooters, and went up in person to warn the king; who began his preparations forthwith.[1] That which Tissaphernes had divined was yet a secret to every man in the army, to Proxenus as well as the rest,— when Cyrus, having confided the provisional management of his satrapy to some Persian kinsmen, and to his admiral the Egyptian Tamos, commenced his march in a south-easterly direction from Sardis, through Lydia and Phrygia.[2] Three days' march, a distance stated at twenty-two parasangs,[3] brought him to

---

[1] Xen. Anab. i, 2, 4; ii, 3, 19.

Diodorus (xiv, 11) citing from Ephorus affirms that the first revelation to Artaxerxes was made by Pharnabazus, who had learnt it from the acuteness of the Athenian exile Alkibiades. That the latter should have had any concern in it, appears improbable. But Diodorus on more than one occasion, confounds Pharnabazus and Tissaphernes.

[2] Diodor. xiv, 19.

[3] The parasang was a Persian measurement of length, but according to Strabo, not of uniform value in all parts of Asia; in some parts, held equivalent to thirty stadia, in others to forty, in others to sixty (Strabo, xi, p. 518; Forbiger, Handbuch der Alten Geograph. vol. i, p. 555). This variability of meaning is no way extraordinary, when we recollect the difference between English, Irish, and German miles, etc.

Herodotus tells us distinctly what *he* meant by a parasang, and what the Persian government of his day recognized as such in their measurement of the great road from Sardis to Susa, as well as in their measurements of territory for purposes of tribute (Herod. v, 53; vi, 43). It was thirty Greek stadia = nearly three and a half English miles, or nearly three geographical miles. The distance between every two successive stations, on the road from Sardis to Susa, (which was "all inhabited and all secure," διὰ οἰκεομένης τε ἄπασα καὶ ἀσφολέος), would seem to have been measured and marked in parasangs and fractions of a parasang. It seems probable, from the account which Herodotus gives of the march of Xerxes (vii, 26), that this road passed from Kappadokia and across the river Halys, through Kelænæ and Kolossæ to Sardis; and therefore that the road which Cyrus took for his march, from Sardis at least as far as Kelænæ, must have been so measured and marked.

Xenophon also in his summing up of the route, (ii, 2, 6; vii, 8, 26) implies the parasang as equivalent to thirty stadia, while he gives for the most part, each day's journey measured in parasangs. Now even at the

the Mæander; one additional march of eight parasangs, after crossing that river, forwarded him to Kolossæ, a flourishing city

---

outset of the march, we have no reason to believe that there was any official measurer of road-progress accompanying the army, like Bæton, ὁ Βηματιστὴς ᾿Αλεξάνδρου, in Alexander's invasion; see Athenæus, x, p. 442, and Geier, Alexandri Magni Histor. Scriptt. p. 357. Yet Xenophon, throughout the whole march, even as far as Trebizond, states the day's march of the army in parasangs; not merely in Asia Minor, where there were roads, but through the Arabian desert between Thapsakus and Pylæ, — through the snows of Armenia, — and through the territory of the barbarous Chalybes. He tells us that in the desert of Arabia they marched ninety parasangs in thirteen days, or very nearly seven parasangs per day, — and that too under the extreme heat of summer. He tells us, farther, that in the deep snows of Armenia, and in the extremity of winter, they marched fifteen parasangs in three days; and through the territory (also covered with snow) of the pugnacious Chalybes, fifty parasangs in seven days, or more than seven parasangs per day. Such marches, at thirty stadia for the parasang, are impossible. And how did Xenophon measure the distance marched over?

The most intelligent modern investigators and travellers, — Major Rennell, Mr. Ainsworth, Mr. Hamilton, Colonel Chesney, Professor Koch, etc.. offer no satisfactory solution of the difficulty. Major Rennell reckons the parasangs as equal to 2.25 geogr. miles; Mr. Ainsworth at three geogr. miles; Mr. Hamilton (travels in Asia Minor, c. 42, p. 200), at something less than two and a half geogr. miles; Colonel Chesney (Euphrat. and Tigris, ch. 8, p. 207) at 2.608 geogr. miles between Sardis and Thapsakus — at 1.98 geogr. miles, between Thapsakus and Kunaxa, — at something less than this, without specifying how much, during the retreat. It is evident that there is no certain basis to proceed upon, even for the earlier portion of the route; much more, for the retreat. The distance between Ikonium and Dana (or Tyana), is one of the quantities on which Mr. Hamilton rests his calculation; but we are by no means certain that Cyrus took the direct route of march; he rather seems to have turned out of his way, partly to plunder Lykaonia, partly to conduct the Kilikian princess homeward. The other item, insisted upon by Mr. Hamilton, is the distance between Kelænæ and Kolossæ, two places the site of which seems well ascertained, and which are by the best modern maps, fifty-two geographical miles apart. Xenophon calls the distance twenty parasangs. Assuming the road by which he marched to have been the same with that now travelled, it would make the parasang of Xenophon = 2.6 geographical miles. I have before remarked that the road between Kolossæ and Kelænæ was probably measured and numbered according to parasangs; so that Xenophon, in giving the number of parasangs between these two places, would be speaking upon official authority.

Even a century and a half afterwards, the geographer Eratosthenes found

in Phrygia, where Menon overtook him with a reinforcement ot
one thousand hoplites, and five hundred peltasts, — Dolopes, Ænianes, and Olynthians.   He then marched three days onward to
Kelænæ, another Phrygian city, "great and flourishing," with a
citadel very strong both by nature and art.   Here he halted no
less than thirty days, in order to await the arrival of Klearchus,
with his division of one thousand hoplites, eight hundred Thracian
peltasts, and two hundred Kretan bowmen; at the same time Sophænetus arrived with one thousand farther hoplites, and Sosias
with three hundred.   This total of Greeks was reviewed by

---

it not possible to obtain accurate measurements, in much of the country
traversed by Cyrus (Strabo, ii, p. 73.)

Colonel Chesney remarks, — "From Sardis to Cunaxa, or the mounds of
Mohammed, cannot be much under or over twelve hundred and sixty-five
geographical miles; making 2.364 geographical miles for each of the five
hundred and thirty-five parasangs given by Xenophon between those two
places."

As a measure of distance, the parasang of Xenophon is evidently untrust-
worthy.   Is it admissible to consider, in the description of this march, that
the parasangs and stadia of Xenophon are measurements rather of time
than of space?   From Sardis to Kelænæ, he had a measured road and
numbered parasangs of distance; it is probable that the same mensuration
and numeration continued for four days farther, as far as Keramôn-Agora,
(since I imagine that the road from Kelænæ to the Halys and Kappadokia
must have gone through these two places,) — and possibly it may have continued even as far as Ikonium or Dana.   Hence, by these early marches,
Xenophon had the opportunity of forming to himself roughly an idea of
the time (measured by the course of the sun) which it took for the army to
march one, two, or three parasangs and when he came to the ulterior portions of the road, he called that length of time by the name of one, two, or
three parasangs.   Five parasangs seem to have meant with him a full day's
march; three or four, a short day; six, seven, or eight, a long, or very long
day.

We must recollect that the Greeks in the time of Xenophon had no portable means of measuring hours, and did not habitually divide the day into
hours, or into any other recognized fraction.   The Alexandrine astrono-
mers, near two centuries afterwards, were the first to use ὥρη in the sense
of hour (Ideler, Handbuch der Chronologie, vol. i, p. 239.)

This may perhaps help to explain Xenophon's meaning, when he talks
about marching five or seven parasangs amidst the deep snows of Armenia
I do not however suppose that he had this meaning uniformly or steadily
present to his mind.   Sometimes, it would seem, he must have used the
word in its usual meaning of distance.

Cyrus in one united body at Kelænæ ; eleven thousand hoplites and two thousand peltasts.[1]

As far as Kelænæ, his march had been directed straight towards Pisidia, near the borders of which territory that city is situated So far, therefore, the fiction with which he started was kept up. But on leaving Kelænæ, he turned his march away from Pisidia, in a direction nearly northward ; first in two days, ten parasangs, to the town of Peltæ ; next in two days farther, twelve parasangs, to Keramôn-Agora, the last city in the district adjoining Mysia. At Peltæ, in a halt of three days, the Arcadian general Xenias celebrated the great festival of his country, the Lykæa, with its usual games and matches, in the presence of Cyrus. From Keramôn-Agora, Cyrus marched in three days the unusual distance of thirty parasangs,[2] to a city called Käystru-Pedion, (the plain

---

[1] Xen. Anab. i, 2, 8, 9.   About Kelænæ, Arrian, Exp. Al. i, 29, 2 ; Quint Curt. iii, 1, 6.

[2] These three marches, each of ten parasangs, from Keramôn-Agora to Käystru-Pedion, — are the longest recorded in the Anabasis.   It is rather surprising to find them so ; for there seems no motive for Cyrus to have hurried forward.   When he reached Käystru-Pedion, he halted five days. Koch (Zug der Zehn Tausend, Leipsic, 1850, p. 19) remarks that the three days' march, which seem to have dropped out of Xenophon's calculation, comparing the items with the total, might conveniently be let in here ; so that these thirty parasangs should have occupied six days' march instead of three ; five parasangs per day.   The whole march which Cyrus had hitherto made from Sardis, including the road from Keramôn-Agora to Käystru-Pedion, lay in the great road from Sardis to the river Halys, Kappadokia, and Susa.   That road (as we see by the March of Xerxes, Herodot. vii, 26 ; v, 52) passed through both Kelænæ and Kolossæ ; though this is a prodigious departure from the straight line.   At Käystru-Pedion, Cyrus seems to have left this great road ; taking a different route, in a direction nearly south-east towards Ikonium.   About the point, somewhere near Synnada, where these different roads crossed, see Mr. Ainsworth, Trav. in the Track, p. 28

I do not share the doubts which have been raised about Xenophon's accuracy, in his description of the route from Sardis to Ikonium ; though the names of several of the places which he mentions are not known to us, and their sites cannot be exactly identified.   There is a great departure from the straight line of bearing.   But we at the present day assign more weight to that circumstance than is suited to the days of Xenophon.   Straight roads, stretching systematically over a large region of country, are not of that age ; the communications were probably all originally made, between

of Käystrus), where he halted for five days. Here his repose
was disturbed by the murmurs of the Greek soldiers, who had
received no pay for three months, (Xenophon had before told us
that they were mostly men who had some means of their own),
and who now flocked around his tent to press for their arrears. So
impoverished was Cyrus by previous disbursements, — perhaps
also by remissions of tribute for the purpose of popularizing himself, — that he was utterly without money, and was obliged to put
them off again with promises. And his march might well have
ended here, had he not been rescued from embarrassment by the
arrival of Epyaxa, wife of the Kilikian prince Syennesis, who
brought to him a large sum of money, and enabled him to give to
the Greek soldiers four months' pay at once. As to the Asiatic
soldiers, it is probable that they received little beyond their maintenance.

Two ensuing days of march, still through Phrygia, brought the
army to Thymbrium ; two more to Tyriæum. Each day's march
is called five parasangs[1]. It was here that Cyrus, halting three
days, passed the army in review, to gratify the Kilikian princess
Epyaxa, who was still accompanying the march. His Asiatic
troops were first made to march in order before him, cavalry and
infantry in their separate divisions ; after which he himself in a
chariot, and Epyaxa in a Harmamaxa, (a sort of carriage or
litter covered with an awning which opened or shut at pleasure),
passed all along the front of the Greek line, drawn up separately.
The hoplites were marshalled four deep, all in their best trim ;
brazen helmets, purple tunics, greaves or leggings, and the shields
rubbed bright, just taken out of the wrappers in which they were

---

one neighboring town and another, without much reference to saving of
distance, and with no reference to any promotion of traffic between distant
places.

It was just about this time that King Archelaus began to "cut straight
roads" in Macedonia, — which Thucydides seems to note as a remarkable
thing (ii, 100).

[1] Neither Thymbrium, nor Tyriæum, can be identified. But it seems
that both must have been situated on the line of road now followed by the
caravans from Smyrna to Konieh (Ikonium,) which line of road follows a
direction between the mountains called Emir Dagh on the north-east, and
those called Sultan Γagh on the south-west (Koch, Der Zug der Zehn
Tausend, p. 21, 22).

carried during a mere march.[1] Klearchus commanded on the left, and Menon on the right; the other generals being distributed in the centre. Having completed his review along the whole line, and taken a station with the Kilikian princess at a certain distance in front of it, Cyrus sent his interpreter to the generals, and desired that he might see them charge. Accordingly, the orders were given, the spears were protended, the trumpets sounded, and the whole Greek force moved forward in battle array with the usual shouts. As they advanced, the pace became accelerated, and they made straight against the victualling portion of the Asiatic encampment. Such was the terror occasioned by the sight, that all the Asiatics fled forthwith, abandoning their property, — Epyaxa herself among the first, quitting her palanquin. Though she had among her personal guards some Greeks from Aspendus, she had never before seen a Grecian army, and was amazed as well as terrified; much to the satisfaction of Cyrus, who saw in the scene an augury of his coming success.[2]

---

[1] Εἶχον δὲ πάντες κράνη χαλκᾶ, καὶ χιτῶνας φοινικοῦς, καὶ κνημῖδας, καὶ τὰς ἀσπίδας ἐκκεκαθαρμένας.

When the hoplite was on march, without expectation of an enemy, the shield seems to have been carried behind him, with his blanket attached to it (see Aristoph. Acharn. 1085, 1089–1149); it was slung by the strap round his neck and shoulder. Sometimes indeed he had an opportunity of relieving himself from the burden, by putting the shield in a baggage-wagon (Xen. Anab. i, 7, 20). The officers generally, and doubtless some soldiers, could command attendants to carry their shields for them (iv, 2, 20; Aristoph. l, c.).

On occasion of this review, the shields were unpacked, rubbed, and brightened, as before a battle (Xen. Hell. vii, 5, 20); then fastened round the neck or shoulders, and held out upon the left arm, which was passed through the rings or straps attached to its concave or interior side.

Respecting the cases or wrappers of the shields, see a curious stratagem of the Syracusan Agathokles (Diodor. xx, 11). The Roman soldiers also carried their shields in leathern wrappers, when on march (Plutarch, Lucull. c. 27).

It is to be remarked that Xenophon, in enumerating the arms of the Cyreians, does not mention *breastplates;* which (though sometimes worn, see Plutarch, Dion. c. 30) were not usually worn by hoplites, who carried heavy shields. It is quite possible that *some* of the Cyreian infantry may have had breastplates as well as shields, since every soldier provided his own arms; but Xenophon states only what was common to all.

Grecian cavalry commonly wore a heavy breastplate, but had no shield.

[2] Xen. Anab. i, 2, 16–19.

Three days of farther march, (called twenty parasangs in all)
brought the army to Ikonium, (now Konieh), the extreme city of
Phrygia; where Cyrus halted three days. He then marched for
five days (thirty parasangs) through Lykaonia; which country,
as being out of his own satrapy, and even hostile, he allowed the
Greeks to plunder. Lykaonia being immediately on the borders
of Pisidia, its inhabitants were probably reckoned as Pisidians,
since they were of the like predatory character:[1] so that Cyrus
would be partially realizing the pretended purpose of his expedi
tion. He thus, too, approached near to Mount Taurus, which
separated him from Kilikia; and he here sent the Kilikian prin
cess, together with Menon and his division, over the mountain, by
a pass shorter and more direct, but seemingly little frequented,
and too difficult for the whole army; in order that they might
thus get straight into Kilikia,[2] in the rear of Syennesis, who was
occupying the regular pass more to the northward. Intending
to enter with his main body through this latter pass, Cyrus first
proceeded through Kappadokia (four days' march, twenty-five
parasangs) to Dana or Tyana, a flourishing city of Kappadokia;
where he halted three days, and where he put to death two
Persian officers, on a charge of conspiring against him.[3]

This regular pass over Taurus, the celebrated Tauri-Pylæ or
Kilikian Gates, was occupied by Syennesis. Though a road fit
for vehicles, it was yet three thousand six hundred feet above the
level of the sea, narrow, steep, bordered by high ground on each
side, and crossed by a wall with gates, so that it could not be
forced if ever so moderately defended.[4] But the Kilikian prince,

---

[1] Xen. Anab. iii, 2, 25.

[2] This shorter and more direct pass crosses the Taurus by Kizil-Ches-
meh, Alan Buzuk, and Mizetli; it led directly to the Kilikian seaport-town
Soli, afterwards called Pompeïopolis. It is laid down in the Peutinger
Tables as the road from Iconium to Pompeiopolis (Ainsworth, p. 40 seq.;
Chesney, Euph. and Tigr. ii, p. 209).

[3] Xen. Anab. i, 2, 20.

[4] Xen. Anab. i, 2, 21; Diodor. xiv, 20. See Mr. Kinneir, Travels in
Asia Minor, p. 116; Col. Chesney, Euphrates and Tigris, vol. i, p. 293–354;
and Mr. Ainsworth, Travels in the Track of the Ten Thousand, p. 40 seq.;
also his other work, Travels in Asia Minor, vol. ii. ch. 30, p. 70–77; and
Koch, Der Zug der Zehn Tausend, p. 26–172, for a description of this mem
orable pass.

alarmed at the news that Menon had already crossed the mountains by the less frequented pass to his rear, and that the fleet of
Cyrus was sailing along the coast, evacuated his own impregnable position, and fell back to Tarsus; from whence he again retired, accompanied by most of the inhabitants, to an inaccessible
fastness on the mountains. Accordingly Cyrus, ascending without opposition the great pass thus abandoned, reached Tarsus
after a march of four days, there rejoining Menon and Epyaxa.
Two lochi or companies of the division of Menon, having dispersed on their march for pillage, had been cut off by the natives;
for which the main body of Greeks now took their revenge,
plundering both the city and the palace of Syennesis. That prince,
though invited by Cyrus to come back to Tarsus, at first refused,
but was at length prevailed upon by the persuasions of his wife,
to return under a safe conduct. He was induced to contract an
alliance, to exchange presents with Cyrus, and to give him a
large sum of money towards his expedition, together with a contingent of troops; in return for which it was stipulated that Kilikia
should be no farther plundered, and that the slaves taken away
might be recovered wherever they were found.[1]

It seems evident, though Xenophon does not directly tell us so,
that the resistance of Syennesis, (this was a standing name or
title of the hereditary princes of Kilikia under the Persian crown),
was a mere feint; that the visit of Epyaxa with a supply of
money to Cyrus, and the admission of Menon and his division
over Mount Taurus, were manœuvres in collusion with him; and
that, thinking Cyrus would be successful, he was disposed to support his cause, yet careful at the same time to give himself the
air of having been overpowered, in case Artaxerxes should prove
victorious.[2]

Alexander the Great, as well as Cyrus, was fortunate enough to find this
impregnable pass abandoned; as it appears, through sheer stupidity or reck-
lessness of the satrap who ought to have defended it, and who had not even
the same excuse for abandoning it as Syennesis had on the approach of
Cyrus (Arrian. E. A. ii. 4; Curtius, iii, 9, 10, 11).

[1] Xen. Anab. i, 2, 23–27.

[2] Diodorus (xiv, 20) represents Syennesis as playing a double game,
though reluctantly. He takes no notice of the proceeding of Epyaxa.

So Livy says, about the conduct of the Macedonian courtiers in regard
to the enmity between Perseus and Demetrius, the two sons of Philip II. of

At first, however, it appeared as if the march of Cyrus was
destined to finish at Tarsus, where he was obliged to remain
twenty days. The army had already passed by Pisidia, the
ostensible purpose of the expedition, for which the Grecian troops
had been engaged; not one of them, either officer or soldier,
suspecting anything to the contrary, except Klearchus, who was
in the secret. But all now saw that they had been imposed
upon, and found out that they were to be conducted against the
Persian king. Besides the resentment at such delusion, they
shrunk from the risk altogether; not from any fear of Persian
armies, but from the terrors of a march of three months inward
from the coast, and the impossibility of return, which had so
powerfully affected the Spartan King Kleomenes,[1] a century before; most of them being (as I have before remarked) men of
decent position and family in their respective cities. Accordingly they proclaimed their determination to advance no farther, as
they had not been engaged to fight against the Great King.[2]

Among the Grecian officers, each (Klearchus, Proxenus, Menon, Xenias, etc.) commanded his own separate division, without
any generalissimo except Cyrus himself. Each of them probably
sympathized more or less in the resentment as well as in the
repugnance of the soldiers. But Klearchus, an exile and a mercenary by profession, was doubtless prepared for this mutiny, and
had assured Cyrus that it might be overcome. That such a man
as Klearchus could be tolerated as a commander of free and
non-professional soldiers, is a proof of the great susceptibility of
the Greek hoplites for military discipline. For though he had
great military merits, being brave, resolute, and full of resource
in the hour of danger, provident for the subsistence of his soldiers,
and unshrinking against fatigue and hardship, — yet his look and
manner were harsh, his punishments were perpetual as well as
cruel, and he neither tried nor cared to conciliate his soldiers;
who accordingly stayed with him, and were remarkable for exactness of discipline, so long as political orders required them, —

Macedon: " Crescente in dies Philippi odio in Romanos, cui Perseus indul-
geret, Demetrius summâ ope adversaretur, prospicientes animo exitum
incaut i a fraude fraternâ juvenis — *adjuvandum, quod futurum erat, rati, foven
damque spem potentioris, Perseo se adjungunt,*" etc. (Livy xl, 5).

1 See Herodot. v. 49.   2 Xen. Anab. i, 3, 1.

but preferred service under other commanders, when they could obtain it.[1] Finding his orders to march forward disobeyed, Klearchus proceeded at once in his usual manner to enforce and punish. But he found resistance universal; he himself with the cattle who carried his baggage, was pelted when he began to move forward, and narrowly escaped with his life. Thus disappointed in his attempt at coercion, he was compelled to convene the soldiers in a regular assembly, and to essay persuasion.

On first appearing before the assembled soldiers, this harsh and imperious officer stood for a long time silent, and even weeping; a remarkable point in Grecian manners, — and exceedingly impressive to the soldiers, who looked on him with surprise and in silence. At length he addressed them : " Be not astonished, soldiers, to see me deeply mortified. Cyrus has been my friend and benefactor. It was he who sheltered me as an exile, and gave me ten thousand Darics, which I expended not on my own profit or pleasure, but upon you, and in defence of Grecian interests in the Chersonese against Thracian depredators. When Cyrus invited me, I came to him along with you, in order to make him the best return in my power for his past kindness. But now, since you will no longer march along with me, I am under the necessity either of renouncing you or of breaking faith with him. Whether I am doing right or not, I cannot say ; but I shall stand by you, and share your fate. No one shall say of me that, having conducted Greek troops into a foreign land, I betrayed the Greeks and chose the foreigner. You are to me country, friends, allies; while you are with me, I can help a friend, and repel an enemy. Understand me well ; I shall go wherever you go, and partake your fortune." [2]

This speech, and the distinct declaration of Klearchus that he would not march forward against the King, was heard by the soldiers with much delight; in which those of the other Greek divisions sympathized, especially as none of the other Greek commanders had yet announced a similar resolution. So strong was this feeling among the soldiers of Xenias and Pasion, that two

[1] Xen. Anab. ii, 6, 5–15.

[2] Xen. Anab. i, 3, 2–7. Here, as on other occasions I translate the sense rather than the words.

thousand of them left their commanders, coming over forthwith
with arms and baggage, to the encampment of Klearchus.

Meanwhile Cyrus himself, dismayed at the resistance encountered, sent to desire an interview with Klearchus. But the latter,
knowing well the game that he was playing, refused to obey the
summons. He, however, at the same time despatched a secret
message to encourage Cyrus with the assurance that everything
would come right at last, — and to desire farther that fresh invi-
tations might be sent, in order that he (Klearchus) might answer
by fresh refusals. He then again convened in assembly both his
own soldiers and those who had recently deserted Xenias to join
him. " Soldiers," (said he), we must recollect that we have now
broken with Cyrus. We are no longer his soldiers, nor he our
paymaster; moreover, I know that he thinks we have wronged
him, — so that I am both afraid and ashamed to go near him.
He is a good friend, — but a formidable enemy; and has a powerful force of his own, which all of you see near at hand. This is
no time for us to slumber. We must take careful counsel whether
to stay or go; and if we go, how to get away in safety, as well as
to obtain provisions. I shall be glad to hear what any man has
to suggest."

Instead of the peremptory tone habitual with Klearchus, the
troops found themselves now, for the first time, not merely released
from his command, but deprived of his advice. Some soldiers
addressed the assembly, proposing various measures suitable to
the emergency; but their propositions were opposed by other
speakers, who, privately instigated by Klearchus himself, set forth
the difficulties either of staying or departing. One among these
secret partisans of the commander even affected to take the opposite side, and to be impatient for immediate departure. " If
Klearchus does not choose to conduct us back (said this speaker)
let us immediately elect other generals, buy provisions, get ready
to depart, and then send to ask Cyrus for merchant-vessels, — or
at any rate for guides in our return march by land. If he re-
fuses both these requests, we must put ourselves in marching
order, to fight our way back; sending forward a detachment without delay to occupy the passes." Klearchus here interposed to
say, that as for himself, it was impossible for him to continue in
command; but he would faithfully obey any other commander

who might be elected. He was followed by another speaker, who demonstrated the absurdity of going and asking Cyrus, either for a guide, or for ships, at the very moment when they were frustrating his projects. How could he be expected to assist them in getting away? Who could trust either his ships or his guides? On the other hand, to depart without his knowledge or concurrence was impossible. The proper course would be to send a deputation to him, consisting of others along with Klearchus, to ask what it was that he really wanted; which no one yet knew. His answer to the question should be reported to the meeting, in order that they might take their resolution accordingly.

To this proposition the soldiers acceded; for it was but too plain that retreat was no easy matter. The deputation went to put the question to Cyrus; who replied that his real purpose was to attack his enemy Abrokomas, who was on the river Euphrates, twelve days' march onward. If he found Abrokomas there, he would punish him as he deserved. If, on the other hand, Abrokomas had fled, they might again consult what step was fit to be taken.

The soldiers, on hearing this, suspected it to be a deception, but nevertheless acquiesced, not knowing what else to do. They required only an increase of pay. Not a word was said about the Great King, or the expedition against him. Cyrus granted increased pay of fifty per cent. upon the previous rate. Instead of one daric per month to each soldier, he agreed to give a daric and a half." [1]

This remarkable scene at Tarsus illustrates the character of the Greek citizen-soldier. What is chiefly to be noted, is, the appeal made to their reason and judgment, — the habit, established more or less throughout so large a portion of the Grecian world, and attaining its maximum at Athens, of hearing both sides and deciding afterwards. The soldiers are indignant, justly and naturally, at the fraud practised upon them. But instead of surrendering themselves to this impulse arising out of the past, they are brought to look at the actualities of the present, and take measure of what is best to be done for the future. To return back from the place where they stood, against the wish of

---

[1] Xen. Anab. i, 3, 16–21.

Cyrus, was an enterprise so full of difficulty and danger, that the decision to which they came was recommended by the best considerations of reason. To go on was the least dangerous course of the two, besides its chances of unmeasured reward.

As the remaining Greek officers and soldiers followed the example of Klearchus and his division, the whole army marched forward from Tarsus, and reached Issus, the extreme city of Kilikia, in five days' march, — crossing the rivers Sarus [1] and Pyramus. At Issus, a flourishing and commercial port in the angle of the Gulf so called, Cyrus was joined by his fleet of fifty triremes, — thirty-five Lacedæmonian and twenty-five Persian triremes; bringing a reinforcement of seven hundred hoplites, under the command of the Lacedæmonian Cheirisophus, said to have been despatched by the Spartan Ephors.[2] He also received a farther reinforcement of four hundred Grecian soldiers; making the total of Greeks in his army fourteen thousand, from which

---

[1] The breadth of the river Sarus (Scihun) is given by Xenophon at three hundred feet; which agrees nearly with the statements of modern travellers (Koch, Der Zug der Zehn Tausend, p. 34).

Compare, for the description of this country, Kinneir's Journey through Asia Minor, p. 135; Col. Chesney, Euphrates and Tigris, ii, p. 211; Mr. Ainsworth, Travels in the Track of the Ten Thousand, p. 54.

Colonel Chesney affirms that neither the Sarus nor the Pyramus is fordable. There must have been bridges; which, in the then flourishing state of Kilikia, is by no means improbable. He and Mr. Ainsworth, however, differ as to the route which they suppose Cyrus to have taken between Tarsus and Issus.

Xenophon mentions nothing about the Amanian Gates, which afterwards appear noticed both in Arrian (ii, 6. ii, 7) and in Strabo (xiv, p. 676). The various data of ancient history and geography about this region are by no means easy to reconcile; see a valuable note of Mützel on Quintus Curtius, iii, 17, 7. An inspection of the best recent maps, either Colonel Chesney's or Kiepert's, clears up some of these better than any verbal description. We see by these maps that Mount Amanus bifurcates into two branches, one of them flanking the Gulf of Issus on its western, the other or its eastern side. There are thus two different passes, each called Pylæ Amanides or Amanian Gates; one having reference to the Western Amanus, the other to the Eastern. The former was crossed by Alexander, the latter by Darius, before the battle of Issus; and Arrian (ii, 6; ii, 7) is equally correct in saying of both of them that they passed the Amanian Gates · though both did not pass the same gates.

[2] Diodor. xiv. 21.

are to be deducted the one hundred soldiers of Menon's division, slain in Kilikia.

The arrival of this last body of four hundred men was a fact of some importance. They had hitherto been in the service of Abrokomas (the Persian general commanding a vast force, said to be three hundred thousand men, for the king, in Phœnicia and Syria), from whom they now deserted to Cyrus. Such desertion was at once the proof of their reluctance to fight against the great body of their countrymen marching upwards, and of the general discouragement reigning amidst the king's army. So great, indeed, was that discouragement, that Abrokomas now fled from the Syrian coast into the interior; abandoning three defensible positions in succession — 1. The Gates of Kilikia and Syria. 2. The pass of Beilan over Mount Amanus. 3. The passage of the Euphrates. — He appears to have been alarmed by the easy passage of Cyrus from Kappadokia into Kilikia, and still more, probably, by the evident collusion of Syennesis with the invader.[1]

Cyrus had expected to find the gates of Kilikia and Syria stoutly defended, and had provided for this emergency by bringing up his fleet to Issus, in order that he might be able to transport a division by sea to the rear of the defenders. The pass was at one day's march from Issus. It was a narrow road for the length of near half a mile, between the sea on one side and the steep cliffs terminating mount Amanus on the other. The two entrances, on the side of Kilikia as well as on that of Syria, were both closed by walls and gates; midway between the two the river Kersus broke out from the mountains and flowed into the sea. No army could force this pass against defenders; but the possession of the fleet doubtless enabled an assailant to turn it. Cyrus was overjoyed to find it undefended.[2] And here we cannot but notice the superior ability and forethought of Cyrus as compared with the other Persians opposed to him. He had looked at this as well as at the other difficulties of his march, beforehand, and had provided the means of meeting them; whereas, on the king's side, all the numerous means and opportunities of defence are succes-

---

[1] Xen. Anab. i, 4, 3–5. 'Αβροκόμας δ' οὐ τοῦτο ἐποίησεν ἀλλ' ἐπεὶ ἤκουσε Κῦρον ἐν Κιλικίᾳ ὄντα, ἀναστρέψας ἐκ Φοινίκης, παρὰ βασιλέα ἀπήλαυνεν, etc.

[2] Diodor. xiv.

sively abandoned; the Persians have no confidence, except in vast numbers,— or when numbers fail, in treachery.

Five parasangs, or one day's march from this pass, Cyrus reached the Phœnician maritime town of Myriandrus; a place of great commerce, with its harbor full of merchantmen. While he ‑ested here seven days, his two generals Xenias and Pasion deserted him; privately engaging a merchant vessel to carry them away with their property. They could not brook the wrong which Cyrus had done them in permitting Klearchus to retain under his command those soldiers who had deserted them at Tarsus, at the time when the latter played off his deceitful manœuvre. Perhaps the men who had thus deserted may have been unwilling to return to their original commanders, after having taken so offensive a step. And this may partly account for the policy of Cyrus in sanctioning what Xenias and Pasion could not but feel as a great wrong, in which a large portion of the army sympathized. The general belief among the soldiers was, that Cyrus would immediately despatch some triremes to overtake and bring back the fugitives. But instead of this, he summoned the remaining generals, and after communicating to them the fact that Xenias and Pasion were gone, added, — " I have plenty of triremes to overtake their merchantmen if I chose, and to bring them back. But I will do no such thing. No one shall say of me, that I make use of a man while he is with me, — and afterwards seize, rob, or ill-use him, when he wishes to depart. Nay, I have their wives and children under guard as hostages, at Tralles;[1] but even these shall be given up to them, in consideration of their good behavior down to the present day. Let them go if they choose, with the full knowledge that they behave worse towards me than I towards them." This behavior, alike judicious and conciliating, was universally admired, and produced the best possible effect upon the spirits of the army; imparting a confidence in Cyrus which did much to outweigh the

---

[1] Xen. Anab. i, 4, 6.   To require the wives or children of generals in service, as hostages for fidelity, appears to have been not unfrequent with Persian kings.   On the other hand, it was remarked as a piece of gross obsequiousness in the Argeian Nikostratus, who commanded the contingent of his countrymen serving under Artaxerxes Ochus in Egypt, that he volunteered to bring up his son to the king as an hostage, without being demanded (Theopompus, Frag. 135 [ed. Wichers] ap. Athenæ. vi, p. 252).

prevailing discouragement, in the unknown march upon which they were entering.[1]

At Myriandrus Cyrus finally quitted the sea, sending back his fleet,[2] and striking with his land-force eastward into the interior. For this purpose it was necessary first to cross mount Amanus, by the pass of Beilan; an eminently difficult road, which he was fortunate enough to find open, though Abrokomas might easily have defended it, if he had chosen.[3] Four days' march brought the army to the Chalus (perhaps the river of Aleppo), full of fish held sacred by the neighboring inhabitants; five more days, to the sources of the river Daradax, with the palace and park of the Syrian satrap Belesys; three days farther, to Thapsakus on the Euphrates. This was a great and flourishing town, a centre of commerce enriched by the important ford or transit of the river Euphrates close to it, in latitude about 35° 40′ N.[4] The river,

---

[1] Xen. Anab. i, 4, 7–9.   [2] Diodor. xiv, 21.

[3] See the remarks of Mr. Ainsworth, Travels in the Track of the Ten Thousand, p. 58–61; and other citations respecting the difficult road through the pass of Beilan, in Mützel's valuable notes on Quintus Curtius, iii, 20, 13, p. 101.

[4] Neither the Chalus, nor the Daradax, nor indeed the road followed by Cyrus in crossing Syria from the sea to the Euphrates, can be satisfactorily made out (Koch, Zug der Zehn Tausend, p. 36, 37).

Respecting the situation of Thapsakus, — placed erroneously by Rennell lower down the river at Deir, where it stands marked even in the map an nexed to Col. Chesney's Report on the Euphrates, and by Reichard higher up the river, near Bir — see Ritter, Erdkunde, part x, B. iii; West Asien, p. 14–17, with the elaborate discussion, p 972–978, in the same volume; also the work of Mr. Ainsworth above cited, p. 70. The situation of Thapsakus is correctly placed in Colonel Chesney's last work (Euphr. and Tigr. p. 213), and in the excellent map accompanying that work; though I dissent from his view of the march of Cyrus between the pass of Beilan and Thapsakus.

Thapsakus appears to have been the most frequented and best-known passage over the Euphrates, throughout the duration of the Seleukid kings. down to 100 B. C. It was selected as a noted point, to which observations and calculations might be conveniently referred, by Eratosthenes and other geographers (see Strabo, ii, p. 79–87). After the time when the Roman empire became extended to the Euphrates. the new Zeugma, higher up the river near Bir or Bihrejik (about the 37th parallel of latitude) became more used and better known, at least to the Roman writers.

The passage at Thapsakus was in the line of road from Palmyra to

when the Cyreians arrived, was four stadia, or somewhat less than half an English mile, in breadth.

Cyrus remained at Thapsakus five days. He was now compelled formally to make known to his soldiers the real object of the march, hitherto, in name at least, disguised. He accordingly sent for the Greek generals, and desired them to communicate publicly the fact, that he was on the advance to Babylon against his brother, — which to themselves, probably, had been for some time well known. Among the soldiers, however, the first announcement excited loud murmurs, accompanied by accusation against the generals, of having betrayed them, in privity with Cyrus. But this outburst was very different to the strenuous repugnance which they had before manifested at Tarsus. Evidently they suspected, and had almost made up their minds to, the real truth; so that their complaint was soon converted into a demand for a donation to each man, as soon as they should reach Babylon; as much as that which Cyrus had given to his Grecian detachment on going up thither before. Cyrus willingly promised them five minæ per head (about £19 5s.), equal to more than a year's pay, at the rate recently stipulated of a daric and a half per month. He engaged to give them, besides, the full rate of pay until they should have been sent back to the Ionian coast. Such ample offers satisfied the Greeks, and served to counterbalance at least, if not to efface, the terrors of that unknown region which they were about to tread.

But before the general body of Greek soldiers had pronounced their formal acquiescence, Menon with his separate division was already in the water, crossing. For Menon had instigated his men to decide separately for themselves, and to execute their decision, before the others had given any answer. " By acting thus (said he) you will confer special obligation on Cyrus, and earn corresponding reward. If the others follow you across, he will suppose

Karrhæ in Northern Mesopotamia; also from Seleukeia (on the Tigris below Bagdad) to the other cities founded in Northern Syria by Seleukus Nikator and his successors, Antioch on the Orontes, Seleukeia in Pieria, Laodikeia, Antioch ad Taurum, etc.

The ford at Thapsakus (says Mr. Ainsworth, p. 69, 70) " is celebrated to this day as the ford of the Anezeh or Beduins. On the right bank of the Euphrates there are the remains of a paved causeway leading to the very banks of the river, and continued on the opposite side."

that they do so because you have set the example. If, on the contrary, the others should refuse, we shall all be obliged to retreat but he will never forget that you, separately taken, have done all that you could for him." Such breach of communion, and avidity for separate gain, at a time when it vitally concerned all the Greek soldiers to act in harmony with each other, was a step suitable to tne selfish and treacherous character of Menon. He gained his point, however, completely; for Cyrus, on learning that the Greek troops had actually crossed, despatched Glus the interpreter to express to them his warmest thanks, and to assure them that he would never forget the obligation; while at the same time, he sent underhand large presents to Menon separately.[1] He passed with his whole army immediately afterwards; no man being wet above the breast.

What had become of Abrokomas and his army, and why did he not defend this passage, where Cyrus might so easily have been arrested? We are told that he had been there a little before, and that he had thought it sufficient to burn all the vessels at Thapsakus, in the belief that the invaders could not cross the river on foot. And Xenophon informs us that the Thapsakenes affirmed the Euphrates to have been never before fordable, — always passed by means of boats; insomuch that they treated the actual low state of the water as a providential interposition of the gods in favor of Cyrus; "the river made way for him to come and take the sceptre." When we find that Abrokomas came too late afterwards for the battle of Kunaxa, we shall be led to suspect that he too, like Syennesis in Kilikia, was playing a double game between the two royal brothers, and that he was content with destroying those vessels which formed the ordinary means of communication between the banks, without taking any means to inquire whether the passage was practicable without them. The assertion of the Thapsakenes, in so far as it was not a mere piece of flattery to Cyrus, could hardly have had any other foundation than the fact, that they had never seen the river crossed on foot (whether practicable or not), so long as there were regular ferry-boats.[2]

---

[1] Xen. Anab. i, 4, 12–18.

[2] Xen. Anab. i, 4, 18. Compare (Plutarch, Alexand. 17) analogous expressions of flattery — from the historians of Alexander, affirming that the sea near Pamphylia providentially made way for him — from the inhabitants on the

After crossing the Euphrates, Cyrus proceeded, for nine days' march,[1] southward along its left bank, until he came to its affluent, the river Araxes or Chaboras, which divided Syria from Arabia. From the numerous and well-supplied villages there situated, he supplied himself with a large stock of provisions, to confront the desolate march through Arabia on which they were about to enter, following the banks of the Euphrates still further southward. It was now that he entered on what may be called the Desert, — an endless breadth or succession of undulations, "like the sea," without any cultivation or even any tree; nothing but wormwood and various aromatic shrubs.[2] Here too the astonished Greeks saw, for the first time, wild asses, antelopes, ostriches, bustards, some of which afforded sport, and occasionally food, to the horsemen who amused themselves by chasing them; though the wild ass was swifter than any horse, and the ostrich altogether unapproachable. Five days' march brought them to Korsôtê, a town which had been abandoned by its inhabitants, — probably, however, leaving

---

banks of the Euphrates, when the river was passed by the Roman legions and the Parthian prince Tiridates, in the reign of the Emperor Tiberius (Tacitus, Annal. vi. 37); and by Lucullus still earlier (Plutarch, Lucull. c. 24).

The time when Cyrus crossed the Euphrates, must probably have been about the end of July or beginning of August. Now the period of greatest height, in the waters of the Euphrates near this part of its course, is from the 21st to the 28th of May; the period when they are lowest, is about the middle of November (see Colonel Chesney's Report on the Euphrates, p. 5) Rennell erroneously states that they are lowest in August and September (Expedit, of Xenophon, p. 277). The waters would thus be at a sort of mean height, when Cyrus passed.

Mr. Ainsworth states that there were only twenty inches of water in the ford at Thapsakus, from October 1841 to February 1842; the steamers Nimrod and Nitocris then struck upon it (p. 72), though the steamers Euphrates and Tigris had passed over it without difficulty in the month of May.

- Xenophon gives these nine days of march as covering fifty parasangs (Anab. i, 4, 19). But Koch remarks that the distance is not half so great as that from the sea to Thapsakus; which latter Xenophon gives at sixty-five parasangs. There is here some confusion; together with the usual difficulty in assigning any given distance as the equivalent of the parasang (Koch, Zug der Zehn Tausend, p. 38).

[2] See the remarkable testimony of Mr. Ainsworth, from personal observation, to the accuracy of Xenophon's description of the country even at the present day.

the provision dealers behind, as had before happened at Tarsus, in Kilikia;[1] since the army here increased their supplies for the onward march. All that they could obtain was required, and was indeed insufficient, for the trying journey which awaited them. For thirteen successive days, and ninety computed parasangs, did they march along the left bank of the Euphrates, without provisions, and even without herbage except in some few places. Their flour was exhausted, so that the soldiers lived for some days altogether upon meat, while many baggage-animals perished of hunger. Moreover the ground was often heavy and difficult, full of hills and narrow valleys, requiring the personal efforts of every man to push the cars and waggons at particular junctures; efforts in which the Persian courtiers of Cyrus, under his express orders, took zealous part, toiling in the dirt with their ornamented attire.[2] After these thirteen days of hardship, they reached Pylæ; near the entrance of the cultivated territory of Babylonia, where they seem to have halted five or six days to rest and refresh.[3] There

---

[1] Xen. Anab. i, 2, 24.   [2] Xen. Anab. i, 5, 4–8.

[3] I infer that the army halted here five or six days, from the story afterwards told respecting the Ambrakiot Silanus, the prophet of the army; who, on sacrificing, had told Cyrus that his brother would not fight for ten days (i, 7, 16). This sacrifice must have been offered, I imagine, during the halt — not during the distressing march which preceded. The ten days named by Silanus, expired on the fourth day after they left Pylæ.

It is in reference to this portion of the course of the Euphrates, from the Chaboras southward down by Anah and Hit (the ancient Is, noticed by Herodotus, and still celebrated from its unexhausted supply of bitumen), between latitude 35½° and 34°— that Colonel Chesney, in his Report on the Navigation of the Euphrates (p. 2), has the following remarks : —

"The scenery above Hit, in itself very picturesque, is greatly heightened, as one is carried along the current, by the frequent recurrence, at very short intervals, of ancient irrigating aqueducts; these beautiful specimens of art and durability are attributed by the Arabs to the times of the ignorant. meaning (as is expressly understood) the Persians, when fire-worshippers, and in possession of the world. They literally cover both banks, and prove that the borders of the Euphrates were once thickly inhabited by a people far advanced indeed in the application of hydraulics to domestic purposes, of the first and greatest utility — the transport of water. The greater portion is now more or less in ruins, but some have been repaired, and kept up for use either to grind corn or to irrigate. The aqueducts are of stone, firmly cemented, narrowing to about two feet or twenty inches at top, placed at

was on the opposite side of the river, at or near this point, a flourishing city named Charmandê; to which many of the soldiers

---

right angles to the current, and carried various distances towards the interior, from two hundred to one thousand two hundred yards.

"But what most concerns the subject of this memoir is, the existence of
a parapet wall or stone rampart in the river, just above the several aqueducts. In general, there is one of the former attached to each of the latter
And almost invariably, between two mills on the opposite banks, one of
them crosses the stream from side to side, with the exception of a passage
left in the centre for boats to pass up and down. The object of these sub-
saqueous walls would appear to be exclusively, to raise the water sufficiently
at low seasons, to give it impetus, as well as a more abundant supply to the
wheels. And their effect at those times is, to create a fall in every part of
the width, save the opening left for commerce, through which the water
rushes with a moderately irregular surface. These dams were probably
from four to eight feet high originally; but they are now frequently a bank
of stones disturbing the evenness of the current, but always affording a sufficient passage for large boats at low seasons."

The marks which Colonel Chesney points out, of previous population
and industry on the banks of the Euphrates at this part of its course, are
extremely interesting and curious, when contrasted with the desolation
depicted by Xenophon ; who mentions that there were no other inhabitants
than some who lived by cutting millstones from the stone quarries near, and
sending them to Babylon in exchange for grain. It is plain that the population, of which Colonel Chesney saw the remaining tokens, either had already long ceased, or did not begin to exist, or to construct their dams and
aqueducts, until a period later than Xenophon. They probably began
during the period of the Seleukid kings, after the year 300 B. C. For this
line of road along the Euphrates began then to acquire great importance
as the means of communication between the great city of Seleukeia (on
the Tigris, below Bagdad) and the other cities founded by Seleukus Nikator
and his successors in the North of Syria and Asia Minor — Seleukeia in
Pieria, Antioch, Laodikeia, Apameia, etc. This route coincides mainly
with the present route from Bagdad to Aleppo, crossing the Euphrates at
Thapsakus. It can hardly be doubted that the course of the Euphrates
was better protected during the two centuries of the Seleukid kings (B. C.
300–100, speaking in round numbers), than it came to be afterwards, when
that river became the boundary line between the Romans and the Parthians.
Even at the time of the Emperor Julian's invasion, however, Ammianus
Marcellinus describes the left bank of the Euphrates, north of Babylonia,
as being in several parts well cultivated, and furnishing ample subsistence,
(Ammian. Marc. xxiv, 1). At the time of Xenophon's Anabasis, there was
nothing to give much importance to the banks of the Euphrates north of
Babylonia.

crossed over (by means of skins stuffed with hay), and procured plentiful supplies, especially of date-wine and millet.[1]

It was during this halt opposite Charmandê that a dispute occurred among the Greeks themselves, menacing to the safety of all. I have already mentioned that Klearchus, Menon, Proxenus, and each of the Greek chiefs, enjoyed a separate command over his own division, subject only to the superior control of Cyrus himself. Some of the soldiers of Menon becoming involved in a quarrel with those of Klearchus, the latter examined into the case, pronounced one of Menon's soldiers to have misbehaved, and caused him to be flogged. The comrades of the man thus punished resented the proceeding to such a degree, that as Klearchus was riding away from the banks of the river to his own tent, attended by a few followers only through the encampment of Menon, — one of the soldiers who happened to be cutting wood, flung the hatchet at him, while others hooted and began to pelt him with stones. Klearchus, after escaping unhurt from this danger to his own division, immediately ordered his soldiers to take arms and put themselves in battle order. He himself advanced at the head of his Thracian peltasts, and his forty horsemen, in hostile attitude against Menon's division; who on their side ran to arms, with Menon himself at their head, and placed themselves in order of defence. A slight accident might have now brought on irreparable disorder and bloodshed, had not Proxenus, coming up at the moment with a company of his hoplites, planted himself in military array between the two disputing par-

---

Mr. Ainsworth describes the country on the left bank of the Euphrates, before reaching Pylæ, as being now in the same condition as it was when Xenophon and his comrades marched through it, — "full of hills and narrow valleys, and presenting many difficulties to the movement of an army. The illustrator was, by a curious accident, left by the Euphrates steamer on this very portion of the river, and on the same side as the Perso-Greek army, and he had to walk a day and a night across these inhospitable regions; so that he can speak feelingly of the difficulties which the Greeks had to encounter." (Travels in the Track, etc. p. 81.)

[1] I incline to think that Charmandê must have been nearly opposite Pylæ, lower down than Hit. But Major Rennell (p. 107) and Mr. Ainsworth (p. 84) suppose Charmandê to be the same place as the modern Hit (the Is of Herodotus). There is no other known town with which we can identify it.

ties, and entreated Klearchus to desist from farther assault. The
latter at first refused. Indignant that his recent insult and narrow escape from death should be treated so lightly, he desired
Proxenus to retire. His wrath was not appeased, until Cyrus
himself, apprised of the gravity of the danger, came galloping up
with his personal attendants and his two javelins in hand. " Klearchus, Proxenus, and all you Greeks (said he), you know not
what you are doing. Be assured that if you now come to blows,
it will be the hour of my destruction, — and of your own also,
shortly after me. For if *your* force be ruined, all these natives
whom you see around, will become more hostile to us even than
the men now serving with the King." On hearing this (says
Xenophon) Klearchus came to his senses, and the troops dispersed without any encounter." [1]

After passing Pylæ, the territory called Babylonia began. The
hills flanking the Euphrates, over which the army had hitherto
been passing, soon ceased, and low alluvial plains commenced.[2]
Traces were now discovered, the first throughout their long march,
of a hostile force moving in their front, ravaging the country and
burning the herbage. It was here that Cyrus detected the treason of a Persian nobleman named Orontes, whom he examined in
his tent, in the presence of various Persians possessing his intimate confidence, as well as of Klearchus with a guard of three

---

[1] Xen. Anab. i, 5, 11-17

[2] The commentators agree in thinking that we are to understand by Pylæ
a sort of gate or pass, marking the spot where the desert country north of
Babylonia — with its undulations of land, and its steep banks along the
river — was exchanged for the flat and fertile alluvium constituting Babylonia proper. Perhaps there was a town near the pass, and named after it.

Now it appears from Col. Chesney's survey that this alteration in the
nature of the country takes place a few miles below Hit. He observes —
(Euphrates and Tigris, vol. i, p. 54) — " Three miles below Hit, the remains
of aqueducts disappear, and the windings become shorter and more frequent,
as the river flows through a tract of country almost level." Thereabouts
it is that I am inclined to place Pylæ.

Colonel Chesney places it lower down, twenty-five miles from Hit. Pro
fessor Koch (Zug der Zehn Tausend, p. 44), lower down still. Mr. Ains
worth places it as much as seventy geographical miles lower than Hit
(Travels in the Track of the Ten Thousand, p. 81); compare Ritter, Erd
kunde. West Asien, x, p. 16; xi, pp. 755–763.

thousand hoplites.   Orontes was examined, found guilty, and privately put to death.[1]

After three days' march, estimated by Xenophon at twelve parasangs, Cyrus was induced by the evidences before him, or by the reports of deserters, to believe that the opposing army was close at hand, and that a battle was impending.   Accordingly, in the middle of the night, he mustered his whole army, Greeks as well as barbarians; but the enemy did not appear as had been expected.   His numbers were counted at this spot, and it was found that there were, of Greeks ten thousand four hundred hoplites, and two thousand five hundred peltasts; of the barbarian or Asiatic force of Cyrus, one hundred thousand men with twenty scythed chariots.   The numbers of the Greeks had been somewhat diminished during the march, from sickness, desertion, or other causes.   The reports of deserters described the army of Artaxerxes at one million two hundred thousand men, besides the six thousand horse-guards commanded by Artagerses, and two hundred scythed chariots, under the command of Abrokomas, Tissaphernes, and two others.   It was ascertained afterwards, however, that the force of Abrokomas had not yet joined, and later accounts represented the numerical estimation as too great by one-fourth.

In expectation of an action, Cyrus here convened the generals as well as the Lochages (or captains) of the Greeks; as well to consult about suitable arrangements, as to stimulate their zeal in his cause.   Few points in this narrative are more striking than the language addressed by the Persian prince to the Greeks, on this as well as on other occasions.

" It is not from want of native forces, men of Hellas, that I have brought you hither, but because I account you better and braver than any number of natives.   Prove yourselves now worthy of the freedom which you enjoy; that freedom for which I envy you, and which I would choose, be assured, in preference to all my possessions a thousand times multiplied.   Learn now from me, who know it well, all that you will have to encounter, — vast numbers and plenty of noise; but if you despise these, I am

---

[1] The description given of this scene (known to the Greeks through the communications of Klearchus) by Xenophon, is extremely interesting (Anab. i, 6).   I omit it from regard to space.

ashamed to tell you what worthless stuff you will find in these native men. Behave well, — like brave men, and trust me for sending you back in such condition as to make your friends at home envy you; though I hope to prevail on many of you to prefer my service to your own homes."

"Some of us are remarking, Cyrus, (said a Samian exile named Gaulitês), that you are full of promises at this hour of danger, but will forget them, or perhaps will be unable to perform them, when danger is over...... As to ability, (replied Cyrus), my father's empire reaches northward to the region of intolerable cold, southward to that of intolerable heat. All in the middle is now apportioned in satrapies among my brother's friends; all, if we are victorious, will come to be distributed among mine. I have no fear of not having enough to give away, but rather of not having friends enough to receive it from me. To each of you Greeks, moreover, I shall present a wreath of gold."

Declarations like these, repeated by Cyrus to many of the Greek soldiers, and circulated among the remainder, filled all of them with confidence and enthusiasm in his cause. Such was the sense of force and superiority inspired, that Klearchus asked him, — "Do you really think, Cyrus, that your brother will fight you?...... Yes, by Zeus, (was the reply); assuredly, if he be the son of Darius and Parysatis, and my brother, I shall not win this prize without a battle." All the Greeks were earnest with him at the same time not to expose his own person, but to take post in the rear of their body.[1] We shall see presently how this advice was followed.

The declarations here reported, as well as the expressions employed before during the dispute between Klearchus and the soldiers of Menon near Charmandê — being, as they are, genuine and authentic, and not dramatic composition such as those of Æschylus in the Persæ, nor historic amplification like the speeches ascribed to Xerxes in Herodotus, — are among the most valuable evidences respecting the Hellenic character generally. It is not merely the superior courage and military discipline of the Greeks which Cyrus attests, compared with the cowardice of Asiatics, — but also their fidelity and sense of obligation which he contrasts with the time-serving treachery of the latter;[2] connect-

---

[1] Xen Anab. i, 7, 2-9.   [2] Xen. Anab. i 5, 16.

ing these superior qualities with the political freedom which they enjoy. To hear this young prince expressing such strong admiration and envy for Grecian freedom, and such ardent personal preference for it above all the splendor of his own position, — was doubtless the most flattering of all compliments which he could pay to the listening citizen-soldiers. That a young Persian prince should be capable of conceiving such a sentiment. is no slight proof of his mental elevation above the level both of his family and of his nation. The natural Persian opinion is expressed by the conversation between Xerxes and Demaratus [1] in Herodotus. To Xerxes, the conception of free citizenship, — and of orderly, self-sufficing courage planted by a public discipline, patriotic as well as equalizing, — was not merely repugnant, but incomprehensible. He understood only a master issuing orders to obedient subjects, and stimulating soldiers to bravery by means of the whip. His descendant Cyrus, on the contrary, had learnt by personal observation to enter into the feeling of personal dignity prevalent in the Greeks around him, based as it was on the conviction that they governed themselves and that there was no man who had any rights of his own over them, — that the law was their only master, and that in rendering obedience to it they were working for no one else but for themselves.[2] Cyrus knew where to touch the sentiment of Hellenic honor, so fatally extinguished after the Greeks lost their political freedom by the hands

---

[1] See Herodot. vii, 102, 103, 209. Compare the observations of the Persian Achæmenês, c. 236.

[2] Herod. vii, 104. Demaratus says to Xerxes, respecting the Lacedæmonians — Ἐλεύθεροι γὰρ ἐόντες, οὐ πάντα ἐλεύθεροί εἰσι· ἔπεστι γάρ σφι δεσπότης, νόμος, τὸν ὑποδειμαίνουσι πολλῷ μᾶλλον ἢ οἱ σοὶ σέ.

Again, the historian observes about the Athenians, and their extraordinary increase of prowess after having shaken off the despotism of Hippias (v. 78) —Δηλοῖ δ' οὐ καθ' ἓν μόνον ἀλλὰ πανταχοῦ, ἡ ἰσηγορίη ὡς ἐστι χρῆμα σπουδαῖον· εἰ καὶ Ἀθηναῖοι τυραννευόμενοι μὲν, οὐδαμῶν τῶν σφέας περιοικεόντων ἦσαν τὰ πολέμια ἀμείνους, ἀπαλλαχθέντες δέ τυράννων, μακρῷ πρῶτοι ἐγένοντο. Δηλοῖ ὦν ταῦτα, ὅτι κατεχόμενοι μὲν ἐθελοκακεέον, ὡς δεσπότῃ ἐργαζόμενοι· ἐλευθερωθέντων δὲ, αὐτὸς ἕκαστος ἑωϋτῷ προθυμέετο ἐργάζεσθαι.

Compare Menander, Fragm. Incert. CL. ap. Meineke, Fragr Comm Græc. vol. iv. p. 268 —

Ἐλεύθερος πᾶς ἑνὶ δεδούλωται, νόμῳ·
Δυσὶν δὲ δοῦλος, καὶ νόμῳ καὶ δεσπότῃ.

of the Macedonians, and exchanged for that intellectual quickness, combined with moral degeneracy, which Cicero and his contemporaries remark as the characteristic of these once high-toned communities.

Having concerted the order of battle with the generals, Cyrus marched forward in cautious array during the next day, anticipating the appearance of the king's forces. Nothing of the kind was seen, however, though abundant marks of their retiring footsteps were evident. The day's march, (called three parasangs) having been concluded without a battle, Cyrus called to him the Ambrakiotic prophet Silanus, and presented him with three thousand darics or ten Attic talents. Silanus had assured him, on the eleventh day preceding, that there would be no action in ten days from that time; upon which Cyrus had told him, — "If your prophecy comes true, I will give you three thousand darics. My brother will not fight at all, if he does not fight within ten days."[1]

In spite of the strong opinion which he had expressed in reply to Klearchus, Cyrus now really began to conceive that no battle would be hazarded by his enemies; especially as in the course of this last day's march, he came to a broad and deep trench (thirty feet broad and eighteen feet deep), approaching so near to the Euphrates as to leave an interval of only twenty feet for passage. This trench had been dug by order of Artaxerxes across the plain, for a length said to be of twelve parasangs (about forty-two English miles, if the parasang be reckoned at thirty stadia), so as to touch at its other extremity what was called the walls of Media.[2] It had been dug as a special measure

---

[1] Xen. Anab. i, 7, 14–17.

[2] From Pylæ to the undefended trench, there intervened three entire days of march, and one part of a day; for it occurred in the fourth day's march.

Xenophon calls the three entire days, twelve parasangs in all. This argues short marches, not full marches. And it does not seem that the space of ground traversed during any one of them can have been considerable. For they were all undertaken with visible evidences of an enemy immediately in front of them; which circumstance was the occasion of the treason of Orontes, who asked Cyrus for a body of cavalry, under pretence of attacking the light troops of the enemy in front, and then wrote a letter to inform Artaxerxes that he was about to desert with his division. The letter was delivered to Cyrus, who thus discovered the treason.

of defence against the approaching invaders. Yet we hear with surprise, and the invaders themselves found with equal surprise, that not a man was on the spot to defend it ; so that the whole Cyreian army and baggage passed without resistance through the narrow breadth of twenty feet. This is the first notice of any defensive measures taken to repel the invasion, — except the precaution of Abrokomas in burning the boats at Thapsakus. Cyrus had been allowed to traverse all this immense space, and to pass through so many defensible positions, without having yet struck a blow. And now Artaxerxes, after having cut a prodigious extent of trench at the cost of so much labor, — provided a valuable means of resistance, especially against Grecian heavy-armed

---

Marching with a known enemy not far off in front, Cyrus must have kept his army in something like battle order, and therefore must have moved slowly. Moreover the discovery of the treason of Orontes must itself have been an alarming fact, well calculated to render both Cyrus and Klearchus doubly cautious for the time. And the very trial of Orontes appears to have been conducted under such solemnities as must have occasioned a halt of the army.

Taking these circumstances, we can hardly suppose the Greeks to have got over so much as thirty English miles of ground in the three entire days of march. The fourth day they must have got over very little ground indeed; not merely because Cyrus was in momentary expectation of the King's main army, and of a general battle (i, 7, 14), but because of the great delay necessary for passing the trench. His whole army (more than one hundred thousand men), with baggage, chariots, etc., had to pass through the narrow gut of twenty feet wide between the trench and the Euphrates. He can hardly have made more than five miles in this whole day's march, getting at night so far as to encamp two or three miles beyond the trench. We may therefore reckon the distance marched over between Pylæ and the trench as about thirty-two miles in all; and two or three miles farther to the encampment of the next night. Probably Cyrus would keep near the river, yet not following its bends with absolute precision ; so that in estimating distance, we ought to take a mean between the straight line and the full windings of the river.

I conceive the trench to have cut the Wall of Media at a much wider angle than appears in Col. Chesney's map ; so that the triangular space included between the trench, the Wall, and the river, was much more extensive. The reason, we may presume, why the trench was cut, was, to defend that portion of the well-cultivated and watered country of Babylonia which lay outside of the Wall of Media — which portion (as we shall see hereafter in the marches of the Greeks after the battle) was very considerable.

soldiers, — and occupied it seemingly until the very last moment,—
throws it up from some unaccountable panic, and suffers a whole
army to pass unopposed through this very narrow gut.   Having
surmounted unexpectedly so formidable an obstacle, Cyrus as well
as the Greeks imagined that Artaxerxes would never think of
fighting in the open plain.   All began to relax in that careful array
which had been observed since the midnight review, insomuch that
he himself proceeded in his chariot instead of on horseback, while
many of the Greek soldiers lodged their arms on the waggons or
beasts of burden.[1]

On the next day but one after passing the undefended trench,
they were surprised, at a spot called Kunaxa,[2] just when they were
about to halt for the mid-day meal and repose, by the sudden in-

---

[1] Xen. Anab. i, 7, 20.   The account given by Xenophon of this long line
of trench, first dug by order of Artaxerxes, and then left useless and undefended, differs from the narrative of Diodorus (xiv, 22), which seems to be
borrowed from Ephorus.   Diodorus says that the king caused a long trench
to be dug, and lined with carriages and waggons as a defence for his baggage ; and that he afterwards marched forth from this entrenchment, with
his soldiers free and unincumbered, to give battle to Cyrus.   This is a
statement more plausible than that of Xenophon, in this point of view, that
it makes out the king to have acted upon a rational scheme; whereas in
Xenophon he appears at first to have adopted a plan of defence, and then
to have renounced it, after immense labor and cost, without any reason, so
far as we can see.   Yet I have no doubt that the account of Xenophon is
the true one.   The narrow passage, and the undefended trench, were both
facts of the most obvious and impressive character to an observing soldier.

[2] Xenophon does not mention the name Kunaxa, which comes to us from
Plutarch (Artaxerx. c. 8), who states that it was five hundred stadia (about
fifty-eight miles) from Babylon ; while Xenophon was informed that the
field of battle was distant from Babylon only three hundred and sixty
stadia.   Now, according to Colonel Chesney (Euphrates and Tigris, vol. i,
p. 57), Hillah (Babylon) is distant ninety-one miles by the river, or sixty-
one and a half miles direct, from Felujah.   Following therefore the distance given by Plutarch (probably copied from Ktesias), we should place
Kunaxa a little lower down the river than Felujah.   This seems the most
probable supposition.

Rennell and Mr. Baillie Fraser so place it (Mesopotamia and Assyria, p.
186, Edin. 1842), I think rightly ; moreover the latter remarks, what most
of the commentators overlook, that the Greeks did not pass through the
Wall of Media until long after the battle.   See a note a little below, near
the beginning of my next chapter, in reference to that Wall.

timation that the king's army was approaching in order of battle on the open plain. Instantly Cyrus hastened to mount on horseback, to arm himself, and to put his forces in order, while the Greeks on their side halted and formed their line with all possible speed.[1] They were on the right wing of the army, adjoining the river Euphrates; Ariæus with the Asiatic forces being on the left, and Cyrus himself, surrounded by a body-guard of six hundred well-armed Persian horsemen, in the centre. Among the Greeks, Klearchus commanded the right division of hoplites, with Paphlagonian horsemen and the Grecian peltasts on the extreme right, close to the river; Proxenus with his division stood next; Menon commanded on the left. All the Persian horsemen around Cyrus had breastplates, helmets, short Grecian swords, and two javelins in their right hands; the horses also were defended by facings both over the breast and head. Cyrus himself, armed generally like the rest, stood distinguished by having an upright tiara instead of the helmet. Though the first news had come upon them by surprise, the Cyreians had ample time to put themselves in complete order; for the enemy did not appear until the afternoon was advanced. First, was seen dust, like a white cloud, — next, an undefined dark spot, gradually nearing, until the armor began to shine, and the component divisions of troops, arranged in dense masses, became discernible. Tissaphernes was on the left, opposite to the Greeks, at the head of the Persian horsemen, with white cuirasses; on his right, stood the Persian bowmen, with their

---

[1] The distance of the undefended trench from the battle-field of Kunaxa would be about twenty-two miles. First, three miles beyond the trench, to the first night-station; next, a full day's march, say twelve miles; thirdly, a half day's march, to the time of the mid-day halt, say seven miles.

The distance from Pylæ to the trench having before been stated at thirty-two miles, the whole distance from Pylæ to Kunaxa will be about fifty-four miles.

Now Colonel Chesney has stated the distance from Hit to Felujah Castle (two known points) at forty-eight miles of straight line, and seventy-seven miles, if following the line of the river. Deduct four miles for the distance from Hit to Pylæ, and we shall then have between Pylæ and Felujah, a rectilinear distance of forty-four miles. The marching route of the Greeks (as explained in the previous note, the Greeks following generally, but not exactly, the windings of the river) will give fifty miles from Pylæ to Felujah, and fifty-three or fifty-four from Pylæ to Kunaxa.

gerrha, or wicker shields, spiked so as to be fastened in the ground
while arrows were shot from behind them; next, the Egyptian
infantry with long wooden shields covering the whole body and
legs.   In front of all was a row of chariots with scythes attached
to the wheels, destined to begin the charge against the Grecian
phalanx.[1]

As the Greeks were completing their array, Cyrus rode to the
front, and desired Klearchus to make his attack with the Greeks
upon the centre of the enemy; since it was there that the king in
person would be posted, and if that were once beaten, the victory
was gained.   But such was the superiority of Artaxerxes in numbers, that his centre extended beyond the left of Cyrus.   Accordingly Klearchus, afraid of withdrawing his right from the river,
lest he should be taken both in flank and rear, chose to keep his
position on the right, — and merely replied to Cyrus, that he would
manage everything for the best.   I have before remarked[2] how
often the fear of being attacked on the unshielded side and on the
rear, led the Greek soldier into movements inconsistent with military expediency; and it will be seen presently that Klearchus,
blindly obeying this habitual rule of precaution, was induced here
to commit the capital mistake of keeping on the right flank, contrary to the more judicious direction of Cyrus.[3]   The latter continued for a short time riding slowly in front of the lines, looking
alternately at the two armies, when Xenophon, one of the small
total of Grecian horsemen, and attached to the division of Proxenus, rode forth from the line to accost him, asking if he had any
orders to give.   Cyrus desired him to proclaim to every one that
the sacrifices were favorable.   Hearing a murmur going through
the Grecian ranks, he inquired from Xenophon what it was; and
received for answer, that the watchword was now being passed
along for the second time.   He asked, with some surprise, who
gave the watchword? and what it was?   Xenophon replied that
it was "Zeus the Preserver, and Victory." — "I accept it," replied Cyrus; "let that be the word;" and immediately rode away
to his own post in the centre, among the Asiatics.

---

[1] Xen. Anab. i, 8, 8–11.

[2] Thucyd. v. 70.   See Vol. VII, ch. lvi, p. 84 of this History.

[3] Plutarch (Artaxerx. c. 8) makes this criticism upon Klearchus; and it
seems quite just.

The vast host of Artaxerxes, advancing steadily and without noise, were now within less than half a mile of the Cyreians, when the Greek troops raised the pæan or usual war-cry, and began to move forward. As they advanced, the shout became more vehement, the pace accelerated, and at last the whole body got into a run.[1] This might have proved unfortunate, had their opponents been other than Grecian hoplites; but the Persians did not stand to await the charge. They turned and fled, when the assailants were yet hardly within bow-shot. Such was their panic, that even the drivers of the scythed chariots in front, deserting their teams, ran away along with the rest; while the horses, left to themselves, rushed apart in all directions, some turning round to follow the fugitives, others coming against the advancing Greeks, who made open order to let them pass. The left division of the king's army was thus routed without a blow, and seemingly without a man killed on either side; one Greek only being wounded by an arrow, and another by not getting out of the way of one of the chariots.[2] Tissaphernes alone, — who, with the body of horse immediately around him, was at the extreme Persian left, close to the river, — formed an exception to this universal flight. He charged and penetrated through the Grecian peltasts, who stood opposite to him between the hoplites and the river. These peltasts, commanded by Episthenes of Amphipolis, opened their ranks to let him pass, darting at the men as they rode by, yet without losing any one themselves. Tissaphernes thus got into the rear of the Greeks, who continued, on their side, to pursue the flying Persians before them.[3]

Matters proceeded differently in the other parts of the field. Artaxerxes, though in the centre of his own army, yet from his superior numbers outflanked Ariæus, who commanded the extreme left of the Cyreians.[4] Finding no one directly opposed to him, he began to wheel round his right wing, to encompass his enemies; not noticing the flight of his left division. Cyrus, on the other hand, when he saw the easy victory of the Greeks on their side, was overjoyed; and received from every one around him salutations, as if he were already king. Nevertheless, he had self-command

---

[1] Xen. Anab. i, 8, 17; Diodor. xiv, 23.   [2] Xen. Anab. i, 8, 17–20.
[3] Xen. Anab i, 10, 4–8.   Xen. Anab. i, 8, 23; i, 9 31

enough not yet to rush forward as if the victory was already gained,[1] but remained unmoved, with his regiment of six hundred horse around him, watching the movements of Artaxerxes. As soon as he saw the latter wheeling round his right division to get upon the rear of the Cyreians, he hastened to check this move ment by an impetuous charge upon the centre, where Artaxerxes was in person, surrounded by the body-guard of six thousand horse, under Artagerses. So vigorous was the attack of Cyrus, that with his six hundred horse, he broke and dispersed this body-guard, killing Artagerses with his own hand. His own six hundred horse rushed forward in pursuit of the fugitives, leaving Cyrus himself nearly alone, with only the select few, called his "Table-Companions," around him. It was under these circumstances that he first saw his brother Artaxerxes, whose person had been ex-posed to view by the flight of the body-guards. The sight filled him with such a paroxysm of rage and jealous ambition,[2] that he lost all thought of safety or prudence,— cried out, " I see the man," — and rushed forward with his mere handful of companions to attack Artaxerxes, in spite of the numerous host behind him. Cyrus made directly at his brother, darting his javelin with so true an aim as to strike him in the breast, and wound him through the cuirass ; though the wound (afterwards cured by the Greek surgeon Ktesias) could not have been very severe, since Artaxerxes did not quit the field, but, on the contrary, engaged in personal com-bat, he and those around him, against this handful of assailants. So unequal a combat did not last long. Cyrus, being severely wounded under the eye by the javelin of a Karian soldier, was cast from his horse and slain. The small number of faithful com-

---

[1] Xen. Anab. i, 8, 21.

Κῦρος δὲ, ὁρῶν τοὺς Ἕλληνας νικῶντας τὸ καθ᾽ αὑτοὺς καὶ διώκοντας, ἡδό-μενος καὶ προσκυνούμενος ἤδη ὡς βασιλεὺς ὑπὸ τῶν ἀμφ᾽ αὑτὸν, οὐδ᾽ ὡς ἐξήχ-θη διώκειν, etc.

The last words are remarkable, as indicating that no other stimulus ex-cept that of ambitious rivalry and fraternal antipathy, had force enough to overthrow the self-command of Cyrus.

[2] Compare the account of the transport of rage which seized the Theban Pelopidas, when he saw Alexander the despot of Pheræ in the opposite army; which led to the same fatal consequences (Plutarch, Pelopidas, c. 32; Cornel. Nepos, Pelop. c. 5). See also the reflections of Xenophon on the conduct of Teleutas before Olynthus. — Hellenic. v. 3, 7.

panions around him all perished in his defence. Artasyras, who stood first among them in his confidence and attachment, seeing him mortally wounded and fallen, cast himself down upon him, clasped him in his arms, and in this position either slew himself, or was slain by order of the king.[1]

The head and the right hand of the deceased prince were immediately cut off by order of Artaxerxes, and doubtless exhibited conspicuously to view. This was a proclamation to every one that the entire contest was at an end; and so it was understood by Ariæus, who, together with all the Asiatic troops of Cyrus, deserted the field and fled back to the camp. Not even there did they defend themselves, when the king and his forces pursued them; but fled yet farther back to the resting-place of the previous night. The troops of Artaxerxes got into the camp and began to plunder it without resistance. Even the harem of Cyrus fell into their power. It included two Grecian women, — of free condition, good family, and education, — one from Phokæa, the other from Miletus, brought to him, by force, from their parents to Sardis. The elder of these two, the Phokæan, named Milto, distinguished alike

---

· Xen. Anab. i, 8, 22–29. The account of this battle and of the death of Cyrus by Ktesias (as far as we can make it out from the brief abstract in Photius — Ktesias, Fragm. c. 58, 59, ed. Bähr) does not differ materially from Xenophon. Ktesias mentions the Karian soldier (not noticed by Xenophon) who hurled the javelin; and adds that this soldier was afterwards tortured and put to death by Queen Parysatis, in savage revenge for the death of Cyrus. He also informs us that Bagapatês, the person who by order of Artaxerxes cut off the head and hand of Cyrus, was destroyed by her in the same way.

Diodorus (xiv, 23) dresses up a much fuller picture of the conflict between Cyrus and his brother, which differs on many points, partly direct and partly implied, from Xenophon.

Plutarch (Artaxerxes, c. 11, 12, 13) gives an account of the battle, and of the death of Cyrus, which he professes to have derived from Ktesias, but which differs still more materially from the narrative in Xenophon. Compare also the few words of Justin, v, 11.

Diodorus (xiv, 24) says that twelve thousand men were slain of the king's army at Kunaxa; the greater part of them by the Greeks under Klearchus, who did not lose a single man. He estimates the loss of Cyrus's Asiatic army at three thousand men. But as the Greeks did not lose a man, so they can hardly have killed many in the pursuit; for they had scarcely any cavalry, and no great number of peltasts, — while hoplites could not have overtaken the flying Persians.

for beauty and accomplished intelligence, was made prisoner and transferred to the harem of Artaxerxes; the other, a younger person, found means to save herself, though without her upper garments,[1] and sought shelter among some Greeks who were left in the camp on guard of the Grecian baggage. These Greeks repelled the Persian assailants with considerable slaughter; preserving their own baggage, as well as the persons of all who fled to them for shelter. But the Asiatic camp of the Cyreians was completely pillaged, not excepting those reserved waggons of provisions which Cyrus had provided in order that his Grecian auxiliaries might be certain, under all circumstances, of a supply.[2]

While Artaxerxes was thus stripping the Cyreian camp, he was joined by Tissaphernes and his division of horse, who had charged through between the Grecian division and the river. At this time, there was a distance of no less than thirty stadia or three and a half miles between him and Klearchus with the Grecian division; so far had the latter advanced forward in pursuit of the Persian fugitives. Apprised, after some time, that the king's troops had been victorious on the left and centre, and were masters of the camp, — but not yet knowing of the death of Cyrus, — Klearchus marched back his troops, and met the enemy's forces also returning. He was apprehensive of being surrounded by superior numbers, and therefore took post with his rear upon the river. In this position, Arta-

---

[1] Xen. Anab. i, 10, 3. The accomplishments and fascinations of this Phokæan lady, and the great esteem in which she was held first by Cyrus and afterwards by Artaxerxes, have been exaggerated into a romantic story, in which we cannot tell what may be the proportion of truth (see Ælian, V. H. xii, 1; Plutarch, Artaxerx. c. 26, 27; Justin, x, 2). Both Plutarch and Justin state that the subsequent enmity between Artaxerxes and his son Darius, which led to the conspiracy of the latter against his father, and to his destruction when the conspiracy was discovered, arose out of the passion of Darius for her. But as that transaction certainly happened at the close of the long life and reign of Artaxerxes, who reigned forty-six years — and as she must have been then sixty years old, if not more — we may fairly presume that the cause of the family tragedy must have been something different.

Compare the description of the fate of Bereikê of Chios, and Monimê of Miletus, wives of Mithridates king of Pontus, during the last misfortunes of that prince (Plutarch, Lucullus, c, 18).

[2] Xen. Anab. i, 10, 17. This provision must probably have been made during the recent halt at Pylæ.

xerxes again marshalled his troops in front, as if to attack him, but the Greeks, anticipating his movement, were first in making the attack themselves, and forced the Persians to take flight even more terror-stricken than before. Klearchus, thus relieved from all enemies, waited awhile in hopes of hearing news of Cyrus. He then returned to the camp, which was found stripped of all its stores; so that the Greeks were compelled to pass the night without supper, while most of them also had had no dinner, from the early hour at which the battle had commenced.[1] It was only or the next morning that they learnt, through Proklês (descendant of the Spartan king Demaratus, formerly companion of Xerxes in the invasion of Greece), that Cyrus had been slain; news which converted their satisfaction at their own triumph into sorrow and dismay.[2]

Thus terminated the battle of Kunaxa, and along with it the ambitious hopes as well as the life of this young prince. His character and proceedings suggest instructive remarks. Both in the conduct of this expedition, and in the two or three years of administration in Asia Minor which preceded it, he displayed qualities such as are not seen in Cyrus called the Great, nor in any other member of the Persian regal family, nor indeed in any other Persian general throughout the history of the monarchy. We observe a large and long-sighted combination, — a power of foreseeing difficulties, and providing means beforehand for overcoming them, — a dexterity in meeting variable exigencies, and dealing with different parties, Greeks or Asiatics, officers or soldiers,— a conviction of the necessity, not merely of purchasing men's service by lavish presents, but of acquiring their confidence by straightforward dealing and systematic good faith, — a power of repressing displeasure when policy commanded, as at the desertion of Xenias and Pasion, and the first conspiracies of Orontes; although usually the punishments which he inflicted were full of Oriental barbarity. How rare were the merits and accomplishments of Cyrus, as a Persian, will be best felt when we contrast this portrait, by Xenophon, with the description of the Persian satraps by Isokrates.[3] That many

---

[1] Xen. Anab. i, 10, 18, 19.   [2] Xen. Anab. ii, 1, 3, 4.

[3] Isokrates, Orat. iv, (Panegyric.) s. 175–182; a striking passage, as describing the way in which political nstitutions work themselves into the individual character and habits.

persons deserted from Artaxerxes to Cyrus, — none, except Oron
tes, from Cyrus to Artaxerxes, — has been remarked by Xenophon
Not merely throughout the march, but even as to the manner of
fighting at Kunaxa, the judgment of Cyrus was sounder than that
of Klearchus. The two matters of supreme importance to the
Greeks, were, to take care of the person of Cyrus, and to strike
straight at that of Artaxerxes with the central division around him.
Now it was the fault of Klearchus, and not of Cyrus, that both
these matters were omitted; and that the Greeks gained only a
victory comparatively insignificant on the right. Yet in spite of
such mistake, not his own, it appears that Cyrus would have been
victorious, had he been able to repress that passionate burst of
antipathy which drove him, like a madman, against his brother.
The same insatiable ambition, and jealous fierceness when power
was concerned, which had before led him to put to death two first
cousins, because they omitted, in his presence, an act of deference
never paid except to the king in person, — this same impulse,
exasperated by the actual sight of his rival brother, and by that
standing force of fraternal antipathy so frequent in regal families,[1]
blinded him, for the moment, to all rational calculation.

---

[1] Diodorus (xiv, 23) notices the legendary pair of hostile brothers, Eteo-
kles and Polyneikes, as a parallel. Compare Tacitus, Annal. iv, 60. "Atrox
Drusi ingenium, super cupidinem potentiæ, et *solita fratribus odia*, accende-
batur invidia, quod mater Agrippina promptior Neroni erat," etc.; and Jus
tin, xlii, 4.

Compare also the interesting narrative of M. Prosper Mérimée, in his
life of Don Pedro of Castile; a prince commonly known by the name of
Peter the Cruel. Don Pedro was dethroned, and slain in personal conflict,
by the hand of his bastard brother, Henri of Transtamare.

At the battle of Navarrete, in 1367, says M. Mérimée, "Don Pédre, pui,
pendant le combat, s'était jété au plus fort de la mêlée, s'acharna long temps
à la poursuite des fuyards. On le voyait galoper dans la plaine, monté sur
un cheval noir, sa bannière armoriée de Castille devant lui, cherchant son
frère partout où l'on combattait encore, et criant, échauffé par le carnage —
'Où est ce bâtard, qui se nomme roi de Castille?'" (Histoire de Don
Pédre, p. 504.)

Ultimately Don Pedro, blocked up and almost starved out in the castle
of Montiel, was entrapped by simulated negotiations into the power of his
enemies. He was slain in personal conflict by the dagger of his brother
Henri, after a desperate struggle, in which he seemed likely to prevail, if
Henri had not been partially aided by a bystander.

We may however remark that Hellas, as a whole, had no cause to regret the fall of Cyrus at Kunaxa. Had he dethroned his brother and become king, the Persian empire would have acquired under his hand such a degree of strength as might probably have enabled him to forestall the work afterwards performed by the Macedonian kings, and to make the Greeks in Europe as well as those in Asia his dependents. He would have employed Grecian military organization against Grecian independence, as Philip and Alexander did after him. His money would have enabled him to hire an overwhelming force of Grecian officers and soldiers, who would (to use the expression of Proxenus as recorded by Xenophon[1]) have thought him a better friend to them than their own country. It would have enabled him also to take advantage of dissension and venality in the interior of each Grecian city, and thus to weaken their means of defence while he strengthened his own means of attack. This was a policy which none of the Persian kings, from Darius son of Hystaspes down to Darius Codomanus, had ability or perseverance enough to follow out; none of them knew either the true value of Grecian instruments, or how to employ them with effect. The whole conduct of Cyrus, in reference to this memorable expedition, manifests a superior intelligence, competent to use the resources which victory would have put in his hands, — and an ambition likely to use them against the Greeks, in avenging the humiliations of Marathon, Salamis, and the peace of Kallias.

This tragical scene (on the night of the 23d of March, 1369) is graphically described by M. Mérimée (p. 564–566).

[1] Xen. Anab. iii, 1, 4. Ὑπισχνεῖτο δὲ αὐτῷ (Ξενοφῶντα Πρόξενος) εἰ ἔλθοι, φίλον Κύρῳ ποιήσειν ὃν αὐτός ἔφη κρείττω ἑαυτῷ νομίζειν τῆς πατρίδος.

CHAPTER LXX.

RETREAT OF THE TEN THOUSAND GREEKS

THE first triumphant feeling of the Greek troops at Kunaxa was exchanged, as soon as they learnt the death of Cyrus, for dismay and sorrow; accompanied by unavailing repentance for the venture into which he and Klearchus had seduced them. Probably Klearchus himself too repented, and with good reason, of having displayed, in his manner of fighting the battle, so little foresight, and so little regard either to the injunctions or to the safety of Cyrus. Nevertheless he still maintained the tone of a victor in the field, and after expressions of grief for the fate of the young prince, desired Proklês and Glus to return to Ariæus, with the reply, that the Greeks on their side were conquerors without any enemy remaining; that they were about to march onward against Artaxerxes; and that if Ariæus would join them, they would place him on the throne which had been intended for Cyrus. While this reply was conveyed to Ariæus by his particular friend Menon along with the messengers, the Greeks procured a meal as well as they could, having no bread, by killing some of the baggage animals; and by kindling fire, to cook their meat, from the arrows, the wooden Egyptian shields which had been thrown away on the field, and the baggage carts.[1]

Before any answer could be received from Ariæus, heralds appeared coming from Artaxerxes; among them being Phalinus, a Greek from Zakynthus, and the Greek surgeon Ktesias of Knidus, who was in the service of the Persian king.[2] Phalinus, an officer

---

[1] Xen. Anab. ii, 1, 5–7.

[2] We know from Plutarch (Artaxer. c. 13) that Ktesias distinctly asserted himself to have been present at this interview, and I see no reason why we should not believe him. Plutarch indeed rejects his testimony as false, affirming that Xenophon would certainly have mentioned him, had he been there; but such an objection seems to me insufficient. Nor is it necessary to construe the words of Xenophon, ἦν δ' αὐτῶν Φαλῖνος εἷς Ἕλλην, ii, 1, 7) so strictly as to negative the presence of one or two other Greeks. Phalinus is thus specified because he was the spokesman of the party — a military man.

of some military experience and in the confidence of Tissaphernes, addressed himself to the Greek commanders; requiring them on the part of the king, since he was now victor and had slain Cyrus, to surrender their arms and appeal to his mercy. To this summons, painful in the extreme to a Grecian ear, Klearchus replied that it was not the practice for victorious men to lay down their arms. Being then called away to examine the sacrifice which was going on, he left the interview to the other officers, who met the summons of Phalinus by an emphatic negative. "If the king thinks himself strong enough to ask for our arms unconditionally, let him come and try to seize them." "The king (rejoined Phalinus) thinks that you are in his power, being in the midst of his territory, hemmed in by impassable rivers, and encompassed by his innumerable subjects." — "Our arms and our valor are all that remain to us (replied a young Athenian); we shall not be fools enough to hand over to you our only remaining treasure, but shall employ them still to have a fight for your treasure."[1] But though several spoke in this resolute tone, there were not wanting others disposed to encourage a negotiation; saying that they had been faithful to Cyrus as long as he lived, and would now be faithful to Artaxerxes, if he wanted their services in Egypt or anywhere else. In the midst of this parley Klearchus returned, and was requested by Phalinus to return a final answer on behalf of all. He at first asked the advice of Phalinus himself; appealing to the common feeling of Hellenic patriotism, and anticipating, with very little judgment, that the latter would encourage the Greeks in holding out. "If (replied Phalinus) I saw one chance out of ten thousand in your favor, in the event of a contest with the king, I should advise you to refuse the surrender of your arms. But as there is no chance of safety for you against the king's consent, I recommend you to look out for safety in the only quarter where it presents itself." Sensible of the mistake which he had made in asking the question, Klearchus rejoined, — "That is *your* opinion; now report our answer: We think we shall be better friends to the king, if we are to be his friends, — or more effective enemies, if we are to be his enemies, — with our arms, than without them."

---

[1] Xen. Anab. ii, 1, 12 μὴ οὖν οἷον τὰ μόνα ἡμῖν ἀγαθὰ ᾖντα ὑμῖν παραδώσειν· ἀλλὰ σὺν τούτοις καὶ περὶ τῶν ὑμετέρων ἀγαθῶν μαχούμεθα.

Phalinus, in retiring, said that the king proclaimed a truce so long as they remained in their present position,— but war, if they moved, either onward or backward. And to this Klearchus acceded, without declaring which he intended to do.[1]

Shortly after the departure of Phalinus, the envoys despatched to Ariæus returned; communicating his reply, that the Persian grandees would never tolerate any pretensions on his part to the crown, and that he intended to depart early the next morning on his return; if the Greeks wished to accompany him, they must join him during the night. In the evening, Klearchus, convening the generals and the lochages (or captains of lochi), acquainted them that the morning sacrifice had been of a nature to forbid their marching against the king, — a prohibition of which he now understood the reason, from having since learnt that the king was on the other side of the Tigris, and therefore out of their reach, — but that it was favorable for rejoining Ariæus. He gave directions accordingly for a night-march back along the Euphrates, to the station where they had passed the last night but one prior to the battle. The other Grecian generals, without any formal choice of Klearchus as chief, tacitly acquiesced in his orders, from a sense of his superior decision and experience, in an emergency when no one knew what to propose. The night-march was successfully accomplished, so that they joined Ariæus at the preceding station about midnight; not without the alarming symptom, however, that Miltokythês the Thracian deserted to the king, at the head of three hundred and forty of his countrymen, partly horse, partly foot.

The first proceeding of the Grecian generals was to exchange solemn oaths of reciprocal fidelity and fraternity with Ariæus. According to an ancient and impressive practice, a bull, a wolf, a boar, and a ram, were all slain, and their blood allowed to run into the hollow of a shield; in which the Greek generals dipped a sword, and Ariæus, with his chief companions, a spear.[2] The latter, besides the

---

[1] Xen. Anab. ii, 1, 14–22. Diodorus (xiv, 25) is somewhat copious in his account of the interview with Phalinus. But he certainly followed other authorities besides Xenophon, if even it be true that he had Xenophon before him. The allusion to the past heroism of Leonidas seems rather in the style of Ephorus.

[2] Xen. Anab. ii. 2, 7–9. Koch remarks, however, with good reason, that it is difficult to see how they could get a wolf in Babylonia for the sacrifice (Zug der Zehn Tausend, p 51).

promise of alliance, engaged also to guide the Greeks, in good faith, down to the Asiatic coast. Klearchus immediately began to ask what route he proposed to take; whether to return by that along which they had come up, or by any other. To this Ariæus replied, that the road along which they had marched was impracticable for retreat, from the utter want of provisions through seventeen days of desert; but that he intended to choose another road, which, though longer, would be sufficiently productive to furnish them with provisions. There was, however, a necessity (he added), that the first two or three days' marches should be of extreme length, in order that they might get out of the reach of the king's forces, who would hardly be able to overtake them afterwards with any considerable numbers.

They had now come ninety-three days' march[1] from Ephesus, or ninety from Sardis.[2] The distance from Sardis to Kunaxa is, according to colonel Chesney, about twelve hundred and sixty-five geographical miles, or fourteen hundred and sixty-four English miles. There had been at least ninety-six days of rest, enjoyed at various places, so that the total of time elapsed must have at least been one hundred and eighty-nine days, or a little more than half a year;[3] but it was probably greater, since some intervals of rest are not specified in number of days.

How to retrace their steps, was now the problem, apparently insoluble. As to the military force of Persia in the field, indeed, not merely the easy victory at Kunaxa, but still more the undisputed march throughout so long a space, left them no serious

---

[1] Such is the sum total stated by Xenophon himself (Anab. ii, 1, 6). It is greater, by nine days, than the sum total which we should obtain by adding together the separate days' march specified by Xenophon from Sardis. But the distance from Sardis to Ephesus, as we know from Herodotus, was three days' journey (Herod. v, 55); and therefore the discrepancy is really only to the amount of six, not of nine. See Krüger ad Anabas. p. 556; Koch, Zug der Z. p. 141.

[2] Colonel Chesney (Euphrates and Tigris, c. ii, p. 208) calculates twelve hundred and sixty-five geographical miles from Sardis to Kunaxa or the Mounds of Mohammed.

[3] For example, we are not told how long they rested at Pylæ, or opposite to Charmandê. I have given some grounds (in the preceding chapter) for believing that it cannot have been less than five days. The army must have been in the utmost need of repose, as well as of provisions.

apprehensions.[1] In spite of this great extent, population, and riches.
they had been allowed to pass through the most difficult and defen
sible country, and to ford the broad Euphrates, without a blow;
nay, the king had shrunk from defending the long trench which he
had specially caused to be dug for the protection of Babylonia.
But the difficulties which stood between them and their homes
were of a very different character. How were they to find their
way back, or obtain provisions, in defiance of a numerous hostile
cavalry, which, not without efficiency even in a pitched battle
would be most formidable in opposing their retreat? The line of
their upward march had all been planned, with supplies furnished,
by Cyrus; — yet even under such advantages, supplies had been
on the point of failing, in one part of the march. They were now,
for the first time, called upon to think and provide for themselves;
without knowledge of either roads or distances, — without trustworthy guides, — without any one to furnish or even to indicate
supplies, — and with a territory all hostile, traversed by rivers
which they had no means of crossing. Klearchus himself knew
nothing of the country, nor of any other river except the Euphrates; nor does he indeed, in his heart, seem to have conceived
retreat as practicable without the consent of the king.[2] The reader
who casts his eye on a map of Asia, and imagines the situation of
this Greek division on the left bank of the Euphrates, near the
parallel of latitude 33° 30′— will hardly be surprised at any measure of despair, on the part either of general or soldiers. And we
may add that Klearchus had not even the advantage of such a map,
or probably of any map at all, to enable him to shape his course.

In this dilemma, the first and most natural impulse was to consult Ariæus who (as has been already stated) pronounced, with
good reason, that return by the same road was impracticable ; and
promised to conduct them home by another road, — longer indeed,
yet better supplied. At daybreak on the ensuing morning, they
began their march in an easterly direction, anticipating that before
night they should reach some villages of the Babylonian territory,
as in fact they did ;[3] yet not before they had been alarmed in the

---

[1] Xen. Anab. i, 5, 9. [2] Xen. Anab. ii, 4, 6, 7.

[3] Xen. Anab. ii, 2, 13. Ἐπεὶ γὰρ ἡμέρα ἐγένετο, ἐπορεύοντο ἐν δεξιᾷ
ἔχοντες τὸν ἥλιον, λογιζόμενοι ἥξειν ἅμα ἡλίῳ δύνοντι εἰς κώμας τῆς
Βαβυλωνίας χώρας· καὶ τοῦτο μὲν οὐκ ἐψεύσθησαν

afternoon by the supposed approach of some of the enemy's horse, and by evidences that the enemy were not far off, which induced them to slacken their march for the purpose of more cautious array. Hence they did not reach the first villages before dark; and these too had been pillaged by the enemy while retreating before them, so that only the first-comers under Klearchus could obtain accommodation, while the succeeding troops, coming up in the dark, pitched as they could without any order. The whole camp was a scene of clamor, dispute, and even alarm, throughout the night. No provisions could be obtained. Early the next morning Klear-

---

Schneider, in his note on this passage, as well as Ritter, (Erdkunde, part. x, 3, p. 17), Mr. Ainsworth (Travels in the Track, p. 103) and Colonel Chesney (Euph. and Tigr. p. 219), understand the words here used by Xenophon in a sense from which I dissent. " When it was day, the army proceeded onward on their march, having the sun on their right hand," — these words they understand as meaning that the army marched *northward;* whereas, in my judgment, the words intimate that the army marched *east-ward.* To have the sun on the right hand, does not so much refer either to the precise point where, or to the precise instant when, the sun rises, — but to his diurnal path through the heavens, and to the general direction of the day's march. This may be seen by comparing the remarkable passage in Herodotus, iv, 42, in reference to the alleged circumnavigation of Africa, from the Red Sea round the Cape of Good Hope to the Straits of Gibraltar, by the Phœnicians under the order of Nekos. These Phœnicians said, " that in sailing round Africa (from the Red Sea) they had the sun on their right hand " — ὡς τὴν Λιβύην περιπλώοντες τὸν ἥέλιον ἐπὶ δεξιᾷ. Herodotus rejects this statement as incredible. Not knowing the phenomena of a southern latitude beyond the tropic of Capricorn, he could not imagine that men in sailing from East to West could possibly have the sun on their *right* hand; any man journeying from the Red Sea to the Straits of Gibraltar must, in his judgment, have the sun on the *left* hand, as he himself had always experienced in the north latitude of the Mediterranean or the African coast. See Vol. III. of this History, ch. xviii, p. 282.

In addition to this reason, we may remark, that Ariæus and the Greeks, starting from their camp on the banks of the Euphrates (the place where they had passed the last night but one before the battle of Kunaxa) and marching *northward,* could not expect to arrive, and could not really arrive, at villages of the Babylonian territory. But they might naturally expect to do so, if they marched *eastward,* towards the Tigris. Nor would they have hit upon the enemy in a northerly march, which would in fact have been something near to a return upon their own previous steps. They would moreover have been stopped by the undefended Trench, which could only be passed at the narrow opening close to the Euphrates.

chus ordered them under arms; and desiring to expose the ground-
less nature of the alarm, caused the herald to proclaim, that whoever would denounce the person who had let the ass into the camp
on the preceding night, should be rewarded with a talent of silver.[1]

What was the project of route entertained by Ariæus, we cannot
ascertain;[2] since it was not farther pursued. For the effect of the
unexpected arrival of the Greeks as if to attack the enemy, — and
even the clamor and shouting of the camp during the night — so
intimidated the Persian commanders, that they sent heralds the
next morning to treat about a truce. The contrast between this
message, and the haughty summons of the preceding day to lay
down their arms, was sensibly felt by the Grecian officers, and
taught them that the proper way of dealing with the Persians was
by a bold and aggressive demeanor. When Klearchus was apprised of the arrival of the heralds, he desired them at first to wait
at the outposts until he was at leisure; then, having put his troops
into the best possible order, with a phalanx compact on every side
to the eye, and the unarmed persons out of sight, he desired the
heralds to be admitted. He marched out to meet them with the
most showy and best-armed soldiers immediately around him, and
when they informed him that they had come from the king with
instructions to propose a truce, and to report on what conditions
the Greeks would agree to it, Klearchus replied abruptly, —
" Well then, — go and tell the king, that our first business must be
to fight; for we have nothing to eat, nor will any man presume to
talk to Greeks about a truce, without first providing dinner for
them." With this reply the heralds rode off, but returned very
speedily; thus making it plain that the king, or the commanding
officer, was near at hand. They brought word that the king
thought their answer reasonable, and had sent guides to conduct
them to a place where they would obtain provisions, if the truce
should be concluded.

After an affected delay and hesitation, in order to impose upon
the Persians, Klearchus concluded the truce, and desired that the

---

[1] Xen. Anab. ii, 2, 20. This seems to have been a standing military jest.
to make the soldiers laugh at their past panic. See the references in Krüger and Schneider's notes.

[2] Diodorus (xvi, 24) tells us that Ariæus intended to guide them towards
Paphlagonia; a very loose indication.

guides would conduct the army to those quarters where provisions could be had. He was most circumspect in maintaining exact order during the march, himself taking charge of the rear guard. The guides led them over many ditches and channels, full of water, and cut for the purpose of irrigation; some so broad and deep that they could not be crossed without bridges. The army had to put together bridges for the occasion, from palm trees either already fallen, or expressly cut down. This was a troublesome business, which Klearchus himself superintended with peculiar strictness. He carried his spear in the left hand, his stick in the right; employing the latter to chastise any soldier who seemed remiss, — and even plunging into the mud and lending his own hands in aid wherever it was necessary.[1] As it was not the usual season of irrigation for crops, he suspected that the canals had been filled on this occasion expressly to intimidate the Greeks, by impressing them with the difficulties of their prospective march; and he was anxious to demonstrate to the Persians that these difficulties were no more than Grecian energy could easily surmount.

At length they reached certain villages indicated by their guides for quarters and provision; and here for the first time they had a sample of that unparalleled abundance of the Babylonian territory, which Herodotus is afraid to describe with numerical precision. Large quantities of corn, — dates not only in great numbers, but of such beauty, freshness, size and flavor, as no Greek had ever seen or tasted, insomuch that fruit like what was imported into Greece, was disregarded and left for the slaves, — wine and vinegar, both also made from the date-palm: these are the luxuries which Xenophon is eloquent in describing, after his recent period of scanty fare and anxious apprehension; not without also noticing the headaches which such new and luscious food, in unlimited quanity, brought upon himself and others.[2]

After three days passed in these restorative quarters, they were visited by Tissaphernes, accompanied by four Persian grandees and a suite of slaves. The satrap began to open a negotiation with Klearchus and the other generals. Speaking through an interpreter, he stated to them that the vicinity of his satrapy

---

[1] Xen. Anab. ii, 3, 7, 13.   [2] Xen. Anab. ii, 3. 14, 17

to Greece impressed him with a strong interest in favor of the Cyreian Greeks, and made him anxious to rescue them out of their present desperate situation; that he had solicited the king's permission to save them, as a personal recompense to himself for having been the first to forewarn him of the schemes of Cyrus, and for having been the only Persian who had not fled before the Greeks at Kunaxa; that the King had promised to consider this point, and had sent him in the meantime to ask the Greeks what their purpose was in coming up to attack him; and that he trusted the Greeks would give him a conciliatory answer to carry back, in order that he might have less difficulty in realizing what he desired for their benefit. To this Klearchus, after first deliberating apart with the other officers, replied, that the army had come together, and had even commenced their march, without any purpose of hostility to the King; that Cyrus had brought them up the country under false pretences, but that they had been ashamed to desert him in the midst of danger, since he had always treated them generously; that since Cyrus was now dead, they had no purpose of hostility against the King, but were only anxious to return home; that they were prepared to repel hostility from all quarters, but would be not less prompt in requiting favor or assistance. With this answer Tissaphernes departed, and returned on the next day but one, informing them that he had obtained the King's permission to save the Grecian army, — though not without great opposition, since many Persian counsellors contended that it was unworthy of the King's dignity, to suffer those who had assailed him to escape. " I am now ready (said he) to conclude a covenant and exchange oaths with you; engaging to conduct you safely back into Greece, with the country friendly, and with a regular market for you to purchase provisions. You must stipulate on your part always to pay for your provisions, and to do no damage to the country. If I do not furnish you with provisions to buy, you are then at liberty to take them where you can find them." Well were the Greeks content to enter into such a covenant, which was sworn, with hands given upon it, by Klearchus, the other generals, and the lochages, on their side, — and by Tissaphernes with the King's brother-in-law on the other. Tissaphernes then left them, saying that he would go back to the King, make preparations, and return to reconduct the Greeks home; going himself to his own satrapy.[1]

The statements of Ktesias, though known to us only indirectly and not to be received without caution, afford ground for believing that Queen Parysatis decidedly wished success to her son Cyrus in his contest for the throne, — that the first report conveyed to her of the battle of Kunaxa, announcing the victory of Cyrus, filled her with joy, which was exchanged for bitter sorrow when she was informed of his death, — that she caused to be slain with horrible tortures all those, who though acting in the Persian army and for the defence of Artaxerxes, had any participation in the death of Cyrus — and that she showed favorable dispositions towards the Cyreian Greeks.[2] It seems probable, farther, that her influence may have been exerted to procure for them an unimpeded retreat, without anticipating the use afterwards made by Tissaphernes (as will soon appear) of the present convention. And in one point of view, the Persian king had an interest in facilitating their retreat. For the very circumstance which rendered retreat difficult, also rendered the Greeks dangerous to him in their actual position. They were in the heart of the Persian empire, within seventy miles of Babylon; in a country not only teeming with fertility, but also extremely defensible; especially against cavalry, from the multiplicity of canals, as Herodotus observed respecting Lower Egypt.[3] And Klearchus might say to his Grecian soldiers, — what Xenophon was afterwards preparing to say to them at Kalpê on the Euxine Sea, and what Nikias also affirmed to the unhappy Athenian army whom he conducted away from Syracuse[4] — that wherever they sat down, they were sufficiently numerous and well-organized to become at once a city. A body of such troops might effectually assist, and would perhaps encourage, the Babylonian population to throw off the Persian yoke, and to exonerate themselves from the prodigious tribute which they now paid to the satrap. For these reasons,

---

[1] Xen. Anab. ii, 3, 18–27.

[2] Ktesiæ Persica, Fragm. c. 59, ed. Bähr; compared with the remarkable Fragment. 18, preserved by the so-called Demetrius Phalêreus: see also Plutarch, Artaxerx. c. 17.

[3] Herodot. i, 193; ii, 108; Strabo, xvii p. 788

[4] Xen. Anab. v, 6, 16; Thucyd. vii.

the advisers of Artaxerxes thought it advantageous to convey the
Greeks across the Tigris out of Babylonia, beyond all possibility
of returning thither. This was at any rate the primary object of
the convention. And it was the more necessary to conciliate the
good-will of the Greeks, because there seems to have been but
one bridge over the Tigris; which bridge could only be reached
by inviting them to advance considerably farther into the interior
of Babylonia.

Such was the state of fears and hopes on both sides, at the
time when Tissaphernes left the Greeks, after concluding his
convention. For twenty days did they await his return, without
receiving from him any communication; the Cyreian Persians
under Ariæus being encamped near them. Such prolonged and
unexplained delay became, after a few days, the source of much
uneasiness to the Greeks; the more so as Ariæus received during
this interval several visits from his Persian kinsmen, and friendly
messages from the king, promising amnesty for his recent services
under Cyrus. Of these messages the effects were painfully felt
in manifest coldness of demeanor on the part of his Persian troops
towards the Greeks. Impatient and suspicious, the Greek soldiers impressed upon Klearchus their fears, that the king had
concluded the recent convention only to arrest their movements,
until he should have assembled a larger army and blocked up
more effectually the roads against their return. To this Klearchus replied, — "I am aware of all that you say. Yet if we
now strike our tents, it will be a breach of the convention and a
declaration of war. No one will furnish us with provisions;
we shall have no guides; Ariæus will desert us forthwith, so
that we shall have his troops as enemies instead of friends.
Whether there be any other river for us to cross, I know not;
but we know that the Euphrates itself can never be crossed, if
there be an enemy to resist us. Nor have we any cavalry, — while
cavalry is the best and most numerous force of our enemies. If
the king, having all these advantages, really wishes to destroy
us, I do not know why he should falsely exchange all these oaths
and solemnities, and thus make his own word worthless in the
eyes both of Greeks and barbarians." [1]

---

[1] Xen. Anab. ii, 4, 3–8.

Such words from Klearchus are remarkable, as they testify his own complete despair of the situation, — certainly a very natural despair, — except by amicable dealing with the Persians ; and also his ignorance of geography and the country to be traversed. This feeling helps to explain his imprudent confidence afterwards in Tissaphernes.

That satrap, however, after twenty days, at last came back, with his army prepared to return to Ionia, — with the king's daughter whom he had just received in marriage, — and with another grandee named Orontas. Tissaphernes took the conduct of the march, providing supplies for the Greek troops to purchase ; while Ariæus and his division now separated themselves altogether from the Greeks, and became intermingled with the other Persians. Klearchus and the Greeks followed them, at the distance of about three miles in the rear, with a separate guide for themselves ; not without jealousy and mistrust, sometimes shown in individual conflicts, while collecting wood or forage, between them and the Persians of Ariæus. After three days' march (that is, apparently, three days, calculated from the moment when they began their retreat with Ariæus) they came to the Wall of Media, and passed through it,[1] prosecuting their march onward through the country on its other or interior side. It was of bricks cemented with bitumen, one hundred feet high, and twenty feet broad ; it was said to extend a length of twenty parasangs (or about seventy miles, if we reckon the parasang at thirty stadia), and to be not far distant

---

[1] Xen. Anab. ii, 4, 12. Διελθόντες δὲ τρεῖς σταθμούς, ἀφίκοντο πρὸς τὸ Μηδίας καλούμενον τεῖχος, καὶ παρῆλθον αὐτοῦ εἴσω. It appears to me that these three days' march or σταθμοὶ can hardly be computed from the moment when they commenced their march under the conduct of Tissaphernes. On the other hand, if we begin from the moment when the Greeks started under conduct of Ariæus, we can plainly trace three distinct *resting places* (σταθμοὺς) before they reached the Wall of Media. First, at the villages where the confusion and alarm arose (ii, 13–21). Secondly, at the villages of abundant supply, where they concluded the truce with Tissaphernes, and waited twenty days for his return (ii, 3, 14 ; ii, 4, 9)   Thirdly, one night's halt under the conduct of Tissaphernes, before they reached the Wall of Media. This makes three distinct stations or halting places, between the station (the first station after passing the undefended trench) from whence they started to begin their retreat under the conduct of Ariæus, — and the point where they traversed the Wall of Media.

from Babylon. Two days of farther march, computed as eight
parasangs, brought them to the Tigris. During these two days
they crossed two great ship canals, one of them over a permanent
bridge, the other over a temporary bridge laid on seven boats.
Canals of such magnitude must probably have been two among
the four stated by Xenophon to be drawn from the river Tigris,
each of them a parasang distant from the other. They were one
hundred feet broad, and deep enough even for heavy vessels ; they
were distributed by means of numerous smaller channels and ditches
for the irrigation of the soil ; and they were said to fall into the
Euphrates ; or rather, perhaps, they terminated in one main larger
canal cut directly from the Euphrates to the Tigris, each of them
joining this larger canal at a different point of its course. Within
less than two miles of the Tigris was a large and populous city
named Sittakê, near which the Greeks pitched their camp, on the
verge of a beautiful park or thick grove full of all kinds of trees ;
while the Persians all crossed the Tigris, at the neighboring bridge.

As Proxenus and Xenophon were here walking in front of the
camp after supper, a man was brought up who had asked for the
former at the advanced posts. This man said that he came with
instructions from Ariæus. He advised the Greeks to be on their
guard, as there were troops concealed in the adjoining grove, for
the purpose of attacking them during the night, — and also to send
and occupy the bridge over the Tigris, since Tissaphernes intended to break it down, in order that the Greeks might be caught
without possibility of escape between the river and the canal.
On discussing this information with Klearchus, who was much
alarmed by it, a young Greek present remarked that the two matters stated by the informant contradicted each other ; for that if
Tissaphernes intended to attack the Greeks during the night, he
would not break down the bridge, so as both to prevent his own
troops on the other side from crossing to aid, and to deprive those
on this side of all retreat if they were beaten, — while, if the
Greeks were beaten, there was no escape open to them, whether
the bridge continued or not. This remark induced Klearchus to
ask the messenger, what was the extent of ground between the
Tigris and the canal. The messenger replied, that it was a great
extent of country, comprising many large cities and villages. Reflecting on this communication, the Greek officers came to the con

clusion that the message was a stratagem on the part of Tissaphernes to frighten them and accelerate their passage across the Tigris; under the apprehension that they might conceive the plan of seizing or breaking the bridge and occupying a permanent position in the spot where they were; which was an island, fortified on one side by the Tigris, — on the other sides, by intersecting canals between the Euphrates and the Tigris.[1] Such an island was

---

[1] I reserve for this place the consideration of that which Xenophon states, in two or three passages, about the Wall of Media and about different canals in connection with the Tigris, — the result of which, as far as I can make it out, stands in my text.

I have already stated, in the preceding chapter, that in the march of the day next but one preceding the battle of Kunaxa, the army came to a deep and broad trench dug for defence across their line of way, with the exception of a narrow gut of twenty feet broad close by the Euphrates; through which gut the whole army passed. Xenophon says, "This trench had been carried upwards across the plain as far as the Wall of Media, where indeed, the canals are situated, flowing from the river Tigris; four canals, one hundred feet in breadth, and extremely deep, so that corn-bearing vessels sail along them. They strike into the Euphrates, they are distant each from the other by one parasang, and there are bridges over them — Παρετέτατο δ' ἡ τάφρος ἄνω διὰ τοῦ πεδίου ἐπὶ δώδεκα παράσαγγας, μέχρι τοῦ Μηδίας τείχους, ἔνθα δὴ (the books print a full stop between τείχους and ἔνθα, which appears to me incorrect, as the sense goes on without interruption) εἰσιν αἱ διώρυχες, ἀπὸ τοῦ Τίγρητος ποταμοῦ ῥέουσαι· εἰσὶ δὲ τέτταρες, τὸ μὲν εὖρος πλεθριαῖαι, βαθεῖαι δὲ ἰσχυρῶς, καὶ πλοῖα πλεῖ ἐν αὐταῖς σιταγωγά· εἰσβάλλουσι δὲ εἰς τὸν Εὐφράτην, διαλείπουσι δ' ἑκάστη παρασάγγην, γέφυραι δ' ἔπεισιν. The present tense — εἰσιν αἱ διώρυχες — seems to mark the local reference of ἔνθα to the Wall of Media, and not to the actual march of the army.

Major Rennell (Illustrations of the Expedition of Cyrus, pp. 79–87, etc.), Ritter, (Erdkunde, x, p. 16), Koch, (Zug der Zehn Tausend, pp. 46, 47), and Mr. Ainsworth (Travels in the Track of the Ten Thousand, p. 88) consider Xenophon to state that the Cyreian army on this day's march (the day but one before the battle) passed through the Wall of Media and over the four distinct canals reaching from the Tigris to the Euphrates. They all, indeed, contest the accuracy of this latter statement; Rennell remarking that the level of the Tigris, in this part of its course, is lower than that of the Euphrates; and that it could not supply water for so many broad canals so near to each other. Col. Chesney also conceives the army to have passed through the Wall of Media before the battle of Kunaxa.

It seems to me, however, that they do not correctly interpret the words of Xenophon, who does not say that Cyrus ever passed either the Wall of Media, or these four canals *before* the battle of Kunaxa, but who says (as

a defensible position, having a most productive territory with numerous cultivators, so as to furnish shelter and means of hostility for all the king's enemies. Tissaphernes calculated that the message

---

Krüger, De Authentiâ Anabaseos, p. 12, prefixed to his edition of the Anabasis, rightly explains him), that these four canals flowing from the Tigris *are* at, or near, the Wall of Media, which the Greeks did not pass through until long *after* the battle, when Tissaphernes was conducting them towards the Tigris, two days' march before they reached Sittakê (Anab. ii, 4, 12).

It has been supposed, during the last few years, that the direction of the Wall of Media could be verified by actual ruins still subsisting on the spot. Dr. Ross and Captain Lynch (see journal of the Geographical Society, vol. ix. pp. 447–473, with Captain Lynch's map annexed) discovered a line of embankment which they considered to be the remnant of it. It begins on the western bank of the Tigris, in latitude 34° 3′, and stretches towards the Euphrates in a direction from N. N. E. to S. S. W. "It is a solitary straight single mound, twenty-five long paces thick, with a bastion on its western face at every fifty-five paces; and on the same side it has a deep ditch, twenty-seven paces broad. The wall is here built of the small pebbles of the country, imbedded in cement of lime of great tenacity; it is from thirty-five to forty feet in height, and runs in a straight line as far as the eye can trace it. The Bedouins tell me that it goes in the same straight line to two mounds called Ramelah on the Euphrates, some hours above Felujah; that it is, in places far inland, built of brick, and in some parts worn down to a level with the desert." (Dr. Ross, l. c. p. 446).

Upon the faith of these observations, the supposed wall (now called Sidd Nimrud by the natives) has been laid down as the Wall of Media reaching from the Tigris to the Euphrates, in the best recent maps, especially that of Colonel Chesney; and accepted as such by recent inquirers.

Nevertheless, subsequent observations, recently made known by Colonel Rawlinson to the Geographical Society, have contradicted the views of Dr. Ross as stated above, and shown that the Wall of Media, in the line here assigned to it, has no evidence to rest upon. Captain Jones, commander of the steamer at Bagdad, undertook, at the request of Colonel Rawlinson a minute examination of the locality, and ascertained that what had been laid down as the Wall of Media was merely a line of mounds; no wall at all, but a mere embankment, extending seven or eight miles from the Tigris, and designed to arrest the winter torrents and drain off the rain water of the desert into a large reservoir, which served to irrigate an extensive valley between the rivers.

From this important communication it results, that there is as yet no evidence now remaining for determining what was the line or position of the Wall of Media; which had been supposed to be a datum positively established, serving as premises from whence to deduce other positions mentioned by Xenophon. As our knowledge now stands, there is not a single point mentioned by Xenophon in Babylonia which can be positively verified, ex. gr.

now delivered would induce the Greeks to become alarmed with their actual position and to cross the Tigris with as little delay as possible. At least this was the interpretation which the Greek officers put upon his proceeding; an interpretation highly plausible, since, in order to reach the bridge over the Tigris, he had been obliged to conduct the Greek troops into a position sufficiently tempting for them to hold, — and since he knew that his own purposes were purely treacherous. But the Greeks, officers as well

---

Babylon itself, — and Pylæ, which is known pretty nearly, as the spot where Babylonia proper commences.

The description which Xenophon gives of the Wall of Media is very plain and specific. I see no reason to doubt that he actually saw it, passed through it, and correctly describes it in height as well as breadth. Its entire length he of course only gives from what he was told. His statement appears to me good evidence that there was a Wall of Media, which reached from the Tigris to the Euphrates, or perhaps to some canal cut from the Euphrates, though there exists no mark to show what was the precise locality and direction of the Wall. Ammianus Marcellinus (xxiv, 2), in the expedition of the emperor Julian, saw near Macepracta, on the left bank of the Euphrates, the ruins of a wall, " which in ancient times had stretched to a great distance for the defence of Assyria against foreign invasion." It is fair to presume that this was the Wall of Media; but the position of Macepracta cannot be assigned.

It is important, however, to remember, — what I have already stated in this note, — that Xenophon did not see, and did not cross either the Wall of Media, or the two canals here mentioned, until many days after the battle of Kunaxa.

We know from Herodotus that all the territory of Babylonia was inter sected by canals, and that there was one canal greater than the rest and navigable, which flowed from the Euphrates to the Tigris, in a direction to the south of east. This coincides pretty well with the direction assigned in Colonel Chesney's map to the Nahr-Malcha or Regium Flumen, into which the four great canals, described by Xenophon as drawn from the Tigris to the Euphrates, might naturally discharge themselves, and still be said to fall into the Euphrates, of which the Nahr-Malcha was as it were a branch. How the level of the two rivers would adjust itself, when the space between them was covered with a network of canals great and small, and when a vast quantity of the water of both was exhausted in fertilizing the earth, is difficult to say.

The *island* wherein the Greeks stood, at their position near Sittakê, before crossing the Tigris, would be a parallelogram formed by the Tigris, the Nahr-Malcha, and the two parallel canals joining them. It might well be called a large island, containing many cities and villages, with a large population.

as soldiers, were animated only by the wish of reaching home
They trusted, though not without misgivings, in the promise of
Tissaphernes to conduct them ; and never for a moment thought
of taking permanent post in this fertile island. They did not,
however, neglect the precaution of sending a guard during the
night to the bridge over the Tigris, which no enemy came to assail.
On the next morning they passed over it in a body, in cautious
and mistrustful array, and found themselves on the eastern bank
of the Tigris, — not only without attack, but even without sight
of a single Persian, except Glûs, the interpreter, and a few others
watching their motions.

After having crossed by a bridge laid upon thirty-seven pon-
toons, the Greeks continued their march to the northward upon the
eastern side of the Tigris, for four days, to the river Physkus ;
said to be twenty parasangs.[1] The Physkus was one hundred
feet wide, with a bridge, and the large city of Opis near it.   Here,
at the frontier of Assyria and Media, the road from the eastern
regions to Babylon joined the road northerly on which the Greeks
were marching.   An illegitimate brother of Artaxerxes was seen
at the head of a numerous force, which he was conducting from
Susa and Ekbatana as a reinforcement to the royal army.   This
great host halted to see the Greeks pass by ; and Klearchus
ordered the march in column of two abreast, employing himself
actively to maintain an excellent array, and halting more than
once.   The army thus occupied so long a time in passing by
the Persian host, that their numbers appeared greater than the
reality, even to themselves : while the effect upon the Persian
spectators was very imposing.[2]   Here Assyria ended and Media
began.   They marched, still in a northerly direction, for six days
through a portion of Media almost unpeopled, until they came to
some flourishing villages which formed a portion of the domain of
queen Parysatis ; probably these villages, forming so marked an
exception to the desert character of the remaining march, were

---

There seems reason to believe that in ancient times the Tigris, above
Bagdad, followed a course more to the westward, and less winding, than it
does now.   The situation of Opis cannot be verified.   The ruins of a large
city were seen by Captain Lynch near the confluence of the river Adhem
with the Tigris, which he supposed to be Opis, in lat. 34°.

[2] Xen. Anab. ii, 4, 26

situated on the Lesser Zab, which flows into the Tigris, and which Xenophon must have crossed. though he makes no mention of it. According to the order of march stipulated between the Greeks and Tissaphernes, the latter only provided a supply of provisions for the former to purchase ; but on the present halt, he allowed the Greeks to plunder the villages, which were rich and full of all sorts of subsistence, — yet without carrying off the slaves. The wish of the satrap to put an insult on Cyrus, as his personal ene-my,[1] through Parysatis, thus proved a sentence of ruin to these unhappy villagers. Five more days' march, called twenty para-sangs, brought them to the banks of the river Zabatus, or the Greater Zab, which flows into the Tigris near a town now called Senn. During the first of these five days, they saw on the oppo-site side of the Tigris a large town called Kænæ, from whence they received supplies of provisions, brought across by the inhabit-ants upon rafts supported by inflated skins.[2]

On the banks of the Great Zab they halted three days, — days of serious and tragical moment. Having been under feelings of mistrust, ever since the convention with Tissaphernes, they had followed throughout the whole march, with separate guides of their own, in the rear of his army, always maintaining their encamp-ment apart. During their halt on the Zab, so many various mani

---

[1] Ktesias, Fragm. 18, ed. Bähr.

[2] Xen. Anab. ii, 5, 26–28.

Mannert, Rennell, Mr. Ainsworth, and most modern commentators, iden tify this town of Καιναί or Kænæ with the modern town Senn ; which lat ter place Mannert (Geogr. der Röm. v. p. 333) and Rennell (Illustrations p. 129) represent to be near the Lesser Zab instead of the greater Zab.

To me it appears that the locality assigned by Xenophon to Καιναί, does not at all suit the modern town of Senn. Nor is there much real similarity of name between the two ; although our erroneous way of pronouncing the Latin name Caenae, creates a delusive appearance of similarity. Mr. Ains-worth shows that some modern writers have been misled in the same man ner by identifying the modern town of Sert with Tigranocerta.

It is a perplexing circumstance in the geography of Xenophon's work, that he makes no mention of the Lesser Zab, which yet he must have crossed. Herodotus notices them both, and remarks on the fact that though distinct rivers, both bore the same name (v, 52). Perhaps in drawing up his narrative after the expedition, Xenophon may have so far forgotten, as to fancy that two synonymous rivers mentioned as distinct in his memo-randa, were only one.

festations occurred to aggravate the mistrust, that hostilities seemed on the point of breaking out between the two camps. To obviate this danger Klearchus demanded an interview with Tissaphernes, represented to him the threatening attitude of affairs, and insisted on the necessity of coming to a clear understanding. He impressed upon the satrap that, over and above the solemn oaths which had been interchanged, the Greeks on their side could have no conceivable motive to quarrel with him; that they had everything to hope from his friendship, and everything to fear, even to the loss of all chance of safe return, from his hostility; that Tissaphernes, also, could gain nothing by destroying them, but would find them, if he chose, the best and most faithful instruments for his own aggrandizement and for conquering the Mysians and the Pisidians, — as Cyrus had experienced while he was alive. Klearchus concluded his protest by requesting to be informed, what malicious reporter had been filling the mind of Tissaphernes with causeless suspicions against the Greeks.[1]

" Klearchus (replied the satrap), I rejoice to hear such excellent sense from your lips. You remark truly, that if you were to meditate evil against me, it would recoil upon yourselves. I shall prove to you, in my turn, that you have no cause to mistrust either the king or me. If we had wished to destroy you, nothing would be easier. We have superabundant forces for the purpose; there are wide plains in which you would be starved, — besides mountains and rivers which you would be unable to pass, without our help. Having thus the means of destroying you in our hands, and having nevertheless bound ourselves by solemn oaths to save you, we shall not be fools and knaves enough to attempt it now, when we should draw upon ourselves the just indignation of the gods. It is my peculiar affection for my neighbors, the Greeks, — and my wish to attach to my own person, by ties of gratitude, the Greek soldiers of Cyrus, — which have made me eager to conduct you to Ionia in safety. For I know that when you are in my service, though the king is the only man who can wear his tiara erect *upon his head*, I shall be able to wear mine erect upon *my heart*, in full pride and confidence." [2]

---

[1] Xen. Anab. ii, 5, 2-15.

[2] Xen. Anab. ii, 5, 17-23. This last comparison is curious, and in all probability the genuine words of the satrap — τὴν μὲν γὰρ ἐπὶ τῇ κεφαλῇ

So powerful was the impression made upon Klearchus by these assurances, that he exclaimed, — " Surely those informers deserve the severest punishment, who try to put us at enmity, when we are such good friends to each other, and have so much reason to be so." " Yes (replied Tissaphernes), they deserve nothing less; and if you, with the other generals and lochages, will come into my tent to-morrow, I will tell you who the calumniators are." " To-be-sure I will (rejoined Klearchus), and bring the other generals with me. I shall tell you at the same time, who are the parties that seek to prejudice us against you." The conversation then ended, the satrap detaining Klearchus to dinner, and treating him in the most hospitable and confidential manner.

On the next morning, Klearchus communicated what had passed to the Greeks, insisting on the necessity that all the generals should go to Tissaphernes pursuant to his invitation; in order to reëstablish that confidence which unworthy calumniators had shaken, and to punish such of the calumniators as might be Greeks. So emphatically did he pledge himself for the good faith and philhellenic dispositions of the satrap, that he overruled the opposition of many among the soldiers; who, still continuing to entertain their former suspicions, remonstrated especially against the extreme imprudence of putting all the generals at once into the power of Tissaphernes. The urgency of Klearchus prevailed. Himself with four other generals, — Proxenus, Menon, Agias, and Sokrates, — and twenty lochages or captains, — went to visit the satrap in his tent; about two hundred of the soldiers going along with them, to make pur chases for their own account in the Persian camp-market.[1]

On reaching the quarters of Tissaphernes,— distant nearly three miles from the Grecian camp, according to habit, — the five generals were admitted into the interior, while the lochages remained at the entrance. A purple flag, hoisted from the top of the tent, betrayed too late the purpose for which they had been invited to come. The lochages and the Grecian soldiers who had accompanied them were surprised and cut down, while the generals in the interior were detained, put in chains, and carried up as prisoners to the Persian court. Here Klearchus, Proxenus, Agias, and

---

τίαραν βασιλεῖ μόνῳ ἔξεστιν ὀρθὴν ἔχειν, τὴν δ' ἐπὶ τῇ καρδίᾳ ἴσως ἂν ὑμῶν παρόντων καὶ ἕτερος εἰπετῶς ἔχοι.

[1] Xen. Anab. ii, 5, 30.

Sokrates were beheaded after a short imprisonment. Queen Parysatis, indeed, from affection to Cyrus, not only furnished many
comforts to Klearchus in the prison. by the hands of her surgeon,
Ktesias, but used all her influence with her son Artaxerxes to save
his life; though her efforts were counteracted, on this occasion, by
the superior influence of queen Stateira, his wife. The rivalry
between these two royal women, doubtless arising out of many
other circumstances besides the death of Klearchus, became soon
afterwards so furious, that Parysatis caused Stateira to be poisoned.[1]

Menon was not put to death along with the other generals.
He appears to have taken credit at the Persian court for the
treason of entrapping his colleagues into the hands of Tissaphernes.
But his life was only prolonged to perish a year afterwards in
disgrace and torture, — probably by the requisition of Parysatis,
who thus avenged the death of Klearchus. The queen-mother
had always power enough to perpetrate cruelties, though not always to avert them.[2]   She had already brought to a miserable
end every one, even faithful defenders of Artaxerxes, concerned
in the death of her son Cyrus.

Though Menon thought it convenient, when brought up to
Babylon, to boast of having been the instrument through whom
the generals were entrapped into the fatal tent, this boast is not to
be treated as matter of fact.   For not only does Xenophon explain the catastrophe differently, but in the delineation which he
gives of Menon, dark and odious as it is in the extreme, he does
not advance any such imputation; indirectly, indeed, he sets it

---

[1] Xen. Anab. ii, 6, 1.   Ktesiæ Frag. Persica, c. 60, ed. Bähr; Plutarch,
Artaxerx. c, 19, 20; Diodor. xiv, 27.

[2] Tacit. Histor. i, 45.   " Othoni nondum auctoritas inerat ad *prohibendum*
scelus ; *jubere* jam poterat.   Ita, simulatione iræ, vinciri jussum (Marium
Celsum) et majores pœnas daturum, affirmans, præsenti exitio subtraxit."

Ktesias (Persica, c, 60 ; compare Plutarch and Diodorus as referred to in
the preceding note) attests the treason of Menon, which he probably derived
from the story of Menon himself.   Xenophon mentions the ignominious
death of Menon, and he probably derived his information from Ktesias (see
Anabasis, ii, 6, 29).

The supposition that it was Parysatis who procured the death of Menon,
in itself highly probable, renders all the different statements consistent and
harmonious

aside.[1] Unfortunately for the reputation of Klearchus, no such reasonable excuse can be offered for his credulity, which brought himself as well as his colleagues to so melancholy an end, and his whole army to the brink of ruin. It appears that the general sentiment of the Grecian army, taking just measure of the character of Tissaphernes, was disposed to greater circumspection in dealing with him. Upon that system Klearchus himself had hith·erto acted; and the necessity of it might have been especially present to *his* mind, since he had served with the Lacedæmonian fleet at Miletus in 411 B. C., and had, therefore, had fuller experience than other men in the army, of the satrap's real character.[2] On a sudden he now turns round, and on the faith of a few verbal declarations, puts all the military chiefs into the most defenceless posture and the most obvious peril, such as hardly the strongest grounds for confidence could have justified. Though the remark of Machiavel is justified by large experience, — that from the short-sightedness of men and their obedience to present impulse, the most notorious deceiver will always find new persons to trust him, — still such misjudgment on the part of an officer of age and experience is difficult to explain.[3] Polyænus intimates that beautiful women, exhibited by the satrap at his first banquet to Klearchus alone, served as a lure to attract him with all his colleagues to the second ; while Xenophon imputes the error to continuance of a jealous rivalry with Menon. The latter,[4] it appears, having always been intimate with Ariæus, had been

---

[1] Xenophon seems to intimate that there were various stories current, which he does not credit, to the disparagement of Menon, — καὶ τὰ μὲν δὴ ἀφανῆ ἔξεστι περὶ αὐτοῦ ψεύδεσθαι, etc. (Anab. ii, 6, 28).

Athenæus (xi, p. 505) erroneously states that Xenophon affirmed Menon to be the person who caused the destruction of Klearchus by Tissaphernes.

[2] Xenophon in the Cyropædia (viii, 8, 3) gives a strange explanation of the imprudent confidence reposed by Klearchus in the assurance of the Persian satrap. It arose (he says) from the high reputation for good faith which the Persians had acquired by the undeviating and scrupulous honor of the first Cyrus (or Cyrus the Great), but which they had since ceased to deserve, though the corruption of their character had not before publicly manifested itself.

This is a curious perversion of history to serve the purpose of his ro mance.

[3] Macciavelli, Principe, c, 18, p. 65.   [4] Polyæn. vii, 18

thus brought into previous communication with Tissaphernes, by whom he had been well received, and by whom he was also encouraged to lay plans for detaching the whole Grecian army from Klearchus, so as to bring it all under his (Menon's) command, into the service of the satrap. Such at least was the suspicion of Klearchus; who, jealous in the extreme of his own military authority, tried to defeat the scheme by bidding still higher himself for the favor of Tissaphernes. Imagining that Menon was the unknown calumniator who prejudiced the satrap against him, he hoped to prevail on the satrap to disclose his name and dismiss him.[1] Such jealousy seems to have robbed Klearchus of his customary prudence. We must also allow for another impression deeply fixed in his mind; that the salvation of the army was hopeless without the consent of Tissaphernes, and, therefore, since the latter had conducted them thus far in safety, when he might have destroyed them before, that his designs at the bottom could not be hostile.[2]

Notwithstanding these two great mistakes, — one on the present occasion, one previously, at the battle of Kunaxa, in keeping the Greeks on the right contrary to the order of Cyrus, — both committed by Klearchus, the loss of that officer was doubtless a great misfortune to the army; while, on the contrary, the re moval of Menon was a signal benefit, — perhaps a condition of ultimate safety. A man so treacherous and unprincipled as Xenophon depicts Menon, would probably have ended by really committing towards the army that treason, for which he falsely took credit at the Persian court in reference to the seizure of the generals.

The impression entertained by Klearchus, respecting the hopeless position of the Greeks in the heart of the Persian territory after the death of Cyrus, was perfectly natural in a military man who could appreciate all the means of attack and obstruction which the enemy had it in their power to employ. Nothing is so unaccountable in this expedition as the manner in which such means were thrown away, — the spectacle of Persian impotence. First, the whole line of upward march, including the passage of the Euphrates, left undefended; next, the long trench dug across the

---

[1] Xen. Anab. ii, 5, 27, 28.   [2] Compare Anab. ii, 4, 6, 7; ii, 5, 9.

frontier of Babylonia, with only a passage of twenty feet wide left near the Euphrates, abandoned without a guard; lastly, the line of the Wall of Media and the canals which offered such favorable positions for keeping the Greeks out of the cultivated territory of Babylonia, neglected in like manner, and a convention concluded, whereby the Persians engaged to escort the invaders safe to the Ionian coast, beginning by conducting them through the heart of Babylonia, amidst canals affording inexpugnable defences if the Greeks had chosen to take up a position among them. The plan of Tissaphernes, as far as we can understand it, seems to have been, to draw the Greeks to some considerable distance from the heart of the Persian empire, and then to open his schemes of treasonable hostility, which the imprudence of Klearchus enabled him to do, on the banks of the Great Zab, with chances of success such as he could hardly have contemplated. We have here a fresh example of the wonderful impotence of the Persians. We should have expected that, after having committed so flagrant an act of perfidy, Tissaphernes would at least have tried to turn it to account; that he would have poured, with all his forces and all his vigor, on the Grecian camp, at the moment when it was unprepared, disorganized, and without commanders. Instead of which, when the generals (with those who accompanied them to the Persian camp) had been seized or slain, no attack whatever was made except by small detachments of Persian cavalry upon individual Greek stragglers in the plain. One of the companions of the generals, an Arcadian named Nikarchus, ran wounded into the Grecian camp where the soldiers were looking from afar at the horsemen scouring the plain without knowing what they were about, — exclaiming that the Persians were massacring all the Greeks, officers as well as soldiers. Immediately the Greek soldiers hastened to put themselves in defence, expecting a general attack to be made upon their camp; but no more Persians came near than a body of about three hundred horse, under Ariæus and Mithridates (the confidential companions of the deceased Cyrus), accompanied by the brother of Tissaphernes. These men, approaching the Greek lines as friends. called for the Greek officers to come forth, as they had a message to deliver from the king. Accordingly, Kleanor and Sophænetus, with an adequate guard, came to the front, accompanied by Xenophon, who was anxious to hear news about Proxenus. Ariæus then acquainted them that Klearchus, having been detected in a breach of the convention to which he had sworn, had been put to death ; that Proxenus and Menon, who had divulged his treason, were in high honor at the Persian quarters. He concluded by saying, — the king calls upon you to surrender your arms, which now (he says) belong to him, since they formerly belonged to his slave Cyrus."[1]

The step here taken seems to testify a belief on the part of these Persians, that the generals being now in their power, the Grecian soldiers had become defenceless, and might be required to surrender their arms, even to men who had just been guilty of the most deadly fraud and injury towards them. If Ariæus entertained such an expectation, he was at once undeceived by the language of Kleanor and Xenophon, who breathed nothing but indignant reproach ; so that he soon retired and left the Greeks to their own reflections.

While their camp thus remained unmolested, every man within it was a prey to the most agonizing apprehensions. Ruin appeared impending and inevitable, though no one could tell in what precise form it would come. The Greeks were in the midst of a hostile country, ten thousand stadia from home, surrounded by enemies, blocked up by impassable mountains and rivers, without guides, without provisions, without cavalry to aid their retreat, without generals to give orders. A stupor of sorrow and conscious helplessness seized upon all. Few came to the evening muster; few lighted fires to cook their suppers ; every man lay down to rest where he was ; yet no man could sleep, for fear, anguish, and yearning after relatives whom he was never again to behold.[2]

Amidst the many causes of despondency which weighed down this forlorn army, there was none more serious than the fact, that not a single man among them had now either authority to command, or obligation to take the initiative. Nor was any ambitious candidate likely to volunteer his pretensions, at a moment when the post promised nothing but the maximum of difficulty as well as of hazard. A new, self-kindled, light — and self-originated stimulus — was required, to vivfy the embers of suspended hope and action, in a mass paralyzed for the moment, but every way capable

---

[1] Xen. Anab. ii, 5, 37, 38.   [2] Xen Anab. iii, 1, 2, 3

of effort. And the inspiration now fell, happily for the army upon one in whom a full measure of soldierly strength and courage was combined with the education of an Athenian, a democrat, and a philosopher.

It is in true Homeric vein, and in something like Homeric language, that Xenophon (to whom we owe the whole narrative of the expedition) describes his dream, or the intervention of Oneirus, sent by Zeus, from which this renovating impulse took its rise.[1] Lying mournful and restless, like his comrades, he caught a short repose; when he dreamt that he heard thunder, and saw the burning thunder-bolt fall upon his paternal house, which became forthwith encircled by flames. Awaking, full of terror, he instantly sprang up; upon which the dream began to fit on and blend itself with his waking thoughts, and with the cruel realities of his position. His pious and excited fancy generated a series of shadowy analogies. The dream was sent by Zeus[2] the King, since it was from him that thunder and lightning proceeded. In one respect, the sign was auspicious, — that a great light had appeared to him from Zeus, in the midst of peril and suffering. But on the other hand, it was alarming, that the house had appeared to be completely encircled by flames, preventing all egress, because this seemed to indicate that he would remain confined where he was in the Persian dominions, without being able to overcome the difficulties which hedged him in. Yet doubtful as the promise was, it was still the message of Zeus addressed to himself, serving as a stimulus to him to break through the common stupor and take the initiative movement.[3] " Why am I lying here? Night is advanc-

---

[1] Xen. Anab. iii, 1, 4–11. Ἦν δέ τις ἐν τῃ στρατιᾷ Ξενοφῶν Ἀθηναῖος ὃς οὔτε στρατηγός, etc.

Homer, Iliad, v, 9 —

Ἦν δέ τις ἐν Τρώεσσι Δάρης, ἀφνειός, ἀμύμων,
Ἱρεὺς Ἡφαίστοιο, etc.

Compare the description of Zeus sending Oneirus to the sleeping Agamemnon, at the beginning of the second book of the Iliad.

[2] Respecting the value of a sign from Zeus Basileus, and the necessity of conciliating him, compare various passages in the Cyropædia, ii, 4, 19; iii, 3, 21; vii, 5, 57.

[3] Xen. Anab. iii, 1, 12, 13. Περίφοβος δ' εὐθὺς ἀνηγέρθη, καὶ τὸ ὄναρ τῇ μὲν ἔκρινεν ἀγαθόν, ὅτι ἐν πόνοις ὢν καὶ κινδύνοις φῶς μέγα ἐκ Διὸς ἰδεῖν ἔδοξε, etc........ Ὁποῖόν μὲν δή ἐστι τὸ τοιοῦτον ὄναρ ἰδεῖν, ἔξεστι σκοπεῖν

ing; at day-break the enemy will be on us, and we shall be put to death with tortures. Not a man is stirring to take measures of defence. Why do I wait for any man older than myself, or for man of a different city, to begin?"

With these reflections, interesting in themselves and given with Homeric vivacity, he instantly went to convene the lochagi or captains who had served under his late friend Proxenus; and impressed upon them emphatically the necessity of standing forward to put the army in a posture of defence. "I cannot sleep, gentlemen; neither, I presume, can you, under our present perils. The enemy will be upon us at day-break,— prepared to kill us all with tortures, as his worst enemies. For my part, I rejoice that his flagitious perjury has put an end to a truce by which we were the great losers; a truce under which we, mindful of our oaths, have passed through all the rich possessions of the king, without touching anything except what we could purchase with our own scanty means. Now, we have our hands free; all these rich spoils stand between us and him, as prizes for the better man. The gods, who preside over the match, will assuredly be on the side of us, who have kept our oaths in spite of strong temptations, against these perjurers. Moreover, our bodies are more enduring, and our spirits more gallant, than theirs. They are easier to wound, and easier to kill, than we are, under the same favor of the gods as we experienced at Kunaxa.

"Probably others also are feeling just as we feel. But let us not wait for any one else to come as monitors to us; let us take the lead, and communicate the stimulus of honor to others. Do you show yourselves now the best among the lochages,— more worthy of being generals than the generals themselves. Begin at once,

---

ἐκ τῶν συμβάντων μετὰ τὸ ὄναρ. Γίγνεται γὰρ τάδε. Εὐθὺς ἐπειδὴ ἀνηγέρθη, πρῶτον μὲν ἐννοια αὐτῷ ἐμπίπτει· Τί κατάκειμαι; ἡ δὲ νὺξ προβαίνει ἅμα δὲ τῇ ἡμέρᾳ εἰκὸς τοὺς πολεμίους ἥξειν, etc.

The reader of Homer will readily recall various passages in the Iliad and Odyssey, wherein the like mental talk is put into language and expanded, — such as Iliad, xi, 403 — and several other passages cited or referred to in Colonel Mure's History of the Language and Literature of Greece, ch. xiv, vol. ii, p. 25 seq.

A vision of light shining brightly out of a friendly house, counts for a favorable sign (Plutarch, De Genio Socratis, p. 587 C.).

and I desire only to follow you. But if you order me into the front rank, I shall obey without pleading my youth as an excuse, — accounting myself of complete maturity, when the purpose is to save myself from ruin."[1]

All the captains who heard Xenophon cordially concurred in his suggestion, and desired him to take the lead in executing it. One captain alone,— Apollonides, speaking in the Bœotian dialect, — protested against it as insane ; enlarging upon their desperate position, and insisting upon submission to the king, as the only chance of safety. " How (replied Xenophon) ? Have you forgotten the courteous treatment which we received from the Persians in Babylonia, when we replied to their demand for the surrender of our arms by showing a bold front? Do not you see the miserable fate which has befallen Klearchus, when he trusted himself unarmed in their hands, in reliance on their oaths ? And yet you scout our exhortations to resistance, again advising us to go and plead for indulgence ! My friends, such a Greek as this man, disgraces not only his own city, but all Greece besides. Let us banish him from our counsels, cashier him, and make a slave of him to carry baggage." — " Nay (observed Agasias of Stymphalus), the man has nothing to do with Greece ; I myself have seen his ears bored, like a true Lydian." Apollonides was degraded accordingly.[2]

Xenophon with the rest then distributed themselves in order to bring together the chief remaining officers in the army, who were presently convened, to the number of about one hundred. The

---

[1] Xen. Anab. iii, 1, 16, 25.

" Vel imperatore, vel milite, me utemini." (Sallust, Bellum Catilinar. c. 20).

[2] Xen. Anab. iii, 1, 26–30. It would appear from the words of Xenophon, that Apollonides had been one of those who had held faint-hearted language (ὑπομαλακιζόμενοι, ii, 1, 14) in the conversation with Phalinus shortly after the death of Cyrus. Hence Xenophon tells him, that this is the second time of his offering such advice — Ἃ σὺ πάντα εἰδὼς, τοὺς μὲν ἀμύνεσθαι κελεύοντας φλυαρεῖν φὴς, πείθειν δὲ πάλιν κελεύεις ἰόντας ;

This helps to explain the contempt and rigor with which Xenophon here treats him. Nothing indeed could be more deplorable, under the actual circumstances, than for a man " to show his acuteness by summing up the perils around." See the remarkable speech of Demosthenes at Pylos (Thucyd. iv, 10).

senior captain of the earlier body next desired Xenophon to repeat to this larger body the topics upon which he had just before been insisting. Xenophon obeyed, enlarging yet more emphatically on the situation, perilous, yet not without hope, — on the proper measures to be taken, — and especially on the necessity that they, the chief officers remaining, should put themselves forward prominently, first fix upon effective commanders, then afterwards submit the names to be confirmed by the army, accompanied with suitable exhortations and encouragement. His speech was applauded and welcomed, especially by the Lacedæmonian general Cheirisophus who had joined Cyrus with a body of seven hundred hoplites a Issus in Kilikia. Cheirisophus urged the captains to retire forthwith, and agree upon other commanders instead of the four who had been seized; after which the herald must be summoned, and the entire body of soldiers convened without delay. Accordingly Timasion of Dardanus was chosen instead of Klearchus; Xanthiklês in place of Sokrates; Kleanor in place of Agias; Philesius in place of Menon; and Xenophon instead of Proxenus.[1] The captains, who had served under each of the departed generals, separately chose a successor to the captain thus promoted. It is to be recollected that the five now chosen were not the only generals in the camp; thus for example, Cheirisophus had the command of his own separate division, and there may have been one or two others similarly placed. But it was now necessary for all the generals to form a Board and act in concert.

At daybreak the newly constituted Board of generals placed proper outposts in advance, and then convened the army in general assembly, in order that the new appointments might be submitted and confirmed. As soon as this had been done, probably on the proposition of Cheirisophus (who had been in command before), that general addressed a few words of exhortation and encouragement to the soldiers. He was followed by Kleanor, who delivered, with the like brevity, an earnest protest against the perfidy of Tissaphernes and Ariæus. Both of them left to Xenophon the task, alike important and arduous at this moment of despondency, of setting forth the case at length, — working up the feelings of the soldiers to that pitch of resolution which the emergency required,

---

[1] Xen. Anab. iii, 1, 36–46.

— and above all, extinguishing all those inclinations to acquiesce in new treacherous proposals from the enemy, which the perils of the situation would be likely to suggest.

Xenophon had equipped himself in his finest military costume at this his first official appearance before the army, when the scales seemed to tremble between life and death. Taking up the protest of Kleanor against the treachery of the Persians, he insisted that any attempt to enter into convention or trust with such liars, would be utter ruin, — but that if energetic resolution were taken to deal with them only at the point of the sword, and punish their misdeeds, there was good hope of the favor of the gods and of ultimate preservation. As he pronounced this last word, one of the soldiers near him happened to sneeze. Immediately the whole army around shouted with one accord the accustomed invocation to Zeus the Preserver; and Xenophon, taking up the accident, continued, — " Since, gentlemen, this omen from Zeus the Preserver has appeared at the instant when we were talking about preservation, let us here vow to offer the preserving sacrifice to that god, and at the same time to sacrifice to the remaining gods as well as we can, in the first friendly country which we may reach. Let every man who agrees with me, hold up his hand." All held up their hands; all then joined in the vow, and shouted the pæan.

This accident, so dexterously turned to profit by the rhetorical skill of Xenophon, was eminently beneficial in raising the army out of the depression which weighed them down, and in disposing them to listen to his animating appeal. Repeating his assurances that the gods were on their side, and hostile to their perjured enemy, he recalled to their memory the great invasions of Greece by Darius and Xerxes, — how the vast hosts of Persia had been disgracefully repelled. The army had shown themselves on the field of Kunaxa worthy of such forefathers; and they would for the future be yet bolder, knowing by that battle of what stuff the Persians were made. As for Ariæus and his troops, alike traitors and cowards, their desertion was rather a gain than a loss. The enemy were superior in horsemen; but men on horseback were, after all, only men, half-occupied in the fear of losing their seats, — incapable of prevailing against infantry firm on the ground, — and only better able to run away. Now that the satrap refused to furnish them with provisions to buy, they on their side were released fiom their covenant, and would take provisions without buying. Then as to the rivers; those were indeed difficult to be crossed in the middle of their course; but the army would march up to their sources, and could then pass them without wetting the knee. Or indeed, the Greeks might renounce the idea of retreat, and establish themselves permanently in the king's own country, defying all his force, like the Mysians and Pisidians. "If (said Xenophon) we plant ourselves here at our ease in a rich country, with these tall, stately, and beautiful Median and Persian women for our companions,[1] — we shall be only too ready, like the Lotophagi, to forget our way home. We ought first to go back to Greece, and tell our countrymen that if they remain poor, it is their own fault, when there are rich settlements in this country awaiting all who choose to come, and who have courage to seize them. Let us burn our baggage-waggons and tents, and carry with us nothing but what is of the strictest necessity. Above all things,

---

[1] Xen. Anab. iii, 2, 25.

'Αλλὰ γὰρ δέδοικα μή ἂν ἅπαξ μάθωμεν ἀργοὶ ζῆν καὶ ἐν ἀφθόνοις βιοτεύειν, καὶ Μήδων δὲ καὶ Περσῶν καλαῖς καὶ μεγάλαις γυναιξὶ καὶ παρθένοις ὁμιλεῖν, μὴ, ὥσπερ οἱ λωτοφάγοι, ἐπιλαθώμεθα τῆς οἴκαδε ὁδοῦ.

Hippokrates (De Aëre, Locis, et Aquis, c. 12) compares the physical characteristics of Asiatics and Europeans, noticing the ample, full-grown, rounded, voluptuous, but inactive forms of the first, — as contrasted with the more compact, muscular, and vigorous type of the second, trained for movement, action, and endurance.

Dio Chrysostom has a curious passage, in reference to the Persian preference for eunuchs as slaves, remarking that they admired even in males an approach to the type of feminine beauty, — their eyes and tastes being under the influence only of aphrodisiac ideas; whereas the Greeks, accustomed to the constant training and naked exercises of the palæstra, boys competing with boys and youths with youths, had their associations of the male beauty attracted towards active power and graceful motion.

Οὐ γὰρ φανερὸν, ὅτι οἱ Πέρσαι εὐνούχους ἐποίουν τοὺς καλοὺς, ὅπως αὑτοῖς ὡς κάλλιστοι ὦσι; Τοσοῦτον διαφέρειν ᾤοντο πρὸς κάλλος τὸ θῆλυ σχεδὸν καὶ πάντες οἱ βάρβαροι, διὰ τὸ μόνον τὰ ἀφροδίσια ἐννοεῖν. Κἀκεῖνοι γυναικός εἶδος περιτιθέασι τοῖς ἄρρεσιν, ἄλλως δ' οὐκ ἐπίστανται ἐρᾶν· ἴσως δὲ καὶ ἡ τροφὴ αἰτία τοῖς Πέρσαις, τῷ μέχρι πολλοῦ τρέφεσθαι ὑπό τε γυναικῶν καὶ εὐνούχων τῶν πρεσβυτέρων· παῖδας δὲ μετὰ παιδῶν, καὶ μειράκια μετὰ μειρακίων μὴ πάνυ συνεῖναι, μηδὲ γυμνοῦσθαι ἐν παλαίστραις καὶ γυμνασίοις, etc. (Orat. xxi, p. 270).

Compare Euripides, Bacchæ, 447 seq.; and the Epigram of Strato in the Anthologia, xxxiv, vol. ii, p. 367 Brunck.

let us maintain order, discipline, and obedience to the commanders, upon which our entire hope of safety depends. Let every man promise to lend his hand to the commanders in punishing any disobedient individuals ; and let us thus show the enemy that we have ten thousand persons like Klearchus, instead of that one whom they have so perfidiously seized. Now is the time for action. If any man, however obscure, has anything better to suggest, let him come forward and state it; for we have all but one object, — the common safety."

It appears that no one else desired to say a word, and that the speech of Xenophon gave unqualified satisfaction ; for when Cheirisophus put the question, that the meeting should sanction his recommendations, and finally elect the new generals proposed, — every man held up his hand. Xenophon then moved that the army should break up immediately, and march to some well-stored villages, rather more than two miles distant; that the march should be in a hollow oblong, with the baggage in the centre ; that Cheirisophus, as a Lacedæmonian, should lead the van; while Kleanor, and the other senior officers, would command on each flank, — and himself with Timasion, as the two youngest of the generals, would lead the rear-guard.

This proposition was at once adopted, and the assembly broke up, proceeding forthwith to destroy, or distribute among one another, every man's superfluous baggage, — and then to take their morning meal previous to the march.

The scene just described is interesting and illustrative in more than one point of view.[1] It exhibits that susceptibility to the influence of persuasive discourse which formed so marked a feature in the Grecian character, — a resurrection of the collective body out of the depth of despair, under the exhortation of one who had no established ascendency, nor anything to recommend him, except his intelligence, his oratorical power, and his community of interest with themselves. Next, it manifests, still more strikingly, the superiority of Athenian training as compared with that of other parts of Greece. Cheirisophus had not only been before in

---

[1] A very meagre abstract is given by Diodorus, of that which passed after the seizure of the generals (xiv, 27). He does not mention the name of Xenophon on this occasion, nor indeed throughout all his account of the march

office as one of the generals, but was also a native of Sparta, whose supremacy and name was at that moment all-powerful. Kleanor had been before, not indeed a general, but a lochage, or one in the second rank of officers; — he was an elderly man, — and he was an Arcadian, while more than the numerical half of the army consisted of Arcadians and Achæans. Either of these two, therefore, and various others besides, enjoyed a sort of pre-rogative, or established starting-point, for taking the initiative in reference to the dispirited army. But Xenophon was compara-tively a young man, with little military experience; — he was not an officer at all, either in the first or second grade, but simply a volunteer, companion of Proxenus; — he was, moreover, a native of Athens, a city at that time unpopular among the great body of Greeks, and especially of Peloponnesians, with whom her recent long war had been carried on. Not only, therefore, he had no advantages compared with others, but he was under positive disad-vantages. He had nothing to start with except his personal quali-ties and previous training; in spite of which we find him not merely the prime mover, but also the ascendent person for whom the others make way. In him are exemplified those peculiarities of Athens, attested not less by the denunciation of her enemies than by the panegyric of her own citizens,[1] — spontaneous and forward impulse, as well in conception as in execution, — confi dence under circumstances which made others despair, — persua-

---

[1] Compare the hostile speech of the Corinthian envoy at Sparta. prior to the Peloponnesian war, with the eulogistic funeral oration of Perikles, in the second year of that war (Thucyd. i, 70, 71; ii, 39, 40).

Οἱ μέν γε (εἰσὶ), νεωτεροποιοὶ (description of the Athenians by the Corinth-ian speaker) καὶ ἐπινοῆσαι ὀξεῖς καὶ ἐπιτελέσαι ἔργῳ ἃ ἂν γνῶ-σιν· ὑμεῖς δὲ (Lacedæmonians), τὰ ὑπάρχοντά τε σώζειν καὶ ἐπιγνῶναι μηδὲν. καὶ ἔργῳ οὐδὲ τἀναγκαῖα ἐξικέσθαι. Αὖθις δὲ, οἱ μὲν, καὶ παρὰ δύναμιν τολ-μηταὶ καὶ παρὰ γνώμην κινδυνευταὶ καὶ ἐπὶ τοῖς δεινοῖς εὐέλπιδες· τὸ δὲ ὑμε-τερον, τῆς τεδυνάμεως ἐνδεᾶ πρᾶξαι, τῆς τε γνώμης μηδὲ ὶ οἷς βεβαίοις πιστεύ-σαι, τῶν τε δεινῶν μηδέποτε οἴεσθαι ἀπολυθήσεσθαι. Καὶ μὴν καὶ ἄοκνοι πῃ ὃς ὑμᾶς μελλήτας, καὶ ἀποδημηταὶ πρὸς ἐνδημοτάτους, etc.

Again, in the oration of Perikles — Καὶ αὐτοὶ ἤτοι κρίνομεν ἢ ἐνθυμού-με θα ὀρθῶς τὰ πράγματα, οὐ τοὺς λόγους τοῖς ἔργοις βλάβην ἡγούμενοι, ἀλλὰ μὴ προδιδαχθῆναι μᾶλλον λόγῳ, πρότερον ἢ ἐπὶ ἃ δεῖ ἔργῳ ἐλθεῖν. Διαφερ-όντως μὲν δὴ καὶ τόδε ἔχομεν, ὥστε τολμᾶν τε οἱ αὐτοὶ μάλιστα καὶ περὶ ὧν ἐπιχιερή:ομεν ἐκλογίζεσθαι· ὃ τοῖς ἄλλοις ἀμαθία μὲν θράσος, λογισμὸς δὲ ὄκνον, φέρει.

sive discourse and publicity of discussion, made subservient to practical business, so as at once to appeal to the intelligence, and stimulate the active zeal, of the multitude. Such peculiarities stood out more remarkably from being contrasted with the oppo site qualities in Spartans, — mistrust in conception, slackness in execution, secrecy in counsel, silent and passive obedience. Though Spartans and Athenians formed the two extremities of the scale, other Greeks stood nearer on this point to the former than to the latter.

If, even in that encouraging autumn which followed immediately upon the great Athenian catastrophe before Syracuse, the inertia of Sparta could not be stirred into vigorous action without the ve- hemence of the Athenian Alkibiades, — much more was it neces- sary under the depressing circumstances which now overclouded the unofficered Grecian army, that an Athenian bosom should be found as the source of new life and impulse. Nor would any one, probably, except an Athenian, either have felt or obeyed the promptings to stand forward as a volunteer at that moment, when there was every motive to decline responsibility, and no special duty to impel him. But if by chance, a Spartan or an Arcadian had been found thus forward, he would have been destitute of such talents as would enable him to work on the minds of others [1] — of that flexibility, resource, familiarity with the temper and move- ments of an assembled crowd, power of enforcing the essential views and touching the opportune chords, which Athenian demo-

---

[1] Compare the observations of Perikles, in his last speech to the Athe nians about the inefficiency of the best thoughts, if a man had not the power of setting them forth in an impressive manner (Thucyd. ii, 60). Καίτοι ἐμοὶ τοιούτῳ ἀνδρὶ ὀργίζεσθε, ὃς οὐδενὸς οἴομαι ἥσσων εἶναι γνῶναί τε τὰ δέοντα καὶ ἑρμηνεῦσαι ταῦτα, φιλόπολίς τε καὶ χρημάτων κρείτ- των ὅ τε γὰρ γνοὺς καὶ μὴ σαφῶς διδάξας, ἐν ἴσῳ καὶ εἰ μὴ ἐνεθυμήθη, etc.

The philosopher and the statesman at Athens here hold the same lan guage. It was the opinion of Sokrates — μόνους ἀξίους εἶναι τιμῆς τοὺς εἰδότας τὰ δέοντα, καὶ ἑρμηνεῦσαι δυναμένους (Xenoph. Mem i, 2, 52).

A striking passage in the funeral harangue of Lysias (Orat. ii, Epitaph s. 19) sets forth the prevalent idea of the Athenian democracy — authorita tive law, with persuasive and instructive speech, as superseding mutual vio lence (νόμος and λόγος, as the antithesis of βία). Compare a similar senti ment in Isokrates (Or. iv, (Panegyr.) s. 53–56).

cratical training imparted. Even Brasidas and Gylippus, individual Spartans of splendid merit, and equal or superior to Xenophon in military resource, would not have combined with it that political and rhetorical accomplishment which the position of the latter demanded. Obvious as the wisdom of his propositions appears, each of them is left to him not only to imitate, but to enforce ; — Cheirisophus and Kleanor, after a few words of introduction, consign to him the duty of working up the minds of the army to the proper pitch. How well he performed this, may be seen by his speech to the army, which bears in its general tenor a remarkable resemblance to that of Perikles addressed to the Athenian public in the second year of the war, at the moment when the miseries of the epidemic, combined with those of invasion, had driven them almost to despair. It breathes a strain of exaggerated confidence, and an undervaluing of real dangers, highly suitable for the occasion, but which neither Perikles nor Xenophon would have employed at any other moment.[1] Throughout the whole of his speech, and especially in regard to the accidental sneeze near at hand which interrupted the beginning of it, Xenophon displayed that skill and practice in dealing with a numerous audience and a given situation, which characterized more or less every educated Athenian. Other Greeks, Lacedæmonians or Arcadians, could act, with bravery and in concert; but the Athenian Xenophon was among the few who could think, speak, and act, with equal efficiency.[2] It was this tripartite accomplishment

---

[1] See the speech of Perikles (Thuc. ii, 60–64). He justifies the boastful tone of it, by the unwonted depression against which he had to contend on the part of his hearers — Δελώσω δὲ καὶ τόδε ὅ μοι δοκεῖτε οὔτ᾽ αὐτοὶ πώποτε ἐνθυμηθῆναι ὑπάρχον ὑμῖν μεγέθους περὶ ἐς τὴν ἀρχὴν οὔτ᾽ ἐγὼ ἐν τοῖς πρὶν λόγοις, οὐδ᾽ ἂν νῦν ἐχρησάμην κομπωδεστέραν ἔχοντι τὴν προσποίησιν, εἰ μὴ καταπεπληγμένους ὑμᾶς παρὰ τὸ εἰκὸς ἑώρων.

This is also the proper explanation of Xenophon's tone.

[2] In a passage of the Cyropædia (v. 5, 46), Xenophon sets forth in a striking manner the combination of the λεκτικὸς καὶ πρακτικός — "Ὥσπερ καὶ ὅταν μάχεσθαι δέῃ, ὁ πλείστους χειρωσάμενος ἀλκιμώτατος δοξάζεται εἶναι, οὕτω καὶ ὅταν πεῖσαι δέῃ, ὁ πλεῖστους ὁμογνώμονας ἡμῖν ποιήσας οὗτος δικαίως ἂν λεκτικώτατος καὶ πρακτικώτατος κρίνοιτο ἂν εἶναι. Μὴ μέντοι ὡς λόγον ἡμῖν ἐπιδειξόμενοι, οἷοι ἂν εἴπο.τε πρὸς κ αστον αὐτῶν, -οὗτο μελετᾶτε—ἀλλ᾽ ὡς τοὺς πεπεισμέ-

which an aspiring youth was compelled to set before himself as an aim, in the democracy of Athens, and which the sophists as well as the democratical institutions, both of them so hardly depreciated, helped and encouraged him to acquire. It was this tripartite accomplishment, the exclusive possession of which, in spite of constant jealousy on the part of Bœotian officers and comrades of Proxenus,[1] elevated Xenophon into the most ascendent person of the Cyreian army, from the present moment until the time when it broke up, — as will be seen in the subsequent history.

I think it the more necessary to notice this fact, — that the accomplishments whereby Xenophon leaped on a sudden into such extraordinary ascendency, and rendered such eminent service to his army, were accomplishments belonging in an especial manner to the Athenian democracy and education, — because Xenophon himself has throughout his writings treated Athens not merely without the attachment of a citizen, but with feelings more like the positive antipathy of an exile. His sympathies are all in favor of the perpetual drill, the mechanical obedience, the secret government proceedings, the narrow and prescribed range of ideas, the silent and deferential demeanor, the methodical, though tardy, action — of Sparta. Whatever may be the justice of his preference, certain it is, that the qualities whereby he was himself enabled to contribute so much both to the rescue of the Cyreian army, and to his own reputation, — were Athenian far more than Spartan.

While the Grecian army, after sanctioning the propositions of Xenophon, were taking their morning meal before they commenced their march, Mithridates, one of the Persians previously attached to Cyrus, appeared with a few horsemen on a mission of pretended friendship. But it was soon found out that his purposes were treacherous, and that he came merely to seduce individual

---

νους ὑφ᾽ ἑκάστου δήλους ἐσομένους οἷς ἂν πράττωσιν, οὕτω παρασκευάζεσθε.

In describing the duties of a Hipparch or commander of the cavalry, Xenophon also insists upon the importance of persuasive speech, as a means of keeping up the active obedience of the sol iiers — Εἰς γε μὴν τὸ εὐπειθεῖς εἶναι τοὺς ἀρχομένους, μέγα μὲν καὶ τὸ λόγῳ διδάσκειν, ὅσα ἀγαθὰ ἔνι ἐν τῷ πειθαρχεῖν, etc. (Xen. Mag. Εϛ i, 24)

[1] See Xenoph. Anab. v, 6, 25.

soldiers to desertion, — with a few of whom he succeeded. Ac
cordingly, the resolution was taken to admit no more heralds or
envoys.

Disembarrassed of superfluous baggage, and refreshed, the
army now crossed the Great Zab River, and pursued their march
on the other side, having their baggage and attendants in the centre,
and Cheirisophus leading the van, with a select body of three hundred hoplites.[1]   As no mention is made of a bridge, we are to
presume that they forded the river, — which furnishes a ford (according to Mr. Ainsworth), still commonly used, at a place between
thirty and forty miles from its junction with the Tigris.   When
they had got a little way forward, Mithridates again appeared with
a few hundred cavalry and bowmen.   He approached them like a
friend; but as soon as he was near enough, suddenly began to
harass the rear with a shower of missiles.   What surprises us
most, is, that the Persians, with their very numerous force, made
no attempt to hinder them from crossing so very considerable a
river; for Xenophon estimates the Zab at four hundred feet broad,
—and this seems below the statement of modern travellers, who
inform us that it contains not much less water than the Tigris ; and
though usually deeper and narrower, cannot be much narrower at
any fordable place.[2]   It is to be recollected that the Persians,
habitually marching in advance of the Greeks, must have reached
the river first, and were, therefore, in possession of the crossing,
whether bridge or ford.   Though on the watch for every opportunity
of perfidy, Tissaphernes did not dare to resist the Greeks even in
the most advantageous position, and ventured only upon sending
Mithridates to harass the rear; which he executed with considerable effect.   The bowmen and darters of the Greeks, few in number, were at the same time inferior to those of the Persians ; and

---

[1] Xen. Anab. iii, 3, 6 ; iii, 5, 43.

[2] Xen. Anab. ii, 5, 1.   Ainsworth, Travels and Researches in Asia Minor,
etc. vol. ii, ch. 44, p. 327 ; also his Travels in the Track of the Ten Thou
sand, p. 119-134.

Professor Koch, who speaks with personal knowledge both of Armenia
and of the region east of the Tigris, observes truly that the Great Zab is
the only point (east of the Tigris) which Xenophon assigns in such a manner as to be capable of distinct local identification.   He also observes, here
as elsewhere, that the number of parasangs specified by Xenophon is essentially delusive as a measure of distance (Zug der Zehn Tausend, p. 64).

when Xenophon employed his rear guard, hoplites and peltasts, to charge and repel them, he not only could never overtake any one, but suffered much in getting back to rejoin his own main body. Even when retiring, the Persian horseman could discharge his arrow or cast his javelin behind him with effect; a dexterity which the Parthians exhibited afterwards still more signally, and which the Persian horsemen of the present day parallel with their carbines. This was the first experience which the Greeks had of marching under the harassing attack of cavalry. Even the small detachment of Mithridates greatly delayed their progress; so that they accomplished little more than two miles, reaching the villages in the evening, with many wounded, and much discouragement.[1]

"Thank Heaven," (said Xenophon in the evening, when Cheirisophus reproached him for imprudence in quitting the main body to charge cavalry, whom yet he could not reach.) "Thank Heaven, that our enemies attacked us with a small detachment only, and not with their great numbers. They have given us a valuable lesson, without doing us any serious harm." Profiting by the lesson, the Greek leaders organized during the night and during the halt of the next day, a small body of fifty cavalry; with two hundred Rhodian slingers, whose slings, furnished with leaden bullets, both carried farther and struck harder than those of the Persians hurling large stones. On the ensuing morning, they started before daybreak, since there lay in their way a ravine difficult to pass. They found the ravine undefended (according to the usual stupidity of Persian proceedings), but when they had got nearly a mile beyond it, Mithridates reappeared in pursuit with a body of four thousand horsemen and darters. Confident from his achievement of the preceding day, he had promised, with a body of that force, to deliver the Greeks into the hands of the satrap. But the latter were now better prepared. As soon as he began to attack them, the trumpet sounded, — and forthwith the horsemen, slingers, and darters, issued forth to charge the Persians, sustained by the hoplites in the rear. So effective was the charge, that the Persians fled in dismay, notwithstanding their superiority in number; while the ravine so impeded their flight that many of them were slain, and eighteen prisoners made. The Greek soldiers of their own

---

[1] Xen Anab iii, 3, 9.

accord mutilated the dead bodies, in order to strike terror into the enemy.[1]   At the end of the day's march they reached the Tigris, near the deserted city of Larissa, the vast, massive, and lofty brick walls of which (twenty-five feet in thickness, one hundred feet high, seven miles in circumference) attested its former grandeur. Near this place was a stone pyramid, one hundred feet in breadth, and two hundred feet high; the summit of which was crowded with fugitives out of the neighboring villages.   Another day's march up the course of the Tigris brought the army to a second deserted city called Mespila, nearly opposite to the modern city of Mosul. Although these two cities, which seem to have formed the continuation or the substitute of the once colossal Nineveh or Ninus, were completely deserted, — yet the country around them was so well furnished with villages and population, that the Greeks not only obtained provisions, but also strings for the making of new bows, and lead for bullets to be used for the slingers.[2]

During the next day's march, in a course generally parallel with the Tigris, and ascending the stream, Tissaphernes, coming up along with some other grandees, and with a numerous army, enveloped the Greeks both in flanks and rear. In spite of his advantage of numbers, he did not venture upon any actual charge, but kept up a fire of arrows, darts, and stones. He was, however, so well answered by the newly-trained archers and slingers of the Greeks, that on the whole they had the advantage, in spite of the superior size of the Persian bows, many of which were taken and effectively employed on the Grecian side. Having passed the night in a well-stocked village, they halted there the next day in order to stock themselves with provisions, and then pursued their march for four successive days along a level country, until, on the fifth day, they reached hilly ground with the prospect of still higher hills beyond. All this march was made under unremitting annoyance from the enemy, insomuch that though the order of the Greeks was never broken, a considerable number of their

---

Xen. Anab. iii, 4, 1–5.

[2] Xen. Anab. iii, 4, 17, 18. It is here, on the site of the ancient Nineveh, that the recent investigations of Mr. Layard have brought to light so many curious and valuable Assyrian remains.   The legend which Xenophon heard on the spot, respecting the way in which these cities were captured and ruined, is of a truly Oriental character.

men were wounded. Experience taught them, that it was inconvenient for the whole army to march in one inflexible, undivided,
hollow square; and they accordingly constituted six lochi or regiments of one hundred men each, subdivided into companies of
fifty, and enômoties or smaller companies of twenty-five, each
with a special officer (conformably to the Spartan practice) to
move separately on each flank, and either to fall back, or fall in,
as might suit the fluctuations of the central mass, arising from
impediments in the road or menaces of the enemy.[1] On reaching the hills, in sight of an elevated citadel or palace, with several
villages around it, the Greeks anticipated some remission of the
Persian attack. But after having passed over one hill, they were
proceeding to ascend the second, when they found themselves assailed with unwonted vigor by the Persian cavalry from the summit of it, whose leaders were seen flogging on the men to the
attack.[2] This charge was so efficacious, that the Greek light
troops were driven in with loss, and forced to take shelter within
the ranks of the hoplites. After a march both slow and full of
suffering, they could only reach their night-quarters by sending a
detachment to get possession of some ground above the Persians,
who thus became afraid of a double attack.

The villages which they now reached (supposed by Mr. Ainsworth to have been in the fertile country under the modern town
called Zakhu),[3] were unusually rich in provisions; magazines of
flour, barley, and wine, having been collected there for the Persian satrap. They reposed here three days, chiefly in order to
tend the numerous wounded, for whose necessities, eight of the
most competent persons were singled out to act as surgeons. On
the fourth day they resumed their march, descending into the
plain. But experience had now satisfied them that it was imprudent to continue in march under the attack of cavalry, so that
when Tissaphernes appeared and began to harass them, they
halted at the first village, and when thus in station, easily repelled him. As the afternoon advanced, the Persian assailants **began**

---

[1] Xen. Anab. iii, 4, 19–23.

I incline to believe that there were six lochi upon *each* flank — **that
is,** twelve lochi in all; though the words of Xenophon are not quite **clear**

[2] Xen. Anab. iii, 4–25. Compare Herodot. vii, 21, 56, 103.

[3] **Professor** Koch (Zug der Zehn Tausend, p. 68) is of the same **opinion.**

to retire; for they were always in the habit of taking up their night-post at a distance of near seven miles from the Grecian position; being very apprehensive of nocturnal attack in their camp, when their horses were tied by the leg and without either saddle or bridle.[1] As soon as they had departed, the Greeks resumed their march, and made so much advance during the night, that the Persians did not overtake them either on the next day or the day after.

On the ensuing day, however, the Persians, having made a forced march by night, were seen not only in advance of the Greeks, but in occupation of a spur of high and precipitous ground overhanging immediately the road whereby the Greeks were to descend into the plain. When Cheirisophus approached, he at once saw that descent was impracticable in the face of an enemy thus posted. He therefore halted, sent for Xenophon from the rear, and desired him to bring forward the peltasts to the van. But Xenophon, though he obeyed the summons in person and galloped his horse to the front, did not think it prudent to move the peltasts from the rear, because he saw Tissaphernes, with another portion of the army, just coming up; so that the Grecian army was at once impeded in front, and threatened by the enemy closing upon them behind. The Persians on the high ground in front could not be directly assailed. But Xenophon observed, that on the right of the Grecian army, there was an accessible mountain-summit yet higher, from whence a descent might be made for a flank attack upon the Persian position. Pointing out this summit to Cheirisophus, as affording the only means of dislodging the troops in front, he urged that one of them should immediately hasten with a detachment to take possession of it, and offered to Cheirisophus the choice either of going, or staying with the army. " Choose yourself," said Cheirisophus. " Well, then, (said Xenophon), I will go; since I am the younger of the

---

[1] Xen. Anab. iii, 4, 35; see also Cyropædia, iii, 3, 37.

The Thracian prince Seuthes was so apprehensive of night attack, that he and his troops kept their horses bridled all night (Xen. Anab. vii, 2, 21.)

Mr. Kinneir (Travels in Asia Minor, etc., p. 481) states that the horses of Oriental cavalry, and even of the English cavalry in Hindostan, are still kept tied and shackled at night, in the same way as Xenophon describes to have been practised by the Persians.

then, (said Xenophon), I will go; since I am the younger of the two." Accordingly, at the head of a select detachment from the van and centre of the army, he immediately commenced his flank march up the steep ascent to this highest summit. So soon as the enemy saw their purpose, they also detached troops on their side, hoping to get to the summit first; and the two detachments were seen mounting at the same time, each struggling with the utmost efforts to get before the other, — each being encouraged by shouts and clamor from the two armies respectively.

As Xenophon was riding by the side of his soldiers, cheering them on and reminding them that their chance of seeing their country and their families all depended upon success in the effort before them, a Sikyonian hoplite in the ranks, named Sotêridas, said to him, — " You and I are not on an equal footing, Xenophon. You are on horseback; I am painfully struggling up on foot, with my shield to carry." Stung with this taunt, Xenophon sprang from his horse, pushed Sotêridas out of his place in the ranks, took his shield as well as his place, and began to march forward afoot along with the rest. Though thus weighed down at once by the shield belonging to an hoplite, and by the heavy cuirass of a horseman (who carried no shield), he nevertheless put forth all his strength to advance, under such double incumbrance, and to continue his incitement to the rest. But the soldiers around him were so indignant at the proceeding of Sotêridas, that they reproached and even struck him, until they compelled him to resume his shield as well as his place in the ranks. Xenophon then remounted and ascended the hill on horseback as far as the ground permitted; but was obliged again to dismount presently, in consequence of the steepness of the uppermost portion. Such energetic efforts enabled him and his detachment to reach the summit first. As soon as the enemy saw this, they desisted from their ascent, and dispersed in all directions; leaving the forward march open to the main Grecian army, which Cheirisophus accordingly conducted safely down into the plain. Here he was rejoined by Xenophon on descending from the summit. All found themselves in comfortable quarters, amidst several well-stocked villages on the banks of the Tigris. They acquired moreover an additional booty of large droves of cattle, intercepted when on the point

of being transported across the river; where a considerable body
of horse were seen assembled on the opposite bank.[1]

Though here disturbed only by some desultory attacks on the
part of the Persians, who burnt several of the villages which lay
in their forward line of march, the Greeks became seriously embarrassed whither to direct their steps; for on their left flank was
the Tigris, so deep that their spears found no bottom, — and on
their right, mountains of exceeding height. As the generals and
the lochages were taking counsel, a Rhodian soldier came to them
with a proposition for transporting the whole army across to the
other bank of the river by means of inflated skins, which could be
furnished in abundance by the animals in their possession. But
this ingenious scheme, in itself feasible, was put out of the question by the view of the Persian cavalry on the opposite bank;
and as the villages in their front had been burnt, the army had
no choice except to return back one day's march to those in which
they had before halted. Here the generals again deliberated,
questioning all their prisoners as to the different bearings of the
country. The road from the south was that in which they had
already marched from Babylon and Media; that to the westward, going to Lydia and Ionia, was barred to them by the inter-
posing Tigris; eastward (they were informed) was the way to
Ekbatana and Susa; northward, lay the rugged and inhospitable
mountains of the Karduchians, — fierce freemen who despised the
Great King, and defied all his efforts to conquer them; having
once destroyed a Persian invading army of one hundred and
twenty thousand men. On the other side of Karduchia, however,
lay the rich Persian satrapy of Armenia, wherein both the Euphrates and the Tigris could be crossed near their sources, and from
whence could choose their farther course easily towards Greece
Like Mysia, Pisidia, and other mountainous regions, Karduchia
was a free territory surrounded on all sides by the dominions of
the Great King, who reigned only in the cities and on the plains.[2]

---

[1] Xen. Anab. iii, 4, 36–49; iii, 5, 3.

[2] Xen. Anab. iii, 5; iv, 1, 3. Probably the place where the Greeks quit
ted the Tigris to strike into the Karduchian mountains, was the neighborhood of Jezireh ibn Omar, the ancient Bezabde. It is here that farther
march, up the eastern side of the Tigris, is rendered impracticable by the

Determining to fight their way across these difficult mountains into Armenia, but refraining from any public announcement, for fear that the passes should be occupied beforehand, — the generals sacrificed forthwith, in order that they might be ready for breaking up at a moment's notice.   They then began their march a little after midnight, so that soon after daybreak they reached the first of the Karduchian mountain-passes, which they found undefended.   Cheirisophus, with his front division and all the light troops, made haste to ascend the pass, and having got over the first mountain, descended on the other side to some villages in the valley or nooks beneath; while Xenophon with the heavy-armed and the baggage, followed at a slower pace, — not reaching the villages until dark, as the road was both steep and narrow. The Karduchians, taken completely by surprise, abandoned the villages as the Greeks approached, and took refuge on the mountains; leaving to the intruders plenty of provisions, comfortable houses, and especially, abundance of copper vessels.   At first the Greeks were careful to do no damage, trying to invite the natives to amicable colloquy.   But none of the latter would come near, and at length necessity drove the Greeks to take what was necessary for refreshment.   It was just when Xenophon and the rear guard were coming in at night, that some few Karduchians first set upon them; by surprise and with considerable success, — so that if their numbers had been greater, serious mischief might have ensued.[1]

Many fires were discovered burning on the mountains, — an earnest of resistance during the next day; which satisfied the Greek generals that they must lighten the army, in order to ensure greater expedition as well as a fuller complement of available hands during the coming march.   They therefore gave orders to burn all the baggage except what was indispensable, and to dismiss all the prisoners; planting themselves in a narrow strait, through which the army had to pass, in order to see that their directions were executed.   The women, however, of whom there

---

mountains closing in.   Here the modern road crosses the Tigris by a bridge, from the eastern bank to the western (Koch, Zug der Zehn Tausend p. 72).

[1] Xen. Anab. iv, 1. 12

were many with the army, could not be abandoned; and it seems farther that a considerable stock of baggage was still retained;[1] nor could the army make more than slow advance, from the narrowness of the road and the harassing attack of the Karduchians, who were now assembled in considerable numbers. Their attack was renewed with double vigor on the ensuing day, when the Greeks were forced, from want of provisions, to hasten forward their march, though in the midst of a terrible snow-storm. Both Cheirisophus in the front and Xenophon in the rear, were hard pressed by the Karduchian slingers and bowmen; the latter, men of consummate skill, having bows three cubits in length, and arrows of more than two cubits, so strong that the Greeks when they took them could dart them as javelins. These archers, amidst the rugged ground and narrow paths, approached so near and drew the bow with such surprising force, resting one extremity of it on the ground, that several Greek warriors were mortally wounded even through both shield and corslet into the reins, and through the brazen helmet into their heads; among them especially, two distinguished men, a Lacedæmonian named Kleonymus, and an Arcadian named Basias.[2] The rear division, more roughly handled than the rest, was obliged continually to halt to repel the enemy, under all the difficulties of the ground, which made it scarcely possible to act against nimble mountaineers. On one occasion, however, a body of these latter were entrapped into an ambush, driven back with loss, and (what was still more fortunate) two of their number were made prisoners.

Thus impeded, Xenophon sent frequent messages entreating Cheirisophus to slacken the march of the van division; but instead of obeying, Cheirisophus only hastened the faster, urging Xenophon to follow him. The march of the army became little better than a rout, so that the rear division reached the halting-place in extreme confusion; upon which Xenophon proceeded to remonstrate with Cheirisophus for prematurely hurrying forward and neglecting his comrades behind. But the other, — pointing out to his attention the hill before them, and the steep path ascending it, forming their future line of march, which was beset with numerous Karduchians, — defended himself by saying that

---

[1] Xen. Anab. iv, 3, 19–30.   [2] Xen. Anab. iv 1, 18; iv, 2, 28.

he had hastened forward in hopes of being able to reach this pass before the enemy, in which attempt however he had not succeeded.[1]

To advance farther on this road appeared hopeless; yet the guides declared that no other could be taken. Xenophon then bethought him of the two prisoners whom he had just captured, and proposed that these two should be questioned also. They were accordingly interrogated apart; and the first of them, — having persisted in denying, notwithstanding all menaces, that there was any road except that before them, — was put to death under the eyes of the second prisoner. This latter, on being then questioned, gave more comfortable intelligence; saying that he knew of a different road, more circuitous, but easier and practicable even for beasts of burden, whereby the pass before them and the occupying enemy might be turned; but that there was one particular high position commanding the road, which it was necessary to master beforehand by surprise, as the Karduchians were already on guard there. Two thousand Greeks, having the guide bound along with them, were accordingly despatched late in the afternoon, to surprise this post by a night-march; while Xenophon, in order to distract the attention of the Karduchians in front, made a feint of advancing as if about to force the direct pass. As soon as he was seen crossing the ravine which led to this mountain, the Karduchians on the top immediately began to roll down vast masses of rock, which bounded and dashed down the roadway, in such manner as to render it unapproachable. They continued to do this all night, and the Greeks heard the noise of the descending masses long after they had returned to their camp for supper and rest.[2]

Meanwhile the detachment of two thousand, marching by the circuitous road, and reaching in the night the elevated position, (though there was another above yet more commanding), held by the Karduchians, surprised and dispersed them, passing the night by their fires. At daybreak, and under favor of a mist, they stole silently towards the position occupied by the other Karduchians in front of the main Grecian army. On coming near they suddenly sounded their trumpets, shouted aloud, and commenced the attack, which proved completely successful. The defenders, taken un-

---

[1] Xen. Anab. iv, 1, 21.

[2] Xen. Anab. iv, 2, 4.

prepared, fled with little resistance, and scarcely any loss, from their activity and knowledge of the country; while Cheirisophus and the main Grecian force, on hearing the trumpet which had been previously concerted as the signal, rushed forward and stormed the height in front; some along the regular path, others climbing up as they could and pulling each other up by means of their spears. The two bodies of Greeks thus joined each other on the summit, so that the road became open for farther advance.

Xenophon, however, with the rear guard, marched on the circuitous road taken by the two thousand, as the most practicable for the baggage animals, whom he placed in the centre of his division, — the whole array covering a great length of ground, since the road was very narrow. During this interval, the dispersed Karduchians had rallied, and reoccupied two or three high peaks, commanding the road, — from whence it was necessary to drive them. Xenophon's troops stormed successively these three positions, the Karduchians not daring to affront close combat, yet making destructive use of their missiles. A Grecian guard was left on the hindermost of the three peaks, until all the baggage train should have passed by. But the Karduchians, by a sudden and well-timed movement, contrived to surprise this guard, slew two out of the three leaders, with several soldiers, and forced the rest to jump down the crags as they could, in order to join their comrades in the road. Encouraged by such success, the assailants pressed nearer to the marching army, occupying a crag over against that lofty summit on which Xenophon was posted. As it was within speaking distance, he endeavored to open a negotiation with them in order to get back the dead bodies of the slain. To this demand the Karduchians at first acceded, on condition that their villages should not be burnt; but finding their numbers every moment increasing, they resumed the offensive. When Xenophon with the army had begun his descent from the last summit, they hurried onward in crowds to occupy it; beginning again to roll down masses of rock, and renew their fire of missiles, upon the Greeks Xenophon himself was here in some danger, having been deserted by his shield-bearer; but he was rescued by an Arcadian hoplite named Eurylochus, who ran to give him the benefit of his own shield as a protection for both in the retreat.[1]

---

[1] Xen. Anab. iv, 3, 17-21.

Afte₁ a march thus painful and perilous, the rear division at ₁ength found themselves in safety among their comrades. in villages with well-stocked houses and abundance of corn and wine. So eager, however, were Xenophon and Cheirisophus to obtain the bodies of the slain for burial, that they consented to purchase them by surrendering the guide, and to march onward without any guide; — a heavy sacrifice in this unknown country, attesting their great anxiety about the burial.[1]

For three more days did they struggle and fight their way through the narrow and rugged paths of the Karduchian mountains, beset throughout by these formidable bowmen and slingers; whom they had to dislodge at every difficult turn, and against whom their own Kretan bowmen were found inferior, indeed, but still highly useful. Their seven days' march through this country, with its free and warlike inhabitants, were days of the utmost fatigue, suffering and peril; far more intolerable than anything which they had experienced from Tissaphernes and the Persians. Right glad were they once more to see a plain, and to find themselves near the banks of the river Kentritês, which divided these mountains from the hillocks and plains of Armenia, — enjoying comfortable quarters in villages, with the satisfaction of talking over past miseries.[2]

Such were the apprehensions of Karduchian invasion, that the Armenian side of the Kentritês, for a breadth of fifteen miles, was unpeopled and destitute of villages.[3] But the approach of the Greeks having become known to Tiribazus, satrap of Armenia, the banks of the river were lined with his cavalry and infantry to oppose their passage; a precaution, which if Tissaphernes had

---

[1] Xen. Anab. iv, 3, 23.

[2] Xen. Anab. iv, 3, 2. His expressions have a simple emphasis which marks how unfading was the recollection of what he had suffered in Karduchia.

Καὶ οἱ Ἕλληνες ἐνταῦθα ἀνεπαύσαντο ἁσμενοι ἰδόντες πέδιον· ἀπεῖχε δὲ τῶν ὁρέων ὁ ποταμὸς ἓξ ἢ ἑπτα στάδια τῶν Καρδούχων. Τότε μὲν οὖν ηὐλίσθησαν μάλα ἡδέως, κιὶ τὰ ἐπιτήδεια ἔχοντες καὶ πολλὰ τῶν παρεληλυθότων πόνων μνημονεύοντες. Ἑπτα γὰρ ἡμέρας, ὑσασπερ ἐπορεύθησαν διὰ τῶν Καρδούχων, πάρας μαχόμενοι διετέλεσαν, καὶ ἔπαθον κακὰ ὅσα οὐδὲ τὰ σύμπαντα ὑπὸ βασιλέως καὶ Τισσαφέρνους. Ὡς οὖν ἀπηλλαγμένοι -ύτων ἡδέως ἐκοιμήθησαν.

[3] Xen. Anab. iv, 4, 1.

taken at the Great Zab at the moment when he perfidiously seized Klearchus and his colleagues, the Greeks would hardly have reached the northern bank of that river. In the face of such obstacles, the Greeks, nevertheless, attempted the passage of the Kentritês, seeing a regular road on the other side. But the river was two hundred feet in breadth (only half the breadth of the Zab), above their breasts in depth, extremely rapid, and with a bottom full of slippery stones; insomuch that they could not hold their shields in the proper position, from the force of the stream, while if they lifted the shields above their heads, they were exposed defenceless to the arrows of the satrap's troops. After various trials, the passage was found impracticable, and they were obliged to resume their encampment on the left bank. To their great alarm they saw the Karduchians assembling on the hills in their rear, so that their situation, during this day and night, appeared nearly desperate. In the night, Xenophon had a dream,— the first, which he has told us, since his dream on the terrific night after the seizure of the generals,— but on this occasion, of augury more unequivocally good. He dreamed that he was bound in chains, but that his chains on a sudden dropped off spontaneously; on the faith of which, he told Cheirisophus at daybreak that he had good hopes of preservation; and when the generals offered sacrifice, the victims were at once favorable. As the army were taking their morning meal, two young Greeks ran to Xenophon with the auspicious news that they had accidentally found another ford near half a mile up the river, where the water was not even up to their middle, and where the rocks came so close on the right bank that the enemy's horse could offer no opposition. Xenophon, starting from his meal in delight, immediately offered libations to those gods who had revealed both the dream to himself in the night, and the unexpected ford afterwards to these youths; two revelations which he ascribed to the same gods.[1]

Presently they marched in their usual order, Cheirisophus commanding the van and Xenophon the rear, along the river to the newly-discovered ford; the enemy marching parallel with them on the opposite bank. Having reached the ford, halted, and grounded arms, Cheirisophus placed a wreath on his head, took it off again,

---

[1] Xen. Anab. iv, 3, 6–13.

and then resumed his arms, ordering all the rest to follow his example.[1]   Each lochus (company of one hundred men) was then
arranged in column or single file, with Cheirisophus himself in the
centre. Meanwhile the prophets were offering sacrifice to the river.
So soon as the signs were pronounced to be favorable, all the soldiers shouted the pæan, and all the women joined in chorus with
their feminine yell.   Cheirisophus then at the head of the army,
entered the river and began to ford it; while Xenophon, with a
large portion of the rear division, made a feint of hastening back to
the original ford, as if he were about to attempt the passage there.
This distracted the attention of the enemy's horse; who became
afraid of being attacked on both sides, galloped off to guard the passage at the other point, and opposed no serious resistance to Cheirisophus. As soon as the latter had reached the other side, and put
his division into order, he marched up to attack the Armenian infantry, who were on the high banks a little way above ; but this
infantry, deserted by its cavalry, dispersed without awaiting his
approach. The handful of Grecian cavalry, attached to the division of Cheirisophus, pursued and took some valuable spoils.[2]

---

[1] Xen. Anab. iv, 3, 17.

...ἔθεντο τὰ ὅπλα, καὶ αὐτὸς πρῶτος Χειρίσοφος, στεφανωσάμενος καὶ ἀπς
δὺς, ἐλάμβανε τὰ ὅπλα, καὶ τοῖς ἄλλοις πᾶσι παρήγγελλε.

I apprehend that the words τὸν στέφανον are here to be understood after
ὑποδὺς — not the words τὰ ὅπλα, as Krüger in his note seems to imagine.
It is surely incredible, that in the actual situation of the Grecian army, the
soldiers should be ordered first to disarm, and then to resume their arms.
I conceive the matter thus : — First, the order is given, to ground arms ; so
that the shield is let down and drops upon the ground, sustained by the left
hand of the soldier upon its upper rim ; while the spear, also resting on the
ground, is sustained by the shield and by the same left hand.   The right
hand of the soldier being thus free, he is ordered first to wreath himself
(the costume usual in offering sacrifice) — next, to take off his wreath —
lastly, to resume his arms.

Probably the operations of wreathing and unwreathing, must here have
been performed by the soldiers symbolically, or by gesture, raising the
hand to the head, as if to crown it.   For it seems impossible that they
could have been provided generally with actual wreaths, on the banks of
the Kentritês, and just after their painful march through the Karduchian
mountains. Cheirisophus himself, however, had doubtless a real wreath,
which he put on and took off · so probably had the prophets and certain
select officiating persons.

[2] Xen. Anab. iv, 3. 20–25.

As soon as Xenophon saw his colleague successfully established on the opposite bank, he brought back his detachment to the ford over which the baggage and attendants were still passing, and proceeded to take precautions against the Karduchians on his own side, who were assembling in the rear. He found some difficulty in keeping his rear division together, for many of them, in spite of orders, quitted their ranks, and went to look after their mistresses or their baggage in the crossing of the water.[1] The peltasts and bowmen, who had gone over with Cheirisophus, but whom that general now no longer needed, were directed to hold themselves prepared on both flanks of the army crossing, and to advance a little way into the water, in the attitude of men just about to re-cross. When Xenophon was left with only the diminished rear-guard, the rest having got over, — the Karduchians rushed upon him, and began to shoot and sling. But on a sudden, the Grecian hoplites charged with their accustomed pæan, upon which the Karduchians took to flight, — having no arms for close combat on the plain. The trumpet now being heard to sound, they ran away so much the faster; while this was the signal, according to orders before given by Xenophon, for the Greeks to suspend their charge, to turn back, and to cross the river as speedily as possible. By favor of this able manœuvre, the passage was accomplished by the whole army, with little or no loss, about mid-day.[2]

They now found themselves in Armenia; a country of even, undulating surface, but very high above the level of the sea, and extremely cold at the season when they entered it, — December. Though the strip of land bordering on Karduchia furnished no supplies, one long march brought them to a village, containing abundance of provisions, together with a residence of the satrap Tiribazus; after which, in two farther marches, they reached the river Teleboas, with many villages on its banks. Here Tiribazus himself, appearing with a division of cavalry, sent forward his interpreter to request a conference with the leaders; which being held, it was agreed that the Greeks should proceed unmolested through his territory, taking such supplies as they required, — but should neither burn nor damage the villages. They accordingly advanced onward for three days, computed at fifteen parasangs, or

---

[1] Xen. Anab. iv, 3, 30.   [2] Xen. Anab. iv, 3, 31–34; iv, 4, 1.

three pretty full days' march; without any hostility from the satrap though he was hovering within less than two miles of them. They then found themselves amidst several villages, wherein were regal or satrapical residences, with a plentiful stock of bread, meat, wine, and all sorts of vegetables. Here, during their nightly bivouac, they were overtaken by so heavy a fall of snow, that the generals, on the next day, distributed the troops into separate quarters among the villages. No enemy appeared near, while the snow seemed to forbid any rapid surprise. Yet at night, the scouts reported that many fires were discernible, together with traces of military movements around; insomuch that the generals thought it prudent to put themselves on their guard, and again collected the army into one bivouac. Here, in the night, they were overwhelmed by a second fall of snow, still heavier than the preceding; sufficient to cover over the sleeping men and their arms, and to benumb the cattle. The men, however, lay warm under the snow and were unwilling to rise, until Xenophon himself set the example of rising, and employing himself, without his arms, in cutting wood and kindling a fire.[1] Others followed his example, and great comfort was found in rubbing themselves with pork-fat, oil of almonds, or of sesame, or turpentine. Having sent out a clever scout named Demokrates, who captured a native prisoner, they learned that Tiribazus was laying plans to intercept them in a lofty mountain-pass lying farther on in their route; upon which they immediately set forth, and by two days of forced march, surprising in their way the camp of Tiribazus, got over the difficult pass in safety. Three days of additional march brought them to the Euphrates river,[2] — that is, to the eastern branch, now called Murad. They found a ford and crossed it, without having the water higher than the navel; and they were informed that its sources were not far off.

---

[1] Xen. Anab. iv, 4, 11.

[2] Xen. Anab. iv, 5, 2.

The recent editors, Schneider and Krüger, on the authority of various MSS., read here ἐπορεύθησαν — ἐπι τὸν Εὐφράτην ποταμόν. The old reading was, as it stands in Hutchinson's edition, παρὰ τὸν Εὐφράτην ποταμόν.

This change may be right, but the geographical data are here too vague to admit of any certainty. See my Appendix annexed to this chapter.

Their four days of march, next on the other side of the Eu-phrates, were toilsome and distressing in the extreme ; through a plain covered with deep snow (in some places six feet deep), and at times in the face of a north wind so intolerably chilling and piercing, that at length one of the prophets urged the necessity of offering sacrifices to Boreas ; upon which (says Xenophon[1]) the severity of the wind abated conspicuously, to the evident conscious-ness of all. Many of the slaves and beasts of burden, and a few even of the soldiers, perished; some had their feet frost-bitten, others became blinded by the snow, others again were exhausted by hunger. Several of these unhappy men were unavoidably left behind ; others lay down to perish, near a warm spring which had melted the snow around, from extremity of fatigue and sheer wretchedness, though the enemy were close upon the rear. It was in vain that Xenophon, who commanded the rear-guard, em ployed his earnest exhortations, prayers, and threats, to induce them to move forward. The sufferers, miserable and motionless, answered only by entreating him to kill them at once. So greatly was the army disorganized by wretchedness, that we hear of one case in which a soldier, ordered to carry a disabled comrade, diso-beyed the order, and was about to bury him alive.[2] Xenophon made a sally, with loud shouts and clatter of spear with shield, in which even the exhausted men joined, — against the pursuing enemy. He was fortunate enough to frighten them away, and drive them to take shelter in a neighboring wood. He then lef: the sufferers lying down, with assurance that relief should be sen. to them on the next day, — and went forward, seeing all along the line of march the exhausted soldiers lying on the snow, without even the protection of a watch. He and his rear-guard, as wel as the rest, were obliged thus to pass the night without either food or fire, distributing scouts in the best way the case admitted Meanwhile, Cheirisophus with the van division had got into a vil lage, which they reached so unexpectedly, that they found the wo

---

[1] Xen. Anab. iv, 5, 4.

Ἔνθα δὴ τῶν μάντεων τις εἶπε σφαγιάσασθαι τῷ Ἀνέμῳ καὶ πᾶσι δὴ περι-φανῶς ἔδοξε λῆξαι τὸ χαλεπὸν τοῦ πνεύματος.

The suffering of the army from the terrible snow and cold of Armenia are set forth in Diodorus, xiv, 28

[2] Xen. Anab. v, 8, 8–11

men fetching water from a fountain outside the wall, and the head-man of the village in his house within. This division here ob tained rest and refreshment, and at daybreak some of their soldiers were sent to look after the rear. It was with delight that Xeno-phon saw them approach, and sent them back to bring up in their arms, into the neighboring village, those exhausted soldiers who had been left behind.[1]

Repose was now indispensable after the recent sufferings. There were several villages near at hand, and the generals, thinking it no longer dangerous to divide the army, quartered the different divisions among them according to lot. Polykrates, an Athenian, one of the captains in the division of Xenophon, requested his permission to go at once and take possession of the village assigned to him, before any of the inhabitants could escape. Accordingly, running at speed with a few of the swiftest soldiers, he came upon the village so suddenly as to seize the headman, with his newly-married daughter, and several young horses intended as a tribute for the king. This village, as well as the rest, was found to con-sist of houses excavated in the ground (as the Armenian villages are at the present day), spacious within, but with a narrow mouth like a well, entered by a descending ladder. A separate entrance was dug for conveniently admitting the cattle. All of them were found amply stocked with live cattle of every kind, wintered upon hay ; as well as with wheat, barley, vegetables, and a sort of bar-ley-wine or beer, in tubs, with the grains of barley on the surface. Reeds or straws, without any joint in them, were lying near, through which they sucked the liquid.[2] Xenophon did his utmost to con-ciliate the headman (who spoke Persian, and with whom he com-municated through the Perso-Grecian interpreter of the army),

---

[1] Xen. Anab. iv, 5, 8–22.

[2] Xen. Anab. iv, 5, 26. Κάλαμοι γόνατα οὐκ ἔχοντες.

This Armenian practice of sucking the beer through a reed, to which the observation of modern travellers supplies analogies (see Krüger's note), illustrates the Fragment of Archilochus (No. 28, ed. Schneidewin, Poetæ Græc. Minor).

$$\text{ὥσπερ αὐλῷ βρύτον ἢ Θρῇιξ ἀνὴρ}$$
$$\text{ἢ Φρὺξ ἔβρυζε, etc.}$$

The similarity of Armenian customs to those of the Thracians and Phrygians, is not surprising.

promising hi n that not one of his relations should be maltreated, and that he should be fully remunerated if he would conduct the army safely out of the country, into that of the Chalybes which he described as being adjacent. By such treatment the headman was won over, promised his aid, and even revealed to the Greeks the subterranean cellars wherein the wine was deposited; while Xenophon, though he kept him constantly under watch, and placed his youthful son as a hostage under the care of Episthenes, yet continued to treat him with studied attention and kindness. For seven days did the fatigued soldiers remain in these comfortable quarters, refreshing themselves and regaining strength. They were waited upon by the native youths, with whom they communicated by means of signs. The uncommon happiness which all of them enjoyed after their recent sufferings, stands depicted in the lively details given by Xenophon; who left here his own exhausted horse, and took young horses in exchange, for himself and the other officers.[1]

After this week of repose, the army resumed its march through the snow. The headman, whose house they had replenished as well as they could, accompanied Cheirisophus in the van as guide, but was not put in chains or under guard; his son remained as an hostage with Episthenes, but his other relations were left unmolested at home. As they marched for three days without reaching a village, Cheirisophus began to suspect his fidelity, and even became so out of humor, though the man affirmed that there were no villages in the track, as to beat him, — yet without the precaution of putting him afterwards in fetters. The next night, accordingly, this headman made his escape; much to the displeasure of Xenophon, who severely reproached Cheirisophus, first for his harshness, and next for his neglect. This was the only point of difference between the two (says Xenophon), during the whole march; a fact very honorable to both, considering the numberless difficulties against which they had to contend. Episthenes retained the headman's youthful son, carried him home in safety, and became much attached to him.[2]

Condemned thus to march without a guide, they could do no better than march up the course of a river; and thus, from the

[1] Xen. Anab. iv, 5, 26–36.   [2] Xen. Anab. iv, 6. 1–3.

villages which had proved so cheering and restorative, they proceeded seven days' march all through snow, up the river Phasis;
a river not verifiable, but certainly not the same as is commonly
known under that name by Grecian geographers; it was one hundred feet in breadth.[1] Two more days' march brought them from
this river to the foot of a range of mountains; near a pass occupied by an armed body of Chalybes, Taochi, and Phasiani.

Observing the enemy in possession of this lofty ground, Chei
risophus halted until all the army came up; in order that the generals might take counsel. Here Kleanor began by advising that
they should storm the pass with no greater delay than was necessary to refresh the soldiers. But Xenophon suggested that it was
far better to avoid the loss of life which must thus be incurred, and
to amuse the enemy by feigned attack, while a detachment should
be sent by stealth, at night, to ascend the mountain at another
point and turn the position. " However (continued he, turning to
Cheirisophus), stealing a march upon the enemy is more your
trade than mine. For I understand that you, the full citizens and
peers at Sparta, practise stealing from your boyhood upward;[2]
and that it is held no way base, but even honorable, to steal such
things as the law does not distinctly forbid. And to the end that
you may steal with the greatest effect, and take pains to do it in
secret, the custom is, to flog you if you are found out. Here, then,
you have an excellent opportunity for displaying your training.
Take good care that we be not found out in stealing an occupation
of the mountain now before us; for if we *are* found out, we shall
be well beaten.

" Why, as for that (replied Cheirisophus), you Athenians, also,
as I learn, are capital hands at stealing the public money, and that
too in spite of prodigious peril to the thief; nay, your most powerful men steal most of all, — at least, if it be the most powerful
men among you who are raised to official command. So that this

---

[1] Xen. Anab. iv, 6, 4.

[2] Xen. Anab. iv, 6, 10–14.

Καὶ οὐκ αἰσχρὸν εἶναι, ἀλλὰ κ α λ ὸ ν κλέπτειν, etc. The reading κ α -
λ ὸ ν is preferred by Schneider to ἀ ν α γ κ α ῖ ο ν, which has been the vul-
gar reading, and is still retained by Krüger. Both are sanctioned by
authority of MSS., and either would be admissible; on the whole, I incline
to side with Schneider

is a time for *you* to exhibit *your* training as well as for me to exhibit mine." [1]

We have here an interchange of raillery between the two Grecian officers, which is not an uninteresting feature in the history of the expedition. The remark of Cheirisophus, especially illustrates that which I noted in a former chapter as true both of Sparta and Athens [2], — the readiness to take bribes, so general in individuals clothed with official power; and the readiness, in official Athenians, to commit such peculation, in spite of serious risk of punishment. Now this chance of punishment proceeded altogether from those accusing orators commonly called demagogues, and from the popular judicature whom they addressed. The joint working of both greatly abated the evil, yet was incompetent to suppress it. But according to the pictures commonly drawn of Athens, we are instructed to believe that the crying public evil was, — too great a license of accusation, and too much judicial trial. Assuredly, such was not the conception of Cheirisophus; nor shall we find it borne out by any fair appreciation of the general evidence. When the peculation of official persons was thus notorious in spite of serious risks, what would it have become if the door had been barred to accusing demagogues, and if the numerous popular dikasts had been exchanged for a few select judges of the same stamp and class as the official men themselves?

Enforcing his proposition, Xenophon now informed his colleagues that he had just captured a few guides by laying an ambush for certain native plunderers who beset the rear; and that these guides acquainted him that the mountain was not inaccessible, but pastured by goats and oxen. He farther offered himself to take command of the marching detachment. But this being overruled by Cheirisophus, some of the best among the captains, Aristonymus, Aristeas, and Nichomachus, volunteered their services and were accepted. After refreshing the soldiers, the generals marched with the main army near to the foot of the pass,

---

Xen. Anab. iv, 6, 16.

Ἀλλὰ μέντοι, ἔφη ὁ Χειρίσοφος, κἀγὼ ὑμᾶς τοὺς Ἀθηναίους ἀκούω δεινοὺς εἶναι κλέπτειν τὰ δημόσια, καὶ μάλα ὄντος δεινοῦ τοῦ κινδύνου τῷ κλέπτοντι καὶ τοὺς κρατίστους μέντοι μάλιστα, εἴπερ ὑμῖν οἱ κράτιστοι ἄρχειν ἀξιοῦνται ὥστε ὥρα καὶ σοὶ ἐπιδείκνυσθαι τὴν παιδειαν.

[2] See Vol. VII, ch. lxi, p. 401 seq.

and there took up their night-station, making demonstrations of a purpose to storm it the next morning. But as soon as it was dark, Aristonymus and his detachment started, and ascending the mountain at another point, obtained without resistance a high position on the flank of the enemy, who soon, however, saw them and despatched a force to keep guard on that side. At daybreak these two detachments came to a conflict on the heights, in which the Greeks were completely victorious, while Cheirisophus was marching up the pass to attack the main body. His light troops, encouraged by seeing this victory of their comrades, hastened on to the charge faster than their hoplites could follow. But the enemy was so dispirited by seeing themselves turned, that they fled with little or no resistance. Though only a few were slain, many threw away their light shields of wicker or wood-work, which became the prey of the conquerors.[1]

Thus masters of the pass, the Greeks descended to the level ground on the other side, where they found themselves in some villages well-stocked with provisions and comforts; the first in the country of the Taochi. Probably they halted here some days; for they had seen no villages, either for rest or for refreshment, during the last nine days' march, since leaving those Armenian villages in which they had passed a week so eminently restorative, and which apparently had furnished them with a stock of provisions for the onward journey. Such halt gave time to the Taochi to carry up their families and provisions into inaccessible strongholds, so that the Greeks found no supplies, during five days' march through the territory. Their provisions were completely exhausted, when they arrived before one of these strongholds, a rock on which were seen the families and the cattle of the Taochi; without houses or fortification, but nearly surrounded by a river, so as to leave only one narrow ascent, rendered unapproachable by vast rocks which the defenders hurled or rolled from the summit. By an ingenious combination of bravery and stratagem, in which some of the captains much distinguished themselves, the Greeks overcame this difficulty, and took the height. The scene which then ensued was awful. The Taochian women seized their children, flung them over the precipice, and then cast

---

[1] Xen. Anab. iv, 6, 20—27

themselves headlong also, followed by the men. Almost every soul thus perished, very few surviving to become prisoners. An Arcadian captain named Æneas, seeing one of them in a fine dress about to precipitate himself with the rest, seized him with a view to prevent it. But the man in return grasped him firmly, dragged him to the edge of the rock, and leaped down to the destruction of both. Though scarcely any prisoners were taken, however, the Greeks obtained abundance of oxen, asses, and sheep, which fully supplied their wants.[1]

They now entered into the territory of the Chalybes, which they were seven days in passing through. These were the bravest warriors whom they had seen in Asia. Their equipment was a spear of fifteen cubits long, with only one end pointed, — a helmet, greaves, stuffed corselet, with a kilt or dependent flaps, — a short sword which they employed to cut off the head of a slain enemy, displaying the head in sight of their surviving enemies with triumphant dance and song. They carried no shield; perhaps because the excessive length of the spear required the constant employment of both hands, — yet they did not shrink from meeting the Greeks occasionally in regular, stand-up fight. As they had carried off all their provisions into hill-forts, the Greeks could obtain no supplies, but lived all the time upon the cattle which they had acquired from the Taochi. After seven days of march and combat, — the Chalybes perpetually attacking their rear, — they reached the river Harpasus (four hundred feet broad), where they passed into the territory of the Skythini. It rather seems that the territory of the Chalybes was mountainous; that of the Skythini was level, and containing villages, wherein they remained three days, refreshing themselves, and stocking themselves with provisions.[2]

Four days of additional march brought them to a sight, the like of which they had not seen since Opis and Sittakê on the Tigris in Babylonia, — a large and flourishing city called Gymnias; an earnest of the neighborhood of the sea, of commerce, and of civilization. The chief of this city received them in a friendly manner, and furnished them with a guide who engaged to conduct them, after five days' march, to a hill from whence they would

---

[1] Xen. Anab. iv, 7, 2-15.   [2] Xen. Anab. iv, 7, 18.

have a view of the sea. This was by no means their nearest way to the sea, for the chief of Gymnias wished to send them through the territory of some neighbors to whom he was hostile; which territory, as soon as they reached it, the guide desired them to burn and destroy. However, the promise was kept, and on the fifth day, marching still apparently through the territory of the Skythini, they reached the summit of a mountain called Thêchês, from whence the Euxine Sea was visible.[1]

An animated shout from the soldiers who formed the van-guard testified the impressive effect of this long-deferred spectacle, assuring as it seemed to do, their safety and their return home. To Xenophon and to the rear-guard, — engaged in repelling the attack of natives who had come forward to revenge the plunder of their territory, — the shout was unintelligible. They at first imagined that the natives had commenced attack in front as well as in the rear, and that the van-guard was engaged in battle. But every moment the shout became louder, as fresh men came to the summit and gave vent to their feelings; so that Xenophon grew anxious, and galloped up to the van with his handful of cavalry to see what had happened. As he approached, the voice of the overjoyed crowd was heard distinctly crying out, *Thalatta, Thalatta* (The sea, the sea), and congratulating each other in ecstasy. The main body, the rear-guard, the baggage-soldiers driving up their horses and cattle before them, became all excited by the sound, and hurried up breathless to the summit. The whole army, officers and soldiers, were thus assembled, manifesting their joyous emotions by tears, embraces, and outpourings of enthusiastic sympathy. With spontaneous impulse they heaped up stones to decorate the spot by a monument and commemorative trophy; putting on the stones such homely offerings as their means afforded, — sticks, hides, and a few of the wicker shields just taken from the natives. To the guide, who had performed his engagement of bringing them in five days within sight of the sea, their gratitude was unbounded. They presented him with a horse, a silver bowl, a Persian costume, and ten darics in money; besides seve-

---

Diodorus (xiv, 29) calls the mountain Χήνοιν — Chenium. He seems to have had Xenophon before him in his brief description of this interesting scene.

ral of the soldiers' rings, which he especially asked for. Thus loaded with presents, he left them, having first shown them a village wherein they could find quarters, — as well as the road which they were to take through the territory of the Makrônes.[1]

When they reached the river which divided the land of the Makrônes from that of the Skythini, they perceived the former assembled in arms on the opposite side to resist their passage. The river not being fordable, they cut down some neighboring trees to provide the means of crossing. While these Makrônes were shouting and encouraging each other aloud, a peltast in the Grecian army came to Xenophon, saying that he knew their language, and that he believed this to be his country. He had been a slave at Athens, exported from home during his boyhood, — he had then made his escape (probably during the Peloponnesian war, to the garrison of Dekeleia), and afterwards taken military service. By this fortunate accident, the generals were enabled to open negotiations with the Makrônes, and to assure them that the army would do them no harm, desiring nothing more than a free passage and a market to buy provisions. The Makrônes, on receiving such assurance in their own language from a countryman, exchanged pledges of friendship with the Greeks, assisted them to pass the river, and furnished the best market in their power during the three days' march across their territory.[2]

The army now reached the borders of the Kolchians, who were found in hostile array, occupying the summit of a considerable mountain which formed their frontier. Here Xenophon, having marshalled the soldiers for attack, with each lochus (company of one hundred men) in single file, instead of marching up the hill in phalanx, or continuous front with only a scanty depth, — addressed to them the following pithy encouragement, — " Now, gentlemen, these enemies before us are the only impediment that keeps us away from reaching the point at which we have been so long aiming. We must even eat them raw, if in any way we can do so."

Eighty of these formidable companies of hoplites, each in single file, now began to ascend the hill; the peltasts and bowmen being partly distributed among them, partly placed on the flanks. Cheirisophus and Xenophon, each commanding on one wing, spread

---

[1] Xen. Anab. iv, 7, 23–27. [2] Xen. Anab. iv 8, 4–7.

their peltasts in such a way as to outflank the Kolchians, who accordingly weakened their centre in order to strengthen their wings. Hence the Arcadian peltasts and hoplites in the Greek centre were enabled to attack and disperse the centre with little resistance; and all the Kolchians presently fled, leaving the Greeks in possession of their camp, as well as of several well-stocked villages in their rear. Amidst these villages the army remained to refresh themselves for several days. It was here that they tasted the grateful, but unwholesome honey, which this region still continues to produce, — unaware of its peculiar properties. Those soldiers who ate little of it were like men greatly intoxicated with wine; those who ate much, were seized with the most violent vomiting and diarrhœa, lying down like madmen in a state of delirium. From this terrible distemper some recovered on the ensuing day, others two or three days afterwards. It does not appear that any one actually died.[1]

Two more days' march brought them to the sea, at the Greek maritime city of Trapezus or Trebizond, founded by the inhabitants of Sinôpê on the coast of the Kolchian territory. Here the Trapezuntines received them with kindness and hospitality, sending them presents of bullocks, barley-meal, and wine. Taking up their quarters in some Kolchian villages near the town, they now enjoyed, for the first time since leaving Tarsus, a safe and undisturbed repose during thirty days, and were enabled to recover in some degree from the severe hardships which they had undergone. While the Trapezuntines brought produce for sale into the camp, the Greeks provided the means of purchasing it by predatory incursions against the Kolchians on the hills. Those Kolchians who dwelt under the hills and on the plain were in a state of semi-dependence upon Trapezus; so that the Trapezuntines mediated on their behalf and prevailed on the

---

[1] Xen. Anab. iv, 8, 15–22. Most modern travellers attest the existence, in these regions, of honey intoxicating and poisonous, such as Xenophon describes. They point out the *Azalea Pontica*, as the flower from which the bees imbibe this peculiar quality. Professor Koch, however, calls in question the existence of any honey thus naturally unwholesome near the Black Sea. He states (Zug der Zehn Tausend, p. 111) that after careful inquiries he could find no trace of any such. Not contradicting Xenophon, he thinks that the honey which the Greeks ate must have been stale or tainted.

Greeks to leave them unmolested, on condition of a contribution of bullocks.

These bullocks enabled the Greeks to discharge the vow which they had made, on the proposition of Xenophon, to Zeus the Preserver, during that moment of dismay and despair which succeeded immediately on the massacre of their generals by Tissaphernes. To Zeus the Preserver, to Heraklês the Conductor, and to various other gods, they offered an abundant sacrifice on their mountain camp overhanging the sea; and after the festival ensuing, the skins of the victims were given as prizes to competitors in running, wrestling, boxing, and the pankration. The superintendence of such festival games, so fully accordant with Grecian usage and highly interesting to the army, was committed to a Spartan named Drakontius; a man whose destiny recalls that of Patroklus and other Homeric heroes, — for he had been exiled as a boy, having unintentionally killed another boy with a short sword. Various departures from Grecian custom, however, were admitted. The matches took place on the steep and stony hill-side overhanging the sea, instead of on a smooth plain; and the numerous hard falls of the competitors afforded increased interest to the by-standers. The captive non-Hellenic boys were admitted to run for the prize, since otherwise a boy-race could not have been obtained. Lastly, the animation of the scene, as well as the ardor of the competitors, was much enhanced by the number of their mistresses present.[1]

---

[1] Xen. Anab. iv, 8, 23–27.

A curious and interesting anecdote in Plutarch's Life of Alexander, (c 41) attests how much these Hetæræ accompanying the soldiers (women for the most part free), were esteemed in the Macedonian army, and by Alexander himself among the rest. A Macedonian of Ægæ named Eurylochus, had got himself improperly put on a list of veterans and invalids, who were on the point of being sent back from Asia to Europe. The imposition was detected, and on being questioned he informed Alexander that he had practised it in order to be able to follow a free Hetæra named Telesippa, who was about to accompany the departing division. " I sympathize with your attachment, Eurylochus (replied Alexander); let us see whether we cannot prevail upon Telesippa either by persuasion or by presents, since she is of free condition, to stay behind" ('Ημᾶς μὲν, ὦ Εὐρύλοχε, συνερῶν-τας ἔχεις· ὅρα δὲ ὅπως πείθωμ.ν ἢ λόγοις ἢ δώροις τὴν Τελεσίππαν, ἐπειδήπ εφ ἐξ ἐλευθέρας ἐστί).

APPENDIX TO CHAPTER LXX.

ON THE GEOGRAPHY OF THE RETREAT OF THE TEN THOUSAND AFTER THEY QUITTED THE TIGRIS AND ENTERED THE KARDU-CHIAN MOUNTAINS.

IT would be injustice to this gallant and long-suffering body of men not to present the reader with a minute description of the full length of their stupendous march. Up to the moment when the Greeks enter Karduchia, the line of march may be indicated upon evidence which, though not identifying special halting-places or localities, makes us certain that we cannot be far wrong on the whole. But after that moment, the evidence gradually disappears, and we are left with nothing more than a knowledge of the terminus, the general course, and a few negative conditions.

Mr. Ainsworth has given, in his Book IV. (Travels in the Track of the Ten Thousand, p. 155 seq.) an interesting topographical comment on the march through Karduchia, and on the difficulties which the Greeks would have to surmount. He has farther shown what may have been their probable line of march through Karduchia; but the most important point which he has established here, seems to be the identity of the river Kentritès with the Buhtan-Chai, an eastern affluent of the Tigris — distinguishing it from the river of Betlis on the west and the river Khabur on the south-east, with both of which it had been previously confounded (p. 167). The Buhtan-Chai falls into the Tigris at a village called Til, and "constitutes at the present day, a natural barrier between Kurdistan and Armenia" (p. 166). In this identification of the Kentritès with the Buhtan-Chai, Professor Koch agrees (Zug der Zehn Tausend, p. 78).

If the Greeks crossed the Kentritès near its confluence with the Tigris, they would march up its right bank in one day to a situation near the modern town of Sert (Mr. Ainsworth thinks), though Xenophon takes no notice of the river of Bitlis, which nevertheless they must have passed. Their next two days of march, assuming a direction nearly north, would carry them (as Xenophon states, iv. 4, 2) beyond the sources of the Tigris ; that is, " beyond the headwaters of the eastern tributaries to the Tigris."

Three days of additional march brought them to the river Teleboas ·-" of no great size, but beautiful" (iv. 4, 4). There appear sufficient reasons to identify this river with the Kara-Su or Black River, which flows through the valley or plain of Mush into the Murad or Eastern

Euphrates (Ainsworth, p. 172; Ritter, Erdkunde, part x. s. 37. p. 682)
Though Kinneir (Journey through Asia Minor and Kurdistan, 1818,
p. 484), Rennell (Illustrations of the Expedition of Cyrus, p. 207)
and Bell (System of Geography, iv. p. 140) identify it with the Ak-Su
or river of Mush — this, according to Ainsworth, is only a small tributary to the Kara-Su, which is the great river of the plain and district."

Professor Koch, whose personal researches in and around Armenia
give to his opinion the highest authority, follows Mr. Ainsworth in
identifying the Teleboas with the Kara-Su. He supposes, however,
that the Greeks crossed the Kentritès, not near its confluence with the
Tigris, but considerably higher up, near the town of Sert or Sort.
From hence he supposes that they marched nearly north-east in the
modern road from Sert to Bitlis, thus getting round the head or near
the head of the river called Bitlis-Su, which is one of the eastern affluents to the Tigris (falling first into the Buhtan-Chai), and which
Xenophon took for the Tigris itself. They then marched farther, in a
line not far distant from the Lake of Van, over the saddle which separates that lake from the lofty mountain Ali-Dagh. This saddle is the
water-shed which separates the affluents to the Tigris from those to the
Eastern Euphrates, of which latter the Teleboas or Kara-Su is one
(Koch, Zuch der Zehn Tausend, p. 82–84).

After the river Teleboas, there seems no one point in the march
which can be identified with anything approaching to certainty. Nor
have we any means even of determining the general line of route,
apart from specific places, which they followed from the river Teleboas to Trebizond.

Their first object was to reach and cross the Eastern Euphrates.
They would of course cross at the nearest point where they could find
a ford. But how low down its course does the river continue to be
fordable, in mid-winter, with snow on the ground? Here professor
Koch differs from Mr. Ainsworth and colonel Chesney. He affirms
that the river would be fordable a little above its confluence with the
Tscharbahur, about latitude 39° 3'. According to Mr. Ainsworth, it
would not be fordable below the confluence with the river of Khanus
(Khinnis). Koch's authority, as the most recent and systematic in-
vestigator of these regions, seems preferable, especially as it puts the
Greeks nearly in the road now travelled over from Mush to Erzerum,
which is said to be the only pass over the mountains open throughout
all the winter, passing by Khinnis and Koili; see Ritter, Erdkunde, x
p. 387. Xenophon mentions a warm spring, which the army passed by
during the third or fourth day after crossing the Euphrates (Anab. iv
5, 15). Professor Koch believes himself to have identif ed this warm
spring — the only one, as he states (p. 90–93), south of the range of
mountains called the Bingöldagh — in the district called Wardo, near
the village of Bashkan.

To lay down, with any certainty, the line which the Greeks followed from the Euphrates to Trebizond, appears altogether impossible. I cannot admit the hypothesis of Mr. Ainsworth, who conducts the army across the Araxes to its northern bank, carries them up northward to the latitude of Teflis in Georgia, then brings them back again across the Harpa Chai (a northern affluent of the Araxes, which he identifies with the Harpasus mentioned by Xenophon) and the Araxes itself, to Gymnias, which he places near the site of Erzerum. Professor Koch (p. 104–108), who dissents with good reason from Mr. Ainsworth, proposes (though with hesitation and uncertainty) a line of his own which appears to me open greatly to the same objection as that of Mr. Ainsworth. It carries the Greeks too much to the northward of Erzerum, more out of their line of march from the place where they crossed the Eastern Euphrates, than can be justified by any probability. The Greeks knew well that, in order to get home they must take a westerly direction (see Anab. iii. 5, 15).

Their great and constant purpose would be to make way to the westward, as soon as they had crossed the Euphrates; and the road from that river, passing near the site of Erzerum to Trebizond, would thus coincide, in the main, with their spontaneous tendency. They had no motive to go northward of Erzerum, nor ought we to suppose it without some proof. I trace out, therefore, a line of march much less circuitous; not meaning it to be understood as the real road which the army can be proved to have taken, but simply because it seems a possible line, and because it serves as a sort of approximation to complete the reader's idea of the entire ground travelled over by the Ten Thousand.

Koch hardly makes sufficient account of the overwhelming hardships with which the Greeks had to contend, when he states (p. 96) that if they had taken a line as straight, or nearly as straight as was practicable, they might have marched from the Euphrates to Trebizond in sixteen or twenty days, even allowing for the bad time of year. Considering that it was mid-winter, in that very high and cold country, with deep snow throughout; that they had absolutely no advantages or assistance of any kind; that their sick and disabled men, together with their arms, were to be carried by the stronger; that there were a great many women accompanying them; that they had beasts to drive along, carrying baggage and plunder, — the prophet Silanus, for example, having preserved his three thousand darics in coin from the field of Kunaxa until his return; that there was much resistance from the Chalybes and Taochi; that they had to take provisions where provisions were discoverable; that even a small stream must have impeded them, and probably driven them out of their course to find a ford, — considering the intolerable accumulation of these and other hardships, we need not wonder at any degree of slowness in their progress. It rarely happens that modern travellers go over these regions in mid-winter; but we may see what travelling is at that season, by the dreadful description which Mr. Baillie Fraser gives of his journey from Tauris to Erzerum in the month of March (Travels in Koordhistan, Letter XV). Mr. Kinneir says (Travels, p. 353) — " The winters are so severe that all communication between Baiburt and the circumja-cent villages is cut off for four months in the year, in consequence of the depth of the snow."

Now if we measure on Kiepert's map the rectilinear distance, — the air-line — from Trebizond to the place where Koch represents the Greeks to have crossed the Eastern Euphrates, — we shall find it one hundred and seventy English miles. The number of days' journey-marches which Xenophon mentions are fifty-four; even if we include the five days of march undertaken from Gymnias (Anab. iv. 7, 20), which, properly speaking, were directed against the enemies of the governor of Gymnias, more than for the promotion of their retreat. In each of those fifty-four days, therefore, they must have made 3.14 miles of rectilinear progress. This surely is not an unreasonably slow progress to suppose, under all the disadvantages of their situ-ation : nor does it imply any very great actual departure from the straightest line practicable. Indeed Koch himself (in his Introduction, p. 4) suggests various embarrassments which must have occurred on the march, but which Xenophon has not distinctly stated.

The river which Xenophon calls the Harpasus seems to be probably the Tchoruk-su, as colonel Chesney and Prof. Koch suppose. At least it is difficult to assign any other river with which the Harpasus can be identified.

I cannot but think it probable that the city which Xenophon calls *Gymnias* (Diodorus, xiv. 29, calls it Gymnasia) was the same as that which is now called Gumisch-Khana (Hamilton), Gumush-Kaneh (Ains-worth), Gemisch-Khaneh (Kinneir). " Gumisch-Khanah (says Mr Hamilton, Travels in Asia Minor, vol. i. ch. xi. p. 168 ; ch. xiv. p. 234) is celebrated as the site of the most ancient and considerable silver-mines in the Ottoman dominions." Both Mr. Kinneir and Mr. Hamil-ton passed through Gumisch-Khana on the road from Trebizond to Erzerum.

Now here is not only great similarity of name, and likelihood of situ-ation, — but the existence of the silver mines furnishes a plausible explanation of that which would otherwise be very strange ; the exist-ence of this " great, flourishing, inhabited, city," inland, in the midst of such barbarians, — the Chalybes, the Skythini, the Makrônes, etc.

Mr. Kinneir reached Gumisch-Khana at the end of the third day after quitting Trebizond ; the two last days having been very long and fatiguing. Mr. Hamilton, who also passed through Gumisch-Khana, reached it at the end of two long days. Both these travellers represent the road near Gumisch-Khana as extremely difficult. Mr. Ains-worth, who did not himself pass through Gumisch-Khana, tells us (what is of some importance in this discussion) that it lies in the *winter-road* from Erzerum to Trebizond (Travels in Asia Minor, vol. ii. p. 394). "The winter-road, which is the longest, passes by Gumisch-Khana, and takes the longer portion of valley; all the others cross over the mountain at various points, to the east of the road by the mines. But whether going by the mountains or the valley, the mule-teers often go indifferently to the west as far as Ash Kaleh, and at other times turn off by the villages of Bey Mausour and Kodjah Bunar, where they take to the mountains."

Mr. Hamilton makes the distance from Trebizond to Gumish-Khana eighteen hours, or fifty-four calculated post miles; that is, about forty English miles (Appendix to Travels in Asia Minor, vol. ii. p. 389).

Now we are not to suppose that the Greeks marched in any direct road from Gymnias to Trebizond. On the contrary, the five days' march which they undertook immediately from Gymnias were con-ducted by a guide sent from that town, who led them over the terri-tories of people hostile to Gymnias, in order that they might lay waste the lands (iv. 7, 20). What progress they made, during these marches, towards Trebizond, is altogether doubtful. The guide promised that on the fifth day he would bring them to a spot from whence they could view the sea, and he performed his promise by leading them to the top of the sacred mountain Thêchê.

Thêchê was a summit (ἄκρον, iv. 7, 25), as might be expected. But unfortunately it seems impossible to verify the particular summit on which the interesting scene described by Xenophon took place. Mr. Ainsworth presumes it to be the mountain called Kop-Dagh; from whence, however, according to Koch, the sea cannot be discerned. D'Anville and some other geographers identify it with the ridge called Tekieh-Dagh, to the east of Gumisch-Khana; nearer to the sea than that place. This mountain, I think, would suit pretty well for the nar-rative in respect to position; but Koch and other modern travellers affirm that it is neither high enough, nor near enough to the sea, to permit any such view as that which Xenophon relates. It stands on Kiepert's map at a distance of full thirty-five English miles from the sea, the view of which, moreover, seems intercepted by the still higher mountain-chain now called Kolath-Dagh, a portion of the ancient Pary-adres, which runs along parallel to the coast. It is to be recollected that in the first half of February, the time of Xenophon's visit, the highest peaks would certainly be all covered with snow, and therefore very difficult to ascend.

There is a striking view obtained of the sea from the mountain called Karakaban. This mountain, more than four thousand feet high, lies rather above twenty miles from the sea, to the south of Trebizond, and immediately north of the still higher chain of Kolath-Dagh. From the Kolath-Dagh chain, which runs east and west, there strike out three or four parallel ridges to the northward, formed of primitive slate, and cut down precipitously so as to leave deep and narrow valleys between. On leaving Trebizond, the traveller ascends the hill immediately above the town, and then descends into the valley on the other side. His road to Karakaban lies partly along the valley, partly along the crest of one of the four ridges just mentioned. But throughout all this road, the sea is never seen; being hidden by the hills immediately above Trebizond. He does not again see the sea until he reaches Karakaban, which is sufficiently high to enable him to see over those hills. The guides (as I am informed by Dr. Holland, who twice went over the spot) point out with great animation this view of the sea, as particularly deserving of notice. It is enjoyed for a short space while the road winds round the mountain, and then again lost.

Here is a view of the sea at once distant, sudden, impressive, and enjoyed from an eminence not too high to be accessible to the Cyreian army. In so far, it would be suitable to the description of Xenophon. Yet again it appears that a person coming to this point from the land-side (as Xenophon of course did), would find it in his descending route, not in his ascending; and this can hardly be reconciled with the description which we read in the Greek historian. Moreover, the subsequent marches which Xenophon mentions after quitting the mountain summit Thêchê, can hardly be reconciled with the supposition that it was the same as what is now called Karakaban. It is, indeed, quite possible, (as Mr. Hamilton suggests), that Thêchê may have been a peak apart from any road, and that the guide may have conducted the soldiers thither for the express purpose of showing the sea, guiding them back again into the road afterwards. This increases the difficulty of identifying the spot. However, the whole region is as yet very imperfectly known. and perhaps it is not impossible that there may be some particular locality even on Tekiah-Dagh, whence, through an accidental gap in the intervening mountains, the sea might become visible.

CHAPTER LXXI.

PROCEEDINGS OF THE TEN THOUSAND GREEKS, FROM THE TIME
THAT THEY REACHED TRAPEZUS, TO THEIR JUNCTION WITH
THE LACEDÆMONIAN ARMY IN ASIA MINOR.

WE now commence a third act in the history of this memorable
body of men. After having followed them from Sardis to Kunaxa
as mercenaries to procure the throne for Cyrus, — then from Kunaxa to Trapezus as men anxious only for escape, and purchasing
their safety by marvellous bravery, endurance, and organization,
we shall now track their proceedings among the Greek colonies
on the Euxine and at the Bosphorus of Thrace, succeeded by their
struggles against the meanness of the Thracian prince Seuthes, as
well as against the treachery and arbitrary harshness of the Lacedæmonian commanders Anaxibius and Aristarchus.

Trapezus, now Trebizond, where the army had recently found
repose, was a colony from Sinôpê, as were also Kerasus and Kotyôra, farther westward; each of them receiving an harmost or
governor from the mother-city, and paying to her an annual tribute. All these three cities were planted on the narrow strip of
land dividing the Euxine from the elevated mountain range which
so closely borders on its southern coast. At Sinôpê itself, the land
stretches out into a defensible peninsula, with a secure harbor, and
a large breadth of adjacent fertile soil. So tempting a site invited
the Milesians, even before the year 600 B. C., to plant a colony
there, and enabled Sinôpê to attain much prosperity and power.
Farther westward, not more than a long day's journey for a rowing vessel from Byzantium, was situated the Megarian colony of
Herakleia, in the territory of the Mariandyni.

The native tenants of this line of coast, upon whom the Greek
settlers intruded themselves (reckoning from the westward), were
the Bithynian Thracians, the Mariandyni, the Paphlagonians, the
Tibarêni, Chalybes, Mosynœki, Drilæ, and Kolchians. Here, as
elsewhere, these natives found the Greek seaports useful, in giving
a new value to inland produce, and in furnishing the great men

with ornaments and luxuries to which they would otherwise have had no access. The citizens of Herakleia had reduced into dependence a considerable portion of the neighboring Mariandyni, and held them in a relation resembling that of the natives of Esthonia and Livonia to the German colonies in the Baltic. Some of the Kolchian villages were also subject, in the same manner, to the Trapezuntines;[1] and Sinôpê doubtless possessed a similar inland dominion of greater or less extent. But the principal wealth of this important city arose from her navy and maritime commerce; from the rich thunny fishery attached to her promontory; from the olives in her immediate neighborhood, which was a cultivation not indigenous, but only naturalized by the Greeks on the seaboard; from the varied produce of the interior, comprising abundant herds of cattle, mines of silver, iron, and copper in the neighboring mountains, wood for ship-building, as well as for house furniture, and native slaves.[2] The case was similar with the three colonies of Sinôpê, more to the eastward, — Kotyôra, Kerasus, and Trapezus; except that the mountains which border on the Euxine, gradually approaching nearer and nearer to the shore, left to each of them a more confined strip of cultivable land. For these cities the time had not yet arrived, to be conquered and absorbed by the inland monarchies around them, as Miletus and the cities on the eastern coast of Asia Minor had been. The Paphlagonians were at this time the only indigenous people in those regions who formed a considerable aggregated force, under a prince named Korylas; a prince tributary to Persia, yet half independent, — since he had disobeyed the summons of Artaxerxes to come up and help in repelling Cyrus[3] — and now on terms of established alliance with Sinôpê, though not without secret designs, which he wanted only force to execute, against that city.[4] The other native tribes to the eastward were mountaineers both ruder and more divided; warlike on their own heights, but little capable of any aggressive combinations.

Though we are told that Perikles had once despatched a detachment of Athenian colonists to Sinôpê,[5] and had expelled from thence the despot Timesilaus, — yet neither that city nor any of

[1] Strabo, xii, p. 542; Xen. Anab. iv, 8, 24.   [2] Strabo, xii, p. 545, 546
[3] Xen. Anab. v, 6, 8.   [4] Xen. Anab. v, 5, 23
[5] Plutarch, Perikles, c. 20.

their neighbors appear to have taken a part in the Peloponnesian war, either for or against Athens ; nor were they among the number of tributaries to Persia. They doubtless were acquainted with the upward march of Cyrus, which had disturbed all Asia ; and probably were not ignorant of the perils and critical state of his Grecian army. But it was with a feeling of mingled surprise, admiration, and alarm, that they saw that army descend from the mountainous region, hitherto only recognized as the abode of Kolchians, Makrônes, and other analogous tribes, among whom was perched the mining city of Gymnias.

Even after all the losses and extreme sufferings of the retreat, the Greeks still numbered, when mustered at Kerasus,[1] eight thousand six hundred hoplites, with peltasts or targeteers, bowmen, slingers, etc., making a total of above ten thousand military persons. Such a force had never before been seen in the Euxine. Considering both the numbers and the now-acquired discipline and self-confidence of the Cyreians, even Sinôpê herself could have raised no force capable of meeting them in the field. Yet they did not belong to any city, nor receive orders from any established government. They were like those mercenary armies which marched about in Italy during the fourteenth century, under the generals called Condottieri, taking service sometimes with one city, sometimes with another. No one could predict what schemes they might conceive, or in what manner they might deal with the established communities on the shores of the Euxine. If we imagine that such an army had suddenly appeared in Sicily, a little time before the Athenian expedition against Syracuse, it would have been probably enlisted by Leontini and Katana in their war against Syracuse. If the inhabitants of Trapezus had wished to throw off the dominion of Sinôpê, — or if Korylas, the Paphlagonian, were meditating war against that city, — here were formidable auxiliaries to second their wishes. Moreover there were various tempting sites, open to the formation of a new colony, which, with so numerous a body of original Greek settlers, would

---

[1] Xen. Anab. v, 3, 3; v, 7, 9, The maximum of the Grecian force, when mustered at Issus after the junction of those three hundred men who deserted from Abrokomas, was thirteen thousand nine hundred men. At the review in Babylonia, three days before the battle of Kunaxa, there were mustered, however, only twelve thousand nine hundred (Anab. i, 7, 10).

probably have ov rtopped Sinôpê herself. There was no restra in-
ing cause to reckon upon, except the general Hellenic sympathies
and education of the Cyreian army; and what was of not less importance, the fact that they were not mercenary soldiers by permanent profession, such as became so formidably multiplied in Greece
during the next generation, — but established citizens who had
come out on a special service under Cyrus, with the full intention,
after a year of lucrative enterprise, to return to their homes and
families.[1] We shall find such gravitation towards home steadily
operative throughout the future proceedings of the army. But at
the moment when they first emerged from the mountains, no one
could be sure that it would be so. There was ample ground for
uneasiness among the Euxine Greeks, especially the Sinopians,
whose supremacy had never before been endangered.

An undisturbed repose of thirty days enabled the Cyreians to
recover from their fatigues, to talk over their past dangers, and
to take pride in the anticipated effect which their unparalleled
achievement could not fail to produce in Greece. Having discharged their vows and celebrated their festival to the gods, they
held an assembly to discuss their future proceedings; when a Thu-
rian soldier, named Antileon, exclaimed, — " Comrades, I am
already tired of packing up, marching, running, carrying arms, falling into line, keeping watch, and fighting. Now that we have the
sea here before us, I desire to be relieved from all these toils, to
sail the rest of the way, and to arrive in Greece outstretched and

---

[1] Xen. Anab. vi, 2, 8.

Τῶν γὰρ στρατιωτῶν οἱ πλεῖστοι ἦσαν οὐ σπάνει βίου ἐκπεπλευκότες ἐπὶ
ταύτην τὴν μισθοφοράν, ἀλλὰ τὴν Κύρου ἀρετὴν ἀκούντες, οἱ μὲν καὶ ἄνδρας
ἄγοντες, οἱ δὲ καὶ προσανηλωκότες χρήματα, καὶ τούτων ἕτεροι ἀποδεδρακότες
πατέρας καὶ μήτερας, οἱ δὲ καὶ τέκνα καταλιπόντες, ὡς χρήματα αὐτοῖς κτησάμενοι ἥξοντες πάλιν, ἀκούοντες καὶ τοὺς ἄλλους τοὺς παρὰ Κύρῳ πολλὰ καὶ
ἀγαθὰ πράττειν. Τοιοῦτοι οὖν ὄντες ἐπόθουν εἰς τὴν Ἑλλάδα σώζεσθαι.

This statement respecting the position of most of the soldiers is more
authentic, as well as less disparaging, than that of Isokrates (Orat. iv, Panegyr. s. 170).

In another oration, composed about fifty years after the Cyreian expedition, Isokrates notices the large premiums which it had been formerly
necessary to give to those who brought together mercenary soldiers, over
and above the pay to the soldiers themselves (Isokrates, Orat. v. ad Philipp.
s. 112); as contrasted with the over-multiplication of unemployed mercenaries during his own later time (Ibid. s. 142 seq.)

asleep, like Odysseus." This pithy address being received with
vehement acclamations, and warmly responded to by all, — Cheirisophus offered, if the army chose to empower him, to sail forthwith
to Byzantium, where he thought he could obtain from his friend
the Lacedæmonian admiral, Anaxibius, sufficient vessels for transport. His proposition was gladly accepted; and he departed to
execute the project.

Xenophon then urged upon the army various resolutions and
measures, proper for the regulation of affairs during the absence
of Cheirisophus. The army would be forced to maintain itself by
marauding expeditions among the hostile tribes in the mountains.
Such expeditions, accordingly, must be put under regulation; neither individual soldiers, nor small companies, must be allowed to
go out at pleasure, without giving notice to the generals; moreover, the camp must be kept under constant guard and scouts, in
the event of surprise from a retaliating enemy. It was prudent
also to take the best measures in their power for procuring vessels;
since, after all, Cheirisophus might possibly fail in bringing an adequate number. They ought to borrow a few ships of war from the
Trapezuntines, and detain all the merchant ships which they saw;
unshipping the rudders, placing the cargoes under guard, and maintaining the crew during all the time that the ships might be required for transport of the army. Many such merchant vessels
were often sailing by;[1] so that they would thus acquire the means
of transport, even though Cheirisophus should bring few or none
from Byzantium. Lastly, Xenophon proposed to require the
Grecian cities to repair and put in order the road along the coast,
for a land-march; since, perhaps, with all their efforts, it would be
found impossible to get together a sufficient stock of transports.

All the propositions of Xenophon were readily adopted by the
army, except the last. But the mere mention of a renewed land-
march excited such universal murmurs of repugnance, that he did
not venture to put that question to the vote. He took upon himself, however, to send messages to the Grecian cities, on his own
responsibility; urging them to repair the roads, in order that the

---

[1] Xen. Anab. v, 1, 3–13.

Ὁρῶ δ' ἐγὼ πλοῖα πολλάκις παραπλέοντα, etc. This is a forcible proof
how extensive was the Grecian commerce with the town and region of Phasis, at the eastern extremity of the Euxine.

departure of the army might be facilitated. And he found the cities ready enough to carry his wishes into effect, as far as Kotyôra.[1]

The wisdom of these precautionary suggestions of Xenophon soon appeared; for Cheirisophus not only failed in his object, but was compelled to stay away for a considerable time. A pente-kor.ter (or armed ship with fifty oars) was borrowed from the Trapezuntines, and committed to the charge of a Lacedæmonian Periœkus, named Dexippus, for the purpose of detaining the merchant vessels passing by. This man having violated his trust, and employed the ship to make his own escape out of the Euxine, a second was obtained and confided to an Athenian, Polykrates; who brought in successively several merchant vessels. These the Greeks did not plunder, but secured the cargoes under adequate guard, and only reserved the vessels for transports. It became, however, gradually more and more difficult to supply the camp with provisions. Though the army was distributed into suitable detachments for plundering the Kolchian villages on the hills, and seizing cattle and prisoners for sale, yet these expeditions did not always succeed ; indeed on one occasion, two Grecian lochi or companies got entangled in such difficult ground, that they were destroyed, to a. man. The Kolchians united on the hills in increased and menacing numbers, insomuch that a larger guard became necessary for the camp; while the Trapezuntines, — tired of the protracted stay of the army, as well as desirous of exempting from pillage the natives in their own immediate neighborhood, — conducted the detachments only to villages alike remote and difficult of access. It was in this manner that a large force under Xenophon himself, attacked the lofty and rugged stronghold of the Drilæ, — the most warlike nation of mountaineers in the neighborhood of the Euxine ; well armed, and troublesome to Trapezus by their incursions. After a difficult march and attack which Xenophon describes in interesting detail, and wherein the Greeks encountered no small hazard of ruinous defeat, — they returned in the end completely successful, and with a plentiful booty.[2]

At Length, after long awaiting in vain the reappearance of Cheirisophus, increasing scarcity and weariness determined them to

---

[1] Xen Anab v. 1. 15.   [2] Xen. Anab. v x

leave Trapezus. A sufficient number of vessels had been collected to serve for the transport of the women, of the sick and wounded, and of the baggage. All these were accordingly placed on board, under the command of Philesius and Sophænetus, the two oldest generals; while the remaining army marched by land, along a road which had been just made good under the representations of Xenophon. In three days they reached Kerasus, another maritime colony of the Sinopeans, still in the territory called Kolchian; there they halted ten days, mustered and numbered the army, and divided the money acquired by the sale of their prisoners. Eight thousand six hundred hoplites, out of a total probably greater than eleven thousand, were found still remaining; besides targeteers and various light troops.[1]

During the halt at Kerasus, the declining discipline of the army became manifest as they approached home. Various acts of outrage occurred, originating now, as afterwards, in the intrigues of treacherous officers. A captain named Klearetus persuaded his company to attempt the plunder of a Kolchian village near Kerasus, which had furnished a friendly market to the Greeks, and which rested secure on the faith of peaceful relations. He intended to make off separately with the booty in one of the vessels; but his attack was repelled, and he himself slain. The injured villagers despatched three elders, as heralds, to remonstrate with the Grecian authorities; but these heralds being seen in Kerasus by some of the repulsed plunderers, were slain. A partial tumult then ensued, in which even the magistrates of Kerasus were in great danger, and only escaped the pursuing soldiers by running

---

[1] Xen. Anab. v, 3, 3. Mr. Kinneir (Travels in Asia Minor, p. 327) and many other authors, have naturally presumed from the analogy of name that the modern town Kerasoun (about long. 38° 40′) corresponds to the Kerasus of Xenophon; which Arrian in his Periplus conceives to be identical with what was afterwards called Pharnakia.

But it is remarked both by Dr. Cramer (Asia Minor, vol. i, p. 281) and by Mr. Hamilton (Travels in Asia Minor, ch. xv, p. 250), that Kerasoun is too far from Trebizond to admit of Xenophon having marched with the army from the one place to the other in three days; or even in less than ten days, in the judgment of Mr. Hamilton. Accordingly Mr. Hamilton places the site of the Kerasus of Xenophon much nearer to Trebizond (about long. 39° 20′, as it stands in Kiepert's map of Asia Minor,) near a river now called the Kerasoun Dere Sú.

into the sea. This enormity, though it occurred under the eyes of the generals, immediately before their departure from Kerasus, remained without inquiry or punishment, from the numbers con- cerned in it.

Between Kerasus and Kotyôra, there was not then (nor is there now any regular road.[1] This march cost the Cyreian army not less than ten days, by an inland track departing from the sea- shore, and through the mountains inhabited by the indigenous tribes Mosynœki and Chalybes. The latter, celebrated for their iron works, were under dependence to the former. As the Mosy- nœki refused to grant a friendly passage across their territory, the army were compelled to fight their way through it as enemies, with the aid of one section of these people themselves; which al- liance was procured for them by the Trapezuntine Timesitheos, who was proxenus of the Mosynœki, and understood their lan- guage. The Greeks took the mountain fastnesses of this people, and plundered the wooden turrets which formed their abodes. Of their peculiar fashions Xenophon gives an interesting description, which I have not space to copy.[2] The territory of the Tibarêni was more easy and accessible. This people met the Greeks with presents, and tendered a friendly passage. But the generals at first declined the presents, — preferring to treat them as enemies

---

[1] It was not without great difficulty that Mr. Kinneir obtained horses to travel from Kotyôra to Kerasoun by land. The aga of the place told him that it was madness to think of travelling by land, and ordered a felucca for him; but was at last prevailed on to furnish horses. There seems, indeed, to have been no regular or trodden road at all; the hills approach close to the sea, and Mr. Kinneir "travelled the whole of the way along the shore alternately over a sandy beach and a high wooded bank. The hills at in- tervals jutting out into the sea, form capes and numerous little bays along the coast; but the nature of the country was still the same, that is to say, studded with fine timber, flowers, and groves of cherry trees" (Travels in Asia Minor, p. 324).

Kerasus is the indigenous country of the cherry tree, and the origin of its name.

Professor Koch thinks, that the number of days' march given by Xeno phon (ten days) between Kerasus and Kotyôra, is more than consists with the real distance even if Kerasus be placed where Mr. Hamilton supposes If the number be correctly stated, he supposes that the Greeks must have halted somewhere (Zug der Zehn Tausend, p. 115, 116).

[2] Xen. Anab. v, 5, 3.

and plunder them; which in fact they would have done, had they not been deterred by inauspicious sacrifices.[1]

Near Kotyôra, which was situated on the coast of the Tibarêni, yet on the borders of Paphlagonia, they remained forty-five days, still awaiting the appearance of Cheirisophus with the transports to carry them away by sea. The Sinopian harmost or governor, did not permit them to be welcomed in so friendly a manner as at Trapezus. No market was provided for them, nor were their sick admitted within the walls. But the fortifications of the town were not so constructed as to resist a Greek force, the like of which had never before been seen in those regions. The Greek generals found a weak point, made their way in, and took possession of a few houses for the accommodation of their sick; keeping a guard at the gate to secure free egress, but doing no farther violence to the citizens. They obtained their victuals partly from the Kotyôrite villages, partly from the neighboring territory of Paphlagonia, until at length envoys arrived from Sinôpê to remonstrate against their proceedings.

These envoys presented themselves before the assembled soldiers in the camp, when Hekatonymus, the chief and the most eloquent among them, began by complimenting the army upon their gallant exploits and retreat. He then complained of the injury which Kotyôra and Sinôpê, as the mother city of Kotyôra, had suffered at their hands, in violation of common Hellenic kinship. If such proceedings were continued, he intimated that Sinôpê would be compelled in her own defence to seek alliance with the Paphlagonian prince Korylas, or any other barbaric auxiliary who would lend them aid against the Greeks.[2] Xenophon replied that if the Kotyôrites had sustained any damage, it was owing to their own ill-will and to the Sinôpian harmost in the place; that the generals were under the necessity of procuring subsistence for the soldiers, with house-room for the sick, and that they had taken nothing more; that the sick men were lying within the town, but at their own cost, while the other soldiers were all encamped without; that they had maintained cordial friendship with the Trapezuntines, and requited all their good offices; that they sought no enemies except through necessity, being anxious

---

[1] Xen. Anab. v, 7, 18–25.   [2] Xen Anab. v, 5, 7–12.

only again to reach Greece ; and that as for the threat respecting
Korylas, they knew well enough that that prince was eager to
become master of the wealthy city of Sinôpê, and would speedily
attempt some such enterprise if he could obtain the Cyreian army
as his auxiliaries.[1]

This judicious reply shamed the colleagues of Hekatonymus so
much, that they went the length of protesting against what he had
said, and of affirming that they had come with propositions of sympathy and friendship to the army, as well as with promises to give
them an hospitable reception at Sinôpê, if they should visit that town
on their way home.   Presents were at once sent to the army by
the inhabitants of Kotyôra, and a good understanding established.

Such an interchange of good will with the powerful city of
Sinôpê was an unspeakable advantage to the army, — indeed, an
essential condition to their power of reaching home. If they continued their march by land, it was only through Sinopian guidance
and mediation that they could obtain or force a passage through
Paphlagonia ; while for a voyage by sea, there was no chance of
procuring a sufficient number of vessels except from Sinôpê, since
no news had been received of Cheirisophus. On the other hand,
that city had also a strong interest in facilitating their transit homeward, and thus removing formidable neighbors for whose ulterior
purposes there could be no guarantee. After some preliminary
conversation with the Sinopian envoys, the generals convoked the
army in assembly, and entreated Hekatonymus and his companions
to advise them as to the best mode of proceeding westward to the
Bosphorus.   Hekatonymus, after apologizing for the menacing insinuations of his former speech, and protesting that he had no other
object in view except to point out the safest and easiest plan of
route for the army, began to unfold the insuperable difficulties of a
march through Paphlagonia.   The very entrance into the country
must be achieved through a narrow aperture in the mountains,
which it was impossible to force if occupied by the enemy.   Even
assuming this difficulty to be surmounted, there were spacious
plains to be passed over, wherein the Paphlagonian horse, the
most numerous and bravest in Asia, would be found almost irresistible.   There were also three or four great rivers, which the

---

[1] Xen. Anab. v, 5, 13–22.

army would be unable to pass, — the Thermôdôn and the Iris each three hundred feet in breadth, — the Halys, two stadia or nearly a quarter of a mile in breadth, — the Parthenius, also very considerable. Such an array of obstacles (he affirmed) rendered the project of marching through Paphlagonia impracticable; whereas the voyage by sea from Kotyôra to Sinôpê, and from Sinôpê to Herakleia, was easy ; and the transit from the latter place, either by sea to Byzantium, or by land across Thrace, yet easier.[1]

Difficulties like these, apparently quite real, were more than sufficient to determine the vote of the army, already sick of marching and fighting, in favor of the sea-voyage; though there were not wanting suspicions of the sincerity of Hekatonymus.   But Xenophon, in communicating to the latter the decision of the army, distinctly apprised him that they would on no account permit themselves to be divided ; that they would either depart or remain all in a body, and that vessels must be provided sufficient for the transport of all.   Hekatonymus desired them to send envoys of their own to Sinôpê to make the necessary arrangements.   Three envoys were accordingly sent, — Ariston, an Athenian, Kalimachus, an Arcadian, and Samolas, an Achæan ; the Athenian, probably, as possessing the talent of speaking in the Sinopian senate or assembly.[2]

During the absence of these envoys, the army still continued near Kotyôra with a market provided by the town, and with traders from Sinôpê and Herakleia in the camp.   Such soldiers as had no money wherewith to purchase, subsisted by pillaging the neighboring frontier of Paphlagonia.[3]   But they were receiving no pay ; every man was living on his own resources ; and instead of carrying back a handsome purse to Greece, as each soldier had hoped when he first took service under Cyrus, there seemed every prospect of their returning poorer than when they left home.[4] Moreover, the army was now moving onward without any definite purpose, with increasing dissatisfaction and decreasing discipline ; insomuch that Xenophon foresaw the difficulties which would beset the responsible commanders when they should come within the stricter restraints and obligations of the Grecian world.

---

[1] Xen. Anab. v, 6, 4–11.

[2] Xen. Anab. v, 6, 14.

[3] Xen. Anab. v, 6, 19; vi, 1, 2.

[4] Xen. Anab. vi, 4, 8 ; vi 2, 4

It was these considerations which helped to suggest to him the idea of employing the army on some enterprise of conquest and colonization in the Euxine itself; an idea highly flattering to his personal ambition, especially as the army was of unrivalled efficiency against an enemy, and no such second force could ever be got together in those distant regions. His patriotism as a Greek was inflamed with the thoughts of procuring for Hellas a new autonomous city, occupied by a considerable Hellenic population, possessing a spacious territory, and exercising dominion over many indigenous neighbors. He seems to have thought first of attacking and conquering some established non-Hellenic city ; an act which his ideas of international morality did not forbid, in a case where he had contracted no special convention with the inhabitants, — though he (as well as Cheirisophus) strenuously protested against doing wrong to any innocent Hellenic community.[1] He contemplated the employment of the entire force in capturing Phasis or some other native city ; after which, when the establishment was once safely effected, those soldiers who preferred going home to remaining as settlers, might do so without emperiling those who stayed, and probably with their own purses filled by plunder and conquest in the neighborhood. To settle as one of the richest proprietors and chiefs, — perhaps even the recognized Œkist, like Agnon at Amphipolis, — of a new Hellenic city such as could hardly fail to become rich, powerful, and important, — was a tempting prospect for one who had now acquired the habits of command. Moreover, the sequel will prove, how correctly Xenophon appreciated the discomfort of leading the army back to Greece without pay and without certain employment.

It was the practice of Xenophon, and the advice of his master Sokrates,[2] in grave and doubtful cases, where the most careful re-

---

[1] Xen. Anab. v, 6, 15–30; vi, 2, 6 ; vii, 1, 25, 29.

Haken and other commentators do injustice to Xenophon when they ascribe to him the design of seizing the Greek city of Kotyôra.

[2] Xen. Memorab. i, 1, 8, 9. Ἔφη δὲ (Sokrates) δεῖν, ἃ μὲν μαθόντας ποι-εῖν ἔδωκαν οἱ θεοί, μανθάνειν· ἃ δὲ μὴ δῆλα τοῖς ἀνθρώποις ἐστὶ, πειρᾶσθαι διὰ μαντικῆς παρὰ τῶν θεῶν πυνθάνεσθαι· τοὺς θεοὺς γὰρ, οἷς ἂν ὦσιν ἵλεω. σημαίνειν.

Compare passages in his Cyropædia, i, 6, 3 ; De Officio Magistr. Equit ix, 9.

" The gods (says Euripidês, in the Sokratic vein) have given us wisdom

flection was at fault, to recur to the inspired authority of an oracle or a prophet, and to offer sacrifice, in full confidence that the gods would vouchsafe to communicate a special revelation to any person whom they favored. Accordingly Xenophon, previous to any communication with the soldiers respecting his new project, was anxious to ascertain the will of the gods by a special sacrifice ; fo. which he invoked the presence of the Ambrakiot Silanus, the chief prophet in the army. This prophet (as I have already mentioned), before the battle of Kunaxa, had assured Cyrus that Artaxerxes would not fight for ten days, — and the prophecy came to pass ; which made such an impression on Cyrus that he rewarded him with the prodigious present of three thousand darics or ten Attic talents. While others were returning poor, Silanus, having contrived to preserve this sum throughout all the hardships of the retreat, was extremely rich, and anxious only to hasten home with his treasure in safety. He heard with strong repug nance the project of remaining in the Euxine, and determined to traverse it by intrigue. As far as concerned the sacrifices, indeed, which he offered apart with Xenophon, he was obliged to admit that the indications of the victims were favorable ;[1] Xenophon

---

to understand and appropriate to ourselves the ordinary comforts of life ; in obscure or untelligible cases, we are enabled to inform ourselves by looking at the blaze of the fire, or by consulting prophets who understand the livers of sacrificial victims and the flight of birds. When they have thus furnished so excellent a provision for life, who but spoilt children can be discontented, and ask for more ? Yet still human prudence, full of self-conceit, will struggle to be more powerful, and will presume itself to be wiser, than the gods."

> Ἃ δ' ἔστ' ἄσημα, κοὐ σαφῆ, γιγνώσκομεν
> Εἰς πῦρ βλέποντες, καὶ κατὰ σπλάγχνων πτύχας
> Μάντεις προσημαίνουσιν οἰωνῶν τ' ἄπο.
> Ἀρ' οὐ τρυφῶμεν, θεοῦ κατασκευὴν βίου
> Δόντος τοιαύτην, οἷσιν οὐκ ἀρκεῖ τάδε ;
> Ἀλλ' ἡ φρόνησις τοῦ θεοῦ μεῖζον σθένειν
> Ζητεῖ· τὸ γαῦρον δ' ἐν χεροῖν κεκ-ημένοι
> Δοκοῦμεν εἶναι δαιμόνων σοφώτεροι (Supplices, 211).

It will be observed that this constant outpouring of special revelations through prophets, omens, etc., was (in the view of these Sokratic thinkers) an essential part of the divine government; indispensable to satisfy their ideas of the benevolence of the gods ; since rational and scientific prediction was so habitually at fault and unable te fathom the phenomena of the fu ture.   [1] Xen. Anab. v, 6, 29

himself being too familiar with the process to be imposed upon
But he at the same time tried to create alarm by declaring that a
nice inspection disclosed evidence of treacherous snares laid for
Xenophon ; which latter indications he himself began to realize,
by spreading reports among the army that the Athenian general
was laying clandestine plans for keeping them away from Greece
without their own concurrence.[1]

Thus prematurely and insidiously divulged, the scheme found
some supporters, but a far larger number of opponents ; especially
among those officers who were jealous of the ascendency of Xenophon.   Timasion and Thorax employed it as a means of alarming
the Herakleotic and Sinopian traders in the camp ; telling them
that unless they provided not merely transports, but also pay for
the soldiers, Xenophon would find means to detain the army in the
Euxine, and would employ the transports when they arrived, not
for the homeward voyage, but for his own projects of acquisition
This news spread so much terror both at Sinôpê and Herakleia,
that large offers of money were made from both cities to Timasion,
on condition that he would ensure the departure of the army, as
soon as the vessels should be assembled at Kotyôra.   Accordingly
these officers, convening an assembly of the soldiers, protested
against the duplicity of Xenophon in thus preparing momentous
schemes without any public debate or decision.   And Timasion,
seconded by Thorax, not only strenuously urged the army to return,
but went so far as to promise to them, on the faith of the assurances from Herakleia and Sinôpê, future pay on a liberal scale, to
commence from the first new moon after their departure ; together
with a hospitable reception in his native city of Dardanus on the
Hellespont, from whence they could make incursions on the rich
neighboring satrapy of Pharnabazus.[2]

It was not, however, until these attacks were repeated from more
than one quarter, — until the Achæans Philêsius and Lykon had

---

[1] Though Xenophon accounted sacrifice to be an essential preliminary to
any action of dubious result, and placed great faith in the indications which
the victims offered, as signs of the future purposes of the gods, — he nevertheless had very little confidence in the professional prophets. He thought
them quite capable of gross deceit (See Xen. Cyrop. i, 6, 2, 3 ; compare So
phokles, Antigone, 1035, 1060 ; and Œdip. Tyrann. 387).

[2] Xen. Anab. v, 6, 19–26.

loudly accused Xenophon of underhand manœuvring to cheat the army into remaining against their will. — that the latter rose to repel the imputation; saying, that all that he had done was, to consult the gods whether it would be better to lay his project before the army or to keep it in his own bosom. The encouraging answer of the gods, as conveyed through the victims and testified even by Silanus himself, proved that the scheme was not ill-conceived; nevertheless, (he remarked) Silanus had begun to lay snares for him, realizing by his own proceedings a collateral indication which he had announced to be visible in the victims. "If (added Xenophon) you had continued as destitute and unprovided as you were just now, — I should still have looked out for a resource in the capture of some city which would have enabled such of you as chose, to return at once; while the rest stay behind to enrich themselves. But now there is no longer any necessity; since Herakleia and Sinôpê are sending transports, and Timasion promises pay to you from the next new moon. Nothing can be better; you will go back safely to Greece, and will receive pay for going thither. I desist at once from my scheme, and call upon all who were favorable to it to desist also. Only let us all keep together until we are on safe ground; and let the man who lags behind or runs off, be condemned as a wrong-doer."[1]

Xenophon immediately put this question to the vote, and every hand was held up in its favor. There was no man more disconcerted with the vote than the prophet Silanus, who loudly exclaimed against the injustice of detaining any one desirous to depart. But the soldiers put him down with vehement disapprobation, threatening that they would assuredly punish him if they caught him running off. His intrigue against Xenophon thus recoiled upon himself, for the moment. But shortly afterwards, when the army reached Herakleia, he took his opportunity for clandestine flight, and found his way back to Greece with the three thousand darics.[2]

If Silanus gained little by his manœuvre, Timasion and his partners gained still less. For so soon as it became known that the army had taken a formal resolution to go back to Greece, and that Xenophon himself had made the proposition, the Sinopians

---

[1] Xen. Anab. v, 6, 30–33   [2] Xen. Anab. v, 6, 34; vi, 4. 13.

and the Herakleots felt at their ease. They sent the transport vessels, but withheld the money which they had promised to Timasion and Thorax. Hence these officers were exposed to dishonor and peril; for, having positively engaged to find pay for the army, they were now unable to keep their word. So keen were their apprehensions, that they came to Xenophon and told him that they had altered their views, and that they now thought it best to employ the newly-arrived transports in conveying the army, not to Greece, but against the town and territory of Phasis at the eastern extremity of the Euxine [1] Xenophon replied, that they might convene the soldiers and make the proposition, if they chose; but that he would have nothing to say to it. To make the very proposition themselves, for which they had so much inveighed against Xenophon, was impossible without some preparation; so that each of them began individually to sound his captains, and get the scheme suggested by them. During this interval, the soldiery obtained information of the manœuvre, much to their discontent and indignation; of which Neon (the lieutenant of the absent Cheirisophus) took advantage, to throw the whole blame upon Xenophon; alleging that it was he who had converted the other officers to his original project, and that he intended as soon as the soldiers were on shipboard, to convey them fraudulently to Phasis instead of to Greece. There was something so plausible in this glaring falsehood, which represented Xenophon as the author of the renewed project, once his own, — and something so improbable in the fact that the other officers should spontaneously have renounced their own strong opinions to take up his, — that we can hardly be surprised at the ready credence which Neon's calumny found among the army. Their exasperation against Xenophon became so intense, that they collected in fierce groups; and there was even a fear that they would break out into mutinous violence, as they had before done against the magistrates of Kerasus.

Well knowing the danger of such spontaneous and informal assemblages, and the importance of the habitual solemnities of convocation and arrangement, to ensure either discussion or legitimate

---

[1] Xen. Anab. v, 6, 36.

I may here note that this *Phasis* in the Euxine means the town of that name, not the river

defence,¹ — Xenophon immediately sent round the herald to summon the army into the regular agora, with customary method and
ceremony. The summons was obeyed with unusual alacrity, and
Xenophon then addressed them, — refraining, with equal generosity and prudence, from saying anything about the last proposition
which Timasion and others had made to him. Had he mentioned
it, the question would have become one of life and death between
him and those other officers.

"Soldiers (said he), I understand that there are some men here
calumniating me, as if I were intending to cheat you and carry you
to Phasis. Hear me, then, in the name of the gods. If I am shown
to be doing wrong, let me not go from hence unpunished ; but if,
on the contrary, my calumniators are proved to be the wrong-doers,
deal with them as they deserve. You surely well know where the
sun rises and where he sets ; you know that if a man wishes to
reach Greece, he must go westward, — if to the barbaric territories,
he must go eastward. Can any one hope to deceive you on this
point, and persuade you that the sun rises on *this* side, and sets on

---

¹ Xen. Anab. v, 7, 1–3.

'Επεὶ δὲ ᾐσθάνετο ὁ Ξενοφῶν, ἔδοξεν αὐτῷ ὡς τάχιστα συναγαγεῖν αὐτῶν
ἀγορὰν, καὶ μὴ ἐᾶσαι συλλεγῆναι αὐτομάτους· καὶ ἐκέλευε τὸν κήρυκα συλλὲ
ξαι ἀγοράν.

The prudence of Xenophon in convoking the assembly at once is incon-
testable. He could not otherwise have hindered the soldiers from getting
together, and exciting one another to action, without any formal summons.

The reader should contrast with this the scene at Athens (described in
Thucydides, ii, 22 ; and in Vol. VI, Ch. xlviii, p. 133 of this History) during the first year of the Peloponnesian war, and the first invasion of Attica
by the Peloponnesians ; when the invaders were at Acharnæ, within sight
of the walls of Athens, burning and destroying the country. In spite of
the most violent excitement among the Athenian people, and the strongest
impatience to go out and fight, Perikles steadily refused to call an assembly, for fear that the people should take the resolution of going out. And
what was much more remarkable — the people even in that state of excitement though all united within the walls, did not meet in any informal
assembly, nor come to any resolution, or to any active proceeding ; which
the Cyreians would certainly have done, had they not been convened in a
regular assembly.

The contrast with the Cyreian army here illustrates the extraordinary
empire exercised by constitutional forms over the minds of the Athenian
citizens.

that? Can any one cheat you into going on shipboard with a wind which blows you away from Greece? Suppose even that I put you aboard when there is no wind at all. How am I to force you to sail with me against your own consent, — I being only in one ship, you in a hundred and more? Imagine, however, that I could even succeed in deluding you to Phasis. When we land there, you will know at once that we are not in Greece; and what fate can I then expect, — a detected impostor in the midst of ten thousand men with arms in their hands? No, — these stories all proceed from foolish men, who are jealous of my influence with you; jealous, too, without reason, — for I neither hinder *them* from outstripping me in your favor, if they can render you greater service, — nor *you* from electing them commanders, if you think fit. Enough of this, now; I challenge any one to come forward and say how it is possible either to cheat, or to be cheated, in the manner laid to my charge."[1]

Having thus grappled directly with the calumnies of his enemies, and dissipated them in such manner as doubtless to create a reaction in his own favor, Xenophon made use of the opportunity to denounce the growing disorders in the army; which he depicted as such that, if no corrective were applied, disgrace and contempt must fall upon all. As he paused after this general remonstrance, the soldiers loudly called upon him to go into particulars; upon which he proceeded to recall, with lucid and impressive simplicity, the outrages which had been committed at and near Kerasus, — the unauthorized and unprovoked attack made by Klearetus and his company on a neighboring village which was in friendly commerce with the army, — the murder of the three elders of the village, who had come as heralds to complain to the generals about such wrong, — the mutinous attack made by disorderly soldiers even upon the magistrates of Kerasus, at the very moment when they were remonstrating with the generals on what had occurred; exposing these magistrates to the utmost peril, and putting the generals themselves to ignominy.[2] " If such are to be our proceedings, (continued Xenophon), look you well into what condition the army will fall. You, the aggregate body,[3] will no longer be

---

[1] Xen. Anab v, 7, 7–11.   [2] Xen. Anab. v, 7, 13–26.
[3] Xen. Anab. v 7, 26–27. Εἰ οὖν ταῦτα τοιαῦτά ἐσ‑α: θεάσασθε οἷα ᾖ

the sovereign authority to make war or peace with whom you please ; each individual among you will conduct the army against any point which he may choose. And even if men should come to you as envoys, either for peace or for other purposes, they may be slain by any single enemy ; so that you will be debarred from all public communications whatever. Next, those whom your univer· sal suffrage shall have chosen commanders, will have no authority , while any self-elected general who chooses to give the word, Cast ! Cast ! (i. e. darts or stones), may put to death, without trial, either officer or soldier, as it suits him ; that is, if he finds you ready to obey him, as it happened near Kerasus. Look, now, what these self-elected leaders have done for you. The magistrate of Kerasus, if he was really guilty of wrong towards you, has been enabled to escape with impunity ; if he was innocent, he has been obliged to run away from you, as the only means of avoiding death without pretence or trial. Those who stoned the heralds to death, have brought matters to such a pass, that you alone, among all Greeks, cannot enter the town of Kerasus in safety, unless in commanding force ; and that we cannot even send in a herald to take up our dead (Klearetus and those who were slain in the attack on the Kerasuntine village) for burial ; though at first those who had slain them in self-defence were anxious to give up the bodies to us. For who will take the risk of going in as herald, from those who have set the example of putting heralds to death ? We generals were obliged to entreat the Kerasuntines to bury the bodies for us."[1]

Continuing in this emphatic protest against the recent disorders and outrages, Xenophon at length succeeded in impressing his own sentiment, heartily and unanimously, upon the soldiers. They

---

κατάστασις ἡμῖν ἔσται τῆς στρατιᾶς. ʽΥμεῖς μὲν οἱ πάντες οὐκ ἔσεσθε κύριοι. οὔτ᾽ ἀνελέσθαι πόλεμον ᾧ ἂν βούλησθε, οὔτε καταλῦσαι· ἰδίᾳ δὲ ὁ βουλόμενος ἄξει στράτευμα ἐφ᾽ ὅ,τι ἂν ἐθέλῃ. Κἄν τινες πρὸς ὑμᾶς ἴωσι πρέσβεις, ἢ εἰρή· νης δεόμενοι ἢ ἄλλου τινος, κατακαίνοντες τούτους οἱ βουλόμενοι, ποιήσουσιν ὑμᾶς τῶν λόγων μὴ ἀκοῦσαι τῶν πρὸς ὑμᾶς ἰόντων. ʽΕπειτα δὲ, οὓς μὲν ἂν ὑμεῖς ἅπαντες ἕλησθε ἄρχοντας, ἐν οὐδεμίᾳ χώρᾳ ἔσονται· ὅστις δ᾽ ἂν ἑαυτὸν ἕληται στρατηγὸν, καὶ ἐθέλῃ λέγειν, Βάλλε, Βάλλε, οὗτος ἔσται ἱκανὸς καὶ ἄρχοντα κατακαίνειν καὶ ἰδιώτην ὃν ἂν ὑμῶν ἐθέλῃ ἄκριτον — ἂν ὦσιν οἱ πεισόμενοι αὐτῷ, ὥσπερ καὶ νῦν ἐγένετο.

[1] Xen. Anab. v 7, 27–30.

passed a vote that the ringleaders of the mutiny at Kerasus should be punished; that if any on : was guilty of similar outrages in future, he should be put upon his trial by the generals, before the lochages or captains as judges, and if condemned by them, put to death ; and that trial should be had before the same persons, for any other wrong committed since the death of Cyrus. A suitable religious ceremony was also directed to be performed, at the instance of Xenophon and the prophets, to purify the army.[1]

This speech affords an interesting specimen of the politica morality universal throughout the Grecian world, though deeper and more predominant among its better sections. In the miscellaneous aggregate, and temporary society, now mustered at Kotyôra, Xenophon insists on the universal suffrage of the whole body, as the legitimate sovereign authority for the guidance of every individual will; the decision of the majority, fairly and formally collected, as carrying a title to prevail over every dissentient minority; the generals chosen by the majority of votes, as the only persons entitled to obedience. This is the cardinal principle to which he appeals, as the anchorage of political obligation in the mind of each separate man or fraction ; as the condition of all success, all safety, and all conjoint action; as the only condition either for punishing wrong or protecting right; as indispensable to keep up their sympathies with the Hellenic communities, and their dignity either as soldiers or as citizens. The complete success of his speech proves that he knew how to touch the right chord of Grecian feeling. No serious acts of individual insubordination occurred afterwards, though the army collectively went wrong on more than one occasion. And what is not less important to notice, — the influence of Xenophon himself, after his unreserved and courageous remonstrance, seems to have been sensibly augmented, — certainly no way diminished.

The circumstances which immediately followed were indeed well calculated to augment it. For it was resolved, on the proposition of Xenophon himself[2] that the generals themselves should be

---

[1] Xen. Anab. v, 7, 34, 35.

[2] Xen. Anab. v, 7, 35.

Παραινοῦντος δὲ Ξενοφῶντος, καὶ τῶν μάντεων συμβουλευόντων, ἔδοξε καὶ καϑᾶραι τὸ στράτευμα· καὶ ἐγένετο καϑαρμός· ἔδοξε δὲ καὶ τοὺς στρατηγοὺς δίκην ὑποσχεῖν τοῦ παρεληλυϑότος χρόνου.

tried before the newly-constituted tribunal of the lochages or captains, in case any one had complaint to make against them for past matters; agreeably to the Athenian habit of subjecting every magistrate to a trial of accountability on laying down his office. In the course of this investigation, Philesius and Xanthiklês were fined twenty minæ, to make good an assignable deficiency of that amount, in the cargoes of those merchantmen which had been detained at Trapezus for the transport of the army; Sophænetus, who had the general superintendence of this property, but had been negligent in that duty, was fined ten minæ. Next, the name of Xenophon was put up, when various persons stood forward to accuse him of having beaten and ill-used them. As commander of the rear-guard, his duty was by far the severest and most difficult, especially during the intense cold and deep snow ; since the sick and wounded, as well as the laggards and plunderers, all fell under his inspection. One man especially was loud in complaints against him, and Xenophon questioned him, as to the details of his case, before the assembled army. It turned out that he had given him blows, because the man, having been intrusted with the task of carrying a sick soldier, was about to evade the duty by burying the dying man alive.[1] This interesting debate (given in the Anabasis at length) ended by full approbation, on the part of the army, of Xenophon's conduct, accompanied with regret that he had not handled the man yet more severely.

The statements of Xenophon himself give us a vivid idea of the internal discipline of the army, even as managed by a discreet and well-tempered officer. " I acknowledge (said he to the soldiers) to have struck many men for disorderly conduct; men who were content to owe their preservation to your orderly march and constant fighting, while they themselves ran about to plunder and enrich themselves at your cost. Had we all acted as they did, we should have perished to a man. Sometimes, too, I struck

---

In the distribution of chapters as made by the editors, chapter the eighth is made to begin at the second ἔδοξε, which seems to me not convenient for comprehending the full sense. I think that the second ἔδοξε, as well as the first, is connected with the words παραινοῦν -ος Ξενοφῶντος, and ought to be included not only in the same chapter with them, but also in the same sentence, without an intervening full stop.

[1] Xen. Anab. v, 8. 3-12.

men who were lagging behind with cold and fatigue, or were stopping the way so as to hinder others from getting forward; I struck them with my fist,[1] in order to save them from the spear of the enemy. You yourselves stood by, and saw me; you had arms in your hands, yet none of you interfered to prevent me. I did it for their good as well as for yours, not from any insolence of disposition; for it was a time when we were all alike suffering from cold, hunger, and fatigue; whereas I now live comparatively well, drink more wine, and pass easy days, — and yet I strike no one. You will find that the men who failed most in those times of hardship, are now the most outrageous offenders in the army. There is Boïskus,[2] the Thessalian pugilist, who pretended sickness during the march, in order to evade the burthen of carrying his .hield, — and now, as I am informed, he has stripped several citizens of Kotyôra of their clothes. If (he concluded) the blows which I have occasionally given, in cases of necessity, are now brought in evidence, — I call upon those among you also, to whom I have rendered aid and protection, to stand up and testify in my favor."[3]

Many individuals responded to this appeal, insomuch that Xenophon was not merely acquitted, but stood higher than before in the opinion of the army. We learn from his defence that for a commanding officer to strike a soldier with his fist, if wanting in duty, was not considered improper; at least under such circumstances as those of the retreat. But what deserves notice still more, is, the extraordinary influence which Xenophon's powers of speaking gave him over the minds of the army. He stood distinguished from the other generals, Lacedæmonian, Arcadian, Achæan, etc.,

---

[1] Xen. Anab. v, 8, 16. ἔπαισα πύξ, ὅπως μὴ λόγχῃ ὑπὸ τῶν πολεμίων παίοιτο.

[2] The idea that great pugilists were not good soldiers in battle, is as old among the Greeks as the Iliad. The unrivalled pugilist of the Homeric Grecian army, Epeius, confesses his own inferiority as a soldier (Iliad, xxiii 667).

> Ἆσσον ἴτω, ὅστις δέπας οἴσεται ἀμφικύπελλον·
> Ἡμίονον δ' οὔ φημί τιν' ἄξεμεν ἄλλον 'Αχαιῶν,
> Πυγμῇ νικήσαντ'· ἐπεὶ εὔχομαι εἶναι ἄριστος.
> Ἦ οὐκ ἅλις, ὅ,ττι μάχης ἐπιδεύομαι; οὐδ' ἄρα πως ἦν
> Ἐν πάντεσσ' ἔργοισι δαήμονα φῶτα γενέσθαι.

Xen. Anab. v, 8, 13–25

by having the power of working on the minds of the soldiers collectively; and we see that he had the good sense, as well as the spirit, not to shrink from telling them unpleasant truths. In spite of such frankness — or rather, partly by means of such frankness, — his ascendency as commander not only remained unabated, as compared with that of the others, but went on increasing. For whatever may be said about the flattery of orators as a means of influence over the people, — it will be found that though particular points may be gained in this way, yet wherever the influence of an orator has been steady and long-continued (like that of Perikles[1] or Demosthenes) it is owing in part to the fact that he has an opinion of his own, and is not willing to accommodate himself constantly to the prepossessions of his hearers. Without the oratory of Xenophon, there would have existed no engine for kindling or sustaining the *sensus communis* of the ten thousand Cyreians assembled at Kotyôra, or for keeping up the moral authority of the aggregate over the individual members and fractions. The other officers could doubtless speak well enough to address short encouragements, or give simple explanations, to the soldiers; without this faculty, no man was fit for military command over Greeks. But the oratory of Xenophon was something of a higher order. Whoever will study the discourse pronounced by him at Kotyôra, will perceive a dexterity in dealing with assembled multitudes, — a discriminating use sometimes of the plainest and most direct appeal, sometimes of indirect insinuation or circuitous transitions to work round the minds of the hearers, — a command of those fundamental political convictions which lay deep in the Grecian mind, but were often so overlaid by the fresh impulses arising out of each successive situation, as to require some positive friction to draw them out from their latent state — lastly, a power of expansion and varied repetition — such as would be naturally imparted both by the education and the practice of an intelligent Athenian, but would rarely be found in any other Grecian city. The energy and judgment displayed by Xenophon in the retreat were doubtless not less essential to his influence than his power of speaking; but in these points we may be sure that other officers were more nearly his equals.

---

[1] See the striking remarks of Thucydides (ii, 65) upon Perikles.

The important public proceedings above described not only re
stored the influence of Xenophon, but also cleared off a great
amount of bad feeling, and sensibly abated the bad habits, which
had grown up in the army. A scene which speedily followed was
not without effect in promoting cheerful and amicable sympathies.
The Paphlagonian prince Korylas, weary of the desultory warfare
carried on between the Greeks and the border inhabitants, sent
envoys to the Greek camp with presents of horses and fine robes,[1]
and with expressions of a wish to conclude peace. The Greek
generals accepted the presents, and promised to submit the proposition to the army. But first they entertained the envoys at a banquet, providing at the same time games and dances, with other
recreations amusing not only to them but also to the soldiers generally. The various dances, warlike and pantomimic, of Thracians,
Mysians, Ænianes, Magnêtes, etc., are described by Xenophon in a
lively and interesting manner. They were followed on the next
day by an amicable convention concluded between the army and
the Paphlagonians.[2]

Not long afterwards, — a number of transports, sufficient for the
whole army, having been assembled from Herakleia and Sinôpê,
— all the soldiers were conveyed by sea to the latter place, passing by the mouth of the rivers Thermodon, Iris, and Halys, which
they would have found impracticable to cross in a land-march
through Paphlagonia. Having reached Sinôpê after a day and a
night of sailing with a fair wind, they were hospitably received,
and lodged in the neighboring seaport of Armênê, where the Sinopians sent to them a large present of barley-meal and wine, and
where they remained for five days.

It was here that they were joined by Cheirisophus, whose ab-

---

[1] Xen. Anab. vi, 1, 2. Πέμπει παρὰ τοὺς Ἕλληνας πρέσβεις, ἔχοντας ἵππους
καὶ στολὰς καλὰς, etc.

The horses sent were doubtless native Paphlagonian; the robes sent were
probably the produce of the looms of Sinôpê and Kotyôra; just as the
Thracian princes used to receive fine woven and metalic fabrics from Ab-
dêra and the other Grecian colonies on their coast — ὑφαντὰ καὶ λεῖα, καὶ
ἡ ἄλλη κατασκευή, etc. (Thucyd. ii, 96). From the like industry probably
proceeded the splendid " regia textilia " and abundance of gold and silver
vessels, captured by the Roman general Paulus Emilius along with Perseus,
the last king of Macedonia (Livy, xlv, 33–35)

[2] Xen. Anab. vi, 1, 10–14.

sence had been so unexpectedly prolonged. But he came with only a single trireme, bringing nothing except a message from Anaxibius, the Lacedæmonian admiral in the Bosphorus; who complimented the army, and promised that they should be taken into pay as soon as they were out of the Euxine. The soldiers, severely disappointed on seeing him arrive thus empty-handed, became the more strongly bent on striking some blow to fill their own purses before they reached Greece. Feeling that it was necessary to the success of any such project that it should be prepared not only skilfully, but secretly, they resolved to elect a single general in place of that board of six (or perhaps more) who were still in function. Such was now the ascendency of Xenophon, that the general sentiment of the army at once turned towards him ; and the lochages or captains, communicating to him what was in contemplation, intimated to him their own anxious hopes that he would not decline the offer. Tempted by so flattering a proposition, he hesitated at first what answer he should give. But at length the uncertainty of being able to satisfy the exigencies of the army, and the fear of thus compromising the reputation which he had already realized, outweighed the opposite inducements. As in other cases of doubt, so in this, — he offered sacrifice to Zeus Basileus ; and the answer returned by the victims was such as to determine him to refusal. Accordingly, when the army assembled, with predetermination to choose a single chief, and proceeded to nominate him, — he respectfully and thankfully declined, on the ground that Cheirisophus was a Lacedæmonian, and that he himself was not; adding that he should cheerfully serve under any one whom they might name. His excuse, however, was repudiated by the army; and especially by the lochages. Several of these latter were Arcadians ; and one of them, Agasias, cried out, with full sympathy of the soldiers, that if that principle were admitted. he, as an Arcadian, ought to resign his command. Finding that his former reason was not approved, Xenophon acquainted the army that he had sacrificed to know whether he ought to accept the command, and that the gods had peremptorily forbidden him to do so.[1]

Cheirisophus was then elected sole commander, and undertook

---

[1] Xen. Anab. vi, ., 22–31

the duty ; saying that he would have willingly served under Xenophon, if the latter had accepted the office, but that it was a good thing for Xenophon himself to have declined, — since Dexippus had already poisoned the mind of Anaxibius against him, although he (Cheirisophus) had emphatically contradicted the calumnies.[1]

On the next day, the army sailed forward, under the command of Cheirisophus, to Herakleia; near which town they were hospitably entertained, and gratified with a present of meal, wine, and bullocks, even greater than they had received at Sinôpê. It now appeared that Xenophon had acted wisely in declining the sole command ; and also that Cheirisophus, though elected commander, yet having been very long absent, was not really of so much importance in the eyes of the soldiers as Xenophon. In the camp near Herakleia, the soldiers became impatient that their generals (for the habit of looking upon Xenophon as one of them still continued) took no measures to procure money for them. The Achæan Lykon proposed that they should extort a contribution of no less than three thousand staters of Kyzikus (about sixty thousand Attic drachmæ, or ten talents, equal to two thousand three hundred pounds) from the inhabitants of Herakleia; another man immediately outbid this proposition, and proposed that they should require ten thousand staters — a full month's pay for the army. It was moved that Cheirisophus and Xenophon should go to the Herakleots as envoys with this demand. But both of them indignantly refused to be concerned in so unjust an extortion from a Grecian city which had just received the army kindly, and sent handsome presents. Accordingly, Lykon with two Arcadian officers undertook the mission, and intimated the demand, not without threats in case of non-compliance, to the Herakleots. The latter replied that they would take it into consideration. But they waited only for the departure of the envoys, and then immediately closed their gates, manned their walls, and brought in their outlying property.

The project being thus baffled, Lykon and the rest turned their displeasure upon Cheirisophus and Xenophon, whom they accused of having occasioned its miscarriage. And they now began to

---

[1] Xen. Anab. vi, 1, 32.

exclaim that it was disgraceful to the Arcadians and Achæans, who formed more than one numerical half of the army and endured all the toil — to obey as well as to enrich generals from other Hellenic cities; especially a single Athenian who furnished no contingent to the army. Here again it is remarkable that the personal importance of Xenophon caused him to be still regarded as a general, though the sole command had been vested, by formal vote, in Cheirisophus. So vehement was the dissatisfaction, that all the Arcadian and Achæan soldiers in the army, more than four thousand and five hundred hoplites in number, renounced the authority of Cheirisophus, formed themselves into a distinct division, and chose ten commanders from out of their own numbers. The whole army thus became divided into three portions — first, the Arcadians and Achæans; secondly, one thousand and four hundred hoplites and seven hundred peltasts, who adhered to Cheirisophus; lastly, one thousand seven hundred hoplites, three hundred peltasts, and forty horsemen, (all the horsemen in the army) attaching themselves to Xenophon; who however was taking measures to sail away individually from Herakleia and quit the army altogether, which he would have done had he not been restrained by unfavorable sacrifices.[1]

The Arcadian division, departing first, in vessels from Herakleia, landed at the harbor of Kalpê; an untenanted promontory of the Bithynian or Asiatic Thrace, midway between Herakleia and Byzantium. From thence they marched at once into the interior of Bithynia, with the view of surprising the villages, and acquiring plunder. But through rashness and bad management, they first sustained several partial losses, and ultimately became surrounded upon an eminence, by a large muster of the indigenous Bithynians from all the territory around. They were only rescued from destruction by the unexpected appearance of Xenophon with his division; who had left Herakleia somewhat later, but heard by accident, during their march, of the danger of their comrades. The whole army thus became re-assembled at Kalpê, where the Arcadians and Achæans, disgusted at the ill-success of their separate expedition, again established the old union and the old generals. They chose Neon in place of Cheirisophus, who, — afflicted by

the humiliation put upon him, in having been first named sole commander and next deposed within a week, — had fallen sick of a
fever and died. The elder Arcadian captains farther moved a resolution, that if any one henceforward should propose to separate the
army into fractions, he should be put to death.[1]

The locality of Kalpê was well suited for the foundation of a
colony, which Xenophon evidently would have been glad to bring
about, though he took no direct measures tending towards it; while
the soldiers were so bent on returning to Greece, and so jealous
lest Xenophon should entrap them into remaining, that they almost
shunned the encampment. It so happened that they were detained there for some days without being able to march forth even
in quest of provisions, because the sacrifices were not favorable.
Xenophon refused to lead them out, against the warning of the
sacrifices — although the army suspected him of a deliberate
manœuvre for the purpose of detention. Neon, however, less scrupulous, led out a body of two thousand men who chose to follow
him, under severe distress for want of provisions. But being surprised by the native Bithynians, with the aid of some troops of the
Persian satrap Pharnabazus, he was defeated with the loss of no
less than five hundred men; a misfortune which Xenophon regards
as the natural retribution for contempt of the sacrificial warning.
The dangerous position of Neon with the remainder of the detachment was rapidly made known at the camp; upon which Xenophon, unharnessing a waggon-bullock as the only animal near at
hand, immediately offered sacrifice. On this occasion, the victim
was at once favorable; so that he led out without delay the greater
part of the force, to the rescue of the exposed detachment, which
was brought back in safety to the camp. So bold had the enemy
become, that in the night the camp was attacked. The Greeks
were obliged on the next day to retreat into stronger ground, surrounding themselves with a ditch and palisade. Fortunately a
vessel arrived from Herakleia, bringing to the camp at Kalpê a
supply of barley-meal, cattle, and wine; which restored the spirits
of the army, enabling them to go forth on the ensuing morning,
and assume the aggressive against the Bithynians and the troops
of Pharnabazus. These troops were completely defeated and dis-

---

[1] Xenoph. Anab. vi, 3, 10–25; vi, 4, 11.

persed, so that the Greeks returned to their camp at Kalpê in the evening, both safe and masters of the country.[1]

At Kalpê they remained some time, awaiting the arrival of Kleander from Byzantium, who was said to be about to bring vessels for their transport. They were now abundantly provided with supplies, not merely from the undisturbed plunder of the neighboring villages, but also from the visits of traders who came with cargoes. Indeed the impression — that they were preparing, at the instance of Xenophon, to found a new city at Kalpê — became so strong, that several of the neighboring native villages sent envoys to ask on what terms alliance would be granted to them. At length Kleander came, but with two triremes only.[2]

Kleander was the Lacedæmonian harmost or governor of Byzantium. His appearance opens to us a new phase in the eventful history of this gallant army, as well as an insight into the state of the Grecian world under the Lacedæmonian empire. He came attended by Dexippus, who had served in the Cyreian army until their arrival at Trapezus, and who had there been entrusted with an armed vessel for the purpose of detaining transports to convey the troops home, but had abused the confidence reposed in him by running away with the ship to Byzantium.

It so happened that at the moment when Kleander arrived, the whole army was out on a marauding excursion. Orders had been already promulgated, that whatever was captured by every one when the whole army was out, should be brought in and dealt with as public property; though on days when the army was collectively at rest, any soldier might go out individually and take to himself whatever he could pillage. On the day when Kleander arrived, and found the whole army out, some soldiers were just coming back with a lot of sheep which they had seized. By right, the sheep ought to have been handed into the public store. But these soldiers, desirous to appropriate them wrongfully, addressed themselves to Dexippus, and promised him a portion if he would enable them to retain the rest. Accordingly the latter interfered, drove away those who claimed the sheep as public property, and denounced them as thieves to Kleander; who desired him to bring them before him. Dexippus arrested one of them, a soldier be-

---

longing to the lochus or company of one of the best friends of
Xenophon, — the Arcadian Agasias. The latter took the man
under his protection; while the soldiers around, incensed not less
at the past than at the present conduct of Dexippus, broke out
into violent manifestations, called him a traitor and pelted him
with stones. Such was their wrath that not Dexippus alone, but
the crew of the triremes also, and even Kleander himself, fled in
alarm; in spite of the intervention of Xenophon and the other
generals, who on the one hand explained to Kleander, that it was
an established army-order which these soldiers were seeking to
enforce — and on the other hand controlled the mutineers. But
the Lacedæmonian harmost was so incensed as well by his own
fright as by the calumnies of Dexippus, that he threatened to sail
away at once, and proclaim the Cyreian army enemies to Sparta,
so that every Hellenic city should be interdicted from giving them
reception.[1] It was in vain that the generals, well knowing the formidable consequences of such an interdict, entreated him to relent.
He would consent only on condition that the soldier who had begun
to throw stones, as well as Agasias the interfering officer, should
be delivered up to him. This latter demand was especially insisted upon by Dexippus, who, hating Xenophon, had already tried
to prejudice Anaxibius against him, and believed that Agasias had
acted by his order.[2]

The situation became now extremely critical; since the soldiers
would not easily be brought to surrender their comrades, — who
had a perfectly righteous cause, though they had supported it by
undue violence, — to the vengeance of a traitor like Dexippus.
When the army was convened in assembly, several of them went
so far as to treat the menace of Kleander with contempt. But
Xenophon took pains to set them right upon this point. "Soldiers
(said he), it will be no slight misfortune if Kleander shall depart
as he threatens to do, in his present temper towards us. We are
here close upon the cities of Greece; now the Lacedæmonians are
the imperial power in Greece, and not merely their authorized
officers, but even each one of their individual citizens, can accomplish what he pleases in the various cities. If then Kleander begins by shutting us out from Byzantium, and next enjoins the Lace-

---

dæmonian harmosts in the other cities to do the same, proclaiming
us lawless and disobedient to Sparta, — if, besides, the same representation should be conveyed to the Lacedæmonian admiral of the
fleet, Anaxibius, — we shall be hard pressed either to remain or to
sail away; for the Lacedæmonians are at present masters, both on
land and at sea.[1] We must not, for the sake of any one or two men,
suffer the whole army to be excluded from Greece. We must obey
whatever the Lacedæmonians command, especially as our cities, to
which we respectively belong, now obey them. As to what concerns myself, I understand that Dexippus has told Kleander that
Agasias would never have taken such a step except by my orders.
Now, if Agasias himself states this, I am ready to exonerate both
him and all of you, and to give myself up to any extremity of punishment. I maintain too, that any other man whom Kleander
arraigns, ought in like manner to give himself up for trial, in order
that you collectively may be discharged from the imputation. It
will be hard indeed, if just as we are reaching Greece, we should
not only be debarred from the praise and honor which we antici
pated, but should be degraded even below the level of others, and
shut out from the Grecian cities."[2]

After this speech from the philo-Laconian Xenophon, — so significant a testimony of the unmeasured ascendency and interference
of the Lacedæmonians throughout Greece, — Agasias rose and proclaimed, that what he had done was neither under the orders, nor
with the privity, of Xenophon; that he had acted on a personal
impulse of wrath, at seeing his own honest and innocent soldier
dragged away by the traitor Dexippus; but that he now willingly
gave himself up as a victim, to avert from the army the displeasure
of the Lacedæmonians. This generous self-sacrifice, which at the

---

[1] Xen. Anab. vi, 6, 12, 13.

Εἰσὶ μὲν γὰρ ἤδη ἐγγὺς αἱ Ἑλληνίδες πόλεις· τῆς δ' Ἑλλάδος Λακεδαιμόνιο
προεστήκασιν· ἱκανοὶ δέ εἰσι καὶ εἰς ἔκαστος Λακεδαιμονίων
ἐν ταῖς πόλεσιν ὅ,τι βούλονται διαπράττεσθαι. Εἰ οὖν
οὖτος πρῶτον μὲν ἡμᾶς Βυζαντίου ἀποκλείσει, ἔπειτα δὲ τοῖς ἄλλοις ἁρμοσταῖς
παραγγελεῖ εἰς τὰς πόλεις μὴ δέχεσθαι, ὡς ἀπιστοῦντας Λακεδαιμονίοις καὶ
ἀνόμους ὄντας — ἔτι δὲ πρὸς 'Αναξίβιον τὸν ναύαρχον οὖτος ὁ λόγος τ ερὶ
ἡμῶν ἥξει — χαλεπὸν ἔσται καὶ μένειν καὶ ἀποπλεῖν· καὶ γὰρ ἐ: τῇ
γῇ ἄρχουσι Λακεδαιμόνιοι καὶ ἐν τῇ θαλάττῃ τὸν νῦν
χρόνον.

[2] Xen. Anab. vi, 6, 12–16.

moment promised nothing less than a fatal result to Agasias, was accepted by the army; and the generals conducted both him and the soldier whom he had rescued, as prisoners to Kleander. Presenting himself as the responsible party, Agasias at the same time explained to Kleander the infamous behavior of Dexippus to the army, and said that towards no one else would he have acted in the same manner; while the soldier whom he had rescued and who was given up at the same time, also affirmed that he had interfered merely to prevent Dexippus and some others from overruling, for their own individual benefit, a proclaimed order of th' entire army. Kleander, having observed that if Dexippus had done what was affirmed, he would be the last to defend him, but that no one ought to have been stoned without trial, — desired that the persons surrendered might be left for his consideration, and at the same time retracted his expressions of displeasure as regarded all the others.[1]

The generals then retired, leaving Kleander in possession of the prisoners, and on the point of taking his dinner. But they retired with mournful feelings, and Xenophon presently convened the army to propose that a general deputation should be sent to Kleander to implore his lenity towards their two comrades. This being cordially adopted, Xenophon, at the head of a deputation comprising Drakontius, the Spartan, as well as the chief officers, addressed an earnest appeal to Kleander, representing that his honor had been satisfied with the unconditional surrender of the two persons required; that the army, deeply concerned for two meritorious comrades, entreated him now to show mercy and spare their lives; that they promised him in return the most implicit obedience, and entreated him to take the command of them, in order that he might have personal cognizance of their exact discipline, and compare their worth with that of Dexippus. Kleander was not merely soothed, but completely won over by this address; and said in reply that the conduct of the generals belied altogether the representations made to him, (doubtless by Dexippus) that they were seeking to alienate the army from the Lacedæmonians. He not only restored the two men in his power, but also accepted the command of the army, and promised to conduct them back into Greece.[2]

---

[1] Xen. Anab. vi, 6, 22-28.   [2] Xen. Anab. vi, 6, 31-36.

The prospects of the army appeared thus greatly improved; the more so, as Kleander, on entering upon his new functions as commander, found the soldiers so cheerful and orderly, that he was highly gratified, and exchanged personal tokens of friendship and hospitality with Xenophon. But when sacrifices came to be offered, for beginning the march homeward, the signs were so unpropitious, for three successive days, that Kleander could not bring himself to brave such auguries at the outset of his career. Accordingly, he told the generals, that the gods plainly forbade him, and reserved it for them, to conduct the army into Greece; that he should therefore sail back to Byzantium, and would receive the army in the best way he could, when they reached the Bosphorus. After an interchange of presents with the soldiers, he then departed with his two triremes.[1]

The favorable sentiment now established in the bosom of Kleander will be found very serviceable hereafter to the Cyreians at Byzantium; but they had cause for deeply regretting the unpropitious sacrifices which had deterred him from assuming the actual command at Kalpê. In the request preferred to him by them that he would march as their commander to the Bosphorus, we may recognize a scheme, and a very well-contrived scheme, of Xenophon; who had before desired to leave the army at Herakleia, and who saw plainly that the difficulties of a commander, unless he were a Lacedæmonian of station and influence, would increase with every step of their approach to Greece. Had Kleander accepted the command, the soldiers would have been better treated, while Xenophon himself might either have remained as his adviser, or might have gone home. He probably would have chosen the latter course.

Under the command of their own officers, the Cyreians now marched from Kalpê across Bithynia to Chrysopolis,[2] (in the territory of Chalkêdon on the Asiatic edge of the Bosphorus, immediately opposite to Byzantium, as Scutari now is to Constantinople) where they remained seven days, turning into money the slaves

---

[1] Xen. Anab. vi, 6, 36, 37

[2] Nearly the same cross march was made by the Athenian general Lamachus, in the eighth year of the Peloponnesian war, after he had lost his triremes by a sudden rise of the water at the mouth of the river Kalex, in the territory of Herakleia (Thucyd. iv, 75).

and plunder which they had collected. Unhappily for them, the Lacedæmonian admiral Anaxibius was now at Byzantium, so that their friend Kleander was under his superior command. And Pharnabazus, the Persian satrap of the north-western regions of Asia Minor, becoming much alarmed lest they should invade his satrapy, despatched a private message to Anaxibius; whom he prevailed upon, by promise of large presents, to transport the army forthwith across to the European side of the Bosphorus.[1] Accordingly, Anaxibius, sending for the generals and the lochages across to Byzantium, invited the army to cross, and gave them his assurance that as soon as the soldiers should be in Europe, he would provide pay for them. The other officers told him that they would return with this message and take the sense of the army; but Xenophon, on his own account, said that he should not return; that he should now retire from the army, and sail away from Byzantium. It was only on the pressing instance of Anaxibius that he was induced to go back to Chrysopolis and conduct the army across; on the understanding that he should depart immediately afterwards.

Here at Byzantium, he received his first communication from the Thracian prince Seuthes; who sent Medosadês to offer him a reward if he would bring the army across. Xenophon replied that the army would cross; that no reward from Seuthes was needful to bring about that movement; but that he himself was about to depart, leaving the command in other hands. In point of fact, the whole army crossed with little delay, landed in Europe, and found themselves within the walls of Byzantium.[2] Xenophon, who had come along with them, paid a visit shortly afterwards to his friend the harmost Kleander, and took leave of him as about to depart immediately. But Kleander told him that he must not think of departing until the army was out of the city, and that he would be held responsible if they stayed. In truth Kleander was very uneasy so long as the soldiers were within the walls, and was well aware that it might be no easy matter to induce them to go away.

---

[1] Xen. Anab. vii, 1, 2. Πέμψας πρὸς ᾿Αναξίβιον τὸν ναύαρχον, ἐδεῖτο διαβιβάσ ι τὸ στράτευμα ἐκ τῆς ᾿Ασίας, καὶ ὑπισχνεῖτο πάντα πι ιήσειν αὐτῷ ὅσα δέοι.

Compare vii, 2, 7, when Anaxibius demanded in vain the fulfilment of this promise.

[2] Xen. Anab. vii, 1, 5–7.

Foɪ Anaxibius had practised a gross fraud in promising them pay, which he had neither the ability nor the inclination to provide. Without handing to them either pay or even means of purchasing supplies, he issued orders that they must go forth with arms and baggage, and muster outside of the gates, there to be numbered for an immediate march ; any one who stayed behind being held as punishable. This proclamation was alike unexpected and offensive to the soldiers, who felt that they had been deluded, and were very backward in obeying. Hence Kleander, while urgent with Xenophon to defer his departure until he had conducted the army outside of the walls, added — " Go forth as if you were about to march along with them ; when you are once outside, you may depart as soon as you please." [1] Xenophon replied that this matter must be settled with Anaxibius, to whom accordingly both of them went, and who repeated the same directions, in a manner yet more peremptory. Though it was plain to Xenophon that he was here making himself a sort of instrument to the fraud which Anaxibius had practised upon the army, yet he had no choice but to obey. Accordingly, he as well as the other generals put themselves at the head of the troops, who followed, however reluctantly, and arrived most of them outside of the gates. Eteonikus (a Lacedæmonian officer of consideration, noticed more than once in my last preceding volume) commanding at the gate, stood close to it in person ; in order that when all the Cyreians had gone forth, he might immediately shut it and fasten it with the bar.[2]

Anaxibius knew well what he was doing. He fully anticipated that the communication of the final orders would occasion an outbreak among the Cyreians, and was anxious to defer it until they were outside. But when there remained only the rearmost companies still in the inside and on their march, all the rest having got out — he thought the danger was over, and summoned to him the generals and captains, all of whom were probably near the gates superintending the march through. It seems that Xenophon, having given notice that he intended to depart, did not answer to this summons as one of the generals, but remained outside among

---

[1] Xen. Anab. vii, 1, 7–10. 'Αλλ' ὁμῶς (ἔφη), ἐγώ σοι συμβουλεύω ἐξελθεῖν ὡς πορευσόμενον· ἐπειδὰν δ' ἔξω γένηται τὸ στράτευμα, τότε ἀπαλλάττεσ θαι.

[2] Xen. Anab. vii, 1, 12.

the soldiers. "Take what supplies you want (said Anaxibius) from the neighboring Thracian villages, which are well furnished with wheat, barley, and other necessaries. After thus providing yourselves, march forward to the Chersonesus, and there Kyniskus will give you pay."[1]

This was the first distinct intimation given by Anaxibius that he did not intend to perform his promise of finding pay for the soldiers. Who Kyniskus was, we do not know, nor was he probably known to the Cyreians; but the march here enjoined was at least one hundred and fifty English miles, and might be much longer. The route was not indicated, and the generals had to inquire from Anaxibius whether they were to go by what was called the Holy Mountain (that is, by the shorter line, skirting the northern coast of the Propontis), or by a more inland and circuitous road through Thrace; — also whether they were to regard the Thracian prince, Seuthes, as a friend or an enemy.[2]

Instead of the pay which had been formally promised to them by Anaxibius if they would cross over from Asia to Byzantium, the Cyreians thus found themselves sent away empty-handed, to a long march, — through another barbarous country, with chance supplies to be ravished only by their own efforts, — and at the end of it a lot unknown and uncertain; while, had they remained in Asia, they would have had at any rate the rich satrapy of Pharnabazus within their reach. To perfidy of dealing was now added a brutal ejectment from Byzantium, without even the commonest manifestations of hospitality; contrasting pointedly with the treatment which the army had recently experienced at Trapezus, Sinôpê, and Herakleia; where they had been welcomed not only by compliments on their past achievements, but also by an ample present of flour, meat, and wine. Such behavior could not fail to provoke the most violent indignation in the bosoms of the soldiery; and Anaxibius had therefore delayed giving the order until the last soldiers were marching out, thinking that the army would hear nothing of it until the generals came out of the gates to inform them; so that the gates would be closed, and the walls manned to resist any assault from without. But his calculations were not realized. Either one of the soldiers passing by heard him give the

---

[1] Xen. Anab. vii, 1, 13.   [2] Xen. Anab. vii. 1, 14

order, or one of the captains forming his audience stole away from the rest, and hastened forward to acquaint his comrades on the outside. The bulk of the army, already irritated by the inhospitable way in which they had been thrust out, needed nothing farther to inflame them into spontaneous mutiny and aggression. While the generals within (who either took the communication more patiently, or at least, looking farther forward, felt that any attempt to resent or resist the ill usage of the Spartan admiral would only make their position worse) were discussing with Anaxibius the details of the march just enjoined, the soldiers without, bursting into spontaneous movement, with a simultaneous and fiery impulse, made a rush back to get possession of the gate. But Eteonikus, seeing their movement, closed it without a moment's delay, and fastened the bar. The soldiers on reaching the gate and finding it barred, clamored loudly to get it opened, threatened to break it down, and even began to knock violently against it. Some ran down to the sea-coast, and made their way into the city round the line of stones at the base of the city wall, which protected it against the sea; while the rearmost soldiers who had not yet marched out, seeing what was passing, and fearful of being cut off from their comrades, assaulted the gate from the inside, severed the fastenings with axes, and threw it wide open to the army.[1] All the soldiers then rushed up, and were soon again in Byzantium.

Nothing could exceed the terror of the Lacedæmonians as well as of the native Byzantines, when they saw the excited Cyreians again within the walls. The town seemed already taken and on the point of being plundered. Neither Anaxibius nor Eteonikus took the smallest means of resistance, nor stayed to brave the approach of the soldiers, whose wrath they were fully conscious of having deserved. Both fled to the citadel — the former first running to the sea-shore, and jumping into a fishing-boat to go thither by sea. He even thought the citadel not tenable with its existing garrison, and sent over to Chalkêdon for a reinforcement. Still more terrified were the citizens of the town. Every man in the market-place instantly fled; some to their houses, others to the merchant vessels in the harbor, others to the triremes or ships of war, which they hauled down to the water, and thus put to sea.[2]

---

[1] Xen. Anab. vii, 1, 15-17.   [2] Xen. Anab. vii, 1, 18, 19.

To the deception and harshness of the Spartan admiral, there was thus added a want of precaution in the manner of execution, which threatened to prove the utter ruin of Byzantium. For it was but too probable that the Cyreian soldiers, under the keen sense of recent injury, would satiate their revenge, and reimburse themselves for the want of hospitality towards them, without distinguishing the Lacedæmonian garrison from the Byzantine citizens; and that too from mere impulse, not merely without orders, but in spite of prohibitions, from their generals. Such was the aspect of the case, when they became again assembled in a mass within the gates; and such would probably have been the reality, had Xenophon executed his design of retiring earlier, so as to leave the other generals acting without him. Being on the outside along with the soldiers, Xenophon felt at once, as soon as he saw the gates forced open and the army again within the town, the terrific emergency which was impending; first, the sack of Byzantium, — next, horror and antipathy, throughout all Greece, towards the Cyreian officers and soldiers indiscriminately, — lastly, unsparing retribution inflicted upon all by the power of Sparta. Overwhelmed with these anxieties, he rushed into the town along with the multitude, using every effort to pacify them and bring them into order. They on their parts, delighted to see him along with them, and conscious of their own force, were eager to excite him to the same pitch as themselves, and to prevail on him to second and methodize their present triumph. "Now is your time, Xenophon, (they exclaimed), to make yourself a man. You have here a city, — you have triremes, — you have money, — you have plenty of soldiers Now then, if you choose, you can enrich us; and we in return can make you powerful." — "You speak well (replied he); I shall do as you propose; but if you want to accomplish anything, you must fall into military array forthwith." He knew that this was the first condition of returning to anything like tranquillity; and by great good fortune, the space called the Thrakion, immediately adjoining the gate inside, was level, open, and clear of houses; presenting an excellent place of arms or locality for a review. The whole army, — partly from their long military practice, — partly under the impression that Xenophon was really about to second their wishes and direct some aggressive operation, — threw themselves almost of their own accord into regular array on the Thrakion.

the hoplites eight deep, the peltasts on each flank. It was in this position that Xenophon addressed them as follows : —

"Soldiers! I am not surprised that you are incensed, and that you think yourselves scandalously cheated and ill-used. But if we give way to our wrath, if we punish these Lacedæmonians now before us for their treachery, and plunder this innocent city, — reflect what will be the consequence. We shall stand proclaimed forthwith as enemies to the Lacedæmonians and their allies; and what sort of a war that will be, those who have witnessed and who still recollect recent matters of history may easily fancy. We Athenians entered into the war against Sparta with a powerful army and fleet, an abundant revenue, and numerous tributary cities in Asia as well as Europe, — among them this very Byzantium in which we now stand. We have been vanquished in the way that all of you know. And what then will be the fate of us soldiers, when we shall have as united enemies, Sparta with all her old allies and Athens besides, — Tissaphernes and the barbaric forces on the coast, — and most of all, the Great King whom we marched up to dethrone and slay, if we were able? Is any man fool enough to think that we have a chance of making head against so many combined enemies? Let us not plunge madly into dishonor and ruin, nor incur the enmity of our own fathers and friends; who are in the cities which will take arms against us, — and will take arms justly, if we, who abstained from seizing any barbaric city, even when we were in force sufficient, shall nevertheless now plunder the first Grecian city into which we have been admitted. As far as I am concerned, may I be buried ten thousand fathoms deep in the earth, rather than see you do such things; and I exhort *you*, too, as Greeks, to obey the leaders of Greece. Endeavor, while thus obedient, to obtain your just rights; but if you should fail in this, rather submit to injustice than cut yourselves off from the Grecian world. Send to inform Anaxibius that we have entered the city, not with a view to commit any violence, but in the hope, if possible, of obtaining from him the advantages which he promised us. If we fail, we shall at least prove to him that we quit the city, not under his fraudulent manœuvres, but under our own sense of the duty of obedience."[1]

---

[1] Xen. Anab. vii, 1, 30-31.

This speech completely arrested the impetuous impulse of the army, brought them to a true sense of their situation, and induced them to adopt the proposition of Xenophon. They remained unmoved in their position on the Thrakion, while three of the captains were sent to communicate with Anaxibius. While they were thus waiting, a Theban named Kœratadas approached, who had once commanded in Byzantium under the Lacedæmonians, during the previous war. He had now become a sort of professional Condottiero or general, looking out for an army to command, wherever he could find one, and offering his services to any city which would engage him. He addressed the assembled Cyreians, and offered, if they would accept him for their general, to conduct them against the Delta of Thrace (the space included between the north-west corner of the Propontis and the south-west corner of the Euxine), which he asserted to be a rich territory presenting great opportunity to plunder; he farther promised to furnish them with ample subsistence during the march. Presently the envoys returned, bearing the reply of Anaxibius, who received the message favorably, promising that not only the army should have no cause to regret their obedience, but that he would both report their good conduct to the authorities at home, and do everything in his own power to promote their comfort.[1] He said nothing farther about taking them into pay; that delusion having now answered its purpose. The soldiers, on hearing his communication, adopted a resolution to accept Kœratadas as their future commander, and then marched out of the town. As soon as they were on the outside, Anaxibius, not content with closing the gates against them, made public proclamation that if any one of them were found in the town, he should be sold forthwith into slavery.

There are few cases throughout Grecian history in which an able discourse has been the means of averting so much evil, as was averted by this speech of Xenophon to the army in Byzantium. Nor did he ever, throughout the whole period of his command, render to them a more signal service. The miserable consequences, which would have ensued, had the army persisted in their aggressive impulse, — first, to the citizens of the town, ultimately to themselves, while Anaxibius, the only guilty person,

---

[1] Xen. Anab. viii, 1, 32–35.

had the means of escaping by sea, ever under the worst circumstances, — are stated by Xenophon rather under than above the
reality. At the same time no orator ever undertook a more difficult case, or achieved a fuller triumph over unpromising conditions.
If we consider the feelings and position of the army at the instant
of their breaking into the town, we shall be astonished that any
commander could have arrested their movements. Though fresh
from all the glory of their retreat, they had been first treacherously
entrapped over from Asia, next roughly ejected, by Anaxibius;
and although it may be said truly that the citizens of Byzantium
had no concern either in the one or the other, yet little heed is
commonly taken, in military operations, to the distinction between
garrison and citizens in an assailed town. Having arms in their
hands, with consciousness of force arising out of their exploits in
Asia, the Cyreians were at the same time inflamed by the opportunity both of avenging a gross recent injury, and enriching themselves in the process of execution; to which we may add, the
excitement of that rush whereby they had obtained the reëntry,
and the farther fact, that without the gates they had nothing to
expect except poor, hard, uninviting service in Thrace. With
soldiers already possessed by an overpowering impulse of this
nature, what chance was there that a retiring general, on the point
of quitting the army, could so work upon their minds as to induce
them to renounce the prey before them? Xenophon had nothing
to invoke except distant considerations, partly of Hellenic reputation, chiefly of prudence; considerations indeed of unquestionable
reality and prodigious magnitude, yet belonging all to a distant future, and therefore of little comparative force, except when set forth
in magnified characters by the orator. How powerfully he worked
upon the minds of his hearers, so as to draw forth these far-removed
dangers from the cloud of present sentiment by which they were
overlaid, — how skilfully he employed in illustration the example
of his own native city, — will be seen by all who study his speech.
Never did his Athenian accomplishments, — his talent for giving
words to important thoughts, — his promptitude in seizing a present situation and managing the sentiments of an impetuous multitude, — appear to greater advantage than when he was thus
suddenly called forth to meet a terrible emergency. His pre-
established reputation and the habit of obeying his orders, were

doubtless essential conditions of success. But none of his colleagues in command would have been able to accomplish the like memorable change on the minds of the soldiers, or to procure obedience for any simple authoritative restraint; nay, it is probable, that if Xenophon had not been at hand, the other generals would have followed the passionate movement, even though they had been reluctant, — from simple inability to repress it.[1] Again, — whatever might have been the accomplishments of Xenophon, it is certain that even *he* would not have been able to work upon the minds of these excited soldiers, had they not been Greeks and citizens as well as soldiers, — bred in Hellenic sympathies and accustomed to Hellenic order, with authority operating in part through voice and persuasion, and not through the Persian whip and instruments of torture. The memorable discourse on the Thrakion at Byzantium illustrates the working of that persuasive agency which formed one of the permanent forces and conspicuous charms of Hellenism. It teaches us that if the orator could sometimes accuse innocent defendants and pervert well-disposed assemblies, — a part of the case which historians of Greece often present as if it were the whole, — he could also, and that in the most trying emergencies, combat the strongest force of present passion, and bring into vivid presence the half-obscured lineaments of long-sighted reason and duty.

After conducting the army out of the city, Xenophon sent, through Kleander, a message to Anaxibius, requesting that he himself might be allowed to come in again singly, in order to take his departure by sea. His request was granted, though not without much difficulty; upon which he took leave of the army, under the strongest expressions of affection and gratitude on their part,[2] and went into Byzantium along with Kleander; while on the next day Kœratadas came to assume the command according to agreement, bringing with him a prophet, and beasts to be offered in

---

[1] So Tacitus says about the Roman general Spurinna (governor of Placentia for Otho against Vitellius), and his mutinous army who marched out to fight the Vitellian generals against his strenuous remonstrance — "Fit *temeritatis alienæ comes* Spurinna, primo coactus, mox *velle simulans*, quo plus auctoritatis inesset consiliis, si **seditio mitesceret**" (Tacitus, Hist. ii. 18).

[2] Xen. Anab. vii, 6, 33.

sacrifice. There followed in his train twenty men carrying sacks of barley-meal, twenty more with jars of wine, three bearing olives, and one man with a bundle of garlic and onions. All these provisions being laid down, Kœratadas proceeded to offer sacrifice, as a preliminary to the distribution of them among the soldiers. On the first day, the sacrifices being unfavorable, no distribution took place; on the second day, Kœratadas was standing with the wreath on his head at the altar, and with the victims beside him, about to renew his sacrifice, — when Timasion and the other officers interfered, desired him to abstain, and dismissed him from the command. Perhaps the first unfavorable sacrifices may have partly impelled them to this proceeding. But the main reason was, the scanty store, inadequate even to one day's subsistence for the army, brought by Kœratadas, — and the obvious insufficiency of his means.[1]

On the departure of Kœratadas, the army marched to take up its quarters in some Thracian villages not far from Byzantium, under its former officers; who however could not agree as to their future order of march. Kleânor and Phryniskus, who had received presents from Seuthes, urged the expediency of accepting the service of that Thracian prince; Neon insisted on going to the Chersonese under the Lacedæmonian officers in that peninsula (as Anaxibius had projected); in the idea that he, as a Lacedæmonian, would there obtain the command of the whole army; while Timasion, with the view of re-establishing himself in his native city of Dardanus, proposed returning to the Asiatic side of the strait.

Though this last plan met with decided favor among the army, it could not be executed without vessels. These Timasion had little or no means of procuring; so that considerable delay took place, during which the soldiers, receiving no pay, fell into much distress. Many of them were even compelled to sell their arms in order to get subsistence; while others got permission to settle in some of the neighboring towns, on condition of being disarmed. The whole army was thus gradually melting away, much to the satisfaction of Anaxibius, who was anxious to see the purposes of Pharnabazus accomplished. By degrees, it would probably have

been dissolved altogether, had not a chai ge of interest on the part
of Anaxibius induced him to promote its reorganization.   He
sailed from Byzantium to the Asiatic coast, to acquaint Pharnabazus that the Cyreians could no longer cause uneasiness, and to
require his own promised reward.   It seems moreover that Xenophon himself departed from Byzantium by the same opportunity.
When they reached Kyzikus, they met the Lacedæmonian Aristarchus; who was coming out as newly-appointed harmost of
Byzantium, to supersede Kleander, and who acquainted Anaxibius that Polus was on the point of arriving to supersede him as
admiral.   Anxious to meet Pharnabazus and make sure of his
bribe, Anaxibius impressed his parting injunction upon Aristarchus to sell for slaves all the Cyreians whom he might find at
Byzantium on his arrival, and then pursued his voyage along the
southern coast of the Propontis to Parium.   But Pharnabazus,
having already received intimation of the change of admirals,
knew that the friendship of Anaxibius was no longer of any value,
and took no farther heed of him; while he at the same time sent
to Byzantium to make the like compact with Aristarchus against
the Cyreian army.[1]

Anaxibius was stung to the quick at this combination of disappointment and insult on the part of the satrap.   To avenge it, he
resolved to employ those very soldiers whom he had first corrupted
and fraudulently brought across to Europe, next cast out from
Byzantium, and lastly, ordered to be sold into slavery, so far as
any might yet be found in that town; bringing them back into
Asia for the purpose of acting against Pharnabazus.   Accordingly he addressed himself to Xenophon, and ordered him without a
moment's delay to rejoin the army, for the purpose of keeping it
together, of recalling the soldiers who had departed, and transporting the whole body across into Asia.   He provided him with
an armed vessel of thirty oars to cross over from Parium to
Perinthus, sending over a peremptory order to the Perinthians to
furnish him with horses in order that he might reach the army

---

Xen. Anab. vii, 2, 7   Φαρνάβαζος δὲ, ἐπεὶ ἤθετο Ἀρίσταρχόν τε ἥκοι-
τα εἰς Βυζάντιον ἁρμοστὴν καὶ Ἀναξίβιον οὐκέτι ναυαρχοῦντα, Ἀναξιβίου
μὲν ἠμέλησε, πρὸς Ἀρίσταρχον δὲ διεπράττετο τὰ αὐτὰ περὶ τοῦ Κυρείου
στρατεύματος ἅπερ καὶ πρὸς Ἀναξίβιον.

with the greatest speed.[1] Perhaps it would not have been safe
for Xenophon to disobey this order, under any circumstances.
But the idea of acting with the army in Asia against Pharnabazus, under Lacedæmonian sanction, was probably very acceptable to him. He hastened across to the army, who welcomed his
return with joy, and gladly embraced the proposal of crossing to
Asia, which was a great improvement upon their forlorn and
destitute condition. He accordingly conducted them to Perinthus,
and encamped under the walls of the town; refusing, in his way
through Selymbria, a second proposition from Seuthes to engage
the services of the army.

While Xenophon was exerting himself to procure transports
for the passage of the army at Perinthus, Aristarchus the new
harmost arrived there with two triremes from Byzantium. It
seems that not only Byzantium, but also both Perinthus and
Selymbria, were comprised in his government as harmost. On
first reaching Byzantium to supersede Kleander, he found there
no less than four hundred of the Cyreians, chiefly sick and wounded;
whom Kleander, in spite of the ill-will of Anaxibius, had not only
refused to sell into slavery, but had billeted upon the citizens, and
tended with solicitude; so much did his good feeling towards Xenophon and towards the army now come into play. We read with
indignation that Aristarchus, immediately on reaching Byzantium
to supersede him, was not even contented with sending these four
hundred men out of the town; but seized them, — Greeks, citizens,
and soldiers as they were, — and sold them all into slavery.[2]

---

[1] Xen. Anab. vii, 2, 8–25.

'Εκ τούτου δὴ ὁ 'Αναξίβιος, καλέσας Ξενοφῶντα, κ ε λ ε ύ ε ι π ά σ η τ έ χ ν η
κ α ὶ μ η χ α ν ῇ π λ ε ῦ σ α ι ἐ π ὶ τ ὸ σ τ ρ ά τ ε υ μ α ὡ ς τ ά χ ι σ τ α, καὶ συνέ-
χειν τε τὸ στράτευμα καὶ συναθροίζειν τῶν διεσπαρμένων ὡς ἂν πλείστους
δύνηται, καὶ παραγαγόντα εἰς τὴν Πέρινθον διαβιβάζειν εἰς τὴν 'Ασίαν ὅ τ ι
τ ά χ ι σ τ α· καὶ δίδωσιν αὐτῷ τριακόντορον, καὶ ἐπιστολὴν καὶ ἄνδρα συμπ-
έμπει κελεύοντα τοὺς Περινθίους ὡς τ ά χ ι σ τ α Ξενοφῶντα προπέμψαι
τοῖς ἵπποις ἐπὶ τὸ στράτευμα.

The vehement interest which Anaxibius took in this new project is marked
by the strength of Xenophon's language; extreme celerity is enjoined three
several times.

[2] Xen. Anab. vii, 2, 6. Καὶ ὁ 'Αναξίβιος τῷ μὲν 'Αριστάρχῳ ἐπιστέλλει
ὁπόσους ἂν εὕροι ἐν Βυζαντίῳ τῶν Κύρου στρατιωτῶν ὑπολελειμμένους, ἀπο-
δόσθαι· ὁ δὲ Κλέανδρος οὐδένα ἐπεπράκει, ἀλλὰ καὶ τοὺς κάμνοντας ἐθερά

Apprised of the movements of Xenophon with the army, he now came to Perinthus to prevent their transit into Asia; laying an embargo on the transports in the harbor, and presenting himself personally before the assembled army to prohibit the soldiers from crossing. When Xenophon informed him that Anaxibius had given them orders to cross, and had sent him expressly to conduct them, — Aristarchus replied, " Anaxibius is no longer in functions as admiral, and I am harmost in this town. If I catch any of you at sea, I will sink you." On the next day, he sent to invite the generals and the captains (lochages) to a conference within the walls. They were just about to enter the gates, when Xenophon, who was among them, received a private warning, that if he went in, Aristarchus would seize him, and either put him to death or send him prisoner to Pharnabazus. Accordingly Xenophon sent forward the others, and remained himself with the army, alleging the obligation of sacrificing. The behavior of Aristarchus, — who, when he saw the others without Xenophon, sent them away, and desired that they would all come again in the afternoon, — confirmed the justice of his suspicions, as to the imminent danger from which he had been preserved by this accidental warning.[1] It need hardly be added that Xenophon disregarded the second invitation no less than the first; moreover a third invitation, which Aristarchus afterwards sent, was disregarded by all.

We have here a Lacedæmonian harmost, not scrupling to lay a snare of treachery as flagrant as that which Tissaphernes had practised on the banks of the Zab to entrap Klearchus and his colleagues, — and that too against a Greek, and an officer of the highest station and merit, who had just saved Byzantium from pillage, and was now actually in execution of orders received

---

πενεν οἰκτείρων, καὶ ἀναγκάζων οἰκίᾳ δέχεσθαι. Ἀρίσταρχος δ' ἐπεὶ ἦλθε τάχιστα, οὐκ ἐλάττους τετρακοσίων ἀπέδοτο.

[1] Xen. Anab. vii, 2, 14–16.

Ἤδη δὲ ὄντων πρὸς τῷ τείχει, ἐξαγγέλλει τις τῷ Ξενοφῶντι ὅτι, εἰ εἴσεισι, συλληφθήσεται· καὶ ἢ αὐτοῦ τι τείσεται, ἢ καὶ Φαρναβάζῳ, παραδοθήσεται Ὁ δὲ, ἀκούσας ταῦτα, τοὺς μὲν προπέμπεται, αὐτὸς δ' εἶπεν, ὅτι θῦσαί τι βούλοιτο.... Οἱ δὲ στρατηγοὶ καὶ οἱ λοχαγοὶ ἥκοντες παρὰ τοῦ Ἀριστάρχου, ἀπήγγελλον ὅτι νῦν μὲν ἀπιέναι σφᾶς κελεύει, τῆς δείλης δὲ ἥκειν· ἔνθα καὶ δῆλη μᾶλλον ἐδόκει [εἶναι] ἡ ἐπιβουλή. Compare vii, 3, 2.

from the Lacedæmonian admiral Anaxibius. Had the accidental
warning been withheld, Xenophon would assuredly have fallen
into this snare, nor could we reasonably have charged him with
imprudence, — so fully was he entitled to count upon straightforward conduct under the circumstances. But the same cannot be
said of Klearchus, who undoubtedly manifested lamentable credulity, nefarious as was the fraud to which he fell a victim.

At the second interview with the other officers, Aristarchus,
while he forbade the army to cross the water, directed them to
force their way by land through the Thracians who occupied the
Holy mountain, and thus to arrive at the Chersonese; where (he
said) they should receive pay. Neon the Lacedæmonian, with
about eight hundred hoplites who adhered to his separate command, advocated this plan as the best. To be set against it, however, there was the proposition of Seuthes to take the army into
pay; which Xenophon was inclined to prefer, uneasy at the
thoughts of being cooped up in the narrow peninsula of the Chersonese, under the absolute command of the Lacedæmonian harmost, with great uncertainty both as to pay and as to provisions.[1]
Moreover it was imperiously necessary for these disappointed
troops to make some immediate movement; for they had been
brought to the gates of Perinthus in hopes of passing immediately
on shipboard; it was mid-winter, — they were encamped in the
open field, under the severe cold of Thrace, — they had neither
assured supplies, nor even money to purchase, if a market had
been near.[2] Xenophon, who had brought them to the neighborhood of Perinthus, was now again responsible for extricating them
from this untenable situation, and began to offer sacrifices, according to his wont, to ascertain whether the gods would encourage
him to recommend a covenant with Seuthes. The sacrifices were
so favorable, that he himself, together with a confidential officer
from each of the generals, went by night and paid a visit to
Seuthes, for the purpose of understanding distinctly his offers and
purposes.

Mæsadês, the father of Seuthes, had been apparently a dependent prince under the great monarchy of the Odrysian Thracians

---

[1] Xen. Anab. vii, 2, 15; vii, 3, 3; vii, 6, 13.

[2] Xen. Anab. vii 6, 24   μέσος δὲ χείμων ἦν, etc. **Probably the month
of December.**

so formidable in the early years of the Peloponnesian war. But
intestine commotions had robbed him of his principality over three
Thracian tribes; which it was now the ambition of Seuthes to
recover, by the aid of the Cyreian army. He offered to each soldier one stater of Kyzikus (about twenty Attic drachmæ, or nearly
the same as that which they originally received from Cyrus) as
pay per month ; twice as much to each lochage or captain, — four
times as much to each of the generals. In case they should incur
the enmity of the Lacedæmonians by joining him, he guaranteed
to them all the right of settlement and fraternal protection in his
territory. To each of the generals, over and above pay, he engaged
to assign a fort on the sea-coast, with a lot of land around it, and
oxen for cultivation. And to Xenophon in particular, he offered
the possession of Bisanthê, his best point on the coast. "I will also
(he added, addressing Xenophon) give you my daughter in marriage; and if you have any daughter, I will buy her from you in
marriage according to the custom of Thrace."[1] Seuthes farther
engaged never on any occasion to lead them more than seven days'
journey from the sea, at farthest.

These offers were as liberal as the army could possibly expect;
and Xenophon himself, mistrusting the Lacedæmonians, as well as
mistrusted by them, seems to have looked forward to the acquisition of a Thracian coast-fortress and territory (such as Miltiades,
Alkibiades, and other Athenian leaders had obtained before him)
as a valuable refuge in case of need.[2] But even if the promise
had been less favorable, the Cyreians had no alternative ; for they
had not even present supplies, — still less any means of subsistence
throughout the winter; while departure by sea was rendered impossible by the Lacedæmonians. On the next day, Seuthes was
introduced by Xenophon and the other generals to the army, who
accepted his offers and concluded the bargain.

They remained for two months in his service, engaged in warfare against various Thracian tribes, whom they enabled him to
conquer and despoil; so that at the end of that period, he was in
possession of an extensive dominion, a large native force, and a
considerable tribute. Though the sufferings of the army from cold
were extreme, during these two months of full winter and amidst

---

[1] Xen. Anab. vii, 2, 17-38.　　　　　[2] Xen. Anab. vii, 6, 34.

the snowy mountains of Thrace, they were nevertheless enabled by their expeditions along with Seuthes to procure plentiful subsistence; which they could hardly have done in any other manner. But the pay which he had offered was never liquidated; at least, in requital of their two months of servi·e, they received pay only for twenty days and a little more. And Xenophon himself, far from obtaining fulfilment of those splendid promises which Seuthes had made to him personally, seems not even to have received his pay as one of the generals. For him, the result was singularly unhappy: since he forfeited the good-will of Seuthes by importunate demand and complaint for the purpose of obtaining the pay due to the soldiers; while they on their side, imputing to his connivance the non-fulfilment of the promise, became thus in part alienated from him. Much of this mischief was brought about by the treacherous intrigues and calumny of a corrupt Greek from Maroneia, named Herakleides; who acted as minister and treasurer to Seuthes.

Want of space compels me to omit the narrative given by Xenophon, both of the relations of the army with Seuthes, and of the warfare carried on against the hostile Thracian tribes,—interesting as it is from the juxtaposition of Greek and Thracian manners. It seems to have been composed by Xenophon under feelings of acute personal disappointment, and probably in refutation of calumnies against himself as if he had wronged the army. Hence we may trace in it a tone of exaggerated querulousness, and complaint that the soldiers were ungrateful to him. It is true that a portion of the army, under the belief that he had been richly rewarded by Seuthes while they had not obtained their stipulated pay, expressed virulent sentiments and falsehoods against him.[1] Until such suspicions were refuted, it is no wonder that the army were alienated; but they were perfectly willing to hear both sides,— and Xenophon triumphantly disproved the accusation. That in the end, their feelings towards him were those of esteem and favor, stands confessed in his own words,[2] proving that the ingratitude of which he complains was the feeling of some indeed, but not of all.

It is hard to say, however, what would have been the fate of this gallant army, when Seuthes, having obtained from their arms in

---

[1] Xen. Anab. vii, 6, 9, 10.   [2] Xen. Anab. vii, 7, 55–57

two months all that he desired, had become only anxious to send
them off without pay, — had they not been extricated by a change
of interest and policy on the part of all-powerful Sparta.   The
Lacedæmonians had just declared war against Tissaphernes and
Pharnabazus, — sending Thimbron into Asia to commence military
operations.   They then became extremely anxious to transport
the Cyreians across to Asia, which their harmost, Aristarchus had
hitherto prohibited, — and to take them into permanent pay ; for
which purpose two Lacedæmonians, Charmînus and Polynîkus
were commissioned by Thimbron to offer to the army the same pay
as had been promised, though not paid, by Seuthes ; and as had been
originally paid by Cyrus.   Seuthes and Herakleides, eager to
hasten the departure of the soldiers, endeavored to take credit with
the Lacedæmonians for assisting their views.[1]   Joyfully did the
army accept this offer, though complaining loudly of the fraud practised upon them by Seuthes ; which Charmînus, at the instance
of Xenophon, vainly pressed the Thracian prince to redress.[2]
He even sent Xenophon to demand the arrear of pay in the name
of the Lacedæmonians, which afforded to the Athenian an opportunity of administering a severe lecture to Seuthes.[3]   But the latter
was found less accessible to the workings of eloquence than the
Cyreian assembled soldiers ; nor did Xenophon obtain anything
beyond a miserable dividend upon the sum due ; — together with
civil expressions towards himself personally, — an invitation to remain in his service with one thousand hoplites instead of going
to Asia with the army, — and renewed promises, not likely now
to find much credit, of a fort and grant of lands.

When the army, now reduced by losses and dispersions to six
thousand men,[4] was prepared to cross into Asia, Xenophon was
desirous of going back to Athens, but was persuaded to remain
with them until the junction with Thimbron.   He was at this time
so poor, having scarcely enough to pay for his journey home, that
he was obliged to sell his horse at Lampsakus, the Asiatic town

---

[1] Xen. Anab. vii, 6, 1–7.   [2] Xen. Anab. vii, 7, 15.

[3] Xen. Anab. vii, 7, 21–47.

  The lecture is of unsuitable prolixity, when we consider the person to
whom, and the circumstances under which, it purports to have been spo
ken.

[4] Xen. Anab. vii, 7, 23.

where the army landed. Here he found Eukleides, a Phliasian prophet with whom he had been wont to hold intercourse and offer sacrifice at Athens. This man, having asked Xenophon how much he had acquired in the expedition, could not believe him when he affirmed his poverty. But when they proceeded to offer sacrifice together, from some animals sent by the Lampsakenes as a present to Xenophon, Eukleides had no sooner inspected the entrails of the victims, than he told Xenophon that he fully credited the state-ment. " I see (he said) that even if money shall be ever on its way to come to you, you yourself will be a hindrance to it, even if there be no other (here Xenophon acquiesced) ; Zeus Meilichios (the Gracious)[1] is the real bar. Have you ever sacrificed to him, with entire burnt-offerings, as we used to do together at Athens ?" " Never (replied Xenophon), throughout the whole march." " Do so now, then (said Eukleides), and it will be for your advantage." The next day, on reaching Ophrynium, Xenophon obeyed the in-junction ; sacrificing little pigs entire to Zeus Meilichios, as was the custom at Athens during the public festival called Diasia. And on the very same day he felt the beneficial effects of the pro-ceeding ; for Biton and another envoy came from the Lacedæmo-nians with an advance of pay to the army, and with dispositions so favorable to himself, that they bought back for him his horse, which he had just sold at Lampsakus for fifty darics. This was equivalent to giving him more than one year's pay in hand (the pay which he would have received as general being four darics per month, or four times that of the soldier), at a time when he was known to be on the point of departure, and therefore would not stay to earn it. The short-comings of Seuthes were now made

---

[1] It appears that the epithet *Meilichios* (the Gracious) is here applied to Zeus in the same euphemistic sense as the denomination *Eumenides* to the avenging goddesses. Zeus is conceived as having actually inflicted, or being in a disposition to inflict, evil ; the sacrifice to him under this surname re-presents a sentiment of fear, and is one of atonement, expiation or purifi-cation, destined to avert his displeasure ; but the surname itself is to be interpreted *proleptice*, to use the word of the critics — it designates, not the actual disposition of Zeus (or of other gods), but that disposition which the sacrifice is intended to bring about in him.

See Pausan. i, 37, 3 ; ii, 20, 3. K. F. Herrmann, Gottesdienstl. Alter-thümer der Griechen. s. 58 ; Van Stegeren, De Græcorum Diebus Festis, p 5 (Utrecht, 1849).

up with immense interest, so that Xenophon became better off than any man in the army; though he himself slurs over the magnitude of the present, by representing it as a delicate compliment to restore to him a favorite horse.

Thus gratefully and instantaneously did Zeus the Gracious respond to the sacrifice which Xenophon, after a long omission, had been admonished by Eukleides to offer. And doubtless Xenophon was more than ever confirmed in the belief, which manifests itself throughout all his writings, that sacrifice not only indicates, by the interior aspect of the immolated victims, the tenor of coming events, — but also, according as it is rendered to the right god and at the right season, determines his will, and therefore the course of events, for dispensations favorable or unfavorable.

But the favors of Zeus the Gracious, though begun, were not yet ended. Xenophon conducted the army through the Troad, and across mount Ida, to Antandrus; from thence along the coast to Lydia, through the plain of Thêbê and the town of Adramyttium, leaving Atarneus on the right hand, to Pergamus in Mysia, a hill-town overhanging the river and plain of Käikus. This district was occupied by the descendants of the Eretrian Gongylus, who, having been banished for embracing the cause of the Persians when Xerxes invaded Greece, had been rewarded (like the Spartan king Demaratus) with this sort of principality under the Persian empire. His descendant, another Gongylus, now occupied Pergamus, with his wife Hellas and his sons Gorgion and Gongylus. Xenophon was here received with great hospitality. Hellas acquainted him that a powerful Persian, named Asidates, was now dwelling, with his wife, family, and property, in a tower not far off, on the plain; and that a sudden night-march, with three hundred men, would suffice for the capture of this valuable booty, to which her own cousin should guide him. Accordingly, having sacrificed and ascertained that the victims were favorable, Xenophon communicated his plan after the evening meal to those captains who had been most attached to him throughout the expedition, wishing to make them partners in the profit. As soon as it became known, many volunteers, to the number of six hundred, pressed to be allowed to join. But the captains repelled them, declining to take more than three hundred, in order that the booty might afford an ampler dividend to each partner.

Beginning their march in the evening, Xenophon and his de-tachment of three hundred reached about midnight the tower of Asidates; it was large, lofty, thickly built, and contained a con-siderable garrison. It served for protection to his cattle and cultivating slaves around, like a baronial castle in the middle ages; but the assailants neglected this outlying plunder, in order to be more sure of taking the castle itself. Its walls however were found much stronger than was expected; and although a breach was made by force about day-break, yet so vigorous was the defence of the garrison, that no entrance could be effected. Signals and shouts of every kind were made by Asidates to procure aid from the Persian forces in the neighborhood; numbers of whom soon began to arrive, so that Xenophon and his company were obliged to retreat. And their retreat was at last only accomplished, after severe suffering and wounds to nearly half of them, through the aid of Gongylus with his forces from Pergamus, and of Prokles (the descendant of Demaratus) from Halisarna, a little farther off seaward.[1]

Though his first enterprise thus miscarried, Xenophon soon laid plans for a second, employing the whole army; and succeeded in bringing Asidates prisoner to Pergamus, with his wife, child-ren, horses, and all his personal property. Thus (says he, anxious above all things for the credit of sacrificial prophecy) the " pre-vious sacrifices (those which had promised favorably before the first unsuccessful attempt) now came true." [2] The persons of this family were doubtless redeemed by their Persian friends for a large ransom;[3] which, together with the booty brought in, made up a prodigious total to be divided.

In making the division, a general tribute of sympathy and ad-miration was paid to Xenophon, to which all the army, — gene-rals, captains, and soldiers, — and the Lacedæmonians besides, — unanimously concurred. Like Agamemnon at Troy, he was al-lowed to select for himself the picked lots of horses, mules, oxen, and other items of booty; insomuch that he became possessor of a

---

[1] Xen. Anab. vii, 8, 10-19.

[2] Xen. Anab. vii, 8, 22. Ἐνταῦθα οἱ περὶ Ξενοφῶντα συμπεριτυγχάνουσιν αὐτῷ καὶ λαμβάνουσιν αὐτὸν ('Ασιδάτην) καὶ γυναῖκα καὶ παῖδας καὶ τοὺς ἴπ-πους καὶ πάντα τὰ ὄντα· καὶ οὕτω τὰ πρότερα ἱερὰ ἀπεβη.

[3] Compare Plutarch, Kimon, c. 9; and Xen. Hellen. iv, 8, 21.

share valuable enough to enrich him at once, in addition to tnd fifty darics which he had before received. " Here then Xenophon (to use his own language[1]) had no reason to complain of the god" (Zeus Meilichios). We may add, — what he ought to have added, considering the accusations which he had before put forth, — that neither had he any reason to complain of the ingratitude of the army.

As soon as Thimbron arrived with his own forces, and the Cyreians became a part of his army, Xenophon took his leave of them. Having deposited in the temple at Ephesus that portion which had been confided to him as general, of the tithe set apart by the army at Kerasus for the Ephesian Artemis,[2] he seems to have executed his intention of returning to Athens.[3] He must have arrived there, after an absence of about two years and a half, within a few weeks, at farthest, after the death of his friend and preceptor Sokrates, whose trial and condemnation have been recorded in my last volume. That melancholy event certainly occurred during his absence from Athens;[4] but whether it had come to his knowledge before he reached the city, we do not know. How much grief and indignation it excited in his mind, we may see by his collection of memoranda respecting the life and conversations of Sokrates, known by the name of Memorabi-lia, and probably put together shortly after his arrival.

That he was again in Asia, three years afterwards, on military service under the Lacedæmonian king Agesilaus, is a fact attested by himself; but at what precise moment he quitted Athens for his second visit to Asia, we are left to conjecture. I incline to believe that he did not remain many months at home, but that he went out again in the next spring to rejoin the Cyreians in Asia, — became again their commander, — and served for two years under the Spartan general Derkyllidas before the arrival of Age

---

[1] Xen. Anab. vii, 8, 23.

Ἐνταῦθα τὸν θεὸν οὐκ ᾐτιάσατο ὁ Ξενοφῶν· συνέπραττον γὰρ καὶ οἱ Λάκ-ωνες καὶ οἱ λοχαγοὶ καὶ οἱ ἄλλοι στρατηγοὶ καὶ οἱ στρατιῶται, ὥστε ἐξαίρετα λαβεῖν καὶ ἵππους καὶ ζεύγη καὶ ἄλλα, ὥστε ἱκανὸν εἶναι καὶ ἄλλον ἤδη εὖ π.ϽΕῖν.

[2] Xen. Anab. v, 3, 6. It seems plain that this deposit must have been first made on the present occasion.

[3] Compare Anabasis, vii, 7, 57; vii, 8, 2.

[4] Xenoph. Memorab. iv, 8, 4 — as well as the opening sentence of the work.

silaus. Such military service would doubtless be very much to his taste; while a residence at Athens, then subject and quiescent, would probably be distasteful to him; both from the habits of command which he had contracted during the previous two years, and from feelings arising out of the death of Sokrates. After a certain interval of repose, he would be disposed to enter again upon the war against his old enemy Tissaphernes; and his service went on when Agesilaus arrived to take the command.[1]

But during the two years after this latter event, Athens became a party to the war against Sparta, and entered into conjunction with the king of Persia as well as with the Thebans and others; while Xenophon, continuing his service as commander of the Cyreians, and accompanying Agesilaus from Asia back into Greece, became engaged against the Athenian troops and their Bœotian allies at the bloody battle of Korôneia. Under these circumstances, we cannot wonder that the Athenians passed sentence of banishment against him; not because he had originally taken part in aid of Cyrus against Artaxerxes, — nor because his political sentiments were unfriendly to democracy, as has been sometimes erroneously affirmed, — but because he was now openly in arms, and in conspicuous command, against his own country.[2]

---

[1] See Xenoph. Hellen. iii. 2, 7 — a passage which Morus refers, I think with much probability, to Xenophon himself.

The very circumstantial details, which Xenophon gives (iii, 1, 11-28) about the proceedings of Derkyllidas against Meidias in the Troad, seem also to indicate that he was serving there in person.

[2] That the sentence of banishment on Xenophon was not passed by the Athenians until after the battle of Korôneia, appears plainly from Anabasis, v. 3, 7. This battle took place in August 394 B. C.

Pausanias also will be found in harmony with this statement, as to the time of the banishment. Ἐδιώχθη δὲ ὁ Ξενοφῶν ὑπὸ Ἀθηναίων, ὡς ἐπὶ βασιλέα τῶν Περσῶν, σφίσιν εὔνουν ὄντα, στρατείας μετασχὼν Κύρῳ πολεμιωτάτῳ τοῦ δήμου (iv, 6, 4). Now it was not until 396 or 395 B. C., that the Persian king began to manifest the least symptoms of good-will towards Athens; and not until the battle of Knidus (a little before the battle of Korôneia in the same year), that he testified his good-will by conspicuous and effective service. If, therefore, the motive of the Athenians to banish Xenophon arose out of the good feeling on the part of the king of Persia toward them, the banishment could not have taken place before 395 B. C., and is not likely to have taken place until after 394 B. C.; which is the intimation of Xenophon himself as above.

Having thus become an exile, Xenophon was allowed by the
Lacedæmonians to settle at Skillûs, one of the villages of Triphylia, near Olympia in Peloponnesus, which they had recently emancipated from the Eleians.   At one of the ensuing Olympic festivals, Megabyzus, the superintendent of the temple of Artemis at
Ephesus, came over as a spectator; bringing with him the money
which Xenophon had dedicated therein to the Ephesian Artemis.
This money Xenophon invested in the purchase of lands at Skillus, to be consecrated in permanence to the goddess; having previously consulted her by sacrifice to ascertain her approval of the
site contemplated, which site was recommended to him by its
resemblance in certain points to that of the Ephesian temple.
Thus, there was near each of them a river called by the same
name Selinûs, having in it fish and a shelly bottom.   Xenophon
constructed a chapel, an altar, and a statue of the goddess made
of cypress-wood: all exact copies, on a reduced scale, of the temple and golden statue at Ephesus.   A column near them was
inscribed with the following words, — " This spot is sacred to
Artemis.   Whoever possesses the property and gathers its fruits,
must sacrifice to her the tithe every year, and keep the chapel

---

Lastly, Diogenes Laërtius (ii, 52) states, what I believe to be the main
truth, that the sentence of banishment was passed against Xenophon by the
Athenians on the ground of his attachment to the Lacedæmonians — ἐπὶ
Λακωνισμῷ.

Krüger and others seem to think that Xenophon was banished because
he took service under Cyrus, who had been the bitter enemy of Athens.   It
is true that Sokrates, when first consulted, was apprehensive beforehand that
this might bring upon him the displeasure of Athens (Xen. Anab. iii, 1, 5).
But it is to be remembered that *at this time*, the king of Persia was just as
much the enemy of Athens as Cyrus was ; and that Cyrus in fact had made
war upon her with the forces and treasures of the king.   Artaxerxes and
Cyrus being thus, at that time, both enemies of Athens, it was of little consequence to the Athenians whether Cyrus succeeded or failed in his enterprise.   But when Artaxerxes, six years afterwards, became their friend,
their feelings towards his enemies were altered.

The passage of Pausanias as above cited, if understood as asserting the
main cause of Xenophon's banishment, is in my judgment inaccurate.
Xenophon was banished *for Laconism*, or attachment to Sparta against his
country; the fact of his having served under Cyrus against Artaxerxes
counted at best only as a secondary motive.

in repair out of the remainder. Should any one omit this duty the goddess herself will take the omission in hand."[1]

Immediately near the chapel was an orchard of every descrip tion of fruit-trees, while the estate around comprised an extensive range of meadow, woodland, and mountain, — with the still loftier mountain called Pholoê adjoining. There was thus abundant pas ture for horses, oxen, sheep, etc., and excellent hunting-ground near for deer and other game; advantages not to be found near the Artemision at Ephesus. Residing hard by on his own pro perty, allotted to him by the Lacedæmonians, Xenophon superin tended this estate as steward for the goddess; looking perhaps to the sanctity of her name for protection from disturbance by the Eleians, who viewed with a jealous eye the Lacedæmonian[2] set tlers at Skillus, and protested against the peace and convention promoted by Athens after the battle of Leuktra, because it recog nized that place, along with the townships of Triphylia, as auto nomous. Every year he made a splendid sacrifice, from the tithe of all the fruits of the property; to which solemnity not only all the Skilluntines, but also all the neighboring villages, were invited. Booths were erected for the visitors, to whom the goddess fur nished (this is the language of Xenophon) an ample dinner of barley-meal, wheaten loaves, meat, game, and sweetmeats;[3] the game being provided by a general hunt, which the sons of Xen ophon conducted, and in which all the neighbors took part if they chose. The produce of the estate, saving this tithe and subject to the obligation of keeping the holy building in repair, was en joyed by Xenophon himself. He had a keen relish for both hunting and horsemanship, and was among the first authors, so far as we know, who ever made these pursuits, with the manage ment of horses and dogs, the subject of rational study and descrip tion.

Such was the use to which Xenophon applied the tithe voted

---

[1] Xen. Anab v, 3, 13. Καὶ στήλη ἕστηκε παρὰ τὸν ναὸν, γράμματα ἔχου-σα — Ἱερὸς ὁ Χῶρος τῆς Αρτέμιδος· τὸν δὲ ἔχοντα καὶ καρπούμενον τὴν μὲν δεκάτην καταθύειν ἑκάστου ἔτους, ἐκ δὲ τοῦ περίττου τόν ναὸν ἐπισκευάζειν ἐὰν δέ τις μὴ ποιῇ ταῦτα, τῇ θεῷ μελήσει.

[2] Xen. Hellen. vi, 5, 2.

[3] Xen. Anab. v, 3, 9. Παρεῖχε δ' ἡ θεὸς τοῖς σκηνοῦσιν ἄλφιτα, ἄρτους οἶνον, τραγήματα, etc.

by the army at Kerasus to the Ephesian Artemis; the other tithe, voted at the same time to Apollo, he dedicated at Delphi in the treasure-chamber of the Athenians, inscribing upon the offering his own name and that of Proxenus. His residence being only at a distance of twenty stadia from the great temple of Olympia, he was enabled to enjoy society with every variety of Greeks, — and to obtain copious information about Grecian politics, chiefly from philo-Laconian informants, and with the Lacedæmonian point of view predominant in his own mind; while he had also leisure for the composition of his various works. The interesting description which he himself gives of his residence at Skillus, implies a state of things not present and continuing,[1] but past and gone; other testimonies too, though confused and contradictory, seem to show that the Lacedæmonian settlement at Skillus lasted no longer than the power of Lacedæmon was adequate to maintain it. During the misfortunes which befel that city after the battle of Leuktra (371 B. C.), Xenophon, with his family and his fellow-settlers, was expelled by the Eleians, and is then said to have found shelter at Corinth. But as Athens soon came to be not only at peace, but in intimate alliance, with Sparta, — the sentence of banishment against Xenophon was revoked; so that the latter part of his life was again passed in the enjoyment of his birthright as an Athenian citizen and Knight.[2] Two of his sons, Gryllus and Diodorus, fought among the Athenian horsemen at the cavalry combat which preceded the battle of Mantineia, where the former was slain, after manifesting distinguished bravery; while his grandson Xenophon became in the next generation the subject of a pleading before the Athenian Dikastery, composed by the orator Deinarchus.[3]

---

[1] Xen. Anab. v, 3, 9.

[2] Diogen. Laërt. ii, 53, 54, 59. Pausanias (v, 6, 4) attests the reconquest of Skillus by the Eleians, but adds (on the authority of the Eleian ἐξηγηταί or show guides) that they permitted Xenophon, after a judicial examination before the Olympic Senate, to go on living there in peace. The latter point I apprehend to be incorrect.

The latter works of Xenophon (De Vectigalibus, De Officio Magistri Equitum, etc.), seem plainly to imply that he had been restored to citizenship, and had come again to take cognizance of politics at Athens.

[3] Diogen. Laërt. ut sup. Dionys. Halic. De Dinarcho, p. 664, ed. Reiske. Dionysius mentions this oration under the title of 'Αποστασίου ἀπολογία

On bringing this accomplished and eminent leader to the close of that arduous retreat which he had conducted with so much honor, I have thought it necessary to anticipate a little on the future, in order to take a glance at his subsequent destiny. To his exile (in this point of view not less useful than that of Thucydides) we probably owe many of those compositions from which so much of our knowledge of Grecian affairs is derived. But to the contemporary world, the retreat, which Xenophon so successfully conducted, afforded a far more impressive lesson than any of his literary compositions. It taught in the most striking manner the impotence of the Persian land-force, manifested not less in the generals than in the soldiers. It proved that the Persian leaders were unfit for any systematic operations, even under the greatest possible advantages, against a small number of disciplined warriors resolutely bent on resistance; that they were too stupid and reckless even to obstruct the passage of rivers, or destroy roads, or cut off supplies. It more than confirmed the contemptuous language applied to them by Cyrus himself, before the battle of Kunaxa; when he proclaimed that he envied the Greeks their freedom, and that he was ashamed of the worthlessness of his own countrymen.[1] Against such perfect weakness and disorgan-

---

Αἰσχύλου πρὸς Ξενοφῶντα. And Diogenes also alludes to it — ὡς φησι Δεί ναρχος ἐν τῷ πρὸς Ξενοφῶντα ἀποστασίου.

Schneider in his Epimetrum (ad calcem Anabaseos, p. 573), respecting the exile of Xenophon, argues as if the person against whom the oration of Deinarchus was directed, was Xenophon himself, the Cyreian commander and author. But this, I think, is chronologically all but impossible; for Deinarchus was not born till 361 B. C., and composed his first oration in 336 B. C.

Yet Deinarchus, in his speech against Xenophon, undoubtedly mentioned several facts respecting the Cyreian Xenophon, which implies that the latter was a relative of the person against whom the oration was directed. I venture to set him down as grandson, on that evidence, combined with the identity of name and the suitableness in point of time. He might well be the son of Gryllus, who was slain fighting at the battle of Mantineia in 362 B. C.

Nothing is more likely than that an orator, composing an oration against Xenophon the grandson, should touch upon the acts and character of Xenophon the grandfather; see for analogy, the oration of Isokrates, de Bigis, among others.

[1] Xen. Anab. i, 7, 4. Compare Plutarch, Artaxerx. c. 20; and Isokrates Panegyr Or iv, s. 168, 169 *seq.*

ization, nothing prevented the success of the Greeks along with
Cyrus, except his own paroxysm of fraternal antipathy.[1] **And**
we shall perceive hereafter the military and political leaders of
Greece, — Agesilaus, Jason of Pheræ,[2] and others down to Philip
and Alexander,[3] — firmly persuaded that with a tolerably numerous and well-appointed Grecian force, combined with exemption
from Grecian enemies, they could succeed in overthrowing or dis-
membering the Persian empire. This conviction, so important in
the subsequent history of Greece, takes its date from the retreat
of the Ten Thousand. We shall indeed find Persia exercising
an important influence, for two generations to come, — and at the
peace of Antalkidas an influence stronger than ever, — over the
destinies of Greece. But this will be seen to arise from the
treason of Sparta, the chief of the Hellenic world, who abandons
the Asiatic Greeks, and even arms herself with the name and the
force of Persia, for purposes of aggrandizement and dominion to
herself. Persia is strong by being enabled to employ Hellenic
strength against the Hellenic cause ; by lending money or a fleet
to one side of the Grecian intestine parties, and thus becoming
artificially strengthened against both. But the Xenophontic Anabasis betrays her real weakness against any vigorous attack; while
it at the same time exemplifies the discipline, the endurance, the
power of self-action and adaptation, the susceptibility of influence
from speech and discussion, the combination of the reflecting obedience of citizens with the mechanical regularity of soldiers, —
which confer such immortal distinction on the Hellenic character.
The importance of this expedition and retreat, as an illustration
of the Hellenic qualities and excellence, will justify the large
space which has been devoted to it in this History.

The last chapter of the Cyropædia of Xenophon (viii, 20, 21–26) expres-
ses strenuously the like conviction, of the military feebleness and disorgan-
ization of the Persian empire, not defensible without Grecian aid.

[1] Isokrates, Orat. v, (Philipp.) s. 104–106. ἤδη δ' ἐγκρατεῖς δοκοῦντας
εἶναι (i. e. the Greeks under Klearchus) διὰ τὴν Κύρου προπέτειαν
ἀτυχῆσαι, etc.

[2] Isokrates, Orat. v, (Philipp.) s. 141 ; Xen. Hellen. vi, 1, 12.

[3] See the stress laid by Alexander the Great upon the adventures of the
Ten Thousand, in his speech to encourage his soldiers before the battle of
Issus (Arrian, E. A. ii, 7, 8).

CHAPTER LXXII.

GREECE UNDER THE LACEDÆMCNIAN EMPIRE

THE three preceding Chapters have been devoted exclusively to the narrative of the Expedition and Retreat, immortalized by Xenophon, occupying the two years intervening between about April 401 B. C. and June 399 B. C. That event, replete as it is with interest and pregnant with important consequences, stands apart from the general sequence of Grecian affairs, — which sequence I now resume.

It will be recollected that as soon as Xenophon with his Ten Thousand warriors descended from the rugged mountains between Armenia and the Euxine to the hospitable shelter of Trapezus, and began to lay their plans for returning to Central Greece, — they found themselves within the Lacedæmonian empire, unable to advance a step without consulting Lacedæmonian dictation, and obliged, when they reached the Bosphorus, to endure without redress the harsh and treacherous usage of the Spartan officers, Anaxibius and Aristarchus.

Of that empire the first origin has been set forth in my last preceding volume. It began with the decisive victory of Ægospotami in the Hellespont (September or October 405 B.C.), where the Lacedæmonian Lysander, without the loss of a man, got possession of the entire Athenian fleet and a large portion of their crews, — with the exception of eight or nine triremes with which the Athenian admiral Konon effected his escape to Euagoras at Cyprus. The whole power of Athens was thus annihilated, and nothing remained for the Lacedæmonians to master except the city itself and Peiræus ; a consummation certain to happen, and actually brought to pass in April 404 B. C., when Lysander entered Athens in triumph, dismantled Peiræus, and demolished a large portion of the Long Walls. With the exception of Athens herself, — whose citizens deferred the moment of subjection by an heroic, though unavailing, struggle against the horrors of famine,

— and of Samos, — no other Grecian city offered any resistance
to Lysander after the battle of Ægospotami; which in fact not
only took away from Athens her whole naval force, but transferred it all over to him, and rendered him admiral of a larger
Grecian fleet than had ever been seen together since the battle
of Salamis.

I have recounted in my sixty-fifth chapter, the sixteen months
of bitter suffering undergone by Athens immediately after her
surrender. The loss of her fleet and power was aggravated by
an extremity of internal oppression. Her oligarchical party and
her exiles, returning after having served with the enemy against
her, extorted from the public assembly, under the dictation of Lysander who attended it in person, the appointment of an omnipotent
council of thirty for the ostensible purpose of framing a new constitution. These thirty rulers, — among whom Kritias was the most
violent, and Theramenes (seemingly) the most moderate, or at
least the soonest satiated, — perpetrated cruelty and spoliation on
the largest scale, being protected against all resistance by a Lacedæmonian harmost and garrison established in the acropolis. Besides numbers of citizens put to death, so many others were driven
into exile with the loss of their property, that Thebes and the
neighboring cities became crowded with them. After about eight
months of unopposed tyranny, the Thirty found themselves for the
first time attacked by Thrasybulus at the head of a small party
of these exiles coming out of Bœotia. His bravery and good conduct, — combined with the enormities of the Thirty, which became
continually more nefarious, and to which even numerous oligarchical citizens, as well as Theramenes himself, successively became
victims, — enabled him soon to strengthen himself, to seize the
Peiræus, and to carry on a civil war which ultimately put down
the tyrants.

These latter were obliged to invoke the aid of a new Lacedæmonian force. And had that force still continued at the disposal
of Lysander, all resistance on the part of Athens would have been
unavailing. But fortunately for the Athenians, the last few months
had wrought material change in the dispositions both of the allies
of Sparta and of many among her leading men. The allies, especially Thebes and Corinth, not only relented in their hatred and
fear of Athens, now that she had lost her power, — but even sym-

pathized with her suffering exiles, and became disgusted with the self-willed encroachments of Sparta; while the Spartan king Pausanias, together with some of the ephors, were also jealous of the arbitrary and oppressive conduct of Lysander. Instead of conducting the Lacedæmonian force to uphold at all price the Lysandrian oligarchy, Pausanias appeared rather as an equitable mediator to terminate the civil war. He refused to concur in any measure for obstructing the natural tendency towards a revival of the democracy. It was in this manner that Athens, rescued from that sanguinary and rapacious *regime* which has passed into history under the name of the Thirty Tyrants, was enabled to reappear as a humble and dependent member of the Spartan alliance, — with nothing but the recollection of her former power, yet with her democracy again in vigorous and tutelary action for internal government. The just and gentle bearing of her democratical citizens, and the absence of reactionary antipathies, after such cruel ill-treatment, — are among the most honorable features in her history.

The reader will find in my last volume, what I can only rapidly glance at here, the details of that system of bloodshed, spoliation, extinction of free speech and even of intellectual teaching, efforts to implicate innocent citizens as agents in judicial assassination, etc., — which stained the year of Anarchy (as it was termed in Athenian annals[1]) immediately following the surrender of the city. These details depend on evidence perfectly satisfactory; for they are conveyed to us chiefly by Xenophon, whose sympathies are decidedly oligarchical. From him too we learn another fact, not less pregnant with instruction; that the knights or horsemen, the body of richest proprietors at Athens, were the mainstay of the Thirty from first to last, notwithstanding all the enormities of their career.

We learn from these dark, but well-attested details, to appreciate the auspices under which that period of history called the Lacedæmonian empire was inaugurated. Such phenomena were by no means confined within the walls of Athens. On the contrary, the year of Anarchy (using that term in the sense in which it was employed by the Athenians) arising out of the same combination

---

[1] Xen. Hellen. ii, 3, 1.

of causes and agents, was common to a very large proportion of
the cities throughout Greece. The Lacedæmonian admiral Lysander, during his first year of naval command, had organized
in most of the allied cites factious combinations of some of the
principal citizens, corresponding with himself personally ; by whose
efforts in their respective cities he was enabled to prosecute the war
vigorously, and whom he repaid, partly by seconding as much as he
could their injustices in their respective cities, — partly by promising to strengthen their hands still farther as soon as victory should
be made sure.[1]   This policy, while it served as a stimulus against
the common enemy, contributed still more directly to aggrandize
Lysander himself; creating for him an ascendency of his own, and
imposing upon him personal obligations towards adherents, apart
from what was required by the interests of Sparta.

The victory of Ægospotami, complete and decisive beyond all
expectations either of friend or foe, enabled him to discharge these
obligations with interest.   All Greece at once made submission
to the Lacedæmonians,[2] except Athens and Samos, — and these
two only held out a few months.   It was now the first business of
the victorious commander to remunerate his adherents, and to take
permanent security for Spartan dominion as well as for his own.
In the greater number of cities, he established an oligarchy of ten
citizens, or a dekarchy,[3] composed of his own partisans ; while he
at the same time planted in each a Lacedæmonian harmost or
governor, with a garrison to uphold the new oligarchy.   The dekarchy of ten Lysandrian partisans, with the Lacedæmonian harmost to
sustain them, became the general scheme of Hellenic government
throughout the Ægean, from Eubœa to the Thracian coast-towns,
and from Myletus to Byzantium.   Lysander sailed round in person, with his victorious fleet, to Byzantium and Chalkêdon, to the
cities of Lesbos, to Thasos, and other places, — while he sent Eteonikus to Thrace, for the purpose of thus recasting the governments everywhere.   Not merely those cities which had hitherto
been on the Athenian side, but also those which had acted as allies

---

[1] Plutarch, Lysand. c. 5.   [2] Xen. Hellen. ii, 2, 6.

[3] These Councils of Ten, organized by Lysander, are sometimes called
Dekarchies — sometimes *Dekadarchies.* I use the former word by preference;
since the word *Dekadarch* is also employed by Xenophon in another and
very different sense — as meaning an officer who commands a *dekad.*

of Sparta, were subjected to the same intestine revolution and the same foreign constraint.[1] Everywhere the new Lysandrian dekarchy superseded the previous governments, whether oligarchical or democratical.

At Thasus, as well as in other places, this revolution was not accomplished without much bloodshed as well as treacherous stratagem, nor did Lysander himself scruple to enforce, personally and by his own presence, the execution and expulsion of suspected citizens.[2] In many places, however, simple terrorism probably sufficed. The new Lysandrian Ten overawed resistance and procured recognition of their usurpation by the menace of inviting the victorious admiral with his fleet of two hundred sail, and by the simple arrival of the Lacedæmonian harmost. Not only was each town obliged to provide a fortified citadel and maintenance for this governor with his garrison, but a scheme of tribute, amounting to one thousand talents annually, was imposed for the future, and assessed ratably upon each city by Lysander.[3]

In what spirit these new dekarchies would govern, consisting as they did of picked oligarchical partisans distinguished for audacity and ambition,[4] — who, to all the unscrupulous lust of power which characterized Lysander himself, added a thirst for personal gain, from which he was exempt, and were now about to reimburse

---

[1] Plutarch, Lysand. c. 13.

Καταλύων δὲ τοὺς δήμους καὶ τὰς ἄλλας πολιτείας, ἕνα μὲν ἁρμοστὴν ἑκάο τῃ Λακεδαιμόνιον κατέλιπε, δέκα δὲ ἄρχοντας ἐκ τῶν ὑπ' αὐτοῦ συγκεκροτημέ νων κατὰ πόλιν ἑταιρειῶν. Καὶ ταῦτα πράττων ὁμοίως ἔν τε ταῖς πολεμίαις καὶ ταῖς συμμάχοις γεγενημέναις πόλεσι, παρέ πλει σχολαίως τρόπον τινα κατασκευαζόμενος ἑαυτῷ τὴν τῆς Ἑλλάδος ἡγεμο νίαν. Compare Xen. Hellen. ii, 2, 2–5 ; Diodor. xiii, 3, 10, 13.

[2] Plutarch, Lysand. c. 13. πολλαῖς παραγινόμενος αὐτὸς σφαγαῖς καὶ συν εκβάλλων τοὺς τῶν φίλων ἐχθροὺς οὐκ ἐπιεικὲς ἐδίδου τοῖς Ἕλλησι δεῖγμα τῆς Λακεδαιμονίων ἀρχῆς, etc.

Plutarch, Lysand. c. 14. Καὶ τῶν μὲν ἄλλων πόλεων ὁμαλῶς ἁπασῶν κατέλυε τὰς πολιτείας καὶ καθίστη δεκαδαρχίας· πολλῶν μὲν ἐν ἑκάστῃ σφατ τομένων, πολλῶν δὲ φευγόντων, etc.

About the massacre at Thasus, see Ἰεpos, Lysand. c. 2 ; Poly æn. i, 45, 4. Compare Plutarch, Lysa- ; and see Vol. VIII, Ch. lxv, p. 220 of this History.

[3] Diodor. xiv, 10. Compare Isokrates, Or. iv, (Panegyr.) s. 151 ; Xen Hellen. iv, 8, 1.

[4] Plutarch, Lysand. c. 13. τοῦ Λυσάνδρου τῶν ὀλίγων τοῖς θρασυτάτοις καὶ φιλονεικοτάτοις τὰς πόλεις ἐγχειρίζοντος.

themselves for services already rendered to him, — the general analogy of Grecian history would sufficiently teach us, though we are without special details. But in reference to this point, we have not merely general analogy to guide us ; we have farther the parallel case of the Thirty at Athens, the particulars of whose rule are well known and have already been alluded to. These Thirty, with the exception of the difference of number, were to all intents and purposes a Lysandrian dekarchy ; created by the same originating force, placed under the like circumstances, and animated by the like spirit and interests. Every subject town would produce its Kritias and Theramenes, and its body of wealthy citizens like the knights or horsemen at Athens to abet their oppressions, under Lacedæmonian patronage and the covering guard of the Lacedæmonian harmost. Moreover, Kritias, with all his vices, was likely to be better rather than worse, as compared with his oligarchical parallel in any other less cultivated city. He was a man of letters and philosophy, accustomed to the conversation of Sokrates, and to the discussion of ethical and social questions. We may say the same of the knights or horsemen at Athens. Undoubtedly they had been better educated, and had been exposed to more liberalizing and improving influences, than the corresponding class elsewhere. If, then, these knights at Athens had no shame in serving as accomplices to the Thirty throughout all their enormities, we need not fear to presume that other cities would furnish a body of wealthy men yet more unscrupulous, and a leader at least as sanguinary, rapacious, and full of antipathies, as Kritias. As at Athens, so elsewhere ; the dekarchs would begin by putting to death notorious political opponents, under the name of " the wicked men ;"[1] they would next proceed to deal in the same manner with men of known probity and courage, likely to take a lead in resisting oppression.[2] Their career of blood would continue, — in spite of remonstrances from more moderate persons among their own num-

---

[1] Xen. Hellen. ii, 3, 13.

... ἔπεισαν Λύσανδρου φρουροὺς σφίσι ξυμπ,ῶᾶξαι ἐλθεῖν, ἕως δὴ τοὺς πο
νηροὺς ἐκποδὼν ποιησάμενοι καταστήσαιντο τὴν πολιτείαν, etc.

[2] Xen. Hellen. ii, 3, 14. Τῶν δὲ φρουρῶν τούτου (the harmost) ξυμπέμπ
οντος αὐτοῖς, οὓς ἐβούλοντο, ξυνελάμβανον (ὑκέτι τοὺς πονηροὺς καὶ ὀλίγους
ἐξίους, ἀλλ᾽ ἤδη οὓς ἐνόμιζον ἥκιστα μὲν παρωθουμένους ἀνέχεσθαι, ὰι τιπρατ
τειν δέ τι ἐπιχειροῦντας πλείστους τοὺς ξυνεθέλοντας λαμβάνειν.

ber, like Theramenes, — until they contrived some stratagem for
disarming the citizens, which would enable them to gratify both
their antipathies and their rapacity by victims still more numerous,
— many of such victims being wealthy men, selected for purposes
of pure spoliation.[1] They would next despatch by force any obtru-
sive monitor from their own number, like Theramenes ; probably
with far less ceremony than accompanied the perpetration of this
crime at Athens, where we may trace the effect of those judicial
forms and habits to which the Athenian public had been habitu-
ated, — overruled indeed, yet still not forgotten. There would
hardly remain any fresh enormity still to commit, over and above
the multiplied executions, except to banish from the city all but
their own immediate partisans, and to reward these latter with
choice estates confiscated from the victims.[2] If called upon to
excuse such tyranny, the leader of a dekarchy would have sufficient invention to employ the plea of Kritias, — that all changes
of government were unavoidably death-dealing, and that nothing
less than such stringent measures would suffice to maintain his
city in suitable dependence upon Sparta.[3]

Of course, it is not my purpose to affirm that in any other city,
precisely the same phenomena took place as those which occurred
in Athens. But we are nevertheless perfectly warranted in re-
garding the history of the Athenian Thirty as a fair sample, from
whence to derive our idea of those Lysandrian dekarchies which
now overspread the Grecian world. Doubtless, each had its own
peculiar march ; some were less tyrannical ; but, perhaps, some
even more tyrannical, regard being had to the size of the city.
And in point of fact, Isokrates, who speaks with indignant horror
of these dekarchies, while he denounces those features which they
had in common with the triakontarchy at Athens, — extrajudicial
murders, spoliations, and banishments, — notices one enormity besides, which we do not find in the latter, violent outrages upon boys
and women.[4] Nothing of this kind is ascribed to Kritias and his

---

[1] Xen. Hellen, ii, 3, 21. [2] Xen. Hellen. ii, 4, 1.

[3] Xen. Hellen. ii, 3, 24–32 Καὶ εἰσὶ μὲν δήπου πᾶσαι μεταβολαὶ πολιτε
ιῶν θαι ατήφε ροι, etc.

[4] Isokrates Orat. iv, (Panegyr.) s. 127–132 (c. 32).

He has been speaking, at some length, and in terms of energetic denun
ciation, against the enormities of the dekarchies. He concludes by saying

companions ;[1] and it is a considerable proof of the restraining force of Athenian manners, that men who inflicted so much evil in gratification of other violent impulses, should have stopped short here. The decemvirs named by Lysander, like the decemvir Appius Claudius at Rome, would find themselves armed with power to satiate their lusts as well as their antipathies, and would not be more likely to set bounds to the former than to the latter. Lysander, in all the overweening insolence of victory, while rewarding his most devoted partisans with an exaltation comprising every sort of license and tyranny, stained the dependent cities with countless murders, perpetrated on private as well as on public grounds.[2] No individual Greek had ever before wielded so prodigious a power of enriching friends or destroying enemies, in this universal reorganization of Greece ;[3] nor was there ever any power more deplorably abused.

It was thus that the Lacedæmonian empire imposed upon each of the subject cities a double oppression ;[4] the native decemvirs, and the foreign harmost ; each abetting the other, and forming together an aggravated pressure upon the citizens, from which scarce any escape was left. The Thirty at Athens paid the greatest possible court to the harmost Kallibius,[5] and put to death

---

— Φυγὰς δὲ καὶ στάσεις καὶ νόμων συγχύσεις καὶ πολιτειῶν μεταβολὰς, ἔτι δὲ παιδῶν ὕβρεις καὶ γυναικῶν αἰσχύνας καὶ χρημάτων ἁρπαγὰς, τίς ἂν δύναιτο διεξελθεῖν ; πλὴν τοσοῦτον εἰπεῖν ἔχω καθ' ἁπάντων, ὅτι τὰ μὲν ἐφ' ἡμῶν δεινὰ ῥαδίως ἄν τις ἑνὶ ψηφίσματι διέλυσε, τὰς δὲ σφαγὰς καὶ τὰς ἀνομίας τὰς ἐπὶ τούτων γενομένας οὐδεὶς ἂν ἰάσασθαι δύναιτο.

See also, of the same author, Isokrates, Orat. v, (Philipp.) s. 110 ; Orat. viii, (de Pace) s. 119–124 ; Or. xii, (Panath.) s. 58, 60, 106.

[1] We may infer that if Xenophon had heard anything of the sort respecting Kritias, he would hardly have been averse to mention it ; when we read what he says (Memorab. i, 2, 29.) Compare a curious passage about Kritias in Dion. Chrysostom. Or. xxvi, p. 270.

[2] Plutarch Lysand. c. 19. Ἦν δὲ καὶ τῶν ἄλλων ἐν ταῖς πόλεσι δημοτικῶν φόνος οὐκ ἀριθμητὸς, ἅτε δὴ μὴ κατ' ἰδίας μόνον αἰτίας αὐτοῦ κτείνοντος, ἀλλὰ πολλαῖς μὲν ἐχθραις, πολλαῖς δὲ πλεονεξίαις, τῶν ἑκασταχοθι φίλων χαριζομένου τὰ τοιαῦτα καὶ συνεργοῦντος ; also Pausanias, vii, 10, 1 ; ix, 32, 6.

[3] Plutarch, Agesilaus, c. 7.

[4] See the speech of the Theban envoys at Athens, about eight years after the surrender of Athens (Xen. Hellen. iii, 5, 13).
... Οὐδὲ γὰρ φυγεῖν ἐξῆν (Plutarch, Lysand. c. 19).

[5] Xen. Hellen. ii, 3, 13.

individual Athenians offensive to him, in order to purchase his co operation in their own violences. The few details which we possess respecting these harmosts (who continued throughout the insular and maritime cities for about ten years, until the battle of Knidus, or as long as the maritime empire of Sparta lasted, — but in various continental dependencies considerably longer, that is, until the defeat of Leuktra in 37¹ B. C.), are all for the most part discreditable. We have seen in the last chapter the description given by the philo-Laconian Xenophon, of the harsh and treacherous manner in which they acted towards the returning Cyreian soldiers, combined with their corrupt subservience to Pharnabazus. We learn from him that it depended upon the fiat of a Lacedæmonian harmost whether these soldiers should be proclaimed enemies and excluded forever from their native cities; and Kleander, the harmost of Byzantium, who at first threatened them with this treatment, was only induced by the most unlimited submission, combined with very delicate management, to withdraw his menace. The cruel proceeding of Anaxibius and Aristarchus, who went so far as to sell four hundred of these soldiers into slavery, has been recounted a few pages above. Nothing can be more arbitrary or reckless than their proceedings. If they could behave thus towards a body of Greek soldiers full of acquired glory, effective either as friends or as enemies, and having generals capable of prosecuting their collective interests and making their complaints heard, — what protection would a private citizen of any subject city, Byzantium or Perinthus, be likely to enjoy against their oppression?

The story of Aristodemus, the harmost of Oreus in Eubœa, evinces that no justice could be obtained against any of their enor-

---

τὸν μὲν Καλλίβιον ἐθεράπευον πάσῃ θεραπείᾳ, ὡς πάντα ἐπαινοίη, ἃ πράττοιεν, etc. (Plutarch, Lysand. c. 15).

The Thirty seem to have outdone Lysander himself. A young Athenian of rank, distinguished as a victor in the pankratium, Autolykus, — having been insulted by Kallibius, resented it, tripped him up, and threw him down. Lysander, on being appealed to, justified Autolykus, and censured Kallibius, telling him that he did not know how to govern freemen. The Thirty, however, afterwards put Autolykus to death, as a means of courting Kallibius (Plutarch, Lysand. c. 15). Pausanias mentions Eteonikus (not Kallibius) as the person who struck Autolykus; but he ascribes the same decision to Lysander (i. 42, 3).

mities from the ephors of Sparta. That harmost, among many other
acts of brutal violence, seized a beautiful youth, son of a free citizen
at Oreus, out of the palæstra, — carried him off, — and after vainly
endeavoring to overcome his resistance, put him to death. The
father of the youth went to Sparta, made known the atrocities,
and appealed to the ephors and Senate for redress. But a deaf
ear was turned to his complaints, and in anguish of mind he slew
himself. Indeed, we know that these Spartan authorities would
grant no redress, not merely against harmosts, but even against
private Spartan citizens, who had been guilty of gross crime out of
their own country. A Bœotian near Leuktra, named Skedasus, preferred complaint that two Spartans, on their way from Delphi, after
having been hospitably entertained in his house, had first violated,
and afterwards killed, his two daughters ; but even for so flagitious
an outrage as this, no redress could be obtained.[1] Doubtless, when
a powerful foreign ally, like the Persian satrap Pharnabazus,[2]
complained to the ephors of the conduct of a Lacedæmonian harmost or admiral, his representations would receive attention ; and
we learn that the ephors were thus induced not merely to recall
Lysander from the Hellespont, but to put to death another officer,
Thorax, for corrupt appropriation of money. But for a private
citizen in any subject city, the superintending authority of Sparta
would be not merely remote but deaf and immovable, so as to
afford him no protection whatever, and to leave him altogether at
the mercy of the harmost. It seems, too, that the rigor of Spartan
training, and peculiarity of habits, rendered individual Lacedæmonians on foreign service more self-willed, more incapable of entering into the customs or feelings of others, and more liable to
degenerate when set free from the strict watch of home, — than
other Greeks generally.[3]

---

[1] Plutarch, Amator. Narration, p. 773 ; Plutarch, Pelopidas, c. 20. In
Diodorus (xv, 54) and Pausanias, (ix, 13, 2), the damsels thus outraged
are stated to have slain themselves. Compare another story in Xenoph.
Hellen. v, 4, 56, 57.

[2] Plutarch, Lysand. c, 19.

[3] This seems to have been the impression not merely of the enemies of
Sparta, but even of the Spartan authorities themselves. Compare two
remarkable passages of Thucydides, i, 77, and i, 95. Ἄμικτα γὰρ (says the
Athenian envoy at Sparta) τά τε καθ᾽ ὑμᾶς αὐτοὺς νόμιμα τοῖς ἄλλοις ἔχετε,

Taking all these causes of evil together, — the dekarchies, the harmosts, and the overwhelming dictatorship of Lysander, — and construing other parts of the Grecian world by the analogy of Athens under the Thirty, — we shall be warranted in affirming that the first years of the Spartan Empire, which followed upon the victory of Ægospotami, were years of all-pervading tyranny and multifarious intestine calamity, such as Greece had never before endured. The hardships of war, severe in many ways, were now at an end, but they were replaced by a state of suffering not the less difficult to bear because it was called peace. And what made the suffering yet more intolerable was, that it was a bitter disappointment, and a flagrant violation of promises proclaimed, repeatedly and explicitly, by the Lacedæmonians themselves.

For more than thirty years preceding, — from times earlier than the commencement of the Peloponnesian war, — the Spartans had professed to interfere only for the purpose of liberating Greece, and of putting down the usurped ascendency of Athens. All the allies of Sparta had been invited into strenuous action, — all those of Athens had been urged to revolt, — under the soul-stirring cry of " Freedom to Greece." The earliest incitements addressed by the Corinthians to Sparta in 432 B. C., immediately after the Korkyræan dispute, called upon her to stand forward in fulfilment of her recognized function as " Liberator of Greece," and denounced her as guilty of connivance with Athens if she held back.[1] Athens was branded as the " despot city;" which had already absorbed the independence of many Greeks, and

---

καὶ προσέτι εἰς ἕκαστος ἐξιὼν οὔτε τούτοις χρῆται, οὐθ᾽ οἷς ἡ ἄλλη Ἑλλὰς νομίζει.

After the recall of the regent Pausanias and of Dorkis from the Hellespont (in 477 B. C.), the Lacedæmonians refuse to send out any successor, φοβούμενοι μὴ σφίσιν οἱ ἐξιόντες χείρους γίγνωνται, ὅπερ καὶ ἐν τῷ Παυσανίᾳ ἐνεῖδον, etc. (i, 95.)

Compare Plutarch Apophtheg. Laconic. p. 220 F.

[1] Thucyd. i, 69. οὐ γὰρ ὁ δουλωσάμενος, ἀλλ᾽ ὁ δυνάμενος μὲν παῦσαι, περιορῶν δὲ, ἀληθέστερον αὐτὸ δρᾷ, εἴπερ καὶ τὴν ἀξίωσιν τῆς ἀρετῆς ὡς ἐλευθερῶν τὴν Ἑλλάδα φέρεται.

To the like purpose the second speech of the Corinthian envoys at Sparta, c. 122-124 — μὴ μέλλετε Ποτιδαιάταις τε ποιεῖσθαι τιμωρίαν . καὶ τῶν ἄλλων μετελθεῖν τὴν ἐλευθερίαν, etc

menaced that of all the rest. The last formal requisition borne
by the Lacedæmonian envoys to Athens in the winter immediately preceding the war, ran thus, — "If you desire the continuance
of peace with Sparta, restore to the Greeks their autonomy." [1]
When Archidamus, king of Sparta, approached at the head of his
army to besiege Platæa, the Platæans laid claim to autonomy as
having been solemnly guaranteed to them by King Pausanias
after the great victory near their town.   Upon which Archidamus
replied, — "Your demand is just; we are prepared to confirm
your autonomy, — but we call upon you to aid us in securing the
like for those other Greeks who have been enslaved by Athens.
This is the sole purpose of our great present effort." [2]   And the
banner of general enfranchisement, which the Lacedæmonians
thus held up at the outset of the war, enlisted in their cause
encouraging sympathy and good wishes throughout Greece.[3]

But the most striking illustration by far, of the seductive promises held out by the Lacedæmonians, was afforded by the conduct of Brasidas in Thrace, when he first came into the neighborhood of the Athenian allies during the eighth year of the war
(424 B. C.).   In his memorable discourse addressed to the public assembly at Akanthus, he takes the greatest pains to satisfy them that
he came only for the purpose of realizing the promise of enfranchisement proclaimed by the Lacedæmonians at the beginning of
the war.[4]   Having expected, when acting in such a cause, nothing

---

[1] Thucyd. i, 139.   Compare Isokrates, Or. iv, Panegyr. c. 34, s. 140; Or.
v, (Philipp.) s. 121 ; Or. xiv, (Plataic.) s. 43.

[2] Thucyd. ii, 72.   Παρασκευὴ δὲ τόσηδε καὶ πόλεμος γεγένηται αὐτῶν ἕνεκα
καὶ τῶν ἄλλων ἐλευθερώσεως.

Read also the speech of the Theban orator, in reply to the Platæan, after
the capture of the town by the Lacedæmonians (iii, 63).

[3] Thucyd. ii, 8.   ἡ δὲ εὔνοια παρὰ πολὺ ἐποίει τῶν ἀνθρώπων μᾶλλοι ἐς
τοὺς Λακεδαιμονίους, ἄλλως τε καὶ προειπόντων ὅτι τὴν Ἑλλάδα ἐλευθεροῦ-
σιν.

See also iii, 13, 14 — the speech of the envoys from the revolted Mitylênê,
to the Lacedæmonians.

The Lacedæmonian admiral Alkidas with his fleet, is announced as crossing over the Ægean to Ionia for the purpose of "liberating Greece;" accordingly, the Samian exiles remonstrate with him for killing his prisoners,
as in contradiction with that object (iii, 32) — ἔλεγον οὐ καλῶς μὴν Ἑλλάδα
ἐλευθεροῦν αὐτὸν, εἰ ἄνδρας διέφθειρεν, etc.

[4] Thucyd iv, 85.   Η μὲν ἐκπεμφίς μου καὶ τῆς στρατιᾶς ὑπὸ Λακεδαιμονίων,

less than a hearty welcome, he is astonished to find their gates closed against him. " I am come (said he) not to injure, but to liberate the Greeks; after binding the Lacedæmonian authorities by the most solemn oaths, that all whom I may bring over shall be dealt with as autonomous allies. We do not wish to obtain you as allies either by force or fraud, but to act as your allies at a time when you are enslaved by the Athenians. You ought not to suspect my purposes, in the face of these solemn assurances; least of all ought any man to hold back through apprehension of private enmities, and through fear lest I should put the city into the hands of a few chosen partisans. I am not come to identify myself with local faction: I am not the man to offer you an unreal liberty by breaking down your established constitution, for the purpose of enslaving either the Many to the Few, or the Few to the Many. That would be more intolerable even than foreign dominion; and we Lacedæmonians should incur nothing but reproach, instead of reaping thanks and honor for our trouble. We should draw upon ourselves those very censures, upon the strength of which we are trying to put down Athens; and that, too, in aggravated measure, worse than those who have never made honorable professions; since to men in high position, specious trick is more disgraceful than open violence.[1] — If (continued Brasidas) in spite of my assurances, you still withhold from me your coöperation, I shall think myself authorized to constrain you by force. We should not be warranted in forcing freedom on any

---

ὦ 'Ακάνθιοι, γεγένηται τὴν αἰτίαν ἐπαληθεύουσα ἣν ἀρχόμενοι τοῦ πολέμου προείπομεν, 'Αθηναίοις ἐλευθεροῦντες τὴν Ἑλλάδα πολεμ ήσειν.

[1] Thucyd. iv, 85. Αὐτός τε οὐκ ἐπὶ κακῷ, ἐπ' ἐλευθερώσει δὲ τῶν Ἑλλήνων παρελήλυθα, ὅρκοις τε Λακεδαιμονίων καταλαβὼν τὰ τέλη τοῖς μεγίστοις, ἦ μὴν οὓς ἂν ἔγωγε προσαγάγωμαι ξυμμάχους ἔσεσθαι αὐτονόμους.......... Καὶ εἴ τις ἰδίᾳ τινα δεδιὼς ἄρα, μὴ ἐγώ τισι προσθῶ τὴν πόλιν, ἀπρόθυμός ἐστι, πάντων μάλιστα πιστευσάτω. Οὐ γὰρ συστασιάσων ἥκω, οὐδὲ ἀσαφῆ τὴν ἐλευθερίαν νομίζω ἐπιφέρειν, εἰ, τὸ πάτριον παρεὶς, τὸ πλέον τοῖς ὀλίγοις, ἢ τὸ ἔλασσον τοῖς πᾶσι, δουλώσαιμι. Χαλεπώτερα γὰρ ἂν τῆς ἀλλοφύλου ἀρχῆς εἴη, καὶ ἡμῖν τοῖς Λακεδαιμονίοις οὐκ ἂν ἀντὶ πόνων χάρις καθίσταιτο, ἀντὶ δὲ τιμῆς καὶ δόξης αἰτία μᾶλλον· οἷς τε τοὺς 'Αθηναίους ἐγκλήμασι καταπολεμοῦμεν, αὐτοὶ ἂν φαινοίμεθα ἐχθίονα ἢ ὁ μὴ ὑποδείξας ἀρετὴν κα τακτώμενοι.

unwilling parties, except with a view to some common good. But
as we seek not empire for ourselves, — as we struggle only to put
down the empire of others, — as we offer autonomy to each and
all, — so we should do wrong to the majority if we allowed you
to persist in your opposition." [1]

Like the allied sovereigns of Europe in 1813, who, requiring
the most strenuous efforts on the part of the people to contend
against the Emperor Napoleon, promised free constitutions and
granted nothing after the victory had been assured, — the Lacedæmonians thus held out the most emphatic and repeated assurances of general autonomy in order to enlist allies against Athens ;
disavowing, even ostentatiously, any aim at empire for themselves.
It is true, that after the great catastrophe before Syracuse, when
the ruin of Athens appeared imminent, and when the alliance
with the Persian satraps against her was first brought to pass,
the Lacedæmonians began to think more of empire,[2] and less of
Grecian freedom ; which, indeed, so far as concerned the Greeks
on the continent of Asia, was surrendered to Persia. Nevertheless the old watchword still continued. It was still currently
believed, though less studiously professed, that the destruction of
the Athenian empire was aimed at as a means to the liberation
of Greece.[3]

The victory of Ægospotami with its consequences cruelly undeceived every one. The language of Brasidas, sanctioned by the
solemn oaths of the Lacedæmonian ephors, in 424 B. C. — and the
proceedings of the Lacedæmonian Lysander in 405–404 B. C., the
commencing hour of Spartan omnipotence, — stand in such literal
and flagrant contradiction, that we might almost imagine the former
to have foreseen the possibility of such a successor, and to have tried
to disgrace and disarm him beforehand. The dekarchies of Ly-

---

[1] Thucyd. iv, 87. Οὐδὲ ὀφείλομεν οἱ Λακεδαιμόνιοι μὴ κοινοῦ τινος
ἀγαθοῦ αἰτίᾳ τοὺς μὴ βουλομένους ἐλευθεροῦν. Οὐδ᾽ αὖ
ἀρχῆς ἐφιέμεθα, παῦσαι δὲ μᾶλλον ἑτέρους σπεύδοντες τοὺς πλείους ἂν
ἀδικοῖμεν, εἰ ξυμπᾶσιν αὐτονομίαν ἐπιφέροντες ὑμᾶς τοὺς ἐναν-
τιουμένους περίδοιμεν. Compare Isokrates, Or. iv, (Panegyr.) s. 140, 141.

[2] Feelings of the Lacedæmonians during the winter immediately succeeding the great Syracusan catastrophe (Thuc. viii, 2) — καὶ καθελόντες ἐκεί-
νους (the Athenians) αὐτοὶ τῆς πάρης Ἑλλάδος ἤδη ἀσφαλῶς ἡγήσεσθαι.

[3] Compare Thucyd. viii, 43, 3 ; viii, 46, 3.

sander realized that precise ascendency of a few chosen partisans which Brasidas repudiates as an abomination worse than foreign dominion; while the harmosts and garrison, installed in the dependent cities along with the native decemvirs, planted the second variety of mischief as well as the first, each aggravating the other. Had the noble-minded Kallikratidas gained a victory at Arginusæ, and lived to close the war, he would probably have tried, with more or less of success, to make some approach to the promises of Brasidas. But it was the double misfortune of Greece, first that the closing victory was gained by such an admiral as Lysander, the most unscrupulous of all power-seekers, partly for his country, and still more for himself, — next, that the victory was so decisive, sudden and imposing, as to leave no enemy standing, or in a position to insist upon terms. The fiat of Lysander, acting in the name of Sparta, became omnipotent, not merely over enemies, but over allies; and to a certain degree even over the Spartan authorities themselves. There was no present necessity for conciliating allies, — still less for acting up to former engagements; so that nothing remained to oppose the naturally ambitious inspirations of the Spartan ephors, who allowed the admiral to carry out the details in his own way. But former assurances, though Sparta was in a condition to disregard them, were not forgotten by others; and the recollection of them imparted additional bitterness to the oppressions of the decemvirs and harmosts.[1]   In perfect consistency

---

[1] This is emphatically set forth in a fragment of Theopompus the historian, preserved by Theodorus Metochita, and printed at the end of the collection of the Fragments of Theopompus the historian, both by Wichers and by M. Didot. Both these editors, however, insert it only as Fragmentum Spurium, on the authority of Plutarch (Lysander, c. 13), who quotes the same sentiment from the comic writer Theopompus. But the passage of Theodorus Metochita presents the express words Θεόπομπος ὁ ἱστορικός. We have, therefore, his distinct affirmation against that of Plutarch; and the question is, which of the two we are to believe.

Now if any one will read attentively the so-called Fragmentum Spurium as it stands at the end of the collections above referred to, he will see (I think) that it belongs much more naturally to the historian than to the comic writer. It is a strictly historical statement, illustrated by a telling, though coarse, comparison. The Fragment is thus presented by Theodorus Metochita (Fragm. Theopomp. 344, ed. Didot).

Θεόπομπος ὁ ἱστορικὸς ἀποσκώπτων εἰς τοὺς Λακεδαιμονίους, εἴκαζεν αὐτοὺς ταῖς φαύλαις καπηλίσιν, αἱ τοῖς χρωμένοις ἐγχέουσαι τὴν ἀρχὴν οἶνον ἡδύν τι

with her misrule throughout Eastern Greece,[1] too, Sparta identified
herself with the energetic tyranny of Dionysius at Syracuse, assisting both to erect and to uphold it; a contradiction to her former
maxims of action which would have astounded the historian Herodotus.

The empire of Sparta thus constituted at the end of 405 B. C.,
maintained itself in full grandeur for somewhat above ten years,
until the naval battle of Knidus,[2] in 394 B. C. That defeat de-

καὶ εὔχρηστον σοφιστικῶς ἐπὶ τῇ λήψει τοῦ ἀργυρίου, μεθύστερον φαυλόν
τινα καὶ ἐκτροπίαν καὶ ὀξίνην κατακιρνῶσι καὶ παρέχονται· καὶ τοὺς Λακεδαιμονίους τοίνυν ἔλεγε, τὸν αὐτὸν ἐκείναις τρόπον, ἐν τῷ κατὰ τῶν Ἀθηναίων
πολέμῳ, τὴν ἀρχὴν ἡδίστῳ πόματι τῆς ἀπ' Ἀθηναίων ἐλευθερίας καὶ προγράμ-
ματι καὶ κηρύγματι τοὺς Ἕλληνας δελεάσαντας, ὕστερον πικρότατα σφίσιν
ἐγχέαι καὶ ἀηδέστατα κράματα βιοτῆς ἐπωδύνου καὶ χρήσεως πραγμάτων ἀλ-
γεινῶν, πάνυ τοι κατατυραννοῦντας τὰς πόλεις δεκαρχίαις καὶ ἁρμοσταῖς βαρυ-
τάτοις, καὶ πραττομένους, ἃ δυσχερὲς εἶναι σφόδρα καὶ ἀνύποιστον φέρειν, καὶ
ἀποκτιννύναι.

Plutarch, ascribing the statement to the comic Theopompus, affirms him
to be silly (ἔοικε ληρεῖν) in saying that the Lacedæmonian empire began by
being sweet and pleasant, and afterwards was corrupted and turned into
bitterness and oppression; whereas the fact was, that it was bitterness and
oppression from the very first.

Now if we read the above citation from Theodorus, we shall see that
Theopompus did not really put forth that assertion which Plutarch contradicts as silly and untrue.

What Theopompus stated was, that the first Lacedæmonians, *during the
war against Athens*, tempted the Greeks with a most delicious draught and
programme and *proclamation* of freedom from the rule of Athens, — and that
they afterwards poured in the most bitter and repulsive mixtures of hard
oppression and tyranny, etc.

The sweet draught is asserted to consist — not, as Plutarch supposes, in
the first taste of the actual Lacedæmonian empire after the war, but — in
the seductive promises of freedom held out by them to the allies *during the
war*. Plutarch's charge of ἔοικε ληρεῖν has thus no foundation. I have
written δελεάσαντας instead of δελεάσοντας which stands in Didot's Fragment, because it struck me that this correction was required to construe
the passage.

[1] Isokrates, Or. iv, (Panegr.) s. 145; Or. viii, (de Pace) s. 122; Diodor.
xiv, 10–44; xv, 23. Compare Herodot. v, 92; Thucyd. i, 18; Isokrates,
Or. iv, (Panegyr.) s. 144.

[2] Isokrates, Panathen. s. 61. Σπαρτιᾶται μὲν γὰρ ἔτη δέκα μόλις ἐπεστά-
τησαν αὐτῶν, ἡμεῖς δὲ πέντε καὶ ἑξήκοντα συνεχῶς κατέσχομεν τὴν ἀρχήν.
I do not hold myself bound to make out the exactness of the chronology
of Isokrates. But here we may remark that his "hardly ten years" is a

stroyed ner fleet and maritime ascendency, yet left her in undiminished power on land, which she still maintained until her defeat by the Thebans[1] at Leuktra in 371 B. C. Throughout all this time, it was her established system to keep up Spartan harmosts and garrisons in the dependent cities on the continent as well as in the islands. Even the Chians, who had been her most active allies during the last eight years of the war, were compelled to submit to this hardship; besides having all their fleet taken away from them.[2] But the native dekarchies, though at first established by Lysander universally throughout the maritime dependencies, did not last as a system so long as the harmosts. Composed as they were to a great degree of the personal nominees and confederates of Lysander, they suffered in part by the reactionary jealousy which in time made itself felt against his overweening ascendency. After continuing for some time, they lost the countenance of the Spartan ephors, who proclaimed permission to the cities (we do not precisely know when) to resume their preëxisting governments.[3] Some of the dekarchies thus became dissolved, or modified in various ways, but several probably still continued to subsist, if they had force enough to maintain themselves; for it does not appear that the ephors ever systematically put them down, as Lysander had systematically set them up.

The government of the Thirty at Athens would never have been overthrown if the oppressed Athenians had been obliged to rely on a tutelary interference of the Spartan ephors to help them in overthrowing it. My last volume has shown that this nefarious

---

term, though less than the truth by some months, if we may take the battle of Ægospotami as the beginning, is very near the truth if we take the surrender of Athens as the beginning, down to the battle of Knidus.

[1] Pausanias, viii, 52, 2; ix, 6, 1.

[2] Diodor. xiv, 84; Isokrates, Orat. viii, (de Pace) s. 121.

[3] Xen. Hellen. iii, 4, 2.

Lysander accompanied King Agesilaus (when the latter was going to his Asiatic command in 396 B. C.). His purpose was — ὅπως τὰς δεκαρχίας τὰς κατασταθείσας ὑπ' ἐκείνου ἐν ταῖς πόλεσιν, ἐκπεπτωκυίας δὲ διὰ τοὺς ἐφόρους, οἱ τὰς πατρίους πολιτείας παρήγγειλαν, πάλιν καταστήσει μετ' Ἀγησιλάου.

It shows the careless construction of Xenophon's Hellenica, or perhaps his reluctance to set forth the discreditable points of the Lacedæmonian rule, that this is the first mention which he makes (and that too, indirectly) of the dekarchies, nine years after they had been first set up by Lysander.

oligarchy came to its end by the unassisted efforts of Thrasybulus and the Athenian democrats themselves. It is true, indeed, that the arrogance and selfishness of Sparta and of Lysander had alienated the Thebans, Corinthians, Megarians, and other neighboring allies, and induced them to sympathize with the Athenian exiles against the atrocities of the Thirty, — but they never rendered any positive assistance of moment. The inordinate personal ambition of Lysander had also offended King Pausanias and the Spartan ephors, so that they too became indifferent to the Thirty, who were his creatures. But this merely deprived the Thirty of that foreign support which Lysander, had he still continued in the ascendent, would have extended to them in full measure. It was not the positive cause of their downfall. That crisis was brought about altogether by the energy of Thrasybulus and his companions, who manifested such force and determination as could not have been put down without an extraordinary display of Spartan military power; a display not entirely safe when the sympathies of the chief allies were with the other side, — and at any rate adverse to the inclinations of Pausanias. As it was with the Thirty at Athens, so it probably was also with the dekarchies in the dependent cities. The Spartan ephors took no steps to put them down; but where the resistance of the citizens was strenuous enough to overthrow them, no Spartan intervention came to prop them up, and the harmost perhaps received orders not to consider his authority as indissolubly linked with theirs. The native forces of each dependent city being thus left to find their own level, the decemvirs, once installed, would doubtless maintain themselves in a great number; while in other cases they would be overthrown, — or, perhaps, would contrive to perpetuate their dominion by compromise and alliance with other oligarchical sections. This confused and unsettled state of the dekarchies, — some still existing, others half-existing, others again defunct, — prevailed in 396 B. C., when Lysander accompanied Agesilaus into Asia, in the full hope that he should have influence enough to reorganize them all.[1]

---

[1] Compare the two passages of Xenophon's Hellenica, iii, 4, 7; iii, 5, 13.

Ἅτε συντεταραγμένων ἐν ταῖς πόλεσι τῶν πολιτειῶν, καὶ οὔτε δημοκρατίας ἔτι οὔσης, ὥσπερ ἐπ' Ἀθηναίων, οὔτε δεκαρχίας, ὥσπερ ἐπὶ Λυσάνδρου.

But that some of these dekarchies still continued, we know from the

We must recollect that no other dependent city would possess the same means of offering energetic resistance to its local decemvirs, as Athens offered to the Thirty; and that the insular Grecian cities were not only feeble individually, but naturally helpless against the lords of the sea.[1]

Such then was the result throughout Greece, when that long war, which had been undertaken in the name of universal autonomy, was terminated by the battle of Ægospotami. In place of imperial Athens was substituted, not the promised autonomy, but yet more imperial Sparta. An awful picture is given by the philo-Laconian Xenophon, in 399 B. C., of the ascendency exercised throughout all the Grecian cities, not merely by the ephors and the public officers, but even by the private citizens, of Sparta. " The Lacedæmonians (says he in addressing the Cyreian army) are now the presidents of Greece; and even any single private Lacedæmonian can accomplish what he pleases." [2] " All the cities (he says in another place) then obeyed whatever order they might receive from a Lacedæmonian citizen." [3] Not merely was the general ascendency thus omnipresent and irresistible, but it was enforced with a stringency of detail, and darkened by a thousand accompaniments of tyranny and individual abuse, such as had never been known under the much-decried empire of Athens.

We have more than one picture of the Athenian empire, in speeches made by hostile orators who had every motive to work up the strongest antipathies in the bosoms of their audience against it. We have the addresses of the Corinthian envoys at Sparta when stimulating the Spartan allies to the Peloponnesian war,[4] —

---

subsequent passage. The Theban envoys say to the public assembly at Athens, respecting the Spartans : —

'Αλλὰ μὴν καὶ οὓς ὑμῶν ἀπέστησαν φανεροί εἰσιν ἐξηπατηκότες· ὑπό τε γὰρ τῶν ἁρμοστῶν τυραννοῦνται, καὶ ὑπὸ δέκα ἀνδρῶν, οὓς Λύσανδρος κατέστησεν ἐν ἑκάστῃ πόλει — where the decemvirs are noted as still subsisting, in 395 B. C. See also Xen. Agesilaus, i, 37.

[1] Xen. Hellen. iii, 5, 15.

[2] Xen. Anab. vi, 6, 12. Εἰσὶ μὲν γὰρ ἤδη ἐγγὺς αἱ Ἑλληνίδες πόλεις· (this was spoken at Kalpê in Bithynia) τῆς δὲ Ἑλλάδος Λακεδαιμόνιοι προεστήκασιν· ἱκανοὶ δέ εἰσι καὶ εἰς ἕκαστος Λακεδαιμονίων ἐν ταῖς πόλεσιν ὅ,τι βούλονται διαπράττεσθαι.

[3] Xen Hellen. iii, 1, 5. Πᾶσαι γὰρ τότε αἱ πόλεις ἐπείθοντο, ὅ,τι Λακεδαιμόνιος ἀνὴρ ἐπιτάττοι.

[4] Thucyd. i, 68–120.

that of the envoys from Mitylênê delivered at Olympia to the
Spartan confederates, when the city had revolted from Athens
and stood in pressing need of support, — the discourse of Brasidas
in the public assembly at Akanthus, — and more than one speech
also from Hermokrates, impressing upon his Sicilian countrymen
hatred as well as fear of Athens.[1]   Whoever reads these dis-
courses, will see that they dwell almost exclusively on the great
political wrong inherent in the very fact of her empire, robbing so
many Grecian communities of their legitimate autonomy, over and
above the tribute imposed.   That Athens had thus already enslaved many cities, and was only watching for opportunities to
enslave many more, is the theme upon which they expatiate.   But
of practical grievances, — of cruelty, oppression, spoliation, multiplied exiles, etc., of high-handed wrong committed by individual
Athenians, — not one word is spoken.   Had there been the smallest
pretext for introducing such inflammatory topics, how much more
impressive would have been the appeal of Brasidas to the sympathies of the Akanthians !   How vehement would have been the
denunciations of the Mitylenæan envoys, in place of the tame and
almost apologetic language which we now read in Thucydides !
Athens extinguished the autonomy of her subject-allies, and punished revolters with severity, sometimes even with cruelty.   But
as to other points of wrong, the silence of accusers, such as those
just noticed, counts as a powerful exculpation.

The case is altered when we come to the period succeeding the
battle of Ægospotami.   Here indeed also, we find the Spartan empire complained of (as the Athenian empire had been before), in
contrast with that state of autonomy to which each city laid claim,
and which Sparta had not merely promised to ensure, but set forth
as her only ground of war.   Yet this is not the prominent grievance,
— other topics stand more emphatically forward.   The decemvirs and the harmosts (some of the latter being Helots), the
standing instruments of Spartan empire, are felt as more sorely
painful than the empire itself; as the language held by Brasidas
at Akanthus admits them to be beforehand.   At the time when
Athens was a subject-city under Sparta, governed by the Lysandrian Thirty and by the Lacedæmonian harmost in the acropolis,

---

[1] Thucyd. iii, 9; iv, 59–85; vi, 76.

— the sense of indignity arising from the fact of subjection was absorbed in the still more terrible suffering arising from the enormities of those individual rulers whom the imperial state had set up. Now Athens set up no local rulers, — no native Ten or native Thirty, — no resident Athenian harmosts or garrisons. This was of itself an unspeakable exemption, when compared with the condition of cities subject, not only to the Spartan empire, but also under that empire to native decemvirs like Kritias, and Spartan harmosts like Aristarchus or Aristodêmus. A city subject to Athens had to bear definite burdens enforced by its own government, which was liable in case of default or delinquency to be tried before the popular Athenian Dikastery. But this same dikastery (as I have shown in a former volume, and as is distinctly stated by Thucydides)[1] was the harbor of refuge to each subject-city; not less against individual Athenian wrong-doers than against misconduct from other cities. Those who complained of the hardship suffered by a subject-city, from the obligation of bringing causes to be tried in the dikastery of Athens, — even if we take the case as they state it, and overlook the unfairness of omitting those numerous instances wherein the city was thus enabled to avert or redress wrong done to its own citizens, — would have complained both more loudly and with greater justice of an ever-present Athenian harmost; especially if there were coexistent a native government of Ten oligarchs, exchanging with him guilty connivances, like the partnership of the Thirty at Athens with the Lacedæmonian harmost Kallibius.[2]

In no one point can it be shown that the substitution of Spartan empire in place of Athenian was a gain, either for the subject-cities or for Greece generally; while in many points, it was a great and serious aggravation of suffering. And this abuse of power is the more deeply to be regretted, as Sparta enjoyed after the battle of Ægospotami a precious opportunity, — such as Athens had never had, and such as never again recurred, — of reorganizing the Grecian world on wise principles, and with a view to Pan-hellenic stability and harmony. It is not her greatest sin to have refused

---

[1] See the remarkable speech of Phrynichus in Thucyd. viii, 48, 5, which I have before referred to.

[2] Xen. Hellen. ii, 3, 14. Compare the analogous case of Thebes, after the Lacedæmonians had got possession of the Kadmeia (v. 2, 34–36).

to grant universal autonomy. She had indeed promised it; but we might pardon a departure from specific performance, had she exchanged the boon for one far greater, which it was within her reasonable power, at the end of 405 B. C., to confer. That universal town autonomy, towards which the Grecian instinct tended, though immeasurably better than universal subjection, was yet accompanied by much internal discord, and by the still more formidable evil of helplessness against any efficient foreign enemy. To ensure to the Hellenic world external safety as well as internal concord, it was not a new empire which was wanted, but a new political combination on equitable and comprehensive principles; divesting each town of a portion of its autonomy, and creating a common authority, responsible to all, for certain definite controlling purposes. If ever a tolerable federative system would have been practicable in Greece, it was after the battle of Ægospotami. The Athenian empire, — which, with all its defects, I believe to have been much better for the subject-cities than universal autonomy would have been, — had already removed many difficulties, and shown that combined and systematic action of the maritime Grecian world was no impossibility. Sparta might now have substituted herself for Athens, not as heir to the imperial power, but as president and executive agent of a new Confederacy of Delos, — reviving the equal, comprehensive, and liberal principles, on which that confederacy had first been organized.

It is true that sixty years before, the constituent members of the original synod at Delos had shown themselves insensible to its value. As soon as the pressing alarm from Persia had passed over, some had discontinued sending deputies, others had disobeyed requisitions, others again had bought off their obligations, and forfeited their rights as autonomous and voting members, by pecuniary bargain with Athens; who, being obliged by the duties of her presidency to enforce obedience to the Synod against all reluctant members, made successively many enemies, and was gradually converted, almost without her own seeking, from President into Emperor, as the only means of obviating the total dissolution of the Confederacy. But though such untoward circumstances had happened before, it does not follow that they would now have happened again, assuming the same experiment to have been retried by Sparta, with manifest sincerity of purpose and tolerable wisdom. The Grecian world, especially the maritime portion of it, had passed through trials not less painful than instructive, during this important interval. Nor does it seem rash to suppose, that the bulk of its members might now have been disposed to perform steady confederate duties, at the call and under the presidency of Sparta, had she really attempted to reorganize a liberal confederacy, treating every city as autonomous and equal, except in so far as each was bound to obey the resolutions of the general synod. However impracticable such a scheme may appear, we must recollect that even Utopian schemes have their transient moments, if not of certain success, at least of commencement not merely possible but promising. And my belief is, that had Kallikratidas, with his ardent Pan-hellenic sentiment and force of resolution, been the final victor over imperial Athens, he would not have let the moment of pride and omnipotence pass over without essaying some noble project like that sketched above. It is to be remembered that Athens had never had the power of organizing any such generous Pan-hellenic combination. She had become depopularized in the legitimate execution of her trust, as president of the Confederacy of Delos, against refractory members;[1] and had been obliged to choose between breaking up the Confederacy, and keeping it together under the strong compression of an imperial chief. But Sparta had not yet become depopularized. She now stood without competitor as leader of the Grecian world, and might at that moment have reasonably hoped to carry the members of it along with her to any liberal and Pan-hellenic organization, had she attempted it with proper earnestness. Unfortunately she took the opposite course, under the influence of Lysander; founding a new empire far more oppressive and odious than that of Athens, with few of the advantages, and none of the excuses, attached to the latter. As she soon became even more unpopular than Athens, her moment of high tide, for beneficent Pan-hellenic combination, passed away also, — never to return.

Having thus brought all the maritime Greeks under her empire, with a tribute of more than one thousand talents imposed upon them, — and continuing to be chief of her landed alliance in

---

[1] Such is the justification offered by the Athenian envoy at Sparta, immediately before the Peloponnesian war (Thucyd. i, 75, 76). And it is borne out in the main by the narrative of Thucydides himself (i, 99).

Central Greece, which now included Athens as a simple unit, — Sparta was the all-pervading imperial power in Greece.[1]   Her new empire was organized by the victorious Lysander; but with so much arrogance, and so much personal ambition to govern all Greece by means of nominees of his own, decemvirs and harmosts, — that he raised numerous rivals and enemies, as well at Sparta itself as elsewhere. The jealousy entertained by king Pausanias, the offended feelings of Thebes and Corinth, and the manner in which these new phenomena brought about (in spite of the opposition of Lysander) the admission of Athens as a revived democracy into the Lacedæmonian confederacy, — has been already related.

In the early months of 403 B. C., Lysander was partly at home, partly in Attica, exerting himself to sustain the falling oligarchy of Athens against the increasing force of Thrasybulus and the Athenian exiles in Peiræus. In this purpose he was directly thwarted by the opposing views of king Pausanias, and three out of the five ephors.[2]   But though the ephors thus checked Lysander in regard to Athens, they softened the humiliation by sending him abroad to a fresh command on the Asiatic coast and the Hellespont; a step which had the farther advantage of putting asunder two such marked rivals as he and Pausanias had now become. That which Lysander had tried in vain to do at Athens, he was doubtless better able to do in Asia, where he had neither Pausanias nor the ephors along with him. He could lend effective aid to the dekarchies and harmosts in the Asiatic cities, against any internal opposition with which they might be threatened. Bitter were the complaints which reached Sparta, both against him and against his ruling partisans. At length the ephors were prevailed upon to disavow the dekarchies; and to proclaim that they would not hinder the cities from resuming their former governments at pleasure.[3]

But all the crying oppressions set forth in the complaints of the maritime cities would have been insufficient to procure the recall of Lysander from his command in the Hellespont, had not Pharnabazus joined his remonstrances to the rest. These last representations so strengthened the enemies of Lysander at Sparta, that a

---

[1] Xen. Hellen. iii, 1, 3.   πάσης τῆς Ἑλλάδος προστάται, etc.

[2] Xen. Hellen. ii, 4, 28–30.   [3] Xen. Hellen. iii, 4, 2

peremptory order was sent to recall him. Constrained to obey, he
came back to Sparta; but the comparative disgrace, and the loss
of that boundless power which he had enjoyed on his command,
was so insupportable to him, that he obtained permission to go on
a pilgrimage to the temple of Zeus Ammon in Libya, under the plea
that he had a vow to discharge.[1] He appears also to have visited
the temples of Delphi and Dodona,[2] with secret ambitious projects
which will be mentioned presently. This politic withdrawal
softened the jealousy against him, so that we shall find him, after
a year or two, reëstablished in great influence and ascendency.
He was sent as Spartan envoy, at what precise moment we do not
know, to Syracuse, where he lent countenance and aid to the
recently established despotism of Dionysius.[3]

The position of the Asiatic Greeks, along the coast of Ionia, Æo-

---

[1] Plutarch, Lysand. c. 19, 20, 21.

The facts, which Plutarch states respecting Lysander, cannot be reconciled with the chronology which he adopts. He represents the recall of
Lysander at the instance of Pharnabazus, with all the facts which preceded
it, as having occurred prior to the reconstitution of the Athenian democracy, which event we know to have taken place in the summer of 403 B.C.

Lysander captured Samos in the latter half of 404 B. C., after the surren
der of Athens. After the capture of Samos, he came home in triumph, in
the autumn of 404 B. C. (Xen. Hellen. iii, 3, 9). He was at home, or serving
in Attica, in the beginning of 403 B. C. (Xen. Hellen. ii, 4, 30).

Now when Lysander came home at the end of 404 B. C., it was his triumphant return; it was not a recall provoked by complaints of Pharnabazus. Yet there can have been no other return before the restoration of the
democracy at Athens.

The recall of Lysander must have been the termination, not of this command, but of a subsequent command. Moreover, it seems to me necessary,
in order to make room for the facts stated respecting Lysander as well as
about the dekarchies, that we should suppose him to have been again sent
out (after his quarrel with Pausanias in Attica) in 403 B. C., to command
in Asia. This is nowhere positively stated, but I find nothing to contradict
it, and I see no other way of making room for the facts stated about Lysander.

It is to be noted that Diodorus has a decided error in chronology as to
the date of the restoration of the Athenian democracy. He places it in
401 B. C. (Diod. xiv, 33), two years later than its real date, which is 403 B.
c.; thus lengthening by two years the interval between the surrender of
Athens and the reëstablishment of the democracy. Plutarch also seems to
have conceived that interval as much longer than it really was.

[2] Plutarch, Lysand. c. 25.   [3] Plutarch, Lysander, c. 2

lis, and the Hellespont, became very peculiar after the triumph of
Sparta at Ægospotami. I have already recounted how, immediately after the great Athenian catastrophe before Syracuse, the
Persian king had renewed his grasp upon those cities, from which
the vigorous hand of Athens had kept him excluded for more than
fifty years ; how Sparta, bidding for his aid, had consented by
three formal conventions to surrender them to him, while her com-
missioner Lichas even reproved the Milesians for their aversion
to this bargain ; how Athens also, in the days of her weakness,
competing for the same advantage, had expressed her willingness
to pay the same price for it.[1] After the battle of Ægospotami, this
convention was carried into effect ; though seemingly not without
disputes between the satrap Pharnabazus on one side, and Lysander and Derkyllidas on the other.[2] The latter was Lacedæmonian
harmost at Abydos, which town, so important as a station on the
Hellespont, the Lacedæmonians seem still to have retained. But
Pharnabazus and his subordinates acquired more complete command of the Hellespontine Æolis and of the Troad, than ever they
had enjoyed before, both along the coast and in the interior.[3]

Another element, however, soon became operative. The condition of the Greek cities on the coast of Ionia, though according to
Persian regulations they belonged to the satrapy of Tissaphernes,
was now materially determined, — first, by the competing claims
of Cyrus, who wished to take them away from him, and tried to
get such transfer ordered at court, — next, by the aspirations of that
young prince to the Persian throne. As Cyrus rested his hope
of success on Grecian coöperation, it was highly important to him
to render himself popular among the Greeks, especially on his
own side of the Ægean. Partly his own manifestations of just
and conciliatory temper, partly the bad name and known perfidy
of Tissaphernes, induced the Grecian cities with one accord to
revolt from the latter. All threw themselves into the arms of Cyrus, except Miletus, where Tissaphernes interposed in time, slew
the leaders of the intended revolt, and banished many of their partisans. Cyrus, receiving the exiles with distinguished favor, levied
an army to besiege Miletus and procure their restoration ; while

---

Thucyd. viii, 5, 18–37, 56–58, 84.

[2] Plutarch, Lysander, c. 19, 20 ; Xen. Hellen. iii, 1, 9.

[3] Xen. Hellen. iii, 1, 13.

he at the same time threw strong Grecian garrisons into the other cities to protect them against attack.[1]

This local quarrel was, however, soon merged in the more comprehensive dispute respecting the Persian succession. Both parties were found on the field of Kunaxa; Cyrus with the Greek soldiers and Milesian exiles on one side, — Tissaphernes on the other. How that attempt, upon which so much hinged in the future history both of Asia Minor and of Greece, terminated, I have already recounted. Probably the impression brought back by the Lacedæmonian fleet which left Cyrus on the coast of Syria, after he had surmounted the most difficult country without any resistance, was highly favorable to his success. So much the more painful would be the disappointment among the Ionian Greeks when the news of his death was afterwards brought; so much the greater their alarm, when Tissaphernes, having relinquished the pursuit of the Ten Thousand Greeks at the moment when they entered the mountains of Karduchia, came down as victor to the seaboard; more powerful than ever, — rewarded[2] by the Great King, for the services which he had rendered against Cyrus, with all the territory which had been governed by the latter, as well as with the title of commander-in-chief over all the neighboring satraps, — and prepared not only to reconquer, but to punish, the revolted maritime cities. He began by attacking Kymê;[3] ravaging the territory, with great loss to the citizens, and exacting from them a still larger contribution, when the approach of winter rendered it inconvenient to besiege their city.

In such a state of apprehension, these cities sent to Sparta, as the great imperial power of Greece, to entreat her protection against the aggravated slavery impending over them.[4] The Lacedæmonians had nothing farther to expect from the king of Persia, with whom they had already broken the peace by lending aid to Cyrus. Moreover, the fame of the Ten Thousand Greeks, who were now coming home along the Euxine towards Byzantium, had become diffused throughout Greece, inspiring signal contempt for Persian military efficiency, and hopes of enrichment by war against the Asiatic satraps. Accordingly, the Spartan ephors were induced

---

[1] Xen. Anab. i, 1, 8.

[2] Xen. Anab. ii, 3, 19; ii 4, 8; Xen. Aellen. iii, 1, 3; iii, 3, 13.

[3] Diodor. xiv, 35.

[4] Diodor. ut sup.

to comply with the petition of their Asiatic countrymen, and to send over to Asia Thimbron at the head of a considerable force: two thousand Neodamodes (or Helots who had been enfranchised) and four thousand Peloponnesians heavy-armed, accompanied by three hundred Athenian horsemen, out of the number of those who had been adherents of the Thirty, four years before; an aid granted by Athens at the special request of Thimbron. Arriving in Asia during the winter of 400–399 B. C., Thimbron was reinforced in the spring of 399 B. C. by the Cyreian army, who were brought across from Thrace as described in my last chapter, and taken into Lacedæmonian pay. With this large force he became more than a match for the satraps, even on the plains where they could employ their numerous cavalry. The petty Grecian princes of Pergamus and Teuthrania, holding that territory by ancient grants from Xerxes to their ancestors, joined their troops to his, contributing much to enrich Xenophon at the moment of his departure from the Cyreians. Yet Thimbron achieved nothing worthy of so large an army. He not only miscarried in the siege of Larissa, but was even unable to maintain order among his own soldiers, who pillaged indiscriminately both friends and foes.[1] Such loud complaints were transmitted to Sparta of his irregularities and inefficiency, that the ephors first sent him order to march into Karia, where Tissaphernes resided, — and next, before that order was executed, despatched Derkyllidas to supersede him; seemingly in the winter 399–398 B. C. Thimbron on returning to Sparta was fined and banished.[2]

It is highly probable that the Cyreian soldiers, though excellent in the field, yet having been disappointed of reward for the prodigious toils which they had gone through in their long march, and having been kept on short allowance in Thrace, as well as cheated by Seuthes, — were greedy, unscrupulous, and hard to be restrained, in the matter of pillage; especially as Xenophon, their most influential general, had now left them. Their conduct greatly improved under Derkyllidas. And though such improvement was doubtless owing partly to the superiority of the latter over Thimbron, yet it seems also partly ascribable to the fact that

---

[1] Xen. Hellen. iii, 1, 5–8 ; Xen. Anab. vii, 8, 8–1(.

[2] Xen. Hellen. iii, 1, 8; Diodor. xiv, 38.

Xenophon, after a few months of residence at Athens, accompanied him to Asia, and resumed the command of his old comrades.

Derkyllidas was a man of so much resource and cunning, as to have acquired the surname of Sisyphus.[2] He had served throughout all the concluding years of the war, and had been harmost at Abydus during the naval command of Lysander, who condemned him, on the complaint of Pharnabazus, to the disgrace of public exposure with his shield on his arm;[3] this was (I presume) a disgrace, because an officer of rank always had his shield carried for him by an attendant, except in the actual encounter of battle. Having never forgiven Pharnabazus for thus dishonoring him, Derkyllidas now took advantage of a misunderstanding between that satrap and Tissaphernes, to make a truce with the latter, and conduct his army, eight thousand strong, into the territory of the former.[4] The mountainous region of Ida generally known as the Troad, — inhabited by a population of Æolic Greeks (who had gradually Hellenized the indigenous inhabitants), and therefore known as the Æolis of Pharnabazus, — was laid open to him by a recent event, important in itself as well as instructive to read.

The entire Persian empire was parcelled into so many satrapies; each satrap being bound to send a fixed amount of annual tribute, and to hold a certain amount of military force ready, for the court at Susa. Provided he was punctual in fulfilling these obligations, little inquiry was made as to his other proceedings, unless in the rare case of his maltreating some individual Persian of high rank. In like manner, it appears, each satrapy was divided into subsatrapies or districts; each of these held by a deputy, who paid to the satrap a fixed tribute and maintained for him a certain military force, — having liberty to govern in other respects as he

---

[1] There is no positive testimony to this; yet such is my belief, as I have stated at the close of the last chapter. It is certain that Xenophon was serving under Agesilaus in Asia three years after this time; the only matter left for conjecture is, at what precise moment he went out the second time. The marked improvement in the Cyreian soldiers, is one reason for the statement in the text; another reason is, the great detail with which the military operations of Derkyllidas are described, rendering it probable that the narrative is from an eye-witness.

[2] Xen. Hellen. iii, 1, 8; Ephorus, ap Athenæ. xi, p. 500.

[3] Xen. Hellen. iii, 1, 9. ἐστάθη τὴν ἀσπίδα ἔχων.

[4] Xen. Hellen. iii, 1, 10; iii, 2, 28.

pleased. Besides the tribute, however, presents of undefined amount were of constant occurrence, both from the satrap to the king, and from the deputy to the satrap. Nevertheless, enough was extorted from the people (we need hardly add), to leave ar ample profit both to the one and to the other.[1]

This region, called Æolis, had been entrusted by Pharnabazus to a native of Dardanus named Zênis, who, after holding the post for some time and giving full satisfaction, died of illness, leaving a widow with a son and daughter still minors. The satrap was on the point of giving the district to another person, when Mania, the widow of Zênis, herself a native of Dardanus, preferred her petition to be allowed to succeed her husband. Visiting Pharnabazus with money in hand, sufficient not only to satisfy himself, but also to gain over his mistresses and his ministers,[2] — she said to him, — " My husband was faithful to you, and paid his tribute so regularly as to obtain your thanks. If I serve you no worse than he, why should you name any other deputy? If I fail in giving you satisfaction, you can always remove me, and give the place to another." Pharnabazus granted her petition, and had no cause to repent it. Mania was regular in her payment of tribute, — frequent in bringing him presents, — and splendid, beyond any of his other deputies, in her manner of receiving him whenever he visited the district.

Her chief residence was at Skêpsis, Gergis, and Kebrên, — inland towns, strong both by position and by fortification, amidst the mountainous region once belonging to the Teukri Gergithes. It was here too that she kept her treasures, which, partly left by her husband, partly accumulated by herself, had gradually reached an enormous sum. But her district also reached down to the coast, comprising among other towns the classical name of Ilium, and prob-

---

See the description of the satrapy of Cyrus (Xenoph. Anab. i, 9, 19, 21, 22). In the main, this division and subdivision of the entire empire into revenue-districts, each held by a nominee responsible for payment of the rent or tribute, to the government or to some higher officer of the government — is the system prevalent throughout a large portion of Asia to the present day.

[2] Xen. Hellen. iii, 1, 10. Ἀναζεύξασα τὸν στόλον, καὶ χρήματα λαβοῦσα, ὥστε καὶ αὐτῷ Φαρναβάζῳ δοῦναι, καὶ ταῖς παλλακίσιν αὐτοῦ χαρίσασθαι καὶ οἷς δυναμένοις μάλιστα παρὰ Φαρναβάζῳ, ἐπορεύετο.

ably her own native city, the neighboring Dardanus. She maintained, besides, a large military force of Grecian mercenaries in regular pay and excellent condition, which she employed both as garrison for each of her dependent towns, and as means for conquest in the neighborhood. She had thus reduced the maritime towns of Larissa, Hamaxitus, and Kolônæ, in the southern part of the Troad; commanding her troops in person, sitting in her chariot to witness the attack, and rewarding every one who distinguished himself. Moreover, when Pharnabazus undertook an expedition against the predatory Mysians or Pisidians, she accompanied him, and her military force formed so much the best part of his army, that he paid her the highest compliments, and sometimes condescended to ask her advice.[1] So, when Xerxes invaded Greece, Artemisia, queen of Halikarnassus, not only furnished ships among the best appointed in his fleet, and fought bravely at Salamis, but also, when he chose to call a council, stood alone, in daring to give him sound opinions contrary to his own leanings; opinions which, fortunately for the Grecian world, he could bring himself only to tolerate, not to follow.[2]

Under an energetic woman like Mania, thus victorious and wellprovided, Æolis was the most defensible part of the satrapy of Pharnabazus, and might probably have defied Derkyllidas, had not a domestic traitor put an end to her life. Her son-in-law, Meidias, a Greek of Skêpsis, with whom she lived on terms of intimate confidence — " though she was scrupulously mistrustful of every one else, as it is proper for a despot to be," [3] — was so inflamed by his own ambition and by the suggestions of evil counsellors, who told him it was a shame that a woman should thus be ruler while

---

[1] Xen. Hellen. iii, 1, 15.   [2] Herod. viii, 69.

[3] Such is the emphatic language of Xenophon (Hellen. iii, 1, 14) — Μει-δίας, θυγατρὸς ἀνὴρ αὐτῆς, ὢν, ἀναπτερωθεὶς ὑπό τινων, ὡς αἰσχρὸν εἴη, γυναῖκα μὲν ἄρχειν, αὐτὸν δ' ἰδιώτην εἶναι, τοὺς μὲν ἄλλους μάλα φυλαττομένης αὐτῆς, ὥσπερ ἐν τυραννίδι προσήκει, ἐκείνῳ δὲ πιστευούσης καὶ ἀσπαζομένης, ὥσπερ ἂν γυνὴ γαμβρὸν ἀσπάζοιτο, — εἰσελθὼν ἀποπνῖξαι αὐτὴν λέγεται.

For the illustration of this habitual insecurity in which the Grecian despot lived, see the dialogue of Xenophon called Hieron (i, 12; ii, 8–10; vii, 10). He particularly dwells upon the multitude of family crimes which stained the houses of the Grecian despots; murders by fathers, sons, brothers, wives, etc. (iii, 8).

he was only a private man, that he strangled her in her chamber.
Following up his nefarious scheme, he also assassinated her son, a
beautiful youth of seventeen. He succeeded in getting possession
of the three strongest places in the district, Kebrên, Skêpsis, and
Gergis, together with the accumulated treasure of Mania; but the
commanders in the other towns refused obedience to his summons,
until they should receive orders from Pharnabazus. To that satrap Meidias instantly sent envoys, bearing ample presents, with a
petition that the satrap would grant to him the district which had
been enjoyed by Mania. Pharnabazus, repudiating the presents,
sent an indignant reply to Meidias,— "Keep them until I come to
seize them, and seize you, too, along with them. I would not
consent to live, if I were not to avenge the death of Mania." [1]

At that critical moment, prior to the coming of the satrap, Derkyllidas presented himself with his army, and found Æolis almost
defenceless. The three recent conquests of Mania, — Larissa,
Hamaxitus, and Kolônæ, surrendered to him as soon as he appeared; while the garrisons of Ilium and some other places, who
had taken special service under Mania, and found themselves
worse off now that they had lost her, accepted his invitation to
renounce Persian dependence, declare themselves allies of Sparta,
and hold their cities for him. He thus became master of most
part of the district, with the exception of Kebrên, Skêpsis, and
Gergis, which he was anxious to secure before the arrival of Pharnabazus. On arriving before Kebrên, however, in spite of this
necessity for haste, he remained inactive for four days,[2] because
the sacrifices were unpropitious; while a rash, subordinate officer,
hazarding an unwarranted attack during this interval, was repulsed
and wounded. The sacrifices at length became favorable, and
Derkyllidas was rewarded for his patience. The garrison, affected
by the example of those at Ilium and the other towns, disobeyed

---

[1] Xen. Hellen. iii, 1, 13.

[2] Xen. Hellen. iii, 1, 18; Diodor. xiv, 38.

The reader will remark here how Xenophon shapes the narrative in such
a manner as to inculcate the pious duty in a general of obeying the warnings furnished by the sacrifice, — either for action or for inaction. I have
already noticed (in my preceding chapters) how often he does this in the
Anabasis.

Such an inference is never (I believe) to be found suggested in Thucydides.

their commander, who tried to earn the satrap's favor by holding out and assuring to him this very strong place. Sending out heralds to proclaim that they would go with Greeks and not with Persians, they admitted the Lacedæmonians at once within the gates. Having thus fortunately captured, and duly secured this important town, Derkyllidas marched against Skêpsis and Gergis, the former of which was held by Meidias himself; who, dreading the arrival of Pharnabazus, and mistrusting the citizens within, thought it best to open negotiations with Derkyllidas. He sent to solicit a conference, demanding hostages for his safety. When he came forth from the town, and demanded from the Lacedæmonian commander on what terms alliance would be granted to him, the atter replied, — " On condition that the citizens shall be left free nd autonomous;" at the same time marching on, without waiting ither for acquiescence or refusal, straight up to the gates of the t⌐wn. Meidias, taken by surprise, in the power of the assailants, and aware that the citizens were unfriendly to him, was obliged to give orders that the gates should be opened; so that Derkyllidas found himself by this manœuvre in possession of the strongest place in the district without either loss or delay, — to the great delight of the Skepsians themselves.[1]

Derkillydas, having ascended the acropolis of Skêpsis to offer a sacrifice of thanks to Athênê, the great patron goddess of Ilium and most of the Teukrian towns, — caused the garrison of Meidias to evacuate the town forthwith, and consigned it to the citizens themselves, exhorting them to conduct their political affairs as became Greeks and freemen. This proceeding, which reminds us of Brasidas in contrast with Lysander, was not less politic than generous; since Derkyllidas could hardly hope to hold an inland town in the midst of the Persian satrapy except by the attachments of the citizens themselves. He then marched away to Gergis, still conducting along with him Meidias, who urgently entreated to be allowed to retain that town, the last of his remaining fortresses. Without giving any decided answer, Derkyllidas took him by his side, and marched with him at the head of his army, arrayed only in double file, so as to carry the appearance of peace, to the foot of the lofty towers of Gergis. The garrison on the

---

Xen. Hellen. iii, , 20–23.

walls, seeing Meidias along with him, allowed him to approach without discharging a single missile. "Now, Meidias (said he), order the gates to be opened, and show me the way in, to the temple of Athênê, in order that I may there offer sacrifice." Again Meidias was forced, from fear of being at once seized as a prisoner, to give the order; and the Lacedæmonian forces found themselves in possession of the town. Derkyllidas, distributing his troops around the walls, in order to make sure of his conquest, ascended to the acropolis to offer his intended sacrifice; after which he proceeded to dictate the fate of Meidias, whom he divested of his character of prince and of his military force, — incorporating the latter in the Lacedæmonian army. He then called upon Meidias to specify all his paternal property, and restored to him the whole of what he claimed as such, though the bystanders protested against the statement given in as a flagrant exaggeration. But he laid hands on all the property, and all the treasures of Mania, — and caused her house, which Meidias had taken for himself, to be put under seal, — as lawful prey; since Mania had belonged to Pharnabazus,[1] against whom the Lacedæmonians were making war. On coming out after examining and verifying the contents of the house, he said to his officers, "Now, my friends, we have here already worked out pay for the whole army, eight thousand men, for nearly a year. Whatever we acquire besides, shall come to you also." He well knew the favorable effect which this intelligence would produce upon the temper, as well as upon the disci-

---

[1] Xen. Hellen. iii, 1, 26. Εἰπέ μοι, ἔφη, Μανία δὲ τίνος ἦν; Οἱ δὲ πάντες εἶπον, ὅτι Φαρναβάζου. Οὐκοῦν καὶ τὰ ἐκείνης, ἔφη, Φαρναβάζου; Μάλιστα, ἔφασαν. Ἡμέτερ᾽ ἂν εἴη, ἔφη, ἐπεὶ κρατοῦμεν· πολέμιος γὰρ ἡμῖν Φαρνάβαζος.

Two points are remarkable here. 1. The manner in which Mania, the administratrix of a large district, with a prodigious treasure and a large army in pay, is treated as *belonging* to Pharnabazus — as the servant or slave of Pharnabazus. 2. The distinction here taken between public property and private property, in reference to the laws of war and the rights of the conqueror. Derkyllidas lays claim to that which had belonged to Mania (or to Pharnabazus); but *not* to that which had belonged to Meidias.

According to the modern rules of international law, this distinction is one allowed and respected, everywhere except at sea. But in the ancient world, it by no means stood out so clearly or prominently; and the observance of 't here deserves notice.

pline of the army. — especially upon the Cyreians, who had tasted the discomfort of irregular pay and poverty.

" And where am I to live?" asked Meidias, who found himself turned out of the house of Mania. "In your rightful place of abode, to be sure (replied Derkyllidas); in your native town Skêpsis, and in your paternal house.¹" What became of the assassin afterwards, we do not hear. But it is satisfactory to find that he did not reap the anticipated reward of his crime; the fruits of which were an important advantage to Derkyllidas and his army, — and a still more important blessing to the Greek cities which had been governed by Mania, — enfranchisement and autonomy.

This rapid, easy, and skilfully managed exploit, — the capture of nine towns in eight days, — is all which Xenophon mentions as achieved by Derkyllidas during the summer. Having acquired pay for so many months, perhaps the soldiers may have been disposed to rest until it was spent. But as winter approached, it became necessary to find winter quarters, without incurring the reproach which had fallen upon Thimbron of consuming the substance of allies. Fearing, however, that if he changed his position, Pharnabazus would employ the numerous Persian cavalry to harass the Grecian cities, he tendered a truce, which the latter willingly accepted. For the occupation of Æolis by the Lacedæmonian general was a sort of watch-post (like Dekeleia to Athens,) exposing the whole of Phrygia near the Propontis (in which was Daskylium the residence of Pharnabazus) to constant attack.² Derkyllidas accordingly only marched through Phrygia, to take up his winter quarters in Bithynia, the north-western corner of Asia Minor, between the Propontis and the Euxine; the same territory through which Xenophon and the Ten Thousand had marched, on their road from Kalpê to Chalkêdon. He procured

---

· Xen. Hellen. iii, 1, 28.

Thus finishes the interesting narrative about Mania, Meidias, and Derkyllidas. The abundance of detail, and the dramatic manner, in which Xenophon has worked it out, impress me with a belief that he was actually present at the scene.

² Xen. Hellen. iii, 2, 1. *νομίζων τὴν Αἰολίδα ἐπιτετειχίσθαι τῇ ἑαυτοῦ οἰκήσει Φρυγίᾳ.*

The word *ἐπιτειχίζειν* is capital and significant, in Grecian warfare.

abundant provisions and booty, slaves as well as cattle, by plundering the Bithynian villages; not without occasional losses on his own side, by the carelessness of marauding parties.[1]

One of these losses was of considerable magnitude. Derkyllidas had obtained from Seuthes in European Thrace (the same prince of whom Xenophon had so much reason to complain) a reinforcement of three hundred cavalry and two hundred peltasts, — Odrysian Thracians. These Odrysians established themselves in a separate camp, nearly two miles and a half from Derkyllidas, which they surrounded with a palisade about man's height. Being indefatigable plunderers, they prevailed upon Derkyllidas to send them a guard of two hundred hoplites, for the purpose of guarding their separate camp with the booty accumulated within it. Presently the camp became richly stocked, especially with Bithynian captives. The hostile Bithynians, however, watching their opportunity when the Odrysians were out marauding, suddenly attacked at daybreak the two hundred Grecian hoplites in the camp. Shooting at them over the palisade with darts and arrows, they killed and wounded some, while the Greeks with their spears were utterly helpless, and could only reach their enemies by pulling up the palisade and charging out upon them ; but the light-armed assailants, easily evading the charge of warriors with shield and spear, turned round upon them when they began to retire, and slew several before they could get back. In each successive sally the same phenomena recurred, until at length all the Greeks were overpowered and slain, except fifteen of them, who charged through the Odrysians in the first sally, and marched onward to join Derkyllidas, instead of returning with their comrades to the palisade. Derkyllidas lost no time in sending a reinforcement, which, however, came too late, and found only the naked bodies of the slain. The victorious Bithynians carried away all their own captives.[2]

At the beginning of spring the Spartan general returned to Lampsakus, where he found Arakus and two other Spartans, just arrived out as commissioners sent by the ephors. Arakus came with instructions to prolong the command of Derkyllidas for another year ; as well as to communicate the satisfaction of the ephors with the Cyreian army, in consequence of the great im-

---

[1] Xen. Hellen. iii, 2, 2–5.   [2] Xen. Hellen. iii, 2, 4.

provement in their conduct, compared with the year of Thimbron. He accordingly assembled the soldiers, and addressed them in a mingled strain of praise and admonition ; expressing his hope that they would continue the forbearance which they had now begun to practise towards all Asiatic allies. The commander of the Cyreians (probably Xenophon himself), in his reply, availed himself of the occasion to pay a compliment to Derkyllidas. " We (said he) are the same men now as we were in the previous year ; but we are under a different general ; you need not look farther for the explanation.[1] " Without denying the superiority of Derkyllidas over his predecessor, we may remark that the abundant wealth of Mania, thrown into his hands by accident (though he showed great ability in turning the accident to account), was an auxiliary circumstance, not less unexpected than weighty, for ensuring the good behavior of the soldiers.

It was among the farther instructions of Arakus to visit all the principal Asiatic Greeks, and report their condition at Sparta ; and Derkyllidas was pleased to see them entering on this survey at a moment when they would find the cities in undisturbed peace and tranquillity.[2] So long as the truce continued both with Tissaphernes and Pharnabazus, these cities were secure from aggression, and paid no tribute ; the land-force of Derkyllidas affording to

---

[1] Xen. Hellen. iii, 2, 6, 7.

Morus supposes (I think, with much probability) that ὁ τῶν Κυρείων προεστηκὼς here means Xenophon himself.

He could not with propriety advert to the fact that he himself had not been with the army during the year of Thimbron.

[2] Xen. Hellen. iii, 2, 9. ἔπεμψεν αὐτοὺς ἀπ' Ἐφέσου διὰ τῶν Ἑλληνιδων πόλεων, ἡδόμενος ὅτι ἔμελλον ὄψεσθαι τὰς πόλεις ἐν εἰρήνῃ εὐδαιμονικῶς διαγούσας. I cannot but think that we ought here to read ἐπ' Ἐφέσου, not ἀπ' Ἐφέσου ; or else ἀπὸ Λαμψάκου.

It was at Lampsakus that this interview and conversation between Derkyllidas and the commissioners took place. The commissioners were to be sent from Lampsakus to Ephesus through the Grecian cities.

The expression ἐν εἰρήνῃ εὐδαιμονικῶς διαγούσας has reference to the foreign relations of the cities, and to their exemption from annoyance by Persian arms, — without implying any internal freedom or good condition. There were Lacedæmonian harmosts in most of them, and dekarchies half broken up or modified in many ; see the subsequent passages (iii, 2, 20 ; iii, t. 7 ; iv, 8, 1)

them a protection[1] analogous to that which had been conferred by Athens and her powerful fleet, during the interval between the formation of the Confederacy of Delos and the Athenian catastrophe at Syracuse. At the same time, during the truce, the army had neither occupation nor subsistence. To keep it together and near at hand, yet without living at the cost of friends, was the problem. It was accordingly with great satisfaction that Derkyllidas noticed an intimation accidentally dropped by Arakus. Some envoys (the latter said) were now at Sparta from the Thracian Chersonesus (the long tongue of land bordering westward on the Hellespont), soliciting aid against their marauding Thracian neighbors. That fertile peninsula, first hellenized a century and a half before by the Athenian Miltiades, had been a favorite resort for Athenian citizens, many of whom had acquired property there during the naval power of Athens. The battle of Ægospotami dispossessed and drove home these proprietors, at the same time depriving the peninsula of its protection against the Thracians. It now contained eleven distinct cities, of which Sestos was the most important; and its inhabitants combined to send envoys to Sparta, entreating the ephors to send out a force for the purpose of building a wall across the isthmus from Kardia to Paktyê; in recompense for which (they said) there was fertile land enough open to as many settlers as chose to come, with coast and harbors for export close at hand. Miltiades, on first going out to the Chersonese, had secured it by constructing a cross-wall on the same spot, which had since become neglected during the period of Persian supremacy; Perikles had afterwards sent fresh colonists, and caused the wall to be repaired. But it seems to have been unnecessary while the Athenian empire was in full vigor,— since the Thracian princes had been generally either conciliated, or kept off, by Athens, even without any such bulwark.[2] Informed that the request of the Chersonesites had been favorably listened to at Sparta, Derkyllidas resolved to execute their project with his own army. Having prolonged his truce with Pharnabazus, he crossed the Hellespont into Europe, and employed his army during the whole summer in constructing this cross-wall, about four and a

---

[1] Compare Xen. Hellen. iv, 2, 5.

[2] Herodot. vi, 36; Plutarch, Perikles, c. 19; Isokrates, Or. v, (Philipp. s. 7

quarter miles in length. The work was distributed in portions to different sections of the army, competition being excited by rewards for the most rapid and workmanlike execution; while the Chersonesites were glad to provide pay and subsistence for the army, during an operation which provided security for all the eleven cities, and gave additional value to their lands and harbors. Numerous settlers seem to have now come in, under Lacedæmonian auspices, — who were again disturbed, wholly or partially, when the Lacedæmonian maritime empire was broken up a few years afterwards.[1]

On returning to Asia in the autumn, after the completion of this work, which had kept his army usefully employed and amply provided during six months, Derkyllidas undertook the siege of Artaneus, a strong post (on the continental coast eastward of Mitylênê) occupied by some Chian exiles, whom the Lacedæmonian admiral Kratesippidas had lent corrupt aid in expelling from their native island a few years before.[2] These men, living by predatory expeditions against Chios and Ionia, were so well supplied with provisions that it cost Derkyllidas a blockade of eight months before he could reduce it. He placed in it a strong garrison well supplied, that it might serve him as a retreat in case of need, — under an Achæan named Drako, whose name remained long terrible from his ravages on the neighboring plain of Mysia.[3]

Derkyllidas next proceeded to Ephesus, where orders presently reached him from the ephors, directing him to march into Karia and attack Tissaphernes. The temporary truce which had hitherto provisionally kept off Persian soldiers and tribute-gatherers from the Asiatic Greeks, was now renounced by mutual consent. These Greeks had sent envoys to Sparta, assuring the ephors that Tissaphernes would be constrained to renounce formally the sovereign rights of Persia, and grant to them full autonomy, if his residence in Karia were vigorously attacked. Accordingly Derkyllidas marched southward across the Mæander into Karia, while the Lacedæmonian fleet under Pharax coöperated along the shore At the same time Tissaphernes, on his side, had received rein forcements from Susa, together with the appointment of generalis simo over all the Persian force in Asia Minor; upon which Phar·

---

[1] Xen. Hellen. iii, 2, 10; iv, 8, 5.   Diodor. xiv, 38.

[2] Diodor. xiii, 65.

[3] Xen. Hellen. iii, 2, 11; Isokrates, Or. iv, (Panegyr.) s. 167,

nabazus (who had gone up to court in the interval to concert more vigorous means of prosecuting the war, but had now returned)[1] joined him in Karia, prepared to commence vigorous operations for the expulsion of Derkyllidas and his army. Having properly garrisoned the strong places, the two satraps crossed the Mæander at the head of a powerful Grecian and Karian force, with numerous Persian cavalry, to attack the Ionian cities. As soon as he heard this news, Derkyllidas came back with his army from Karia, to cover the towns menaced. Having recrossed the Meander, he was marching with his army in disorder, not suspecting the enemy to be near, when on a sudden he came upon their scouts, planted on some sepulchral monuments in the road. He also sent some scouts up to the neighboring monuments and towers, who apprised him that the two satraps, with their joint force in good order, were planted here to intercept him. He immediately gave orders for his hoplites to form in battle array of eight deep, with the peltasts, and his handful of horsemen, on each flank. But such was the alarm caused among his troops by this surprise, that none could be relied upon except the Cyreians and the Peloponnesians. Of the insular and Ionian hoplites, from Priênê and other cities, some actually hid their arms in the thick standing corn, and fled; others, who took their places in the line, manifested dispositions which left little hope that they would stand a charge; so that the Persians had the opportunity of fighting a battle not merely with superiority of number, but also with advantage of position and circumstances. Pharnabazus was anxious to attack without delay. But Tissaphernes, who recollected well the valor of the Cyreian troops, and concluded that all the remaining Greeks were like them, forbade it; sending forward heralds to demand a conference. As they approached, Derkyllidas, surrounding himself with a body-guard of the finest and best-equipped soldiers,[2] advanced to the front of the line to meet them; saying that he, for his part, was prepared

---

[1] Diodor. xiv, 39.

[2] Xen. Hellen. iii, 2, 18.

In the Anabasis (ii, 3, 3) Xenophon mentions the like care on the part of Klearchus, to have the best armed and most imposing soldiers around him, when he went to his interview with Tissaphernes.

Xenophon gladly avails himself of the opportunity, to pay an indirect compliment to the Cyreian army.

right, — but since a conference was demanded, he had no objection to grant it, provided hostages were exchanged. This having been assented to, and a place named for conference on the ensuing day, both armies were simultaneously withdrawn; the Persians to Tralles, the Greeks to Leukophrys, celebrated for its temple of Artemis Leukophryne.[1]

This backwardness on the part of Tissaphernes even at a time when he was encouraged by a brother satrap braver than himself, occasioned to the Persians the loss of a very promising moment, and rescued the Grecian army out of a position of much peril. It helps to explain to us the escape of the Cyreians, and the manner in which they were allowed to cross rivers and pass over the most difficult ground without any serious opposition; while at the same time it tended to confirm in the Greek mind the same impressions of Persian imbecility as that escape so forcibly suggested.

The conference, as might be expected, ended in nothing. Derkyllidas required on behalf of the Asiatic Greeks complete autonomy, — exemption from Persian interference and tribute; while the two satraps on their side insisted that the Lacedæmonian army should be withdrawn from Asia, and the Lacedæmonian harmosts from all the Greco-Asiatic cities. An armistice was concluded, to allow time for reference to the authorities at home; thus replacing matters in the condition in which they had been at the beginning of the year.[2]

Shortly after the conclusion of this truce, Agesilaus, king of Sparta, arrived with a large force, and the war in all respects began to assume larger proportions, — of which more in the next chapter.

But it was not in Asia alone that Sparta had been engaged in war. The prostration of the Athenian power had removed that common bond of hatred and alarm which attached the allies to her headship; while her subsequent conduct had given positive offence, and had even excited against herself the same fear of unmeasured imperial ambition which had before run so powerfully against Athens. She had appropriated to herself nearly the whole of the Athenian maritime empire, with a tribute scarcely inferior, if at all inferior, in amount. How far the total of one thousand talents was actually realised during each successive year, we are not in a

---

Xen. Hellen. iii, 2, 19; Diodo: xiv, 39.   [2] Xen. Hellen. iii, 2, 20.

condition to say; but such was the assessment imposed and the scheme laid down by Sparta for her maritime dependencies, — enforced too by omnipresent instruments of rapacity and oppression, decemvirs and harmosts, such as Athens had never paralleled. When we add to this great maritime empire the prodigious ascendency on land which Sparta had enjoyed before, we shall find a total of material power far superior to that which Athens had enjoyed, even in her day of greatest exaltation, prior to the truce of 445 B. C.

This was not all. From the general dulness of character pervading Spartan citizens, the full resources of the state were hardly ever put forth. Her habitual short-comings at the moment of action are keenly criticised by her own friends, in contrast with the ardor and forwardness which animated her enemies. But at and after the battle of Ægospotami, the entire management of Spartan foreign affairs was found in the hands of Lysander; a man not only exempt from the inertia usual in his countrymen, but of the most unwearied activity and grasping ambition, as well for his country as for himself. Under his direction the immense advantages which Sparta enjoyed from her new position were at once systematized and turned to the fullest account. Now there was enough in the new ascendency of Sparta, had it been ever so modestly handled, to spread apprehension through the Grecian world. But apprehension became redoubled, when it was seen that her ascendency was organized and likely to be worked by her most aggressive leader for the purposes of an insatiable ambition. Fortunately for the Grecian world, indeed, the power of Sparta did not long continue to be thus absolutely wielded by Lysander, whose arrogance and overweening position raised enemies against him at home. Yet the first impressions received by the allies respecting Spartan empire, were derived from his proceedings and his plans of dominion, manifested with ostentatious insolence; and such impressions continued, even after the influence of Lysander himself had been much abated by the counterworking rivalry of Pausanias and others.

While Sparta separately had thus gained so much by the close of the war, not one of her allies had received the smallest remuneration or compensation, except such as might be considered to be involved in the destruction of a formidable enemy. Even the

pecuniary result or residue which Lysander had brought home
with him (four hundred and seventy talents remaining out of the
advances made by Cyrus), together with the booty acquired at
Dekeleia, was all detained by the Lacedæmonians themselves.
Thebes and Corinth indeed presented demands, in which the other
allies did not (probably durst not) join, to be allowed to share.
But though all the efforts and sufferings of the war had fallen upon
these allies no less than upon Sparta, the demands were refused,
and almost resented as insults.[1]   Hence there arose among the
allies not merely a fear of the grasping dominion, but a hatred of
the monopolizing rapacity, of Sparta. Of this new feeling, an early
manifestation, alike glaring and important, was made by the Thebans and Corinthians, when they refused to join Pausanias in his
march against Thrasybulus and the Athenian exiles in Peiræus,[2]
— less than a year after the surrender of Athens, the enemy whom
these two cities had hated with such extreme bitterness down to
the very moment of surrender.   Even Arcadians and Achæans
too, habitually obedient as they were to Lacedæmon, keenly felt
the different way in which she treated them, as compared with the
previous years of war, when she had been forced to keep alive
their zeal against the common enemy.[3]

The Lacedæmonians were however strong enough not merely
to despise this growing alienation of their allies, but even to take
revenge upon such of the Peloponnesians as had incurred their
displeasure.   Among these stood conspicuous the Eleians ; now
under a government called democratical, of which the leading man
was Thrasydæus, — a man who had lent considerable aid in 404
B. C. to Thrasybulus and the Athenian exiles in Peiræus.   The
Eleians, in the year 420 B. C., had been engaged in a controversy
with Sparta, — had employed their privileges as administrators

---

[1] Xenoph. Hellen. iii, 5, 5 ; Plutarch, Lysand. c. 27 ; Justin, v, 10.

[2] Xen. Hellen. ii, 4, 30.

[3] Xen. Hellen. iii, 5, 12.   Κορινθίους δὲ καὶ ᾽Αρκαδας καὶ ᾽Αχαίους τι φῶ-
μεν ; οἱ ἐν μὲν τῷ πρὸς ὑμᾶς (it is the Theban envoys who are addressing
the public assembly at Athens) πολέμῳ μάλα λιπαρούμενοι ὑπ᾽ ἐκε
ίνων (the Lacedæmonians), πάντων καὶ πόνων καὶ κινδύνων καὶ δαπανημά-
των μετεῖχον· ἐπεὶ δ᾽ ἔπραξαν ἃ ἐβούλοντο οἱ Λακεδαιμόνιοι, ποίας ἢ ἀρχῆς ἢ
τιμῆς ἢ ποίων χρημάτων μετσδεδώκασιν αὐτοῖς ; ἀλλὰ τοὺς μὲν εἱλώτας ἁρμοσ
τὰς καθιστάναι ἀξιοῦσι, τῶν δὲ ξυμμάχων ἐλευθέριν ὄντων, ἐπεὶ εὐτύχησαν
δεσπόται ἀναπεφήνασιν.

of the Olympic festival to exclude her from attendance on that occasion, — and had subsequently been in arms against her along with Argos and Mantineia. To these grounds of quarrel, now of rather ancient date, had been added afterwards, a refusal to furnish aid in the war against Athens since the resumption of hostilities in 414 B. C., and a recent exclusion of king Agis, who had come in person to offer sacrifice and consult the oracle of Zeus Olympius; such exclusion being grounded on the fact that he was about to pray for victory in the war then pending against Athens, contrary to the ancient canon of the Olympic temple, which admitted no sacrifice or consultation respecting hostilities of Greek against Greek.[1] These were considered by Sparta as affronts ; and the season was now favorable for resenting them, as well as for chastising and humbling Elis.[2] Accordingly Sparta sent an embassy, requiring the Eleians to make good the unpaid arrears of the quota assessed upon them for the cost of the war against Athens ; and farther, — to relinquish their authority over their dependent townships or Perioeki, leaving the latter autonomous.[3] Of these dependencies there were several, no one very considerable individually, in the region called Triphylia, south of the river Alpheus, and north of the Neda. One of them was Lepreum, the autonomy of which the Lacedæmonians had vindicated against Elis in 420 B. C., though during the subsequent period it had again become subject.

---

[1] Xen. Hellen. iii, 2, 22.

Τούτων δ᾽ ὕστερον, καὶ Ἄγιδος πεμφθέντος θῦσαι τῷ Διὶ κατὰ μαντείαν τινα, ἐκώλυον οἱ Ἠλεῖοι, μὴ προσεύχεσθαι νίκην πολέμου, λέγοντες, ὡς καὶ τὸ ἀρχαῖον εἴη οὕτω νόμιμον, μὴ χρηστηριάζεσθαι τοὺς Ἕλληνας ἐφ᾽ Ἕλληνωι πολέμῳ· ὥστε ἄθυτος ἀπῆλθεν.

This canon seems not unnatural, for one of the greatest Pan-hellenic temples and establishments. Yet it was not constantly observed at Olympia (compare another example — Xen. Hellen. iv, 7, 2) ; nor yet at Delphi, which was not less Pan-hellenic than Olympia (see Thucyd. i, 118). We are therefore led to imagine that it was a canon which the Eleians invoked only when they were prompted by some special sentiment or aversion.

[2] Xen. Hellen. iii, 2, 23. Ἐκ τούτων οὖν πάντων ὀργιζομένοις, ἔδοξε τοῖς ἐφόροις καὶ τῇ ἐκκλησίᾳ, σωφρονίσαι αὐτούς.

[3] Diodorus (xiv, 17) mentions this demand for the arrears ; which appears very probable. It is not directly noticed by Xenophon, who however mentions (see the passage cited in the note of page preceding) the general assessment levied by Sparta upon all her Peloponnesian allies during the war

The Eleians refused compliance with the demand thus sent, alleging that their dependent cities were held by the right of conquest. They even retorted upon the Lacedæmonians the charge of enslaving Greeks;[1] upon which Agis marched with an army to invade their territory, entering it from the north side where it joined Achaia. Hardly had he crossed the frontier river Larissus and begun his ravages, when an earthquake occurred. Such an event, usually construed in Greece as a divine warning, acted on this occasion so strongly on the religious susceptibilities of Agis, that he not only withdrew from the Eleian territory, but disbanded his army. His retreat gave so much additional courage to the Eleians, that they sent envoys and tried to establish alliances among those cities which they knew to be alienated from Sparta. Not even Thebes and Corinth, however, could be induced to assist them; nor did they obtain any other aid except one thousand men from Ætolia.

In the next summer Agis undertook a second expedition, accompanied on this occasion by all the allies of Sparta; even by the Athenians, now enrolled upon the list. Thebes and Corinth alone stood aloof. On this occasion he approached from the opposite or southern side, that of the territory once called Messenia; passing through Aulon, and crossing the river Neda. He marched through Triphylia to the river Alpheius, which he crossed, and then proceeded to Olympia, where he consummated the sacrifice from which the Eleians had before excluded him. In his march he was joined by the inhabitants of Lepreum, Makistus, and other dependent towns, which now threw off their subjection to Elis. Thus reinforced, Agis proceeded onward towards the city of Elis, through a productive country under flourishing agriculture, enriched by the crowds and sacrifices at the neighboring Olympic temple, and for

---

[1] Diodor. xiv, 17.

Diodorus introduces in these transactions King Pausanias, not King Agis, as the acting person.

Pausanias states (iii, 8, 2) that the Eleians, in returning a negative answer to the requisition of Sparta, added that they would enfranchise their Periœki, when they saw Sparta enfranchise her own. This answer appears to me highly improbable, under the existing circumstances of Sparta and her relations to the other Grecian states. Allusion to the relations between Sparta and her Periœki was a novelty, even in 371 B. C., at the congress which preceded the battle of Leuktra.

a long period unassailed. After attacking, not very vigorously, the half-fortified city, — and being repelled by the Ætolian auxiliaries, — he marched onward to the harbor called Kyllênê, still plundering the territory. So ample was the stock of slaves, cattle, and rural wealth generally, that his troops not only acquired riches for themselves by plunder, but were also joined by many Arcadian and Achæan volunteers, who crowded in to partake of the golden harvest.[1]

The opposition or wealthy oligarchical party in Elis availed themselves of this juncture to take arms against the government; hoping to get possession of the city, and to maintain themselves in power by the aid of Sparta. Xenias their leader, a man of immense wealth, with several of his adherents, rushed out armed, and assailed the government-house, in which it appears that Thrasydæus and his colleagues had been banqueting. They slew several persons, and among them one, whom, from great personal resemblance, they mistook for Thrasydæus. The latter was however at that moment intoxicated, and asleep in a separate chamber.[2] They then assembled in arms in the market-place, believing themselves to be masters of the city; while the people, under the like impression that Thrasydæus was dead, were too much dismayed to offer resistance. But presently it became known that he was yet alive; the people crowded to the government-house " like a swarm of bees,"[3] and arrayed themselves for his protection as well as under his guidance. Leading them forth at once to battle, he completely defeated the oligarchical insurgents, and forced them to flee for protection to the Lacedæmonian army.

---

[1] Xen. Hellen. iii, 2, 23, 26 ; Diodor. xiv, 17.

[2] Xen. Hellen. iii, 2, 27 ; Pausanias, iii, 8, 2 ; v, 4, 5.

The words of Xenophon are not very clear — Βουλόμενοι δὲ οἱ περὶ Ξενίαν ὁν λεγόμενον μεδίμνῳ ἀπομετρήσασθαι τὸ παρὰ τοῦ πατρὸς ἀργύριον (τὴν πόλιν) δι' αὐτῶν προσχωρῆσαι Λακεδαιμονίοις, ἐκπεσόντες ἐξ οἰκίας ξίφη ἔχοντες σφαγὰς ποιοῦσι, καὶ ἄλλους τέ τινας κτείνουσι, καὶ ὁμοιόν τινα Θρασυδαίῳ ἀποκτείναντες, τῷ τοῦ δήμου προστάτῃ, ᾤοντο Θρασυδαῖον ἀπεκτονέναι...Ὁ δὲ Θρασυδαῖος ἔτι καθεύδων ἐτύγχανεν, οὖπερ ἐμεθύσθη.

Both the words and the narrative are here very obscure. It seems as if a sentence had dropped out, when we come suddenly upon the mention of the drunken state of Thrasydæus, without having before been told of any circumstance either leading to or implying this condition.

[3] Xen. Hellen. iii, 2, 28.

Agis presently evacuated the Eleian territory, yet not without planting a Lacedæmonian harmost and a garrison, together with Xenias and the oligarcl. exiles, at Epitalium, a little way south of the river Alpheius. Occupying this fort (analogous to Dekeleia in Attica), they spread ravage and ruin all around throughout the autumn and winter, to such a degree, that in the early spring, Thrasydæus and the Eleian government were compelled to send to Sparta and solicit peace. They consented to raze the imperfect fortifications of their city, so as to leave it quite open. They farther surrendered their harbor of Kyllênê with their ships of war, and relinquished all authority over the Triphylian townships, as well as over Lasion, which was claimed as an Arcadian town.[1] Though they pressed strenuously their claim to preserve the town of Epeium (between the Arcadian town of Heræa and the Triphylian town of Makistus), on the plea that they had bought it from its previous inhabitants at the price of thirty talents paid down, — the Lacedæmonians, pronouncing this to be a compulsory bargain imposed upon weaker parties by force, refused to recognize it. The town was taken away from them, seemingly without any reimbursement of the purchase money either in part or in whole. On these terms the Eleians were admitted to peace, and enrolled again among the members of the Lacedæmonian confederacy.[2]

---

[1] Xen. Hellen. iii, 2, 30. There is something perplexing in Xenophon's description of the Triphylian townships which the Eleians surrendered. First, he does not name Lepreum or Makistus, both of which neverthelesss had joined Agis on his invasion, and were the most important places in Triphylia (iii, 2, 25). Next, he names Letrini, Amphidoli, and Marganeis, as Triphylian; which yet were on the north of the Alpheius, and are elsewhere distinguished from Triphylian. I incline to believe that the words in his text, καὶ τὰς Τριφυλίδας πόλεις ἀφεῖναι, must be taken to mean Lepreum and Makistus, perhaps with some other places which we do not know; but that a καὶ after ἀφεῖναι, has fallen out of the text, and that the cities, whose names follow, are to be taken as *not* Triphylian. Phrixa and Epitalium were both south, but only just south, of the Alpheius; they were not on the borders of Triphylia, —and it seems doubtful whether they were properly Triphylian.

[2] Xen. Hellen. iii, 2, 30; Diodor. xiv, 34; Pausan. iii, 8. 2.

This war between Sparta and Elis reaches over three different years; it began in the first, occupied the whole of the second, and was finished in the third. Which years these three were (out of the seven which separate B C. 403–396), critics have not been unanimous.

The time of the Olympic festival seems to have been now approaching, and the Eleians were probably the more anxious to obtain peace from Sparta, as they feared to be deprived of their privilege as superintendents. The Pisatans, — inhabitants of the district immediately around Olympia, — availed themselves of the Spartan invasion of Elis to petition for restoration of their original privilege, as administrators of the temple of Zeus at Olympia with its great periodical solemnity, — by the dispossession of the Eleians as usurpers of that privilege. But their request met with no success. It was true indeed that such right had belonged to the Pisatans in early days, before the Olympic festival had acquired its actual Pan-hellenic importance and grandeur ; and that the Eleians had only appropriated it to themselves after conquering

---

Following the chronology of Diodorus, who places the beginning of the war in 402 B. C., I differ from Mr. Clinton, who places it in 401 B. C. (Fasti Hellen. ad ann.), and from Sievers (Geschichte von Griechenland bis zur Schlacht von Mantinea, p. 382), who places it in 398 B. C.

According to Mr. Clinton's view, the principal year of the war would have been 400 B. C., the year of the Olympic festival. But surely, had such been the fact, the coincidence of war in the country with the Olympic festival, must have raised so many complications, and acted so powerfully on the sentiments of all parties, as to be specifically mentioned. In my judgment, the war was brought to a close in the early part of 400 B. C., before the time of the Olympic festival arrived. Probably the Eleians were anxious, on this very ground, to bring it to a close before the festival did arrive.

Sievers, in his discussion of the point, admits that the date assigned by Diodorus to the Eleian war, squares both with the date which Diodorus gives for the death of Agis, and with that which Plutarch states about the duration of the reign of Agesilaus, — better than the chronology which he himself (Sievers) prefers. He founds his conclusion on Xenophon, Hell. iii, 2, 21. Τούτων δὲ πραττομένων ἐν τῇ 'Ασίᾳ ὑπὸ Δερκυλλίδα, Λακεδαιμόνιοι κατὰ τὸν αὐτὸν χρόνον πάλαι ὀργιζόμενοι τοῖς 'Ηλείοις, etc.

This passage is certainly of some weight; yet I think in the present case it is not to be pressed with rigid accuracy as to date. The whole third Book down to these very words, has been occupied entirely with the course of Asiatic affairs. Not a single proceeding of the Lacedæmonians in Peloponnesus, since the amnesty at Athens, has yet been mentioned. The command of Derkyllidas included only the last portion of the Asiatic exploits, and Xenophon has here loosely refe red to it as if it comprehended the whole. Sievers moreover compresses the whole Eleian war into one year and a fraction ; an interval, shorter, I think, than that which is implied in the statements of Xenophon.

the territory of Pisa. But taking the festival as it then stood, the Pisatans, mere villagers without any considerable city, were incompetent to do justice to it, and would have lowered its dignity in the eyes of all Greece.

Accordingly the Lacedæmonians, on this ground, dismissed the claimants, and left the superintendence of the Olympic games still in the hands of the Eleians.[1]

This triumphant dictation of terms to Elis, placed the Lacedæmonians in a condition of overruling ascendency throughout Peloponnesus, such as they had never attained before. To complete their victory, they rooted out all the remnants of their ancient enemies the Messenians, some of whom had been planted by the Athenians at Naupaktus, others in the island of Kephallenia. All of this persecuted race were now expelled, in the hour of Lacedæmonian omnipotence, from the neighborhood of Peloponnesus, and forced to take shelter, some in Sicily, others at Kyrênê.[2] We shall in a future chapter have to commemorate the turn of fortune in their favor.

---

[1] Xen. Hellen. iii, 2, 31.   [2] Diodor. xiv, 34 ; Pausan. iv, 26, 2.

CHAPTER LXXIII.

AGESILAUS KING OF SPARTA. — THE CORINTHIAN WAR.

THE close of the Peloponnesian war, with the victorious organization of the Lacedæmonian empire by Lysander, has already been described as a period carrying with it increased sufferings to those towns which had formerly belonged to the Athenian empire, as compared with what they had endured under Athens, — and harder dependence, unaccompanied by any species of advantage, even to those Peloponnesians and inland cities which had always been dependent allies of Sparta. To complete the melancholy picture of the Grecian world during these years, we may add (what will be hereafter more fully detailed) that calamities of a still more deplorable character overtook the Sicilian Greeks; first, from the invasion of the Carthaginians, who sacked Himera, Selinus, Agrigentum, Gela, and Kamarina, — next from the over-ruling despotism of Dionysius at Syracuse.

Sparta alone had been the gainer; and that to a prodigious extent, both in revenue and power. It is from this time, and from the proceedings of Lysander, that various ancient authors dated the commencement of her degeneracy, which they ascribe mainly to her departure from the institutions of Lykurgus by admitting gold and silver money. These metals had before been strictly prohibited; no money being tolerated except heavy pieces of iron, not portable except to a very trifling amount. That such was the ancient institution of Sparta, under which any Spartan having in his possession gold and silver money, was liable, if detected, to punishment, appears certain. How far the regulation may have been in practice evaded, we have no means of determining. Some of the ephors strenuously opposed the admission of the large sum brought home by Lysander as remnant of what he had received from Cyrus towards the prosecution of the war. They contended that the admission of so much gold and silver into the public treasury was a flagrant transgression of the Lykurgean ordinances. But their resistance was unavailing, and the new acquisitions were received; though it still continued to be a penal offence (and was even made a capital offence, if we may trust Plutarch) for any individual to be found with gold and silver in his possession.[1]   To enforce such a prohibition, however, even if practicable before, ceased to be practicable so soon as these metals were recognized and tolerated in the possession, and for the purposes of the government.

There can be no doubt that the introduction of a large sum of coined gold and silver into Sparta was in itself a striking and important phenomenon, when viewed in conjunction with the peculiar customs and discipline of the state.   It was likely to raise strong antipathies in the bosom of an old fashioned Spartan, and probably king Archidamus, had he been alive, would have taken part with the opposing ephors.   But Plutarch and others have criticised it too much as a phenomenon by itself; whereas, it was really one characteristic mark and portion·of a new assemblage of circumstances, into which Sparta had been gradually arriving during the last years of the war, and which were brought into the most effective action by the decisive success at Ægospotami. The institutions of Lykurgus, though excluding all Spartan citizens, by an unremitting drill and public mess, from trade and industry, from ostentation, and from luxury, — did not by any means extinguish in their bosoms the love of money;[2] while it had a positive tendency to exaggerate, rather than to abate, the love of power.   The Spartan kings, Leotychides and Pleistoanax, had

---

[1] Plutarch, Lysand. c. 17.   Compare Xen. Rep. Laced. vii, 6.

Both Ephorus and Theopompus recounted the opposition to the introduction of gold and silver into Sparta, each mentioning the name of one of the ephors as taking the lead in it.

There was a considerable body of ancient sentiment, and that too among high-minded and intelligent men, which regarded gold and silver as a cause of mischief and corruption, and of which the stanza of Horace (Od. iii, 3) is an echo:—

> Aurum irrepertum, et sic melius situm
> Cum terra celat, spernere fortior
> Quam cogere humanos in usus,
> Omne sacrum rapiente dextrâ.

[2] Aristotel. Politic. ii, 6, 23.

Ἀποβέβηκε δὲ τοὐνάντιον τῷ νομοθέτῃ τοῦ συμφέροντος· τὴν μὲν γὰρ πόλιν πεποίηκεν ἀχρήματον, τοὺς δ' ἰδιώτας φιλοχρηματους

both been guilty of receiving bribes; Tissaphernes had found means (during the twentieth year of the Peloponnesian war) to corrupt not merely the Spartan admiral Astyochus, but also nearly all the captains of the Peloponnesian fleet, except the Syracusan Hermokrates; Gylippus, as well as his father Kleandrides, had degraded himself by the like fraud; and Anaxibius at Byzantium was not at all purer. Lysander, enslaved only by his appetite for dominion, and himself a remarkable instance of superiority to pecuniary corruption, was thus not the first to engraft that vice on the minds of his countrymen. But though he found it already diffused among them, he did much to impart to it a still more decided predominance, by the immense increase of opportunities, and enlarged booty for peculation, which his newly-organized Spartan empire furnished. Not merely did he bring home a large residue in gold and silver, but there was a much larger annual tribute imposed by him on the dependent cities, combined with numerous appointments of harmosts to govern these cities. Such appointments presented abundant illicit profits, easy to acquire, and even difficult to avoid, since the decemvirs in each city were eager thus to purchase forbearance or connivance for their own misdeeds. So many new sources of corruption were sufficient to operate most unfavorably on the Spartan character, if not by implanting any fresh vices, at least by stimulating all its inherent bad tendencies.

To understand the material change thus wrought in it, we have only to contrast the speeches of king Archidamus and of the Corinthians, made in 432 B. C. at the beginning of the Peloponnesian war, with the state of facts at the end of the war, — during the eleven years between the victory of Ægospotami and the defeat of Knidus (405–394 B. C.) At the former of the two epochs, Sparta had no tributary subjects, nor any funds in her treasury, while her citizens were very reluctant to pay imposts.[1] About 334 B. C., thirty-seven years after her defeat at Leuktra and her loss of Messenia, Aristotle remarks the like fact, which had then again become true;[2] but during the continuance of her empire

---

[1] Thucyd. i, 80. ἀλλὰ πολλῷ ἔτι πλέον τούτου (χρημα-ων) ἐλλίπομεν καὶ οὔτε ἐν κοίνῳ ἔχομεν, οὔτε ἐτοίμως ἐκ τῶν ἰδίων φέρομεν

[2] Aristotel. Polit. ii, 6, 23. Φαύλως δ' ἔχει καὶ περὶ τὰ κοινὰ χρήματα τοῖς

between 405 and 394 B. C., she possessed a large public revenue, derived from the tribute of the dependent cities. In 432 B. C., Sparta is not merely cautious but backward ; especially averse to any action at a distance from home.[1] In 404 B. C., after the close of the war, she becomes aggressive, intermeddling, and ready for dealing with enemies, or making acquisitions remote as well as near.[2] In 432 B. C., her unsocial and exclusive manners, against the rest of Greece, with her constant expulsion of other Greeks from her own city, stand prominent among her attributes ;[3] while at the end of the war, her foreign relations had acquired such great development as to become the principal matter of attention for her leading citizens as well as for her magistrates; so that the influx of strangers into Sparta, and the efflux of Spartans into other parts of Greece became constant and inevitable. Hence the strictness of the Lykurgean discipline gave way on many points, and the principal Spartans especially struggled by various shifts to evade its obligations. It was to these leading men that the great prizes fell, enabling them to enrich themselves at the expense either of foreign subjects or of the public treasury, and tending more and more to aggravate that inequality of wealth among the Spartans which Aristotle so emphatically notices in his time;[4] since the smaller citizens had no similar opportunities opened to them, nor any industry of their own, to guard their properties against gradual subdivision and absorption, and to keep them in a permanent state of ability to furnish that contribution to the mess-table, for themselves and their sons, which formed the groundwork of Spartan political franchise. Moreover, the spec-

---

Σπαρτιάταις· οὔτε γὰρ ἐν τῷ κοινῷ τῆς πόλεως ἐστιν οὐδὲν, πολέμους μεγά-λους ἀναγκαζομένους φέρειν· εἰσφέρουσί τε κακῶς, etc.

Contrast what Plato says in his dialogue of Alkibiades, i, c. 39, p. 122 E. about the great quantity of gold and silver then at Sparta. The dialogue must bear date at some period between 400–371 B. C.

[1] See the speeches of the Corinthian envoys and of King Archidamus at Sparta (Thucyd. i, 70–84 ; compare also viii, 24–96).

[2] See the criticisms upon Sparta, about 395 B. C. and 372 B. C. (Xenoph. Hellen. iii, 5, 11–15 ; vi, 3, 8–11).

[3] Thucyd. i, 77. Ἄμικτα γὰρ τά τε καθ' ὑμᾶς αὐτοὺς νόμιμα τοῖς ἄλλοις ἔχετε, etc. About the ξενηλασίαι of the Spartans — see the speech of Perikles in Thucyd. i, 138.

[4] Aristotel. Politic. ii, 6, 10.

tacle of such newly-opened lucrative prizes, — accessible only to that particular section of influential Spartan families who gradually became known apart from the rest under the title of the Equals or Peers, — embittered the discontent of the energetic citizens beneath that privileged position, in such a manner as to menace the tranquillity of the state, — as will presently be seen. That sameness of life, habits, attainments, aptitudes, enjoyments, fatigues, and restraints, which the Lykurgean regulations had so long enforced, and still continued to prescribe, — divesting wealth of its principal advantages, and thus keeping up the sentiment of personal equality among the poorer citizens, — became more and more eluded by the richer, through the venality as well as the example of ephors and senators; [1] while for those who had no means of corruption, it continued unrelaxed, except in so far as many of them fell into a still more degraded condition by the loss of their citizenship.

It is not merely Isokratês,[2] who attests the corruption wrought in the character of the Spartans by the possession of that foreign empire which followed the victory of Ægospotami, — but also their earnest panegyrist Xenophon. After having warmly extolled the laws of Lykurgus or the Spartan institutions, he is constrained to admit that his eulogies, though merited by the past, have become lamentably inapplicable to that present which he himself witnessed. " Formerly (says he,[3]) the Lacedæmonians used to prefer their

---

[1] Aristot. Politic. ii, 6, 16–18; ii, 7, 3.   [2] Isokrates, de Pace, s. 118–127.
[3] Xen. de Republ. Laced. c. 14.

Οἶδα γὰρ πρότερον μὲν Λακεδαιμονίους αἱρουμένους, οἴκοι τὰ μέτρια ἔχοντας ἀλλήλοις συνεῖναι μᾶλλον, ἢ ἁρμόζοντας ἐν ταῖς πόλεσι καὶ κολακευομένους διαφθείρεσθαι. Καὶ πρόσθεν μὲν οἶδα αὐτοὺς φοβουμένους, χρύσιον ἔχοντας φαίνεσθαι· νῦν δ᾽ ἐστιν οὓς καὶ καλλωπιζομένους ἐπὶ τῷ κεκτῆσθαι. Ἐπίσταμαι δὲ καὶ πρόσθεν τούτου ἕνεκα ξενηλασίας γιγνομένας, καὶ ἀποδημεῖν οὐκ ἐξὸν, ὅπως μὴ ῥᾳδιουργίας οἱ πολῖται ἀπὸ τῶν ξένων ἐμπίμπλαιντο· νῦν δ᾽ ἐπίσταμαι τοὺς δοκοῦντας πρώτους εἶναι ἐσπουδακότας ὡς μηδέποτε παύωνται ἁρμόζοντες ἐπὶ ξένης. Καὶ ἦν μὲν, ὅτε ἐπεμελοῦντο, ὅπως ἄξιοι εἶεν ἡγεῖσθαι· νῦν δὲ πολὺ μᾶλλον πραγματεύονται, ὅπως ἄρξουσιν, ἢ ὅπως ἄξιοι τούτου ἔσονται. Τοιγαροῦν οἱ Ἕλληνες πρότερον μὲν ἰόντες εἰς Λακεδαίμονα ἐδέοντο αὐτῶν, ἡγεῖσθαι ἐπὶ τοὺς δοκοῦντας ἀδικεῖν· νῦν δὲ πολλοὶ παρακαλοῦσιν ἀλλήλους ἐπὶ τὸ διακωλύειν ἄρξαι πάλιν αὐτούς. Οὐδὲν μέντοι δεῖ θαυμάζειν τούτων τῶν ἐπιφόγων αὐτοῖς γιγνομένων, ἐπειδὴ φανεροί εἰσιν οὔτε τῷ θεῷ πειθόμενοι οὔτε τοῖς Λυκούργου νόμοις.

The expression, "taking measures to hinder the Lacedæmonians from again exercising empire," — marks this treatise as probably composed some

own society and moderate way of life at home, to appointments as harmosts in foreign towns, with all the flattery and all the corruption attending them. Formerly, they were afraid to be seen with gold in their possession; now, there are some who make even an ostentatious display of it. Formerly, they enforced their (Xenêlasy or) expulsion of strangers, and forbade foreign travel, in order that their citizens might not be filled with relaxed habits of life from contact with foreigners; but now, those who stand first in point of influence among them, study above all things to be in perpetual employment as harmosts abroad. There was a time when they took pains to be worthy of headship; but now they strive much rather to get and keep the command, than to be properly qualified for it. Accordingly, the Greeks used in former days to come and solicit, that the Spartans would act as their leaders against wrong-doers; but now they are exhorting each other to concert measures for shutting out Sparta from renewed empire. Nor can we wonder that the Spartans have fallen into this discredit, when they have manifestly renounced obedience both to the Delphian god, and to the institutions of Lykurgus!"

This criticism (written at some period between 394–371 B. C.) from the strenuous eulogist of Sparta is highly instructive. We know from other evidences how badly the Spartan empire worked for the subject cities; we here learn how badly it worked for the character of the Spartans themselves, and for those internal institutions which even an enemy of Sparta, who detested her foreign policy, still felt constrained to admire.[1] All the vices, here insisted upon by Xenophon, arise from various incidents connected with her empire. The moderate, home-keeping, old-fashioned, backward disposition, — of which the Corinthians complain,[2] but

time between their naval defeat at Knidus, and their land-defeat at Leuktra. The former put an end to their maritime empire, — the latter excluded them from all possibility of recovering it; but during the interval between the two, such recovery was by no means impossible.

[1] The Athenian envoy at Melos says, — Λακεδαιμόνιοι γὰρ πρὸς μὲν σφᾶς αὐτοὺς καὶ τὰ ἐπιχώρια νόμιμα, πλεῖστα ἀρετῇ χρῶνται· πρὸς δὲ τοὺς ἄλλους — ἐπιφανέστατα ὧν ἴσμεν τὰ μὲν ἡδέα καλὰ νομίζουσι, τὰ δὲ ξυμφέροντα δίκαια (Thucyd. v. 105). A judgment almost exactly the same, is pronounced by Polybius (vi, 48).

[2] Thucyd. i, 69, 70, 71, 34. ἀρχαιότροπα ὑμῶν τὰ ἐπιτηδεύματα — ἄοκνοι πρὸς ὑμᾶς μελλητὰς καὶ ἀποδημηταὶ πρὸς ἐνδημοτάτους: also viii, 24

for which king Archidamus takes credit, at the beginning of the
Peloponnesian war, — is found exchanged, at the close of the war,
for a spirit of aggression and conquest, for ambition public as well
as private, and for emancipation of the great men from the subduing[1] equality of the discipline enacted by Lykurgus.

Agis the son of Archidamus (426–399 B. C.), and Pausanias
son of Pleistoanax (408–394 B. C.), were the two kings of Sparta
at the end of the war. But Lysander, the admiral or commander
of the fleet, was for the time[2] greater than either of the two kings,
who had the right of commanding only the troops on land. I have
already mentioned how his overweening dictation and insolence
offended not only Pausanias, but also several of the ephors and
leading men at Sparta, as well as Pharnabazus the Persian
satrap ; thus indirectly bringing about the emancipation of Athens
from the Thirty, the partial discouragement of the dekarchies
throughout Greece, and the recall of Lysander himself from his
command. It was not without reluctance that the conqueror of
Athens submitted to descend again to a private station. Amidst
the crowd of flatterers who heaped incense on him at the moment
of his omnipotence, there were not wanting those who suggested
that he was much more worthy to reign than either Agis or Pausanias ; that the kings ought to be taken, not from the first-
born of the lineage of Eurysthenês and Proklês, but by selection
out of all the Herakleids, of whom Lysander himself was one ;[3]

---

[1] Σπάρτην δαμασίμβροτον (Simonides ap. Plutarch. Agesilaum, c. 1).

[2] See an expression of Aristotle (Polit. ii, 6, 22) about the function of
admiral among the Lacedæmonians, — ἐπὶ γὰρ τοῖς βασιλεῦσιν, οὖσι στρατη-
γοῖς ἀϊδίοις, ἡ ναυαρχία σχεδόν ἑτέρα βασιλεία καθέστηκε.

This reflection, — which Aristotle intimates that he has borrowed from
some one else, though without saying from whom, — must in all probability
have been founded upon the case of Lysander ; for never after Lysander,
was there any Lacedæmonian admiral enjoying a power which could by
possibility be termed exorbitant or dangerous. We know that during the
later years of the Peloponnesian war, much censure was cast upon the Lace-
dæmanian practice of annually changing the admiral (Xen. Hellen. i, 6, 4).

The Lacedæmonians seem to have been impressed with these criticisms,
for in the year 395 B. C. (the year before the battle of Knidus) they conferred
upon King Agesilaus, who was then commanding the land army in Asia
Minor, the command of the fleet also — in order to secure unity of operations. This had never been done before (Xen. Hellen. iii, 4, 28).

[3] Plutarch, Lysand. c. 24. Perhaps he may have been simply a member

and that the person elected ought to be not merely a descendant of Hêraklês, but a worthy parallel of Hêraklês himself, while pæans were sung to the honor of Lysander at Samos,[1] — while Chœrilus and Antilochus composed poems in his praise, — while Antimachus (a poet highly esteemed by Plato) entered into a formal competition of recited epic verses called *Lysandria*, and was surpassed by Nikêratus, there was another warm admirer, a rhetor or sophist of Halikarnassus, named Kleon,[2] who wrote a discourse proving that Lysander had well earned the regal dignity, — that personal excellence ought to prevail over legitimate descent, and that the crown ought to be laid open to election from the most worthy among the Herakleids. Considering that rhetoric was neither employed nor esteemed at Sparta, we cannot reasonably believe that Lysander really ordered the composition of this discourse as an instrument of execution for projects preconceived by himself, in the same manner as an Athenian prosecutor or defendant before the dikastery used to arm himself with a speech from Lysias or Demosthenes. Kleon would make his court professionally through such a prose composition, whether the project were first recommended by himself, or currently discussed among a circle of admirers; while Lysander would probably requite the compliment by a reward not less munificent than that which he gave to the indifferent poet Antilochus.[3] And the composition would be put into the form of an harangue from the admiral to his countrymen, without any definite purpose that it should be ever so delivered. Such hypothesis of a speaker and an audience was frequent with the rhetors in their writings, as we may see in Isokrates, — especially in his sixth discourse, called Archidamus.

Either from his own ambition, or from the suggestions of others, Lysander came now to conceive the idea of breaking the succession of the two regal families, and opening for himself a door to reach the crown. His projects have been characterized as revolu-

---

of the tribe called Hylleis, who, probably, called themselves Herakleids. Some affirmed that Lysander wished to cause the kings to be elected out of all the Spartans, not simply out of the Herakleids. This is less probable.

[1] Duris ap. Athenæum, xv, p. 696.

[2] Plutarch, Lysand. c. 18; Plutarch, Agesil. c. 20.

[3] Plutarch, Lysand. c. 17.

tionary; but there seems nothing in them which fairly merits the appellation, in the sense which that word now bears, if we consider accurately what the Spartan kings were in the year 400 B. C. In this view the associations connected with the title of king, are to a modern reader misleading. The Spartan kings were not kings at all, in any modern sense of the term; not only they were not absolute, but they were not even constitutional kings. They were not sovereigns, nor was any Spartan their subject; every Spartan was the member of a free Grecian community. The Spartan king did not govern; nor did he reign, in the sense of having government carried on in his name and by his delegates. The government of Sparta was carried on by the ephors, with frequent consultation of the senate, and occasional, though rare appeals, to the public assembly of citizens. The Spartan king was not legally inviolable. He might be, and occasionally was, arrested, tried, and punished for misbehavior in the discharge of his functions. He was a self-acting person, a great officer of state; enjoying certain definite privileges, and exer cising certain military and judicial functions, which passed as an *universitas* by hereditary transmission in his family; but subject to the control of the ephors as to the way in which he performed these duties.[1] Thus, for example, it was his privilege to command the army when sent on foreign service; yet a law was made, requiring him to take deputies along with him, as a council of war, without whom nothing was to be done. The ephors recalled Agesilaus when they thought fit; and they brought Pausanias to trial

---

[1] Aristotle (Polit. v, 1, 5) represents justly the schemes of Lysander as going πρὸς τὸ μέρος τι κινῆσαι τῆς πολιτείας· οἷον ἀρχήν τινα καταστῆσαι ἢ ἀνελεῖν. The Spartan kingship is here regarded as ἀρχή τις — one office of state, among others. But Aristotle regards Lysander as having intended to destroy the kingship — καταλῦσαι τὴν βασιλείαν — which does not appear to have been the fact. The plan of Lysander was to retain the kingship, but to render it elective instead of hereditary. He wished to place the Spartan kingship substantially on the same footing, as that on which the office of the kings or suffetes of Carthage stood; who were not hereditary, nor confined to members of the same family or Gens, but chosen out of the principal families or Gentes. Aristotle, while comparing the βασιλεῖς at Sparta with those at Carthage, as being generally analogous, pronounces in favor of the Carthaginian election as better than the Spartan hereditary transmission. (Arist. Polit. ii, 8, 2.)

and punishment, for alleged misconduct in his command.[1] The only way in which the Spartan kings formed part of the sovereign power in the state, or shared in the exercise of government properly so called, was that they had votes *ex officio* in the Senate, and could vote there by proxy when they were not present. In ancient times, very imperfectly known, the Spartan kings seem really to have been sovereigns; the government having then beer really carried on by them, or by their orders. But in the year 400 B. C., Agis and Pausanias had become nothing more than great and dignified hereditary officers of state, still bearing the old title of their ancestors. To throw open these hereditary functions to all the members of the Herakleid Gens, by election from their number, might be a change better or worse; it was a startling novelty (just as it would have been to propose, that any of the various priesthoods, which were hereditary in particular families, should be made elective), because of the extreme attachment of the Spartans to old and sanctified customs; but it cannot properly be styled revolutionary. The ephors, the senate, and the public assembly, might have made such a change in full legal form, without any appeal to violence; the kings might vote against it, but they would have been outvoted. And if the change had been made, the Spartan government would have remained, in form as well as in principle, just what it was before; although the Eurystheneid and Prokleid families would have lost their privileges. It is not meant here to deny that the Spartan kings were men of great importance in the state, especially when (like Agesilaus) they combined with their official station a marked personal energy. But it is not the less true, that the associations, connected with the title of *king* ir the modern mind, do not properly apply to them.

To carry his point at Sparta, Lysander was well aware that agencies of an unusual character must be employed. Quitting Sparta soon after his recall, he visited the oracles of Delphi, Dodona, and Zeus Ammon in Libya,[2] in order to procure, by persuasion or corruption, injunctions to the Spartans, countenancing his projects. So great was the general effect of oracular injunctions on the Spartan mind, that Kleomenes had thus obtained the deposition of king Demaratus, and the exiled Pleistoanax, his own

[1] Thucyd. v, 63; Xen. Hellen. iii, 5, 25; iv, 2, 1.

[2] Diodor. xiv, 13; Cicero, de Divinat. i, 43, 96; Cornel. Nepos, Lysand. c. 5.

return ;[1] bribery having been in both cases the moving impulse
But Lysander was not equally fortunate. None of these oracles
could be induced, by any offers, to venture upon so grave a sentence as that of repealing the established law of succession to the
Spartan throne. It is even said that the priests of Ammon, not
content with refusing his offers, came over to Sparta to denounce
his proceeding; upon which accusation Lysander was put on his
trial, but acquitted. The statement that he was thus tried and acquitted, I think untrue. But his schemes so far miscarried, —
and he was compelled to resort to another stratagem, yet still appealing to the religious susceptibilities of his countrymen. There
had been born some time before, in one of the cities of the Euxine,
a youth named Silenus, whose mother affirmed that he was the son
of Apollo; an assertion which found extensive credence, notwithstanding various difficulties raised by the sceptics. While making
at Sparta this new birth of a son to the god, the partisans of Lysander also spread abroad the news that there existed sacred
manuscripts and inspired records, of great antiquity, hidden and
yet unread, in the custody of the Delphian priests; not to be
touched or consulted until some genuine son of Apollo should come
forward to claim them. With the connivance of some among the
priests, certain oracles were fabricated agreeable to the views of
Lysander. The plan was concerted that Silenus should present
himself at Delphi, tender the proofs of his divine parentage, and
then claim the inspection of these hidden records; which the
priests, after an apparently rigid scrutiny, were prepared to grant.
Silenus would then read them aloud in the presence of all the
spectators; and one would be found among them, recommending
to the Spartans to choose their kings out of all the best citizens.[2]

So nearly did this project approach to consummation, that Silenus actually presented himself at Delphi, and put in his claim.
But one of the confederates either failed in his courage, or broke
down, at the critical moment; so that the hidden records still
remained hidden. Yet though Lysander was thus compelled to
abandon his plan, nothing was made public about it until after his

---

[1] Plutarch, Lysand. c. 25, from Ephorus. Compare Herodot. vi, 66;
Thucyd. v, 12.

[2] Plutarch, Lysand. c. 26.

death. It might probably have succeeded, had he found temple-confederates of proper courage and cunning, — when we consider the profound and habitual defe1 ence of the Spartans to Delphi; upon the sanction of which oracle the Lykurgean institutions themselves were mainly understood to rest. And an occasion presently arose, on which the proposed change might have been tried with unusual facility and pertinence; though Lysander himself, having once miscarried, renounced his enterprise, and employed his influence, which continued unabated, in giving the sceptre to another instead of acquiring it for himself,[1] — like Mucian in reference to the emperor Vespasian.

It was apparently about a year after the campaigns in Elis, that king Agis, now an old man, was taken ill at Heræa in Arcadia, and carried back to Sparta, where he shortly afterwards expired. His wife Mimæa had given birth to a son named Leotychides, now

---

[1] Tacit. Histor. i, 10. "Cui expeditius fuerit tradere imperium, quam obtinere."

The general fact of the conspiracy of Lysander to open for himself a way to the throne, appears to rest on very sufficient testimony, — that of Ephorus; to whom perhaps the words φασί τινες in Aristotle may allude, where he mentions this conspiracy as having been narrated (Polit. v, 1, 5). But Plutarch, as well as K. O. Müller (Hist. of Dorians, iv, 9, 5) and others, erroneously represent the intrigues with the oracle as being resorted to after Lysander returned from accompanying Agesilaus to Asia; which is certainly impossible, since Lysander accompanied Agesilaus out, in the spring of 396 B.C. — did not return to Greece until the spring of 395 B.C. — and was then employed, with an interval not greater than four or five months, on that expedition against Bœotia wherein he was slain.

The tampering of Lysander with the oracle must undoubtedly have taken place prior to the death of Agis, — at some time between 403 B.C. and 399 B.C. The humiliation which he received in 396 B.C. from Agesilaus might indeed have led him to revolve in his mind the renewal of his former plans; but he can have had no time to do anything towards them. Aristotle (Polit. v, 6, 2) alludes to the humiliation of Lysander by the kings as an example of incidents *tending to* raise disturbance in an aristocratical government; but this humiliation, probably, alludes to the manner in which he was thwarted in Attica by Pausanias in 403 B.C. — which proceeding is ascribed by Plutarch to both kings, as well as to their jealousy of Lysander (see Plutarch, Lysand. c. 21) — not to the treatment of Lysander by Agesilaus in 396 B.C. The mission of Lysander to the despot Dionysius at Syracuse (Plutarch, Lysand. c. 2) must also have taken place prior to the death of Agis in 399 B.C.; whether before or after the failure of the stratagem at Delphi, is uncertain; perhaps after it.

a youth about fifteen years of age.[1] But the legitimacy of this youth
had always been suspected by Agis, who had pronounced, when
the birth of the child was first made known to him, that it could
not be his. He had been frightened out of his wife's bed by the
shock of an earthquake, which was construed as a warning from
Poseidon, and was held to be a prohibition of intercourse for a certain time; during which interval Leotychides was born. This was
one story; another was, that the young prince was the son of Alkibiades, born during the absence of Agis in his command at
Dekeleia. On the other hand, it was alleged that Agis, though
originally doubtful of the legitimacy of Leotychides, had afterwards retracted his suspicions, and fully recognized him; especially,
and with peculiar solemnity, during his last illness.[2] As in the
case of Demaratus about a century earlier,[3] — advantage was
taken of these doubts by Agesilaus, the younger brother of Agis,
powerfully seconded by Lysander, to exclude Leotychides, and
occupy the throne himself.

Agesilaus was the son of king Archidamus, not by Lampito the
mother of Agis, but by a second wife named Eupolia. He was now
at the mature age of forty,[4] and having been brought up without
any prospect of becoming king, — at least until very recent times,
— had passed through the unmitigated rigor of Spartan drill and
training. He was distinguished for all Spartan virtues; exemplary
obedience to authority, in the performance of his trying exercises,
military as well as civil, — intense emulation, in trying to surpass
every competitor, — extraordinary courage, unremitting energy,
as well as facility in enduring hardship, — perfect simplicity and
frugality in all his personal habits, — extreme sensibility to the
opinion of his fellow-citizens. Towards his personal friends or

---

[1] The age of Leotychides is approximately marked by the date of the
presence of Alkibiades at Sparta 414–413 B. C. The mere rumor, true or
false, that this young man was the son of Alkibiades, may be held sufficient
as chronological evidence to certify his age.

[2] Xen. Hellen. iii, 3, 2; Pausanias, iii, 8, 4; Plutarch, Agesilaus, c. 3.

[3] Herodot. v, 66.

[4] I confess I do not understand how Xenophon can say, in his Agesilaus,
¬ 6, Ἀγησίλαος τοίνυν ἔτι μὲν νέος ὢν ἔτυχε τῆς βασιλείας. For he himself
says (ii, 28), and it seems well established, that Agesilaus died at the age of
above 80 (Plutarch, Agesil. c. 40); and his death must have been about 360
B. C.

adherents, he was remarkable for fervor of attachment, even for unscrupulous partisanship, with a readiness to use all his influence in screening their injustices or short-comings ; while he was comparatively placable and generous in dealing with rivals at home, notwithstanding his eagerness to be first in every sort of competition.[1] His manners were cheerful and popular, and his physiognomy pleasing; though in stature he was not only small but mean, and though he labored under the additional defect of lameness on one leg,[2] which accounts for his constant refusal to suffer his statue to be taken.[3] He was indifferent to money, and exempt from excess of selfish feeling, except in his passion for superiority and power.

In spite of his rank as brother of Agis, Agesilaus had never yet been tried in any military command, though he had probably served in the army either at Dekeleia or in Asia. Much of his character, therefore, lay as yet undisclosed. And his popularity may perhaps have been the greater at the moment when the throne became vacant, inasmuch as, having never been put in a position to excite jealousy, he stood distinguished only for accomplishments, efforts, endurances, and punctual obedience, wherein even the poorest citizens were his competitors on equal terms. Nay, so complete was the self-constraint, and the habit of smothering emotions, generated by a Spartan training, that even the cunning Lysander himself did not at this time know him. He and Agesilaus had been early and intimate friends,[4] both having been placed as boys in the same herd or troop for the purposes of discipline ; a strong illustration of the equalizing character of this discipline, since we know that Lysander was of poor parents and condition.[5] He made the mistake of supposing Agesilaus to be of a disposition particularly gentle and manageable ; and this was his main inducement for espousing the pretensions of the latter to the throne, after the

---

[1] Plutarch, Agesilaus, c. 2–5 ; Xenoph. Agesil. vii, 3 ; Plutarch, Apophth. Laconic. p. 212 D.

[2] Plutarch, Agesil. c. 2 ; Xenoph. Agesil. viii, 1.

It appears that the mother of Agesilaus was a very small woman, and that Archidamus had incurred the censure of the ephors, on that especial ground, for marrying her.

[3] Xenoph. Agesil. xi, 7 ; Plutarch, Agesil. c. 2

[4] Plutarch, Agesil. c. 2. [5] Plutarch, Lysand. c. 2.

decease of Agis. Lysander reckoned, if by his means Agesilaus became king, on a great increase of his own influence, and especially on a renewed mission to Asia, if not as ostensible general, at least as real chief under the tutelar headship of the new king.

Accordingly, when the imposing solemnities which always marked the funeral of a king of Sparta were terminated,[1] and the day arrived for installation of a new king, Agesilaus, under the promptings of Lysander, stood forward to contest the legitimacy and the title of Leotychides, and to claim the sceptre for himself, — a true Herakleid, brother of the late king Agis. In the debate, which probably took place not merely before the ephors and the senate but before the assembled citizens besides, Lysander warmly seconded his pretensions. Of this debate unfortunately we are not permitted to know much. We cannot doubt that the mature age and excellent reputation of Agesilaus would count as a great recommendation, when set against an untried youth ; and this was probably the real point (since the relationship of both was so near) upon which decision turned ;[2] for the legitimacy of Leotychides was positively asseverated by his mother Timæa,[3] and we do not find that the question of paternity was referred to the Delphian oracle, as in the case of Demaratus.

There was, however, one circumstance which stood much in the way of Agesilaus, — his personal deformity. A lame king of Sparta had never yet been known. And if we turn back more than a century to the occurrence of a similar deformity in one of the Battiad princes at Kyrênê,[4] we see the Kyrenians taking it so deeply to heart, that they sent to ask advice from Delphi, and invited over the Mantineian reformer Demônax. Over and above this sentiment of repugnance, too, the gods had specially forewarned Sparta to beware of " a lame reign." Deiopeithes, a prophet and religious

---

[1] Xen. Hellen. iii, 3, 1.

[2] Plutarch, Lysand. c. 22; Plutarch, Agesil. c. 3; Xen. Hellen. iii, 3, 2 ; Xen. Agesil. 1, 5 — κρίνασα ἡ πόλις ἀνεπικλετότερον εἶναι Ἀγησίλαον καὶ τῷ γένει καὶ τῇ ἀρετῇ, etc.

[3] Xen. Hellen. iii, 3, 2. This statement contradicts the talk imputed to Timæa by Duris (Plutarch, Agesil. c. 3 ; Plutarch, Alkibiad. c. 23).

[4] Herodot. iv, 161. Διεδέξατο δὲ τὴν βασιληίην τοῦ Ἀρκεσίλεω ὁ παῖς Βάττος, χωλός τε ἐὼν καὶ οὐκ ἀρτίπους. Οἱ δὲ Κυρηναῖοι πρὸς τὴν καταλαβοῦσαν συμφορὴν ἔπεμπον ἐς Δελφοὺς, ἐπιφησομένους ὄντινα τρόπον καταστησάμενοι κάλλιστα ἂν οἰκέοιεν

adviser of high reputation, advocated the cause of Leotychides. He produced an ancient oracle, telling Sparta, that "with all her pride she must not suffer a lame reign to impair her stable footing;[1] for if she did so, unexampled suffering and ruinous wars would long beset her." This prophecy had already been once invoked, about eighty years earlier,[2] but with a very different interpretation. To Grecian leaders, like Themistokles or Lysander, it was an accomplishment of no small value to be able to elude inconvenient texts or intractable religious feelings, by expository ingenuity. And Lysander here raised his voice (as Themistokles had done on the momentous occasion before the battle of Salamis),[3] to combat the professional expositors; contending that by "a lame reign," the god meant, not a bodily defect in the king, — which might not even be congenital, but might arise from some positive hurt,[4] — but the reign of any king who was not a genuine descendant of Hêraklês.

The influence of Lysander,[5] combined doubtless with a preponderance of sentiment already tending towards Agesilaus, caused this effort of interpretative subtlety to be welcomed as convincing, and led to the nomination of the lame candidate as king. There was, however, a considerable minority, to whom this decision appeared a sin against the gods and a mockery of the oracle. And though the murmurs of such dissentients were kept down by the ability and success of Agesilaus during the first years of his reign; yet when, in his ten last years, calamity and humiliation were poured thickly upon this proud city, the public sentiment came decidedly round to their view. Many a pious Spartan then

---

[1] Plutarch, Lysand. c. 22; Plutarch, Agesil. c. 3; Pausanias, iii, 8, 5.
[2] Diodor. xi, 50.   [3] Herodot. vii, 143.
[4] Xen. Hellen. iii, 3, 3. ὡς οὐκ οἴοιτο, τὸν θεὸν τοῦτο κελεύειν φυλάξασθαι, μὴ προσπταίσας τις χωλεύσῃ, ἀλλὰ μᾶλλον, μὴ οὐκ ὢν τοῦ γένους βασιλεύσῃ.

Congenital lameness would be regarded as a mark of divine displeasure, and therefore a disqualification from the throne, as in the case of Battus of Kyrênê above noticed. But the words χωλὴ βασίλεια were general enough to cover both the cases, — superinduced as well as congenital lameness. It is upon this that Lysander founds his inference — that the god did not mean to allude to bodily lameness at all.

[5] Pausanias, iii, 8, 5; Plutarch, Agesil. c. 3; Plutarch, Lysand. c. 22. Justin, vi, 2.

exclaimed, with feelings of bitter repentance, that the divine word never failed to come true at last,[1] and that Sparta was justly punished for having wilfully shut her eyes to the distinct and merciful warning vouchsafed to her, about the mischiefs of a " lame reign."[2]

Besides the crown, Agesilaus at the same time acquired the large property left by the late king Agis; an acquisition which enabled him to display his generosity by transferring half of it at once to his maternal relatives, — for the most part poor persons.[3] The popularity acquired by this step was still farther increased by his manner of conducting himself towards the ephors and senate. Between these magistrates and the kings, there was generally a bad understanding. The kings, not having lost the tradition of the plenary power once enjoyed by their ancestors, displayed as much haughty reserve as they dared, towards an authority now become essentially superior to their own. But Agesilaus, — not less from his own preëstablished habits, than from anxiety to make up for the defects of his title, — adopted a line of conduct studiously opposite. He not only took pains to avoid collision with the ephors, but showed marked deference both to their orders and to their persons. He rose from his seat whenever they appeared; he conciliated both ephors and senators by timely presents.[4] By such judicious proceeding, as well as by his exact observance of the laws and customs,[5] he was himself the greatest gainer. Combined with that ability and energy in which he was never deficient, it ensured to him more real power than had ever fallen to the lot of any king of Sparta; power not merely over the military operations abroad

---

[1] Ἰδ' οἷον, ὦν παῖδες, προσέμιξεν ἄφαρ
Τούπος τὸ θεόπροπον ἡμῖν
Τῆς παλαιφάτου προνοίας,
Ὃν ἔλακεν, etc.

This is a splendid chorus of the Trachiniæ of Sophokles (822) proclaiming their sentiments on the awful death of Herakles, in the tunic of Nessus, which has just been announced as about to happen.

[2] Plutarch, Agesil. c. 30; Plutarch, Compar. Agesil. and Pomp. c. 1
Ἀγησίλαος δὲ τὴν βασίλειαν ἔδοξε λαβεῖν, οὔτε τὰ πρὸς τοὺς θεοὺς ἄμεμπτ᾽ης, οὔτε τὰ πρὸς ἀνθρώπους, κρίνας νοθείας Λεωτυχίδην, ὃν υἱὸν αὑτοῦ ἀπέδειξεν ὁ ἀδελφὸς γνήσιον, τὸν δὲ χρησμὸν κατειρωνευσάμενος τὸν περὶ τῆς χωλότητος. Again, ib. c. 2. δι᾽ Ἀγησίλαον ἐπεσκότησε τῷ χρησμῷ Λύσανδρος

[3] Xen. Agesil. iv, 5; Plutarch, Ages. c. 4.

[4] Plutarch, Agesil. c. 4.

[5] Xen. Agesil. vii, 2.

which usually fell to the kings, — but also over the policy of the state at home. On the increase and maintenance of that rea! power, his chief thoughts were concentrated ; new dispositions generated by kingship, which had never shown themselves in him before. Despising, like Lysander, both money, luxury, and all the outward show of power, — he exhibited, as a king, an ultra-Spar tan simplicity, carried almost to affectation, in diet, clothing, and general habits. But like Lysander also, he delighted in the exer cise of dominion through the medium of knots or factions of de voted partisans, whom he rarely scrupled to uphold in all their career of injustice and oppression. Though an amiable man, with no disposition to tyranny, and still less to plunder, for his own bene fit, — Agesilaus thus made himself the willing instrument of both, for the benefit of his various coadjutors and friends, whose power and consequence he identified with his own.[1]

At the moment when Agesilaus became king, Sparta was at the maximum of her power, holding nearly all the Grecian towns as subject allies, with or without tribute. She was engaged in the task (as has already been mentioned) of protecting the Asiatic Greeks against the Persian satraps in their neighborhood. And the most interesting portion of the life of Agesilaus consists in the earnestness with which he espoused, and the vigor and ability with which he conducted, this great Pan-hellenic duty. It will be seen that success in his very promising career was intercepted [2] by his bad, factious subservience to partisans, at home and abroad, — by his unmeasured thirst for Spartan omnipotence, — and his indiffer ence or aversion to any generous scheme of combination with the cities dependent on Sparta.

His attention, however, was first called to a dangerous inter nal conspiracy with which Sparta was threatened. The " lame reign" was as yet less than twelve months old, when Agesilaus, be ing engaged in sacrificing at one of the established state solemnities, was apprised by the officiating prophet, that the victims exhibited menacing symptoms, portending a conspiracy of the most formida-

---

[1] Isokrates, Orat. v, (Philipp.) s. 100; Plutarch, Agesilaus, c. 3, 13–23 ; Plutarch, Apophthegm. Laconica, p. 209 F—212 D.

See the incident alluded to by Theopompus ap. Athenæum, xiii, p 609.

[2] Isokrates (Orat. v, *ut sup.*) makes a remark in substance the same

ble character. A second sacrifice gave yet worse promise; and on the third, the terrified prophet exclaimed, "Agesilaus, the revelation before us imports that we are actually in the midst of our enemies." They still continued to sacrifice, but victims were now offered to the averting and preserving gods, with prayers that these latter, by tutelary interposition, would keep off the impending peril At length, after much repetition, and great difficulty, favorable victims were obtained; the meaning of which was soon made clear. Five days afterwards, an informer came before the ephors, communicating the secret, that a dangerous conspiracy was preparing, organized by a citizen named Kinadon.[1]

The conspirator thus named was a Spartan citizen, but not one of that select number called The Equals or The Peers. It has already been mentioned that inequalities had been gradually growing up among qualified citizens of Sparta, tending tacitly to set apart a certain number of them under the name of The Peers, and all the rest under the correlative name of The Inferiors. Besides this, since the qualification of every family lasted only so long as the citizen could furnish a given contribution for himself and his sons to the public mess-table, and since industry of every kind was inconsistent with the rigid personal drilling imposed upon all of them,— the natural consequence was, that in each generation a certain number of citizens became disfranchised and dropped off. But these disfranchised men did not become Periœki or Helots. They were still citizens, whose qualification, though in abeyance, might be at any time renewed by the munificence of a rich man;[2] so that they too, along with the lesser citizens, were known under the denomination of The Inferiors. It was to this class that Kinadon belonged. He was a young man of remarkable strength and courage, who had discharged with honor his duties in the Lykurgean discipline,[3] and had imbibed from it that sense of personal

---

[1] Xenoph. Hellen. iii, 3, 4.

[2] See Vol. II, Ch. vi, p. 359 of this History.

[3] Xen. Hellen. iii, 3, 5. Οὗτος (Kinadon) δ' ἦν νεανίσκος καὶ τὸ εἶδος καὶ τὴν ψυχὴν εὔρωστος, οὐ μέντοι τῶν ὁμοίων.

The meaning of the term Οἱ ὅμοιοι fluctuates in Xenophon; it sometimes, as here, is used to signify the privileged Peers — again De Repub. Laced. xiii, 1; and Anab iv, 6, 14. Sometimes again it is used agreeably to the Lykurgean theory; whereby every citizen, who rigorously discharged his duty in the public drill, belonged to the number (De Rep. Lac. x, 7).

There was a variance between the theory and the practice

equality, and that contempt of privilege, which its theory as well
as its practice suggested. Notwithstanding all exactness of duty
performed, he found that the constitution, as practically worked,
excluded him from the honors and distinctions of the state; re-
serving them for the select citizens known under the name of
Peers. And this exclusion had become more marked and galling
since the formation of the Spartan empire after the victory of
Ægospotami; whereby the number of lucrative posts (harmosties
and others) all monopolized by the Peers, had been so much multiplied. Debarred from the great political prizes, Kinadon was still
employed by the ephors, in consequence of his high spirit and
military sufficiency, in that standing force which they kept for
maintaining order at home.[1] He had been the agent ordered on
several of those arbitrary seizures which they never scrupled to
employ towards persons whom they regarded as dangerous. But
this was no satisfaction to his mind; nay, probably, by bringing
him into close contact with the men in authority, it contributed to
lessen his respect for them. He desired " to be inferior to no man
in Sparta,"[2] and his conspiracy was undertaken to realize this
object by breaking up the constitution.

It has already been mentioned that amidst the general insecurity
which pervaded the political society of Laconia, the ephors maintained a secret police and system of espionage which reached its
height of unscrupulous efficiency under the title of the Krypteia.
Such precautions were now more than ever requisite; for the
changes in the practical working of Spartan politics tended to
multiply the number of malcontents, and to throw the Inferiors as
well as the Periœki and the Neodamodes (manumitted Helots),
into one common antipathy with the Helots, against the exclusive
partnership of the Peers. Informers were thus sure of encouragement and reward, and the man who now came to the ephors either

---

[1] Xen. Hellen. iii, 3, 9. Ὑπηρετήκει δὲ καὶ ἄλλ᾽ ἤδη ὁ Κινάδων τοῖς Ἐφόροις τοιαῦτα. iii, 3, 7. Οἱ συντεταγμένοι ἡμῶν (Kinadon says) αὐτοὶ ὅπλα
κεκτήμεθα.

[2] Xen. Hellen. iii, 3, 11. μηδενὸς ἥττων εἶναι τῶν ἐν Λακεδαίμονι — was
the declaration of Kinadon when seized and questioned by the ephors con-
cerning his purposes. Substantially it coincides with Aristotle (Polit. v, 6,
2) — ἢ ὅταν ἀνδρώδης τις ὢν μὴ μετέχῃ τῶν τιμῶν, οἷον Κινάδων ὁ τὴν ἐπ
Ἀγησιλάου συστήσας ἐπίθεσιν ἐπὶ τοὺς Σπαρτιάτας.

was really an intimate friend of Kinadon, or had professed himself
such in order to elicit the secret. " Kinadon (said he to the ephors)
brought me to the extremity of the market-place, and bade me
count how many Spartans there were therein. I reckoned up
about forty, besides the king, the ephors and the senators. Upon
my asking him why he desired me to count them, he replied, —
Because these are the men, and the only men, whom you have
to look upon as enemies; [1] all others in the market-place, more
than four thousand in number, are friends and comrades. Kina
don also pointed out to me the one or two Spartans whom we met
in the roads, or who were lords in the country districts, as our only
enemies; every one else around them being friendly to our purpose." " How many did he tell you were the accomplices actually
privy to the scheme ? " — asked the ephors. " Only a few (was
the reply) ; but those thoroughly trustworthy; these confidants
themselves, however, said that all around them were accomplices,
— Inferiors, Periœki, Neodamodes, and Helots, all alike; for
whenever any one among the classes talked about a Spartan, he
could not disguise his intense antipathy, — he talked as if he could
eat the Spartans raw." [2]

" But how (continued the ephors) did Kinadon reckon upon getting arms ? " " His language was (replied the witness) — We of
the standing force have our own arms all ready ; and here are
plenty of knives, swords, spits, hatchets, axes and scythes — on sale
in this market-place, to suit an insurgent multitude ; besides, every
man who tills the earth, or cuts wood and stone, has tools by him
which will serve as weapons in case of need ; especially in a struggle with enemies themselves unarmed." On being asked what was
the moment fixed for execution, the witness could not tell ; he had
been instructed only to remain on the spot, and be ready.[3]

---

[1] Xen. Hellen. iii, 3, 5.

[2] Xen. Hellen. iii, 3, 6. Αὐτοὶ μέντοι πᾶσιν ἔφασαν συνειδέναι καὶ εἵλωσι
καὶ νεοδαμώδεσι, καὶ τοῖς ὑπομείοσι, καὶ τοῖς 1 εριοίκοις· ὅπου γὰρ ἐν τούτοις
τις λόγος γένοιτο περὶ Σπαρτιατῶν, οὐδένα δύνασθαι κρύπτειν τὸ μὴ οὐχ
ἡδέως ἂν καὶ ὠμῶν ἐσθίειν αὐτῶν.

The expression is Homeric — ὠμὸν βεβρώθοις Πρίαμον, etc. (Iliad. iv, 35).
The Greeks did not think themselves obliged to restrain the full expression
of vindictive feeling. The poet Theognis wishes, " that he may one day
come to drink the blood of those who had ill-used him" v. 349 Gaisf.)

[2] Xen. Hellen. iii, 3, 7. ὅτι ἐπιδημεῖν οἱ παρηγγελμένον εἴη.

It does not appear that this man knew the name of any person concerned, except Kinadon himself. So deeply were the ephors alarmed, that they refrained from any formal convocation even of what was called the Lesser Assembly, — including the senate, of which the kings were members *ex officio*, and, perhaps, a few other principal persons besides. But the members of this assembly were privately brought together to deliberate on the emergency; Agesilaus, probably, among them. To arrest Kinadon at once in Sparta appeared imprudent; since his accomplices, of number as yet unknown, would be thus admonished either to break out in insurrection, or at least to make their escape. But an elaborate stratagem was laid for arresting him out of Sparta, without the knowledge of his accomplices. The ephors, calling him before them, professed to confide to him (as they had done occasionally before) a mission to go to Aulon (a Laconian town on the frontier towards Arcadia and Triphylia) and there to seize some parties designated by name in a formal skytalê or warrant; including some of the Aulonite Periœki,— some Helots, — and one other person by name, a woman of peculiar beauty, resident at the place, whose influence was understood to spread disaffection among all the Lacedæmonians who came thither, old as well as young.[1] When Kinadon inquired what force he was to take with him on the mission, the ephors, to obviate all suspicion that they were picking out companions with views hostile to him, desired him to go to the Hippagretês (or commander of the three hundred youthful guards called horsemen, though they were not really mounted) and ask for the first six or seven men of the guard[2] who might happen to be in the way. But they (the ephors) had already held secret communication with the Hippagretês, and had informed him both whom they wished to be sent, and what the persons sent were to

---

[1] Xen. Hellen. iii, 3, 8. Ἀγαγεῖν δὲ ἐκέλευον καὶ τὴν γυναῖκα, ἣ καλλίστη μὲν ἐλέγετο αὐτόθι εἶναι, λυμαίνεσθαι δὲ ἐφκει τοὺς ἀφικνουμένους Λακεδαιμονίων καὶ πρεσβυτέρους καὶ νεωτέρους.

[2] Xen. Hellen. iii, 3, 9, 10.

The persons called Hippeis at Sparta, were not mounted; they were a select body of three hundred youthful citizens, employed either on home police or on foreign service.

See Herodot. viii, 124; Strabo, x, p. 481; K. O. Müller, History of the Dorians, B. iii, ch. 12, s. 5, 6.

do. They then despatched Kinadon on his pretended mission
telling him that they should place at his disposal three carts, in
order that he might more easily bring home the prisoners.

Kinadon began his journey to Aulon, without the smallest suspicion of the plot laid for him by the ephors; who, to make their
purpose sure, sent an additional body of the guards after him, to
quell any resistance which might possibly arise. But their stratagem succeeded as completely as they could desire. He was seized
on the road, by those who accompanied him ostensibly for his
pretended mission. These men interrogated him, put him to the
torture,[1] and heard from his lips the names of his accomplices;

---

[1] Xen. Hellen. iii, 3, 9.

Ἔμελλον δὲ οἱ συλλαβόντες αὐτὸν μὲν κατέχειν, τοὺς δὲ ξυνειδότας, πι-
θόμενοι αὐτοῦ, γράψαντες ἀποπέμπειν τὴν ταχίστην τοῖς ἐφόροις. Οὕτω δ᾽ εἶχον οἱ ἔφοροι πρὸς τὸ πρᾶγμα, ὥστε καὶ μορὰν ἱππέων ἐπεμψαν τοῖς ἐπ᾽ Αὐλῶνος. Ἐπεὶ δ᾽ εἰλημμένου τοῦ ἀνδρὸς ἧκεν ἱππεὺς, φέρων
τὰ ὀνόματα ὧν Κινάδων ἀπέγραψε, παραχρῆμα τόν τε μάντιν Τισ-
άμενον καὶ τοὺς ἐπικαιριωτάτους ξυνελάμβανον. Ὡς δ᾽ ἀνήχθη ὁ Κινάδων,
καὶ ἠλέγχετο, καὶ ὡμολόγει πάντα, καὶ τοὺς ξυνειδότας ἔλεγε, τέλος
αὐτὸν ἤροντο, τί καὶ βουλόμενος ταῦτα πράττοι;

Polyænus (ii, 14, 1) in his account of this transaction, expressly mentions
that the Hippeis or guards who accompanied Kinadon, put him to the torture (στρεβλώσαντες) when they seized him, in order to extort the names of
his accomplices. Even without express testimony, we might pretty confidently have assumed this. From a man of spirit like Kinadon, they were
not likely to obtain such betrayal without torture.

I had affirmed that in the description of this transaction given by Xen
ophon, it did not appear whether Kinadon was able to write or not. My
assertion was controverted by Colonel Mure (in his Reply to my Appendix),
who cited the words φέρων τὰ ὀνόματα ὧν Κινάδων ἀπέγραψε, as containing an affirmation from Xenophon that Kinadon could write.

In my judgment, these words, taken in conjunction with what precedes,
and with the probabilities of the fact described, do not contain such an affirmation.

The guards were instructed to seize Kinadon, and after *having heard from
Kinadon who his accomplices were, to write the names down and send them to the
ephors*. It is to be presumed that they executed these instructions as given;
the more so, as what they were commanded to do, was at once the safest
and the most natural proceeding. For Kinadon was a man distinguished
for personal *stature and courage* (τὸ εἶδος καὶ τὴν ψυχὴν εὔρωστος, iii, 3, 5)
so that those who seized him would find it an indispensable precaution to
pinion his arms. Assuming even that Kinadon could write, — yet, if he
were to write, he must have his right arm free. And why should the guards

the list of whom they wrote down, and forwarded by one of the guards to Sparta. The ephors, on receiving it, immediately arrested the parties principally concerned, especially the prophet Tisamenus ; and examined them along with Kinadon, as soon as

---

take this risk, when all which the ephers required was, that Kinadon should *pronounce* the names, to be written down by others ? With a man of the qualities of Kinadon, it probably required the most intense pressure to force him to betray his comrades, even by word of mouth ; it would probably be more difficult still, to force him to betray them by the more deliberate act of writing.

I conceive that ἥκει ἱππεὺς, φέρων τὰ ὀνόματα ὧν ὁ Κινάδων ἀπέγραψε is to be construed with reference to the preceding sentence, and announces the carrying into effect of the instructions then reported as given by the ephors. " A guard came, bearing the names of those whom Kinadon had given in." It is not necessary to suppose that Kinadon had written down these names with his own hand.

In the beginning of the Oration of Andokides (De Mysteriis), Pythoni-kus gives information of a mock celebration of the mysteries, committed by Alkibiades and others ; citing as his witness the slave Andromachus ; who is accordingly produced, and states to the assembly *vivâ voce* what he had seen and who were the persons present— Πρῶτος μὲν οὗτος (Androma-chus) ταῦτα ἐμήνυσε, καὶ ἀπέγραψε τούτους (s. 13). It is not here meant to affirm that the slave Andromachus wrote down the names of these persons, which he had the moment before publicly announced to the assem-bly. It is by the words ἀπέγραψε τούτους that the orator describes the pub-lic oral announcement made by Andromachus, which was formally taken note of by a secretary, and which led to legal consequences against the persons whose names were given in.

So again, in the old law quoted by Demosthenes (adv. Makast. p. 1068), Ἀπογραφέτω δὲ τὸν μὴ ποιοῦντα ταῦτα ὁ βουλόμενος πρὸς τὸν ἄρχοντα ; and in Demosthenes adv. Nikostrat. p. 1247. Ἁ ἐκ τῶν νόμων τῷ ἰδιώτῃ τῷ ἀπογράψαντι γίγνεται, τῇ πόλει ἀφίημι : compare also Lysias, De Bonis Aristophanis, Or. xix, s. 53 ; it is not meant to affirm that ὁ ἀπογράφων was required to perform his process in writing, or was necessarily able to write. A citizen who could not write might do this, as well as one who could. He *informed against* a certain person as delinquent ; he *informed of* certain arti-cles of property, as belonging to the estate of one whose property had been confiscated to the city. The information, as well as the name of the in-former, was taken down by the official person, — whether the informer could himself write or not.

It appears to me that Kinadon, having been interrogated, *told* to the guards who first seized him, the names of his accomplices, — just as he *told* these names afterwards to the ephors (καὶ τοὺς ξυνειδότας ἔλεγε) ; and this, whether he was, or was not, able to write ; a point, which the passage of Xenophon noway determines.

he was brought prisoner. They asked the latter, among other questions, what was his purpose in setting on foot the conspiracy; to which he replied, — "I wanted to be inferior to no man at Sparta." His punishment was not long deferred. Having been manacled with a clog round his neck to which his hands were made fast, — he was in this condition conducted round the city, with men scourging and pricking him during the progress. His accomplices were treated in like manner, and at length all of them were put to death.[1]

Such is the curious narrative, given by Xenophon, of this unsuccessful conspiracy. He probably derived his information from Agesilaus himself; since we cannot easily explain how he could have otherwise learnt so much about the most secret manœuvres of the ephors, in a government proverbial for constant secrecy, like that of Sparta. The narrative opens to us a glimpse, though sadly transient and imperfect, of the internal dangers of the Spartan government. We were aware, from earlier evidences, of great discontent prevailing among the Helots, and to a certain extent among the Periœki. But the incident here described presents to us the first manifestation of a body of malcontents among the Spartans themselves; malcontents formidable both from energy and position, like Kinadon and the prophet Tisamenus. Of the state of disaffected feeling in the provincial townships of Laconia, an impressive proof is afforded by the case of that beautiful woman who was alleged to be so active in political proselytism at Aulon ; not less than by the passionate expressions of hatred revealed in the deposition of the informer himself. Though little is known about the details, yet it seems that the tendency of affaris at Sparta was to concentrate both power and property in the hands of an oligarchy ever narrowing among the citizens ; thus aggravating the dangers at home, even at the time when the power of the state was greatest abroad, and preparing the way for that irreparable humiliation which began with the defeat of Leuktra.

It can hardly be doubted that much more wide-spread discontent came to the knowledge of the ephors than that which is specially indicated in Xenophon. And such discovery may probably have been one of the motives (as had happened in 424 B. C. on occasion

---

[1] Xenoph. Hellen. iii, 3, 11.

of the expedition of Brasidas into Thrace) which helped to bring about the Asiatic expedition of Agesilaus, as an outlet for brave malcontents on distant and lucrative military service.

Derkyllidas had now been carrying on war in Asia Minor for near three years, against Tissaphernes and Pharnabazus, with so much efficiency and success, as both to protect the Asiatic Greeks on the coast, and to intercept all the revenues which those satraps either transmitted to court or enjoyed themselves. Pharnabazus had already gone up to Susa (during his truce with Derkyllidas in 397 B. C.), and besides obtaining a reinforcement which acted under himself and Tissaphernes in 396 B. C. against Derkyllidas in Lydia, had laid schemes for renewing the maritime war against Sparta.[1]

It is now that we hear again mentioned the name of **Konon**, who, having saved himself with nine triremes from the defeat of Ægospotami, had remained for the last seven years under the protection of Evagoras, prince of Salamis, in Cyprus, Konon, having married at Salamis, and having a son[2] born to him there, indulged but faint hopes of ever returning to his native city, when, fortunately for him as well as for Athens, the Persians again became eager for an efficient admiral and fleet on the coast of Asia Minor. Through representations from Pharnabazus, as well as from Evagoras in Cyprus, — and through correspondence of the latter with the Greek physician Ktesias, who wished to become personally employed in the negotiation, and who seems to have had considerable influence with queen Parysatis,[3] — orders were obtained, and funds provided, to equip in Phœnicia and Kilikia a numerous fleet, under the command of Konon. While that officer began to show himself, and to act with such triremes as he

---

[1] Diodor. xiv, 39 ; Xen. Hellen. iii, 3, 13.

[2] Lysias, Orat. xix, (De Bonis Aristophanis) s. 38.

[3] See Ktesias, Fragmenta, Persica, c. 63, ed. Bähr; Plutarch, Artax. c. 21

We cannot make out these circumstances with any distinctness ; but the general fact is plainly testified, and is besides very probable. Another Grecian surgeon (besides Ktesias) is mentioned as concerned, — Polykritus of Mendê; and a Kretan dancer named Zeno, — both established at the Persian court.

There is no part of the narrative of Ktesias, the loss of which is so much to be regretted as this ; relating transactions, in which he was himself concerned, and seemingly giving original letters.

found in readiness (about forty in number) along the southern coast
of Asia Minor from Kilikia to Kaunus,[1] — further preparations
were vigorously prosecuted in the Phœnician ports, in order to
make up the fleet to three hundred sail.[2]

It was by a sort of accident that news of such equipment reached
Sparta, — in an age of the world when diplomatic residents were
as yet unknown. A Syracusan merchant named Herodas, having
visited the Phœnician ports for trading purposes, brought back to
Sparta intelligence of the preparations which he had seen, sufficient
to excite much uneasiness. The Spartans were taking counsel
among themselves, and communicating with their neighboring
allies, when Agesilaus, at the instance of Lysander, stood forward
as a volunteer to solicit the command of a land-force for the purpose of attacking the Persians in Asia. He proposed to take with
him only thirty full Spartan citizens or peers, as a sort of Board
or Council of Officers ; two thousand Neodamodes or enfranchised
Helots, whom the ephors were probably glad to send away, and
who would be selected from the bravest and most formidable ; and
six thousand hoplites from the land-allies, to whom the prospect
of a rich service against Asiatic enemies would be tempting. Of
these thirty Spartans, Lysander intended to be the leader ; and
thus, reckoning on his preëstablished influence over Agesilaus, to
exercise the real command himself, without the name. He had
no serious fear of the Persian arms, either by land or sea. He
looked upon the announcement of the Phœnician fleet to be an
empty threat, as it had so often proved in the mouth of Tissaphernes during the late war ; while the Cyreian expedition had
inspired him further with ardent hopes of another successful Anabasis, or conquering invasion of Persia from the sea-coast inwards.
But he had still more at heart to employ his newly-acquired
ascendency in reëstablishing everywhere the dekarchies, which
had excited such intolerable hatred and exercised so much oppression, that even the ephors had refused to lend positive aid in
upholding them, so that they had been in several places broken up
or modified.[3] If the ambition of Agesilaus was comparatively less
stained by personal and factious antipathies, and more Pan-hellenic

---

[1] Diodor. xiv, 39–79.   [2] Xen. Hellen. iii, 4, 1
[3] Xen. Hellen. iii, 4, 2.

in its aim, than that of Lysander,—it was at the same time yet more unmeasured in respect to victory over the Great King, whom he dreamed of dethroning, or at least of expelling from Asia Minor and the coast.[1] So powerful was the influence exercised by the Cyreian expedition over the schemes and imagination of energetic Greeks: so sudden was the outburst of ambition in the mind of Agesilaus, for which no one before had given him credit.

Though this plan was laid by two of the ablest men in Greece, it turned out to be rash and improvident, so far as the stability of the Lacedæmonian empire was concerned. That empire ought to have been made sure by sea, where its real danger lay, before attempts were made to extend it by new inland acquisitions. And except for purposes of conquest, there was no need of farther reinforcements in Asia Minor; since Derkyllidas was already there with a force competent to make head against the satraps. Nevertheless, the Lacedæmonians embraced the plan eagerly; the more so, as envoys were sent from many of the subject cities, by the partisans of Lysander and in concert with him, to entreat that Agesilaus might be placed at the head of the expedition, with as large a force as he required.[2]

No difficulty probably was found in levying the proposed number of men from the allies, since there was great promise of plunder for the soldiers in Asia. But the altered position of Sparta with respect to her most powerful allies was betrayed by the refusal of Thebes, Corinth, and Athens to take any part in the expedition. The refusal of Corinth, indeed, was excused professedly on the ground of a recent inauspicious conflagration of one of the temples in the city ; and that of Athens, on the plea of weakness and exhaustion not yet repaired. But the latter, at least, had already begun to conceive some hope from the projects of Konon.[3]

The mere fact that a king of Sparta was about to take the command and pass into Asia, lent peculiar importance to the enterprise. The Spartan kings, in their function of leaders of Greece, conceived themselves to have inherited the sceptre of Agamemnon

---

Xen. Hellen. iii, 5, 1. ἐλπίδας ἔχοντα μεγάλας αἱρήσειν βασιλέα, etc Compare iv, 2, 3.

Xen. Agesilaus, i, 36. ἐπινοῶν καὶ ἐλπίζων καταλύσειν τὴν ἐπὶ τὴν Ἑλ ιάδα στρατεύσασαν πρότερον ἀρχὴν, etc.

[2] Plutarch, Agesil. c. 5.   [3] Xen. Hellen. iii, 5, 5 , Pausan. iii, 9, 1.

and Orestes ;[1] and Agesilaus, especially, assimilated his expedition to a new Trojan war, — an effort of united Greece, for the purpose of taking vengeance on the common Asiatic enemy of the Hellenic name. The sacrifices having been found favorable, Agesilaus took measures for the transit of the troops from various ports to Ephesus. But he himself, with one division, touched in his way at Geræstus, the southern point of Eubœa; wishing to cross from thence and sacrifice at Aulis, (the port of Bœotia nearly opposite to Geræstus on the other side of the strait) where Agamemnon had offered his memorable sacrifice immediately previous to departure for Troy. It appears that he both went to the spot, and began the sacrifice, without asking permission from the Thebans ; moreover, he was accompanied by his own prophet, who conducted the solemnities in a manner not consistent with the habitual practice of the temple or chapel of Artemis at Aulis. On both these grounds, the Thebans, resenting the proceeding as an insult, sent a body of armed men, and compelled him to desist from the sacrifice.[2] Not taking part themselves in the expedition, they probably considered that the Spartan king was presumptuous in assuming to himself the Pan-hellenic character of a second Agamemnon ; and they thus inflicted a humiliation which Agesilaus never forgave.

Agesilaus seems to have reached Asia about the time when Derkyllidas had recently concluded his last armistice with Tissaphernes and Pharnabazus ; an armistice, intended to allow time for mutual communication both with Sparta and the Persian court. On being asked by the satrap what was his purpose in coming, Agesilaus merely renewed the demand which had before been made by Derkyllidas — of autonomy for the Asiatic Greeks. Tissaphernes replied by proposing a continuation of the same armistice, until he could communicate with the Persian court, — adding that he hoped to be empowered to grant the demand. A fresh armistice was accordingly sworn to on both sides, for three months ; Derkyllidas (who with his army came now under the command of Agesilaus) and Herippidas being sent to the satrap to receive his oath, and take oaths to him in return.[3]

---

[1] Herodot. i, 68; vii, 159; Pausan. iii, 16, 6.

[2] Xen. Hellen. iii, 4, 3, 4 ; iii, 5, 5 ; Plutarch, Agesilaus, c. 6; Pausan. iii, 9, 2.

[3] Xen. Hellen. iii, 4, 5, 6 ; Xen. Agesilaus, i, 10.

The term of three months is specified only in the latter passage. The

While the army was thus condemned to temporary inaction at Ephesus, the conduct and position of Lysander began to excite intolerable jealousy in the superior officers; and most of all Agesilaus. So great and established was the reputation of Lysander, — whose statue had been erected at Ephesus itself in the temple of Artemis,[1] as well as in many other cities, — that all the Asiatic Greeks looked upon him as the real chief of the expedition. That *he* should be real chief, under the nominal command of another, was nothing more than what had happened before, in the year wherein he gained the great victory of Ægospotami, — the Lacedæmonians having then also sent him out in the ostensible capacity of secretary to the admiral Arakus, in order to save the inviolability of their own rule, that the same man should not serve twice as admiral.[2] It was through the instigation of Lysander, and with a view to his presence, that the decemvirs and other partisans in the subject cities had sent to Sparta to petition for Agesilaus; a prince as yet untried and unknown. So that Lysander, — taking credit, with truth, for having ensured to Agesilaus first the crown, next this important appointment, — intended for himself, and was expected by others, to exercise a fresh turn of command, and to renovate in every town the discomfited or enfeebled dekarchies. Numbers of his partisans came to Ephesus to greet his arrival, and a crowd of petitioners were seen following his steps everywhere; while Agesilaus himself appeared comparatively neglected. Moreover, Lysander resumed all that insolence of manner which he had contracted during his former commands, and which on this occasion gave the greater offence, since the manner of Agesilaus was both courteous and simple in a peculiar degree.[3]

The thirty Spartan counsellors, over whom Lysander had been named to preside, finding themselves neither consulted by him, nor solicited by others, were deeply dissatisfied. Their complaints

---

former armistice of Derkyllidas had probably not expired when Agesilaus first arrived.

[1] Pausan. vi, 3, 6.

[2] Xen. Hellen. ii, 1, 7. This rule does not seem to have been adhered to afterwards. Lysander was sent out again as commander in 403 B. C. It is possible, indeed, that he may have been again sent out as nominal secretary to some other person named as commander.

[3] Plutarch, Agesilaus, c 7

helped to encourage Agesilaus, who was still more keenly wounded in his own personal dignity, to put forth a resolute and imperious strength of will, such as he had not before been known to possess. He successively rejected every petition preferred to him by or through Lysander; a systematic purpose which, though never formally announced,[1] was presently discerned by the petitioners, by the Thirty, and by Lysander himself. The latter thus found himself not merely disappointed in all his calculations, but humiliated to excess, though without any tangible ground of complaint. He was forced to warn his partisans, that his intervention was an injury and not a benefit to them; that they must desist from obsequious attentions to him, and must address themselves directly to Agesilaus. With that prince he also remonstrated on his own account, — "Truly, Agesilaus, you know how to degrade your friends." — "Ay, to be sure (was the reply), those among them who want to appear greater than I am; but such as seek to uphold me, I should be ashamed if I did not know how to repay with due honor." — Lysander was constrained to admit the force of this reply, and to request, as the only means of escape from present and palpable humiliation, that he might be sent on some mission apart; engaging to serve faithfully in whatever duty he might be employed.[2]

This proposition, doubtless even more agreeable to Agesilaus than to himself, being readily assented to, he was despatched on a mission to the Hellespont. Faithful to his engagement of forgetting past offences and serving with zeal, he found means to gain over a Persian grandee named Spithridates, who had received some offence from Pharnabazus. Spithridates revolted openly, carrying a regiment of two hundred horse to join Agesilaus; who was thus enabled to inform himself fully about the sa

---

[1] The sarcastic remarks which Plutarch ascribes to Agesilaus, calling Lysander "my meat-distributor" (κρεοδαίτην), are not warranted by Xenophon, and seem not to be probable under the circumstances (Plutarch. Lysand. c. 23 ; Plutarch, Agesil. c. 8).

[2] Xen. Hellen. iii, 4, 7–10; Plutarch, Agesilaus, c 7–8; Plutarch, Lysand. c. 23.

It is remarkable that in the Opusculum of Xenophon, a special Panegyric called *Agesilaus*, not a word is said about this highly characteristic proceeding between Agesilaus and Lysander at Ephesus ; nor indeed is the name of Lysander once mentioned.

trapy of Pharnabazus, comprising the territory called Phrygia, in the neighborhood of the Propontis and the Hellespont.[1]

The army under Tissaphernes had been already powerful at the moment when his timidity induced him to conclude the first armistice with Derkyllidas. But additional reinforcements, received since the conclusion of the second and more recent armistice, had raised him to such an excess of confidence, that even before the stipulated three months had expired, he sent to insist on the immediate departure of Agesilaus from Asia, and to proclaim war forthwith, if such departure were delayed. While this message, accompanied by formidable reports of the satrap's force, filled the army at Ephesus with mingled alarm and indignation, Agesilaus accepted the challenge with cheerful readiness; sending word back that he thanked the satrap for perjuring himself in so flagrant a manner, as to set the gods against him and ensure their favor to the Greek side.[2] Orders were forthwith given, and contingents summoned from the Asiatic Greeks, for a forward movement southward, to cross the Mæander, and attack Tissaphernes in Karia, where he usually resided. The cities on the route were required to provide magazines, so that Tissaphernes, fully anticipating attack in this direction, caused his infantry to cross into Karia, for the purpose of acting on the defensive; while he kept his numerous cavalry in the plain of the Mæander, with a view to overwhelm Agesilaus, who had no cavalry, in his march over that level territory towards the Karian hills and rugged ground. But the Lacedæmonian king, having put the enemy on this false scent, suddenly turned his march northward towards Phrygia and the satrapy of Pharnabazus. Tissaphernes took no pains to aid his brother satrap, who on his side had made few preparations for defence. Accordingly Agesilaus, finding little or no resistance, took many towns and villages, and collected abundance of provisions, plunder, and slaves. Profiting by the guidance of the revolted Spithridates, and marching as little as possible over the plains, he carried on lucrative and unopposed incursions as far as the neighborhood of Daskylium, the residence of the satrap himself, near the Propontis. Near the satrapic residence, however, his small

---

[1] Xen. Hellen. iii, 4, 10.

[2] Xen. Hellen. iii, 4, 11, 12 Xen. Agesil. i, 12–14; Plutarch, Agesil. c. 9.

body of cavalry, ascending an eminence, came suddenly upon an equal detachment of Persian cavalry, under Rhathines and Bagæus; who attacked them vigorously, and drove them back with some loss, until they were protected by Agesilaus himself coming up with the hoplites. The effect of such a check (and there were probably others of the same kind, though Xenophon does not specify them) on the spirits of the army was discouraging. On the next morning, the sacrifices being found unfavorable for farther advance, Agesilaus gave orders for retreating towards the sea. He reached Ephesus about the close of autumn; resolved to employ the winter in organizing a more powerful cavalry, which experience proved to be indispensable.[1]

This autumnal march through Phrygia was more lucrative than glorious. Yet it enables Xenophon to bring to view different merits of his hero Agesilaus; in doing which he exhibits to us ancient warfare and Asiatic habits on a very painful side. In common both with Kallikratidas and Lysander, though not with the ordinary Spartan commanders, Agesilaus was indifferent to the acquisition of money for himself. But he was not the less anxious to enrich his friends, and would sometimes connive at unwarrantable modes of acquisition for their benefit. Deserters often came in to give information of rich prizes or valuable prisoners; which advantages, if he had chosen, he might have appropriated to himself. But he made it a practice to throw both the booty and the honor in the way of some favorite officer; just as we have seen (in a former chapter) that Xenophon himself was allowed by the army to capture Asidates and enjoy a large portion of his ransom.[2] Again, when the army in the course of its march was at a considerable distance from the sea, and appeared to be advancing farther inland, the authorized auctioneers, whose province it was to sell the booty, found the buyers extremely slack. It was difficult to keep or carry what was bought, and opportunity for resale did not

---

[1] Xen. Hellen. iii, 4, 13–15; Xen. Agesil. i, 23. Ἐπεὶ μέντοι οὐδὲ ἐν τῇ Φρυγίᾳ ἀνὰ τὰ πέδια ἐδύνατο στρατεύεσθαι, διὰ τὴν Φαρναβάζου ἱππείαν, etc. Plutarch, Agesil. c. 9.

These military operations of Agesilaus are loosely adverted to in the early part of c. 79 of the fourteenth Book of Diodorus.

[2] Xen. Agesil. i, 19; Xen. Anabas. vii, 8, 20–23; Plutarch, Reipub. Gerend. Præcept. p. 809, B. See above, Chapter lxxii, of this History.

seem at hand. Agesilaus, while he instructed the auctioneers to sell upon credit, without insisting on ready money, — at the same time gave private hints to a few friends that he was very shortly about to return to the sea. The friends thus warned, bidding for the plunder on credit and purchasing at low prices, were speedily enabled to dispose of it again at a seaport, with large profits.[1]

We are not surprised to hear that such lucrative graces procured for Agesilaus many warm admirers; though the eulogies of Xenophon ought to have been confined to another point in his conduct, now to be mentioned. Agesilaus, while securing for his army the plunder of the country over which he carried his victorious arms, took great pains to prevent both cruelty and destruction of property. When any town surrendered to him on terms, his exactions were neither ruinous nor grossly humiliating.[2] Amidst all the plunder realized, too, the most valuable portion was the adult natives of both sexes, hunted down and brought in by the predatory light troops of the army, to be sold as slaves. Agesilaus was vigilant in protecting these poor victims from ill-usage; inculcating upon his soldiers the duty, "not of punishing them like wrong-doers, but simply of keeping them under guard as men.[3]" It was the practice of the poorer part of the native population often to sell their little children for exportation to travelling slave-merchants, from inability to maintain them. The children thus purchased, if they promised to be handsome, were often mutilated, and fetched large prices as eunuchs, to supply the large demand for the harems and religious worship of many Asiatic towns. But in their haste to get out of the way of a plundering army, these slave-merchants were forced often to leave by the way-side the little children whom they had purchased, exposed to the wolves, the dogs, or starvation. In this wretched condition, they were found by Agesilaus on his march. His humane disposition prompted him to see them carried to a place of safety, where he gave them in charge of those old natives whom age and feebleness had

---

[1] Xen. Agesil. i, 18.   πάντες παμπλήθη χρήματα ἔλαβον.

[2] Xen. Agesil. i, 20–22.

[3] Xen. Hellen. iii, 4, 19; Xen. Agesil. i, 28.   τοὺς ὑπὸ τῶν λῃστῶν ἁλισ κομένους βαρβάρους.

So the word λῃστής, used in reference to the fleet, means the commander of a predatory vessel or privateer (Xen. Hellen. ii, 1, 30).

caused to be left behind as not worth carrying off. By such active kindness, rare, indeed, in a Grecian general, towards the conquered, he earned the gratitude of the captives, and the sympathies of every one around.[1]

This interesting anecdote, imparting a glimpse of the ancient world in reference to details which Grecian historians rarely condescend to unveil, demonstrates the compassionate disposition of Agesilaus. We find in conjunction with it another anecdote, illustrating the Spartan side of his character. The prisoners who had been captured during the expedition were brought to Ephesus, and

---

[1] Xen. Agesil. i, 21. Καὶ πολλάκις μὲν προηγόρευε τοῖς στρατιώταις τοὺς ἁλισκομένους μὴ ὡς ἀδίκους τιμωρεῖσθαι, ἀλλ᾽ ὡς ἀνθρώπους ὄντας φυλάσσειν. Πολλάκις δὲ, ὁπότε μεταστρατοπεδεύοιτο, εἰ αἴσθοιτο καταλελειμμένα παιδάρια μικρὰ ἐμπόρων, (ἃ πολλοὶ ἐπώλουν, διὰ τὸ νομίζειν μὴ δύνασθαι ἂν φέρειν αὐτὰ καὶ τρέφειν) ἐπεμέλετο καὶ τούτων, ὅπως συγκομίζοιτό ποι· τοῖς δ᾽ αὖ διὰ γῆρας καταλελειμμένοις αἰχμαλώτοις προσέταττεν ἐπιμελεῖσθαι αὐτῶν, ὡς μήτε ὑπὸ κυνῶν, μήθ᾽ ὑπὸ λύκων, διαφθείροιντο. Ὥστε οὐ μόνον οἱ πυνθανόμενοι ταῦτα, ἀλλὰ καὶ αὐτοὶ οἱ ἁλισκόμενοι, εὐμενεῖς αὐτῷ ἐγίγνοντο.

Herodotus affirms that the Thracians also sold their children for exportation, — πωλεῦσι τὰ τέκνα ἐπ᾽ ἐξαγωγῇ (Herod. v, 6): compare Philostratus, Vit. Apollon. viii, 7–12, p. 346; and Ch. xvi, Vol. III, p. 216 of this History.

Herodotus mentions the Chian merchant Panionius (like the " Mitylenæus mango" in Martial, — " Sed Mitylenæi roseus mangonis ephebus " Martial, vii, 79) — as having conducted on a large scale the trade of purchasing ooys, looking out for such as were handsome, to supply the great demand in the East for eunuchs, who were supposed to make better and more attached servants. Herodot. viii, 105. ὅκως γὰρ κτήσαιτο (Panionius) παῖδας εἴδεος ἐπαμμένους, ἐκτάμνων, ἀγινέων ἐπώλεε ἐς Σάρδις τε καὶ Ἔφεσον χρη ιάτων μεγάλων· παρὰ γὰρ τοῖσι βαρβάροισι τιμιώτεροί εἰσι οἱ εὐνοῦχοι, πίσ- "ιος εἴνεκα τῆς πάσης, τῶν εὐνούχων. Boys were necessary, as the operation was performed in childhood or youth, — παῖδες ἐκτομίαι (Herodot. vi, 6–32 : compare iii, 48). The Babylonians, in addition to their large pecuniary tribute, had to furnish to the Persian court annually five hundred παῖδας ἐκτομίας (Herodot. iii, 92). For some farther remarks on the preference of the Persians both for the persons and the services of εὐνοῦχοι, see Dio Chrysostom, Orat. xxi, p. 270 ; Xenoph. Cyropæd. vii, 5, 61–65. Hellanikus (Fr. 169, ed. Didot) affirmed that the Persians had derived both the persons so employed, and the habit of employing them, from the Babylonians.

When Mr. Hanway was travelling near the Caspian, among the Kal mucks, little children of two or three years of age, were often tendered to oim for sale, at two rubles per head (Hanway's Travels, ch. xvi, pp. 65, 66)

sold during the winter as slaves for the profit of the army. Agesilaus,— being then busily employed in training his troops to military efficiency, especially for the cavalry service during the ensuing campaign,— thought it advisable to impress them with contempt for the bodily capacity and prowess of the natives. He therefore directed the heralds who conducted the auction, to put the prisoners up to sale in a state of perfect nudity. To have the body thus exposed, was a thing never done, and even held disgraceful by the native Asiatics; while among the Greeks the practice was universal for purposes of exercise,— or at least, had become universal during the last two or three centuries,— for we are told that originally the Asiatic feeling on this point had prevailed throughout Greece. It was one of the obvious differences between Grecian and Asiatic customs,[1]— that in the former, both the exercises of the palæstra, as well as the matches in the solemn games, required competitors of every rank to contend naked. Agesilaus himself stripped thus habitually; Alexander, prince of Macedon, had done so, when he ran at the Olympic stadium,[2] — also the combatants out of the great family of the Diagorids of Rhodes, when they gained their victories in the Olympic pankratium, — and all those other noble pugilists, wrestlers, and runners, descended from gods and heroes, upon whom Pindar pours forth his complimentary odes.

On this occasion at Ephesus, Agesilaus gave special orders to put up the Asiatic prisoners to auction naked; not at all by way of insult, but in order to exhibit to the eye of the Greek soldier, as he contemplated them, how much he gained by his own bodily training and frequent exposure, and how inferior was the condition of men whose bodies never felt the sun or wind. They displayed a white skin, plump and soft limbs, weak and undeveloped muscles, like men accustomed to be borne in carriages instead of walking or running; from whence we indirectly learn that many of them were men in wealthy circumstances. And the purpose of Agesilaus was completely answered; since his soldiers, when they witnessed such evidences of bodily incompetence, thought that "the

---

[1] Herodot. i, 10. παρὰ γὰρ τοῖσι Λυδοῖσι, σχεδὸν δὲ παρὰ τοῖσι ἄλλοισι βαρβάροισι, καὶ ἄνδρα ὀφθῆναι γυμνὸν, ἐς αἰσχύνην μεγάλην φέρει. Compare Thucyd. i, 6; Plato, Republic, v, 3, p. 452, D.

[2] Herodot. v, 22.

enemies against whom they had to contend were not more formida‑
ble than women." [1] Such a method of illustrating the difference
between good and bad physical training, would hardly have oc‑
curred to any one except a Spartan, brought up under the Ly‑
kurgean rules.

While Agesilaus thus brought home to the vision of his soldiers
the inefficiency of untrained bodies, he kept them throughout the
winter under hard work and drill, as well in the palæstra as in
arms. A force of cavalry was still wanting. To procure it, he
enrolled all the richest Greeks in the various Asiatic towns, as
conscripts to serve on horseback; giving each of them leave to
exempt himself, however, by providing a competent substitute and
equipment, — man, horse, and arms.[2] Before the commencement
of spring, an adequate force of cavalry was thus assembled at
Ephesus, and put into tolerable exercise. Throughout the whole
winter, that city became a place of arms, consecrated to drilling
and gymnastic exercises. On parade as well as in the palæstra,
Agesilaus himself was foremost in setting the example of obedience
and hard work. Prizes were given to the diligent and improving
among hoplites, horsemen, and light troops; while the armorers,
braziers, leather-cutters, etc., — all the various artisans, whose
trade lay in muniments of war, were in the fullest employment.
"It was a sight full of encouragement (says Xenophon, who was
doubtless present and took part in it), to see Agesilaus and the
soldiers leaving the gymnasium, all with wreaths on their heads,

---

[1] Xen. Hellen. iii, 4, 19. Ἡγούμενος δὲ, καὶ τὸ καταφρονεῖν τῶν πολεμίων
ῥώμην τινα ἐμβάλλειν πρὸς τὸ μάχεσθαι, προεῖπε τοῖς κήρυξι, τοὺς ὑπὸ τῶν
λῃστῶν ἁλισκομένους βαρβάρους γυμνοὺς πωλεῖ . Ὁρῶντες οὖν οἱ στρατιῶ‑
ται λευκοὺς μὲν, διὰ τὸ μηδέποτε ἐκδύεσθαι, μαλακοὺς δὲ καὶ ἀπό‑
νους, διὰ τὸ ἀεὶ ἐπ' ὀχημάτων εἶναι, ἐνόμισαν, οὐδὲν 'ιοίσειν τὸν πόλεμον ἢ
εἰ γυναιξὶ δέοι μάχεσθαι.

Xen. Agesil. i, 28 — where he has it — πίονας οι καὶ ἀπόνους, διὰ τὸ αε
ἐπ' ὀχημάτων εἶναι (Polyænus, ii, 1, 5; Plutarch, Agesil. c. 9).

Frontinus (i, 18) recounts a proceeding somewhat similar on the part of
Gelon, after his great victory over the Carthaginians at Himera in Sicily
— "Gelo Syracusarum tyrannus, bello adversus Pœnos suscepto, cum mul‑
tos cepisset, infirmissimum quemque præcipue ex auxiliaribus, qui nigerri
mi erant, nudatum in conspectu suorum produxit. ut persuaderet contem
nendos."

[2] Xen. Hellen. iii, 4, 15; Xen. Agesil. i, 23. Compare what is related
about Scipio Africanus — Livy, xxix, 1.

and marching to the temple of Artemis to dedicate their wreaths to the goddess."[1]

Before Agesilaus was in condition to begin his military operations for the spring, the first year of his command had passed over. Thirty fresh counsellors reached Ephesus from Sparta, superseding the first thirty under Lysander, who forthwith returned home. The army was now not only more numerous, but better trained, and more systematically arranged than in the preceding campaign. Agesilaus distributed the various divisions under the command of different members of the new Thirty; the cavalry being assigned to Xenokêls, the Neodamode hoplites to Skythês, the Cyreians to Herippidas, the Asiatic contingents to Migdon. He then gave out that he should march straight against Sardis. Nevertheless, Tissaphernes, who was in that place, construing this proclamation as a feint, and believing that the real march would be directed against Karia, disposed his cavalry in the plain of the Mæander as he had done in the preceding campaign; while his infantry were sent still farther southward within the Karian frontier. On this occasion, however, Agesilaus marched as he had announced in the direction of Sardis. For three days he plundered the country without seeing an enemy; nor was it until the fourth day that the cavalry of Tissaphernes could be summoned back to oppose him; the infantry being even yet at a distance. On reaching the banks of the river Paktôlus, this Persian cavalry found the Greek light troops dispersed for the purpose of plunder, attacked them by surprise, and drove them in with considerable loss. Presently, however, Agesilaus came up, and ordered his cavalry to charge, anxious to bring on a battle before the Persian infantry could arrive in the field. In efficiency, it appears, the Persian cavalry was a full match for his cavalry, and in number apparently superior. But when he brought up his infantry, and caused his peltasts and younger hoplites to join the cavalry in a vigorous attack, — victory soon declared on his side. The Persians were put to flight and many of them drowned in the Paktôlus. Their camp, too, was taken, with a valuable booty; including several camels, which Agesilaus afterwards took with him into Greece. This success ensured to him the unopposed mastery of all the ter

---

[1] Xen. Hellen. iii, 4 17, 18; Xen. Agesil. i, 26, 27

ritory around Sardis. He carried his ravages to the very gates of that city, plundering the gardens and ornamented ground, proclaiming liberty to those within, and defying Tissaphernes to come out and fight.[1]

The career of that timid and treacherous satrap now approached its close. The Persians in or near Sardis loudly complained of him as leaving them undefended, from cowardice and anxiety for his own residence in Karia; while the court of Susa was now aware that the powerful reinforcement which had been sent to him last year, intended to drive Agesilaus out of Asia, had been made to achieve absolutely nothing. To these grounds of just dissatisfaction was added a court intrigue; to which, and to the agency of a person yet more worthless and cruel than himself, Tissaphernes fell a victim. The queen mother, Parysatis, had never forgiven him for having been one of the principal agents in the defeat and death of her son Cyrus. Her influence being now reëstablished over the mind of Artaxerxes, she took advantage of the existing discredit of the satrap to get an order sent down for his deposition and death. Tithraustes, the bearer of this order, seized him by stratagem at Kolossæ in Phrygia, while he was in the bath, and caused him to be beheaded.[2]

The mission of Tithraustes to Asia Minor was accompanied by increased efforts on the part of Persia for prosecuting the war against Sparta with vigor, by sea as well as by land; and also for fomenting the anti-Spartan movement which burst out into hostilities this year in Greece. At first, however, immediately after the death of Tissaphernes, Tithraustes endeavored to open negotiations with Agesilaus, who was in military possession of the country around Sardis, while that city itself appears to have been occupied by Ariæus, probably the same Persian who had formerly been

---

[1] Xen. Hellen. iii, 4, 21–24; Xen. Agesil. i, 32, 33; Plutarch, Agesil. c. 10.

Diodorus (xiv, 80) professes to describe this battle; but his description is hardly to be reconciled with that of Xenophon, which is better authority. Among other points of difference, Diodorus affirms that the Persians had fifty thousand infantry; and Pausanias also states (iii, 9, 3) that the number of Persian infantry in this battle was greater than had ever been got together since the times of Darius and Xerxes. Whereas, Xenophon expressly states that the Persian infantry had not come up, and took no part in the battle.

[2] Plutarch, Artaxerx. c. 23; Diodor. xiv, 80; Xen. Hellen. iii, 4, 25.

general under Cyrus, and who had now again revolted from Arta
xerxes.[1] Tithraustes took credit to the justice of the king for
having punished the late satrap ; out of whose perfidy (he affirmed)
the war had arisen.   He then summoned Agesilaus, in the king's
name, to evacuate Asia, leaving the Asiatic Greeks to pay their
original tribute to Persia, but to enjoy complete autonomy, subject
to that one condition.   Had this proposition been accepted and
executed, it would have secured these Greeks against Persian occupation or governors ; a much milder fate for them than that to
which the Lacedæmonians had consented in their conventions with
Tissaphernes sixteen years before,[2] and analogous to the position
in which the Chalkidians of Thrace had been placed with regard
to Athens, under the peace of Nikias ;[3] subject to a fixed tribute,
yet autonomous, — with no other obligation or interference. Agesilaus replied that he had no power to entertain such a proposition
without the authorities at home, whom he accordingly sent to consult.   But in the interim he was prevailed upon by Tithraustes to
conclude an armistice for six months, and to move out of his satrapy
into that of Pharnabazus ; receiving a contribution of thirty talents
towards the temporary maintenance of the army.[4] These satraps
generally acted more like independent or even hostile princes, than
coöperating colleagues ; one of the many causes of the weakness
of the Persian empire.

When Agesilaus had reached the neighborhood of Kymê, on
his march northward to the Hellespontine Phrygia, he received a
despatch from home, placing the Spartan naval force in the Asiatic
seas under his command, as well as the land-force, and empower-
ing him to name whomsoever he chose as acting admiral.[5]   For
the first time since the battle of Ægospotami, the maritime empire
of Sparta was beginning to be threatened, and increased efforts on
her part were becoming requisite. Pharnabazus, going up in person to the court of Artaxerxes, had by pressing representations
obtained a large subsidy for fitting out a fleet in Cyprus and Phœnicia, to act under the Athenian admiral Konon against the Lacedæmonians.[6]   That officer, — with a fleet of forty triremes, before

---

[1] Xen. Hellen. iii, 14, 25 ; iv, 1, 27.   [2] Thucyd. viii, 18, 37, 58.
[3] Thucyd. v, 18, 5.
[4] Xen. Hellen. iii, 4, 26 ; Diodor. xiv, 80.   ἐξαμηνιαίυς ἀνοχάς.
[5] Xen. Hellen. iii, 4, 27.   [6] Diodor. xiv, 39 , Justin, vi, 1

the equipment of the remainder was yet complete, — had ad ancea along the southern coast of Asia Minor to Kaunus, at the south western corner of the peninsula, on the frontier of Karia and Ly· kia. In this port he was besieged by the Lacedæmonian fleet of one hundred and twenty triremes under Pharax. But a Persian reinforcement strengthened the fleet of Konon to eighty sail, and put the place out of danger ; so that Pharax, desisting from the siege, retired to Rhodes.

The neighborhood of Konon, however, who was now with his fleet of eighty sail near the Chersonesus of Knidus, emboldened the Rhodians to revolt from Sparta. It was at Rhodes that the general detestation of the Lacedæmonian empire, disgraced in so many different cities by the local dekarchies and by the Spartan harmosts, first manifested itself. And such was the ardor of the Rhodian population, that their revolt took place while the fleet of Pharax was (in part at least) actually in the harbor, and they drove him out of it.[1] Konon, whose secret encouragements had helped to excite this insurrection, presently sailed to Rhodes with his fleet, and made the island his main station. It threw into his hands an unexpected advantage ; for a numerous fleet of vessels arrived there shortly afterwards, sent by Nephareus, the native king of Egypt (which was in revolt against the Persians), with marine stores and grain to the aid of the Lacedæmonians. Not having been apprized of the recent revolt, these vessels entered the harbor of Rhodes as if it were still a Lacedæmonian island ; and their cargoes were thus appropriated by Konon and the Rhodians.[2]

In recounting the various revolts of the dependencies of Athens which took place during the Peloponnesian war, I had occasion to point out more than once that all of them took place not merely in the absence of any Athenian force, but even at the instigation

---

Diodor. xiv, 79 'Ρόδιοι δὲ ἐκβαλόντες τὸν τῶν Πελοποννησίων στόλον, ὑπέστησαν ἀπὸ Λακεδαιμονίων· καὶ τὸν Κόνωνα προσεδέξαντο μετὰ τοῦ στόλου παντὸς εἰς τὴν πόλιν.

Compare Androtion apud Pausaniam, vi, 7, 2.

[2] Diodor. xiv, 79 ; Justin (vi, 2) calls this native Egyptian king Hercynion.

It seems to have been the uniform practice, for the corn-ships coming from Egypt to Greece to halt at Rhodes (Demosthen. cont. Dionysodo' 1285 : compare Herodot. ii, 182).

'in most cases) of a present hostile force, — by the contrivance of a local party, — and without privity or previous consent of the bulk of the citizens. The present revolt of Rhodes, forming a remarkable contrast on all these points, occasioned the utmost surprise and indignation among the Lacedæmonians. They saw themselves about to enter upon a renewed maritime war, without that aid which they had reckoned on receiving from Egypt, and with aggravated uncertainty in respect to their dependencies and tribute. It was under this prospective anxiety that they took the step of nominating Agesilaus to the command of the fleet as well as of the army, in order to ensure unity of operations; [1] though a distinction of functions, which they had hitherto set great value upon maintaining, was thus broken down, — and, though the two commands had never been united in any king before Agesilaus.[2] Pharax, the previous admiral, was recalled.[3]

But the violent displeasure of the Lacedæmonians against the revolted Rhodians was still better attested by another proceeding. Among all the great families at Rhodes, none were more distinguished than the Diagoridæ. Its members were not only generals and high political functionaries in their native island, but had attained even Pan-hellenic celebrity by an unparalleled series of victories at the Olympic and other great solemnities. Dorieus, a member of this family, had gained the victory in the pankration at Olympia on three successive solemnities. He had obtained seven prizes in the Nemean, and eight in the Isthmian games. He had carried off the prize at one Pythian solemnity without a contest, — no one daring to stand up against him in the fearful struggle of the pankration. As a Rhodian, while Rhodes was a subject ally of Athens during the Peloponnesian war, he had been so pronounced in his attachment to Sparta as to draw on himself a sentence of banishment; upon which he had retired to Thurii, and had been active in hostility to Athens after the Syracusan

---

[1] Xen. Hellen. iii, 4, 27.

[2] Plutarch, Agesil. c. 10; Aristotel. Politic. ii, 6, 22.

[3] The Lacedæmonian named Pharax, mentioned by Theopompus (Fragm. 218, ed. Didot: compare Athenæus, xii, p. 536) as a profligate and extravagant person, is more probably an officer who served under Dionysius in Sicily and Italy, about forty years after the revolt of Rhodes. The difference of time appears so great, that we must probably suppose two different men bearing the same name.

catastrophe. Serving against her in ships fitted out at his own cost, he had been captured in 407 B. C. by the Athenians, and brought in as prisoner to Athens. By the received practice of war in that day, his life was forfeited; and over and above such practice, the name of Dorieus was peculiarly odious to the Athenians. But when they saw before the public assembly a captive enemy, of heroic lineage, as well as of unrivalled athletic majesty and renown, their previous hatred was so overpowered by sympathy and admiration, that they liberated him by public vo⊀ ., and dismissed him unconditionally.[1]

This interesting anecdote, which has already been related in ɯυ eighth volume,[2] is here again noticed as a contrast to the treatment which the same Dorieus now underwent from the Lacedæmonians. What he had been doing since, we do not know; but at the time when Rhodes now revolted from Sparta, he was not only absent from the island, but actually in or near Peloponnesus. Such, however, was the wrath of the Lacedæmonians against Rhodians generally, that Dorieus was seized by their order, brought to Sparta, and there condemned and executed.[3] It seems hardly possible that he can have had any personal concern in the revolt. Had such been the fact, he would have been in the island, — or would at least have taken care not to be within the reach of the Lacedæmonians when the revolt happened. Perhaps, however, other members of the Diagoridæ, his family, once so much attached to Sparta, may have taken part in it; for we know, by the example of the Thirty at Athens, that the Lysandrian dekarchics and Spartan harmosts made themselves quite as formidable to oligarchical as to democratical politicians, and it is very conceivable that the Diagoridæ may have become less philo-Laconian in their politics.

This extreme difference in the treatment of the same man by Athens and by Sparta raises instructive reflections. It exhibits the difference both between Athenian and Spartan sentiment, and between the sentiment of a multitude and that of a few. The

---

[1] Xen. Hellen. i, 5, 19.

Compare a similar instance of merciful dealing, on the part of the Syracusan assembly, towards the Sikel prince Duketius (Diodor xi, 92).

[2] Hist. of Greece, Vol. VIII, Ch. lxiv, p. 159.

[3] Pausanias, vi, 7, 2.

grand and sacred personality of the Hieronike Dorieus, when exhibited to the senses of the Athenian multitude, — the spectacle of a man in chains before them, who had been proclaimed victor and crowned on so many solemn occasions before the largest assemblages of Greeks ever brought together, — produced an overwhelming effect upon their emotions; sufficient not only to efface a strong preëstablished antipathy founded on active past hostility, but to countervail a just cause of revenge, speaking in the language of that day. But the same appearance produced no effect at all on the Spartan ephors and senate; not sufficient even to hinder them from putting Dorieus to death, though he had given them no cause for antipathy or revenge, simply as a sort of retribution for the revolt of the island. Now this difference depended partly upon the difference between the sentiment of Athenians and Spartans, but partly also upon the difference between the sentiment of a multitude and that of a few. Had Dorieus been brought before a select judicial tribunal at Athens, instead of before the Athenian public assembly, — or, had the case been discussed before the assembly in his absence, — he would have been probably condemned, conformably to usage, under the circumstances; but the vehement emotion worked by his presence upon the multitudinous spectators of the assembly, rendered such a course intolerable to them. It has been common with historians of Athens to dwell upon the passions of the public assembly as if it were susceptible of excitement only in an angry or vindictive direction; whereas, the truth is, and the example before us illustrates, that they were open-minded in one direction as well as in another, and that the present emotion, whatever it might be, merciful or sympathetic as well as resentful, was intensified by the mere fact of multitude. And thus, where the established rule of procedure happened to be cruel, there was some chance of moving an Athenian assembly to mitigate it in a particular case, though the Spartan ephors or senate would be inexorable in carrying it out, — if, indeed, they did not, as seems probable in the case of Dorieus, actually go beyond it in rigor.

While Konon and the Rhodians were thus raising hostilities against Sparta by sea, Agesilaus, on receiving at Kymê the news of his nomination to the double command, immediately despatched orders to the dependent maritime cities and islands, requiring the

construction and equipment of new triremes. Such was the influence of Sparta, and so much did the local governments rest upon
its continuance, that these requisitions were zealously obeyed.
Many leading men incurred considerable expense, from desire to
acquire his favor; so that a fleet of one hundred and twenty new
triremes was ready by the ensuing year. Agesilaus, naming his
brother-in-law, Peisander, to act as admiral, sent him to superin-
tend the preparations; a brave young man, but destitute both of
skill and experience.[1]

Meanwhile, he himself pursued his march (about the beginning
of autumn) towards the satrapy of Pharnabazus, — Phrygia south
and south-east of the Propontis. Under the active guidance of his
new auxiliary, Spithridates, he plundered the country, capturing
some towns, and reducing others to capitulate; with considerable
advantage to his soldiers.   Pharnabazus, having no sufficient army
to hazard a battle in defence of his satrapy, concentrated all his
force near his own residence at Daskylium, offering no opposition
to the march of Agesilaus; who was induced by Spithridates to
traverse Phrygia and enter Paphlagonia, in hopes of concluding
an alliance with the Paphlagonian prince Otys. That prince, in
nominal dependence on Persia, could muster the best cavalry in
the Persian empire. But he had recently refused to obey an invitation from the court at Susa, and he now not only welcomed
the appearance of Agesilaus, but concluded an alliance with him,
strengthening him with an auxiliary body of cavalry and peltasts.
Anxious to requite Spithridates for his services, and vehemently
attached to his son, the beautiful youth Megabates, — Agesilaus
persuaded Otys to marry the daughter of Spithridates. He even
caused her to be conveyed by sea in a Lacedæmonian trireme,
— probably from Abydos to Sinopê.[2]

---

[1] Xen. Hellen. iii, 4, 28, 29 ; Plutarch, Agesil. c. 10.

[2] Xen. Hellen. iv, 1, 1–15.

The negotiation of this marriage by Agesilaus is detailed in a curious
and interesting manner by Xenophon. His conversation with Otys took
place in the presence of the thirty Spartan counsellors, and probably in
the presence of Xenophon himself.

The attachment of Agesilaus to the youth Megabazus or Megabates, is
marked in the Hellenica (iv, 1, 6–28) — but is more strongly brought out
in the Agesilaus of Xenophon (v, 6), and in Plutarch, Agesil. c. 11.

In the retreat of the Ten Thousand Greeks (five years before) along the

Reinforced by the Paphlagonian auxiliaries, Agesilaus prosecuted the war with augmented vigor against the satrapy of Pharnabazus. He now approached the neighborhood of Daskylium, the residence of the satrap himself, inherited from his father Pharnakês, who had been satrap before him. This was a well-supplied country, full of rich villages, embellished with parks and gardens for the satrap's hunting and gratification: the sporting tastes of Xenophon lead him also to remark that there were plenty of birds for the fowler, with rivers full of fish.[1] In this agreeable region Agesilaus passed the winter. His soldiers, abundantly supplied with provisions, became so careless, and straggled with so much contempt of their enemy, that Pharnabazus, with a body of four hundred cavalry and two scythed chariots, found an opportunity of attacking seven hundred of them by surprise; driving them back with considerable loss, until Agesilaus came up to protect them with the hoplites.

This partial misfortune, however, was speedily avenged. Fearful of being surrounded and captured, Pharnabazus refrained from occupying any fixed position. He hovered about the country, carrying his valuable property along with him, and keeping his place of encampment as secret as he could. The watchful Spithridates, nevertheless, having obtained information that he was encamped for the night in the village of Kanê, about eighteen miles distant, Herippidas (one of the thirty Spartans) undertook a night-march with a detachment to surprise him. Two thousand Grecian hoplites, the like number of light-armed peltasts, and Spithridates with the Paphlagonian horse, were appointed to accompany him. Though many of these soldiers took advantage of the darkness to evade attendance, the enterprise proved completely successful. The camp of Pharnabazus was surprised at break of day; his Mysian advanced guards were put to the sword, and he himself, with all his troops, was compelled to take flight with scarcely any resistance. All his stores, plate, and personal furniture, together with a large baggage-train and abundance of prisoners, fell into the hands

---

southern coast of the Euxine, a Paphlagonian prince named Korylas is mentioned (Xen. Anab. v, 5, 22 ; v, 6, 8). Whether there was more than one Paphlagonian prince — or whether Otys was successor of Korylas — we cannot tell.

[1] Xen. Hellen. iv, 1, 16–33.

of the victors. As the Paphlagonians under Spithridates formed the cavalry of the victorious detachment, they naturally took more spoil and more prisoners than the infantry. They were proceeding to carry off their acquisitions, when Herippidas interfered and took everything away from them ; placing the entire spoil of every description, under the charge of Grecian officers, to be sold by formal auction in a Grecian city ; after which the proceeds were to be distributed or applied by public authority. The orders of Herippidas were conformable to the regular and systematic proceeding of Grecian officers ; but Spithridates and the Paphlagonians were probably justified by Asiatic practice in appropriating that which they had themselves captured. Moreover, the order, disagreeable in itself, was enforced against them with Lacedæmonian harshness of manner,[1] unaccompanied by any guarantee that they would be allowed, even at last, a fair share of the proceeds. Resenting the conduct of Herippidas as combining injury with insult, they deserted in the night and fled to Sardis, where the Persian Ariæus was in actual revolt against the court of Susa. This was a serious loss, and still more serious chagrin, to Agesilaus. He was not only deprived of valuable auxiliary cavalry, and of an enterprizing Asiatic informant ; but the report would be spread that he defrauded his Asiatic allies of their legitimate plunder, and others would thus be deterred from joining him. His personal sorrow too was aggravated by the departure of the youth Megabazus, who accompanied his father Spithridates to Sardis.[2]

It was towards the close of this winter that a personal conference took place between Agesilaus and Pharnabazus, managed by the intervention of a Greek of Kyzikus named Apollophanês ; who was connected by ties of hospitality with both, and served to each as guarantee for the good faith of the other. We have from Xenophon, himself probably present, an interesting detail of this interview. Agesilaus, accompanied by his thirty Spartan counsel-

---

[1] Plutarch, Agesil. c. 11. πικρὸς ὢν ἐξεταστὴς τῶν κλαπέντων, etc.

[2] Xen. Hellen. iv, 1, 27 ; Plutarch, Agesil. c. 11.

Since the flight of Spithridates took place secretly by night, the scene which Plutarch asserts to have taken place between Agesilaus and Megabazus cannot have occurred on the departure of the latter, but must belong to some other occasion ; as, indeed, it seems to be represented by Xenophon (Agesil. v 4).

lors, being the first to arrive at the place of appointment, all of
them sat down upon the grass to wait. Presently came Pharnabazus, with splendid clothing and retinue. His attendants were
beginning to spread fine carpets for him, when the satrap, observing how the Spartans were seated, felt ashamed of such a luxury
for himself, and sat down on the grass by the side of Agesilaus.
Having exchanged salutes, they next shook hands; after which
Pharnabazus, who as the older of the two had been the first to
tender his right hand, was also the first to open the conversation.
Whether he spoke Greek well enough to dispense with the neces
sity of an interpreter, we are not informed. " Agesilaus (said he),
I was the friend and ally of you Lacedæmonians while you were
at war with Athens; I furnished you with money to strengthen
your fleet, and fought with you myself ashore on horseback, chas
ing your enemies into the sea. You cannot charge me with having
ever played you false, like Tissaphernes, either by word or deed.
Yet, after this behavior, I am now reduced by you to such a condition, that I have not a dinner in my own territory, except by
picking up your leavings, like the beasts of the field. I see the fine
residences, parks, and hunting-grounds, bequeathed to me by my
father, which formed the charm of my life, cut up or burnt down
by you. Is this the conduct of men mindful of favors received,
and eager to requite them ? Pray answer me this question ; for,
perhaps, I have yet to learn what is holy and just."

The thirty Spartan counsellors were covered with shame by this
emphatic appeal. They all held their peace; while Agesilaus,
after a long pause, at length replied, — " You are aware, Pharnabazus, that in Grecian cities, individuals become private friends
and guests of each other. Such guests, if the cities to which they
belong go to war, fight with each other, and sometimes by accident
even kill each other, each in behalf of his respective city. So then
it is that we, being at war with your king, are compelled to hold
all his dominions as enemy's land. But in regard to you, we would
pay any price to become your friends. I do not invite you to
accept us as masters, in place of your present master ; I ask you
to become our ally, and to enjoy your own property as a freeman,
— bowing before no man and acknowledging no master. Now
freedom is in itself a possession of the highest value. But this is
not all. We do not call upon you to be a freeman, and yet poor

We offer you our alliance, to acquire fresh territory, not for the king, but for yourself; by reducing those who are now your fellow-slaves to become your subjects. Now tell me, — if you thus continue a freeman and become rich, what can you want farther to make you a thoroughly prosperous man?"

"I will speak frankly to you in reply (said Pharnabazus). If the king shall send any other general, and put me under him, I shall willingly become your friend and ally. But if he imposes the duty of command on me, so strong is the point of honor, that I shall continue to make war upon you to the best of my power. Expect nothing else."[1]

Agesilaus, struck with this answer, took his hand and said, — "Would that with such high-minded sentiments you *could* become our friend! At any rate, let me assure you of this, — that I will immediately quit your territory; and for the future, even should the war continue, I will respect both you and all your property, as long as I can turn my arms against any other Persians."

Here the conversation closed; Pharnabazus mounted his horse, and rode away. His son by Parapita, however, — at that time still a handsome youth, — lingered behind, ran up to Agesilaus, and exclaimed, — "Agesilaus, I make you my guest." — "I accept it with all my heart," — was the answer. "Remember me by this," — rejoined the young Persian, — putting into the hands of Agesilaus the fine javelin which he carried. The latter immediately took off the ornamental trappings from the horse of his secretary Idæus, and gave them as a return present; upon which the young man rode away with them, and rejoined his father.[2]

There is a touching interest and emphasis in this interview as described by Xenophon, who here breathes into his tame Hellenic chronicle something of the romantic spirit of the Cyropædia. The pledges exchanged between Agesilaus and the son of Pharnabazus were not forgotten by either. The latter, — being in after days impoverished and driven into exile by his brother, during the

---

[1] Xen. Hellen. iv, 1, 38. Ἐὰν μέντοι μοι τὴν ἀρχὴν προστάττῃ τοιοῦτόν τι, ὡς ἔοικε, φιλοτιμία ἐστί, εὖ χρὴ εἰδέναι, ὅτι πολεμήσω ὑμῖν ὡς ἂν δύνωμαι ἄριστα.

Compare about φιλοτιμία, Herodot. iii, 53.

[2] Xen. Hellen. iv, 1, 29–41; Plutarch, Agesil c. 13, 14; Xen. Agesil ii, 5.

Absence of Pharnabazus in Egypt, — was compelled to take refuge in Greece; where Agesilaus provided him with protection and a home, and even went so far as to employ influence in favor of an Athenian youth, to whom the son of Pharnabazus was attached. This Athenian youth had outgrown the age and size of the boy-runners in the Olympic stadium; nevertheless Agesilaus, by strenuous personal interference, overruled the reluctance of the Eleian judges, and prevailed upon them to admit him as a competitor with the other boys.[1] The stress laid by Xenophon upon this favor illustrates the tone of Grecian sentiment, and shows us the variety of objects which personal ascendency was used to compass. Disinterested in regard to himself, Agesilaus was unscrupulous both in promoting the encroachments, and screening the injustices, of his friends.[2] The unfair privilege which he procured for this youth, though a small thing in itself, could hardly fail to offend a crowd of spectators familiar with the established conditions of the stadium, and to expose the judges to severe censure.

Quitting the satrapy of Pharnabazus, — which was now pretty well exhausted, while the armistice concluded with Tithraustes must have expired, — Agesilaus took up his camp near the temple of Artemis, at Astyra in the plain of Thêbê (in the region commonly known as Æolis, near the Gulf of Elæus. He here employed himself in bringing together an increased number of troops, with a view to penetrate farther into the interior of Asia Minor during the summer. Recent events had greatly increased the belief entertained by the Asiatics in his superior strength; so that he received propositions from various districts in the interior, inviting his presence, and expressing anxiety to throw off the Persian yoke. He sought also to compose the dissensions and misrule which had arisen out of the Lysandrian dekarchies in the Greco-Asiatic cities, avoiding as much as possible sharp inflictions of death or exile. How much he achieved in this direction, we cannot tell,[3] nor can it have been possible, indeed, to achieve

---

[1] Xen. Hellen. iv, 1, 40. πάντ' ἐποίησεν, ὅπως ἂν δι' ἐκεῖνον ἐγκριθείη εἰς τὸ στάδιον ἐν 'Ολυμπίᾳ, μέγιστος ὢν παιδῶν.

[2] Plutarch, Agesil. c. 5–13.

[3] Xen. Hellen. iv, 1, 41 ; Xen. Agesil. i, 35–38 ; Plutarch, Agesil. c. 14. 15 Isokrates, Or. v, (Philipp.) s. 100,

much, without dismissing the Spartan harmosts and lessening the political power of his own partisans; neither of which he did.

His plans were now all laid for penetrating farther than ever into the interior, and for permanent conquest, if possible, of the western portion of Persian Asia. What he would have permanently accomplished towards this scheme, cannot be determined; for his aggressive march was suspended by a summons home, the reason of which will appear in the next chapter.

Meanwhile, Pharnabazus had been called from his satrapy to go and take the command of the Persian fleet in Kilikia and the south of Asia Minor, in conjunction with Konon. Since the revolt of Rhodes from the Lacedæmonians, (in the summer of the preceding year, 395 B. C.) that active Athenian had achieved nothing The burst of activity, produced by the first visit of Pharnabazus at the Persian court, had been paralyzed by the jealousies of the Persian commanders, reluctant to serve under a Greek, — by peculation of officers who embezzled the pay destined for the troops, — by mutiny in the fleet from absence of pay, — and by the many delays arising while the satraps, unwilling to spend their own revenues in the war, waited for orders and remittances from court.[1] Hence Konon had been unable to make any efficient use of his fleet, during those months when the Lacedæmonian fleet was increased to nearly double its former number. At length he resolved, — seemingly at the instigation of his countrymen at home[2] as well as of Euagoras prince of Salamis in Cyprus, and through the encouragement of Ktesias, one of the Grecian physicians resident at the Persian court, — on going himself into the interior to communicate personally with Artaxerxes. Landing on the Kilikian coast, he crossed by land to Thapsakus on the Eu-

---

[1] Compare Diodor. xv, 41 *ad fin.*; and Thucyd. viii, 45.

[2] Isokrates Or. viii, De Pace, s. 82) alludes to "many embassies" as having been sent by Athens to the king of Persia, to protest against the Lacedæmonian dominion. But this mission of Konon is the only one which we can verify, prior to the battle of Knidus.

Probably Demus, the son of Pyrilampês, an eminent citizen and trierarch of Athens, must have been one of the companions of Konon in this mission. He is mentioned in an oration of Lysias as having received from the Great King a present of a golden drinking-bowl or ($\phi\iota\acute{\alpha}\lambda\eta$); and I do not know on what other occasion he can have received it, except in this embassy (Lysias, Or. xix, De Bonis Aristoph. s. 27).

♦hrates (as the Cyreian army had marched), from whence he sailed down the river in a boat to Babylon. It appears that he did not see Artaxerxes, from repugnance to that ceremony of prostration which was required from all who approached the royal person. But his messages, transmitted through Ktesias and others, — with his confident engagement to put down the maritime empire of Sparta and counteract the projects of Agesilaus, if the Persian forces and money were put into efficient action, — produced a powerful effect on the mind of the monarch; who doubtless was not merely alarmed at the formidable position of Agesilaus in Asia Minor, but also hated the Lacedæmonians as main agents in the aggressive enterprise of Cyrus. Artaxerxes not only approved his views, but made to him a large grant of money, and transmitted peremptory orders to the coast that his officers should be active in prosecuting the maritime war.

What was of still greater moment, Konon was permitted to name any person whom he chose, as admiral jointly with himself. It was by his choice that Pharnabazus was called from his satrapy, and ordered to act jointly as commander of the fleet. This satrap, the bravest and most straightforward among all the Persian grandees, and just now smarting with resentment at the devastation of his satrapy[1] by Agesilaus, coöperated heartily with Konon. A powerful fleet, partly Phœnician, partly Athenian or Grecian, was soon equipped, superior in number even to the newly-organized Lacedæmonian fleet under Peisander.[2] Euagoras, prince of Sa-

---

[1] Xen. Hellen. iv, 8, 6.

[2] The measures of Konon and the transactions preceding the battle of Knidus, are very imperfectly known to us; but we may gather them generally from Diodorus, xiv, 81 ; Justin, vi, 3, 4 ; Cornelius Nepos, Vit. Conon. c. 2, 3 ; Ktesiæ Fragment, c. 62, 63, ed. Bähr.

Isokrates (Orat. iv, (Panegyr.) s. 165; compare Orat. ix, (Euagor.) s. 77) speaks loosely as to the duration of time that the Persian fleet remained blocked up by the Lacedæmonians before Konon obtained his final and vigorous orders from Artaxerxes, unless we are to understand his *three years* as referring to the first news of outfit of ships of war in Phœnicia, brought to Sparta by Hêrodas. as Schneider understands them ; and even then the statement that the Persian fleet remained πολιορκούμενον for all this time, would be much exaggerated. Allowing for exaggeration, however, Isokrates coincides generally with the authorities above noticed.

It would appear that Ktesias the physician obtained about this time per mission to quit the court of Persia and come back to Greece. Perhaps he

lamis in Cyprus,[1] not only provided many triremes, but served himself, personally, on board.

It was about the month of July, 394 B. C., that Pharnabazus and Konon brought their united fleet to the south-western corner of Asia Minor; first, probably, to the friendly island of Rhodes, next, off Loryma[2] and the mountain called Dorion on the peninsula of Knidus.[3]   Peisander, with the fleet of Sparta and her allies, sailed out from Knidus to meet them, and both parties prepared for a battle.   The numbers of the Lacedæmonians are reported by Diodorus at eighty-five triremes; those of Konon and Pharnabazus at above ninety.   But Xenophon, without particularizing the number on either side, seems to intimate the disparity as far greater; stating that the entire fleet of Peisander was considerably inferior even to the Grecian division under Konon, without reckoning the Phœnician ships under Pharnabazus.[4]   In spite of such inferiority, Peisander did not shrink from the encounter. Though a young man without military skill, he possessed a full measure of Spartan courage and pride; moreover,— since the Spartan maritime empire was only maintained by the assumed superior-

---

may have been induced (like Demokêdes of Kroton, one hundred and twenty years before) to promote the views of Konon in order to get for himself this permission.

In the meagre abstract of Ktesias given by Photius (c. 63) mention is made of some Lacedæmonian envoys who were now going up to the Persian court, and were watched or detained on the way. This mission can hardly have taken place before the battle of Knidus; for then Agesilaus was in the full tide of success, and contemplating the largest plans of aggression against Persia.   It must have taken place, I presume, after the battle.

[1] Isokrates, Or. ix, (Euagoras) s. 67.   Εὐαγόρου δὲ αὐτόν τε παρασ-χόντος, καὶ τῆς δυνάμεως τὴν πλείστην παρασκευάσαντος. Compare s. 83 of the same oration. Compare Pausanias, i, 3, 1.

[2] Diodor. xiv, 83. διέτριβον περὶ Λώρυμα τῆς Χερσονήσου.

It is hardly necessary to remark, that the word Chersonesus here (and in xiv, 89) does not mean the peninsula of Thrace commonly known by that name, forming the European side of the Hellespont, — but the peninsula on which Knidus is situated.

[3] Pausan. vi, 3, 6.   περὶ Κνίδον καὶ ὄρος τὸ Δώριον ὀνομαζόμενον.

[4] Xen. Hellen. iv, 3, 12. Φαρνάβαζον, ναυαρχὸν ὄντα, ξὺν ταῖς Φοινίσσαις εἶναι. Κόνωνα δὲ, τὸ Ἑλληνικὸν ἔχοντα, τετάχθαι ἔμπροσθεν αὐτοῦ. Ἀν τιπαραταξαμένου δὲ τοῦ Πεισάνδρου, καὶ πολὺ ἐλαττόνων αὐτῷ τῶν νεῶν φανεισῶν ·ὦν αὐτοῦ τοῦ μετὰ Κόνωνος Ἑλληνικοῦ etc.

rty of his fleet, — had he confessed himself too weak to fight, his enemies would have gone unopposed around the islands to excite revolt. Accordingly, he sailed forth from the harbor of Knidus. But when the two fleets were ranged opposite to each other, and the battle was about to commence, — so manifest and alarming was the superiority of the Athenians and Persians, that his Asiatic allies on the left division, noway hearty in the cause, fled almost without striking a blow. Under such discouraging circumstances, he nevertheless led his fleet into action with the greatest valor. But his trireme was overwhelmed by numbers, broken in various places by the beaks of the enemy's ships, and forced back upon the land, together with a large portion of his fleet. Many of the crews jumped out and got to land, abandoning their triremes to the conquerors. Peisander, too, might have escaped in the same way; but disdaining either to survive his defeat or to quit his ship, fell gallantly fighting aboard. The victory of Konon and Pharnabazus was complete. More than half of the Spartan ships were either captured or destroyed, though the neighborhood of the land enabled a large proportion of the crews to escape to Knidus, so that no great number of prisoners were taken.[1] Among the allies of Sparta, the chief loss of course fell upon those who were most attached to her cause ; the disaffected or lukewarm were those who escaped by flight at the beginning.

Such was the memorable triumph of Konon at Knidus ; the reversal of that of Lysander at Ægospotami eleven years before. Its important effects will be recounted in the coming chapter.

---

[1] Xen. Hellen. iv, 3 11–14; Diodor. xiv, 83 ; Cornelius Nepos, Conon, c 4 ; Justin, vi, 3.

CHAPTER LXXIV.

FROM THE BATTLE OF KNIDUS TO THE REBUILDING OF THE
LONG WALLS OF ATHENS.

HAVING in my last chapter carried the series of Asiatic events
down to the battle of Knidus, in the beginning of August, B. C. 394,
at which period war was already raging on the other side of the
Ægean, in Greece Proper, — I now take up the thread of events
from a period somewhat earlier, to show how this last-mentioned
war, commonly called the Corinthian war, began.

At the accession of Agesilaus to the throne, in 398 B. C., the
power of Sparta throughout all Greece from Laconia to Thessaly,
was greater than it had ever been, and greater than any Grecian
state had ever enjoyed before.   The burden of the long war against
Athens she had borne in far less proportion than her allies ; its
fruits she had reaped exclusively for herself.   There prevailed
consequently among her allies a general discontent, which Thebes
as well as Corinth manifested by refusing to take part in the recent
expeditions ; either of Pausanias against Thrasybulus and the
Athenian exiles in Peiræus, — or of Agis against the Eleians, —
or of Agesilaus against the Persians in Asia Minor.   The Eleians
were completely humbled by the invasions of Agis ; all the other
cities in Peloponnesus, from apprehension, from ancient habit, and
from being governed by oligarchies who leaned on Sparta for support, were obedient to her authority, - - with the single exception
of Argos, which remained, as before, neutral and quiet, though in
sentiment unfriendly.   Athens was a simple unit in the catalogue
of Spartan allies, furnishing her contingent, like the rest, to be
commanded by the xenâgus,—or officer sent from Sparta for
the special purpose of commanding such foreign contingents.

In the northern regions of Greece, the advance of Spartan power
is yet more remarkable.   Looking back to the year 419 B. C.
(about two years after the peace of Nikias), Sparta had been so
unable to protect her colony of Herakleia, in Trachis on the Ma-
liac Gulf, near the strait of Thermopylæ, that the Bœotians were

obliged to send a garrison thither, in order to prevent it from falling into the hands of Athens. They even went so far as to dismiss the Lacedæmonian harmost.[1] In the winter of 409–408 B. C., another disaster had happened at Herakleia, in which the Lacedæmonian harmost was slain.[2] But about 399 B. C., we find Sparta exercising an energetic ascendency at Herakleia, and even making that place a central post for keeping down the people in the neighborhood of Mount Œta and a portion of Thessaly. Herippidas, the Lacedæmonian, was sent thither to repress some factious movements, with a force sufficient to enable him to overawe the public assembly, to seize the obnoxious party in the place, and to put them to death, five hundred in number, outside of the gates.[3] Carrying his arms farther against the Œtæans and Trachinians in the neighborhood, who had been long at variance with the Laconian colonists at Herakleia, he expelled them from their abodes, and forced them to migrate with their wives and children into Thessaly.[4] Hence, the Lacedæmonians were enabled to extend their influence into parts of Thessaly, and to place a harmost with a garrison in Pharsalus, resting upon Herakleia as a basis, — which thus became a position of extraordinary importance for their dominion over the northern regions.

With the real power of Sparta thus greatly augmented on land, in addition to her vast empire at sea, bringing its ample influx of tribute, — and among cities who had not merely long recognized her as leader, but had never recognized any one else, — it required an unusual stimulus to raise any formidable hostile combination against her, notwithstanding a large spread of disaffection and antipathy. The stimulus came from Persia, from whose treasures the means had been before furnished to Sparta herself for subduing Athens. The news that a formidable navy was fitting out in Phœnicia, which had prompted the expedition of Agesilaus in the spring of 396 B. C., was doubtless circulated and heard with satisfaction among the Grecian cities unfriendly to Sparta; and the refusal of Thebes, Corinth, and Athens, to take service under that

---

[1] Thucyd. v, 52.   [2] Xen. Hellen. i, 2, 18.

[3] Diodor. xiv, 38; Polyæn. ii, 21.

[4] Diodorus, *ut sup.*; compare xiv, 81. τοὺς Τραχινίους φεύγοντας ἐκ τῶν ... ρίδων ὑπὸ Λακεδαιμονίων, etc

prince, — aggravated in the case of the Thebans oy a positive
offence given to him on the occasion of his sacrifice at Aulis, —
was enough to warn Sparta of the dangerous sentiments and tendencies by which she was surrounded near home.

It was upon these tendencies that the positive instigation and
promises of Persia were brought to bear, in the course of the following year ; and not merely promises, but pecuniary supplies,
with news of revived naval warfare threatening the insular dominion
of Sparta. Tithraustes, the new satrap, who had put to death and
succeeded Tissaphernes, had no sooner concluded the armistice
mentioned above, and prevailed upon Agesilaus to remove his
army into the satrapy of Pharnabazus, than he employed active
measures for kindling war against Sparta in Greece, in order to
create a necessity for the recall of Agesilaus out of Asia. He sent
a Rhodian named Timokrates into Greece, as envoy to the cities
most unfriendly to the Lacedæmonians, with a sum of fifty talents ;[1]
directing him to employ this money in gaining over the leading
men in these cities, and to exchange solemn oaths of alliance and
aid with Persia, for common hostility against Sparta. The island
of Rhodes having just revolted from the Spartan dominion, had
admitted Konon with the Persian fleet (as I have mentioned in
the last chapter), so that probably the Rhodian envoy was on a
mission to Tithraustes on behalf of his countrymen. He was an
appropriate envoy on this occasion, as having an animated interest
in raising up new enemies to Sparta, and as being hearty in stirring up among the Thebans and Corinthians the same spirit which
had led to the revolt of Rhodes. The effect which that revolt
produced in alarming and exasperating the Spartans, has been

---

[1] Xen. Hellen. iii, 5, 1. Πέμπει Τιμοκράτην 'Ρόδιον ἐς τὴν 'Ελλάδα, δοὺς
χρυσίον ἐς πεντήκοντα τάλαντα ἀργυρίου, καὶ κελεύει πειρᾶσθαι, πιστὰ τὰ
μέγιστα λαμβάνοντα, διδόναι τοῖς προεστηκόσιν ἐν ταῖς πόλεσιν, ἐφ' ᾧ τε πόλεμον ἐξοίσειν πρὸς Λακεδαιμονίους.

Timokrates is ordered to give the money; yet not absolutely, but only
on a certain condition, in case he should find that such condition could be
realized ; that is, if by giving it he could procure from various leading
Greeks sufficient assurances and guarantees that they would raise war
against Sparta. As this was a matter more or less doubtful, Timokrates is
ordered to *try to give the money for this purpose*. Though the construction
of πειρᾶσθαι couples it with διδόναι, the sense of the word more properly
belongs to ἐξοίσειν — which designates the purpose to be accomplished.

already noticed; and we may fairly presume that its effect on the other side, in encouraging their Grecian enemies, was considerable. Timokrates visited Thebes, Corinth, and Argos, distributing his funds. He concluded engagements on behalf of the satrap, with various leading men in each, putting them into communication with each other; Ismenias, Androkleidas, and others in Thebes, — Timolaus and Polyanthes at Corinth, — Kylon and others at Argos. It appears that he did not visit Athens; at least, Xenophon expressly says that none of his money went there. The working of this mission, — coupled, we must recollect, with the renewed naval warfare on the coast of Asia, and the promise of a Persian fleet against that of Sparta, — was soon felt in the more pronounced manifestation of anti-Laconian sentiments in these various cities, and in the commencement of attempts to establish alliance between them.[1]

With that Laconian bias which pervades his Hellenica, Xenophon represents the coming war against Sparta, as if it had been brought about mainly by these bribes from Persia to the leading men in these various cities. I have stated on more than one occasion, that the average public morality of Grecian individual politicians in Sparta, Athens, and other cities, was not such as to exclude personal corruption; that it required a morality higher than the average, when such temptation was resisted, — and a morality considerably higher than the average, if it were systematically resisted, and for a long life, as by Perikles and Nikias. There would be nothing therefore surprising, if Ismenias and the rest had received bribes under the circumstances here mentioned. But it appears highly improbable that the money given by Timokrates could have been a bribe; that is, given privately, and for the separate use of these leaders. It was furnished for the promotion of a certain public object, which could not be accomplished without heavy disbursements; it was analogous to that sum of thirty talents which (as Xenophon himself tells us) Tithraustes had just given to Agesilaus, as an inducement to carry away his army into the satrapy of Pharnabazus (not as a present for the private purse of the Spartan king, but as a contribution to the

---

[1] Xen. Hellen. iii, 5, 2; Pausan. iii, 9, 4; Plutarch, Artaxerxes, c. 20

wants of the army),[1] or to that which the satrap Tiribazus **gave** to Antalkidas afterwards,[2] also for public objects. Xenophon affirms, that Ismenias and the rest, having received these presents from Timokrates, accused the Lacedæmonians and rendered them odious, — each in his respective city.[3] But it is certain, from his own showing, that the hatred towards them existed in these cities, before the arrival of Timokrates. In Argos, such hatred was of old standing ; in Corinth and Thebes, though kindled only since the close of the war, it was not the less pronounced. Moreover, Xenophon himself informs us, that the Athenians, though they received none of the money,[4] were quite as ready for war as the other cities. If we therefore admit his statement as a matter of fact, that Timokrates gave private presents to various leading politicians, which is by no means improbable, — we must dissent from the explanatory use which he makes of this fact by setting it out prominently as the cause of the war. What these leading men would find it difficult to raise was, not hatred to Sparta, but confidence and courage to brave the power of Sparta. And for this purpose the mission of Timokrates would be a valuable aid, by conveying assurances of Persian coöperation and support against Sparta. He must have been produced publicly either before the people, the senate, or at least the great body of the anti-Laconian party in each city. And the money which he brought with him, though a portion of it may have gone in private presents, would serve to this party as the best warrant for the sincerity of the satrap.

Whatever negotiations may have been in progress between the cities visited by Timokrates, no union had been brought about between them when the war, kindled by an accident, broke out as

---

[1] Xen. Hellen. iii, 4, 26.   [2] Xen. Hellen. iv, 8, 16.

[3] Xen. Hellen. iii, 5, 2. Οἱ μὲν δὴ δεξαμενοι τὰ χρήματα ἐς τὰς οἰκείας πόλεις διέβαλλον τοὺς Λακεδαιμονίους· ἐπεὶ δὲ ταύτας ἐς μῖσος αὐτῶν προήγαγον, συνίστασαν καὶ τὰς μεγίστας πόλεις πρὸς ἀλλήλας.

[4] Xenophon, *ut sup.*

Pausanias (iii, 9, 4) names some Athenians as having received part of the money. So Plutarch also, in general terms (Agesil. c. 15).

Diodorus mentions nothing respecting either the mission or the presents of Timokrates.

a "Bœotian war,"[1] between Thebes and Sparta separately. Between the Opuntian Lokrians and the Phokians, north of Bœotia,
there was a strip of disputed border land; respecting which the
Phokians, imputing wrongful encroachment to the Lokrians, invaded their territory. The Lokrians, allied with Thebes, entreated
her protection; upon which a body of Bœotians invaded Phokis:
while the Phokians on their side threw themselves upon Lacedæmon, invoking her aid against Thebes.[2] "The Lacedæmonians
(says Xenophon) were delighted to get a pretence for making war
against the Thebans, — having been long angry with them on
several different grounds. They thought that the present was an
excellent time for marching against them, and putting down their
insolence; since Agesilaus was in full success in Asia, and there
was no other war to embarrass them in Greece."[3] The various

---

[1] Πόλεμος Βοιωτικός (Diodor. xiv, 81).

[2] Xenophon (Hellen. iii, 5, 5) says, — and Pausanias (iii, 9, 4) follows
him, — That the Theban leaders, wishing to bring about a war with Sparta,
and knowing that Sparta would not begin it, purposely incited the Lokrians
to encroach upon this disputed border, in order that the Phokians might
resent it, and that thus a war might be lighted up. I have little hesitation
in rejecting this version, which I conceive to have arisen from Xenophon's
philo-Laconian and miso-Theban tendency, and in believing that the fight
between the Lokrians and Phokians, as well as that between the Phokians
and Thebans, arose without any design on the part of the latter to provoke
Sparta. So Diodorus recounts it, in reference to the war between the Phokians and the Thebans; for about the Lokrians he says nothing (xiv, 81).

The subsequent events, as recounted by Xenophon himself, show that the
Spartans were not only ready in point of force, but eager in regard to will,
to go to war with the Thebans; while the latter were not at all ready to go
to war with Sparta. They had not a single ally; for their application to
Athens, in itself doubtful, was not made until after Sparta had declared
war against them.

[3] Xen. Hellen. iii, 5, 5. Οἱ μέντοι Λακεδαιμόνιοι ἄσμενοι ἔλαβον
προφάσιν στρατεύειν ἐπὶ τοὺς Θηβαίους, πάλαι ὀργιζόμε-
νοι αὐτοῖς, τῆς τε ἀντιλήψεως τῆς τοῦ Ἀπόλλωνος δεκάτης ἐν Δεκελείᾳ, καὶ
τοῦ ἐπὶ τὸν Πειραιᾶ μὴ ἐθελῆσαι ἀκολουθῆσαι· ᾐτιῶντο δ' αὐτοὺς, καὶ Κορινθίους πεῖσαι μὴ συστρατεύειν. Ἀνεμιμνήσκοντο δὲ καὶ, ὡς θύοντ' ἐν Αὐλίδι
τὸν Ἀγησίλαον οὐκ εἴων, καὶ τὰ τεθυμένα ἱερὰ ὡς ἔρριψαν ἀπὸ τοῦ βωμοῦ
καὶ ὅτι οὐδ' εἰς τὴν Ἀσίαν συνεστράτευον Ἀγησιλάῳ. Ἐλογίζοντο δὲ καὶ
καλὸν εἶναι τοῦ ἐξάγειν στρατιὰν ἐπ' αὐτοὺς, καὶ παῦσαι τῆς ἐς αὐτοὺς ὕβρεως·
τά τε γὰρ ἐν τῇ Ἀσίᾳ καλῶς σφίσιν ἔχειν, κρατοῦντος Ἀγησιλάου, καὶ ἐν τῇ
Ἑλλάδι οὐδένα ἄλλον πόλεμον ἐμποδὼν σφίσιν εἶναι. Compare vii, 1, 34.

The description here given by Xenophon himself, — of the past dealing

grounds on which the Lacedæmonians rested their displeasure against Thebes, begin from a time immediately succeeding the close of the war against Athens, and the sentiment was now both established and vehement. It was they who now began the Bœotian war; not the Thebans, nor the bribes brought by Timokrates.

The energetic and ambitious Lysander, who had before instigated the expedition of Agesilaus across the Ægean, and who had long hated the Thebans, — was among the foremost advisers of the expedition now decreed by the ephors against Thebes,[1] as well as the chief commander appointed to carry it into execution. He was despatched with a small force to act on the north of Bœotia. He was directed to start from Herakleia, the centre of Lacedæmonian influence in those regions, — to muster the Herakleots, together with the various dependent populations in the neighborhood of Œta, Œtæans, Malians, Ænianes, etc. — to march towards Bœotia, taking up the Phokians in his way, — and to attack Haliartus. Under the walls of this town king Pausanias engaged to meet him on a given day, with the native Lacedæmonian force and the Peloponnesian allies. For this purpose, having obtained favorable border sacrifices, he marched forth to Tegea, and there employed himself in collecting the allied contingents from Peloponnesus.[2] But the allies generally were tardy and reluctant in the cause; while the Corinthians withheld all concurrence and support,[3] — though neither did they make any manifestation in favor of Thebes.

Finding themselves thus exposed to a formidable attack on two sides, from Sparta at the height of her power, and from a Spartan officer of known ability, — being, moreover, at the same time without a single ally, — the Thebans resolved to entreat succor from Athens. A Theban embassy to Athens for any purpose, and especially for this purpose, was itself among the strongest marks of the revolution which had taken place in Grecian politics.

---

and established sentiment between Sparta and Thebes, — refutes his allegation, that it was the bribes brought by Timokrates to the leading Thebans which first blew up the hatred against Sparta; and shows farther, that Sparta did not need any circuitous manœuvres of the Thebans, to furnish her with a pretext for going to war.

[1] Plutarch, Lysand. c. 28.   [2] Xen. Hellen. iii, 5, 6, 7.
[3] Xen. Hellen. iii, 5, 23.

The conduct of the Corinthians here contributes again to refute the assertion of Xenophon about the effect of the bribes of Timokrates

The antipathy between the two cities had been so long and virulent, that the Thebans, at the close of the war, had endeavored to
induce Sparta to root out the Athenian population. Their conduct
subsequently had been favorable and sympathizing towards Thrasybulus in his struggle against the Thirty, and that leader had
testified his gratitude by dedicating statues in the Theban Herakleion.[1] But it was by no means clear that Athens would feel
herself called upon, either by policy or by sentiment, to assist
them in the present emergency; at a moment when she had no
Long Walls, no fortifications at Peiræus, no ships, nor any protection against the Spartan maritime power.

It was not until Pausanias and Lysander were both actually
engaged in mustering their forces, that the Thebans sent to address
the Athenian assembly. The speech of the Theban envoy sets
forth strikingly the case against Sparta as it then stood. Dis-
claiming all concurrence with that former Theban deputy, who,
without any instructions, had taken on himself to propose, in the
Spartan assembly of allies, extreme severity towards the conquered Athenians, — he reminded the Athenians that Thebes had
by unanimous voice declined obeying the summons of the Spartans,
to aid in the march against Thrasybulus and the Peiræus; and
that this was the first cause of the anger of the Spartans against
her. On that ground, then, he appealed to the gratitude of democratical Athens against the Lacedæmonians. But he likewise invoked against them, with yet greater confidence, the aid of
oligarchical Athens, — or of those who at that time had stood
opposed to Thrasybulus and the Peiræus; for it was Sparta who,
having first set up the oligarchy at Athens, had afterwards refused
to sustain it, and left its partisans to the generosity of their democratical opponents, by whom alone they were saved harmless.[2]
Of course Athens was eager, if possible (so he presumed), to regain
her lost empire; and in this enterprise he tendered the cordial aid

---

[1] Pausanias, ix, 11, 4.

[2] Xen. Hellen. iii, 5, 9.

Πολὺ δ' ἔτι μᾶλλον ἀξιοῦμεν, ὅσοι τῶν ἐν ἄστει ἐγένεσθε, προθύμως ἐπὶ
τοὺς Λακεδαιμονίους ἰέναι. Ἐκεῖνοι γὰρ, καταστήσαντες ὑμᾶς ἐς ὀλιγαρχίαν
καὶ ἐς ἔχθραν τῷ δήμῳ, ἀφικόμενο· πολλῇ δυνάμει, ὡς ὑμῖν σύμμαχοι, παρέ-
δοσαν ὑμᾶς τῷ πλήθει· ὥστε τὸ μὲν ἐπ' ἐκείνοις εἶναι, ἀπολώλατε, ὁ δὲ δῆμος
οὑτοσὶ ὑμᾶς ἔσωσε.

of Thebes as an ally. He pointed out that it was by no means an impracticable enterprise; looking to the universal hatred which Sparta had now drawn upon herself, no less on the part of ancient allies than of prior enemies. The Athenians knew by experience that Thebes could be formidable as a foe; she would now show that she could be yet more effective as a friend, if the Athenians would interfere to rescue her. Moreover, she was now about to fight, not for Syracusans or Asiatics, but for her own preservation and dignity. "We hesitate not to affirm, men of Athens (concluded the Theban speaker), that what we are now invoking at your hands is a greater benefit to you than it is to ourselves."[1]

Eight years had now elapsed since the archonship of Eukleides and the renovation of the democracy after the crushing visitation of the Thirty. Yet we may see, from the important and well-turned allusion of the Theban speaker to the oligarchical portion of the assembly, that the two parties still stood in a certain measure distinguished. Enfeebled as Athens had been left by the war, she had never since been called upon to take any decisive and emphatic vote on a question of foreign policy; and much now turned upon the temper of the oligarchical minority, which might well be conceived likely to play a party game and speculate upon Spartan countenance. But the comprehensive amnesty decreed on the reëstablishment of the democratical constitution, — and the wise and generous forbearance with which it had been carried out, in spite of the most torturing recollections, — were now found to have produced their fruits. Majority and minority, — democrats and oligarchs, — were seen confounded in one unanimous and hearty vote to lend assistance to Thebes, in spite of all risk from hostility with Sparta. We cannot indeed doubt that this vote was considerably influenced also by the revolt of Rhodes, by the reappearance of Konon with a fleet in the Asiatic seas, and by private communications from that commander intimating his hope of acting triumphantly against the maritime power of Sparta, through enlarged aid from Persia. The vote had thus a double meaning. It proclaimed not merely the restored harmony between democrats and oligarchs at Athens, but also their common resolution to break the chain by which they were held as mere satellites

---

[1] Xen. Hellen. iii, 5, 9, 16.

and units in the regiment of Spartan allies, and to work out anew the old traditions of Athens as a self-acting and primary power at least, — if not once again an imperial power. The vote proclaimed a renovated life in Athens, and its boldness under the existing weakness of the city, is extolled two generations afterwards by Demosthenes.[1]

After having heard the Theban orator (we are told even by the philo-Laconian Xenophon),[2] "very many Athenian citizens rose and spoke in support of his prayer, and the whole assembly with one accord voted to grant it." Thrasybulus proposed the resolution, and communicated it to the Theban envoys.

He told them that Athens knew well the risk which she was incurring while Peiræus was undefended ; but nevertheless she was prepared to show her gratitude by giving more in requital than she had received ; for she was prepared to give the Thebans positive aid, in case they were attacked — while the Thebans had done nothing more for *her* than to refuse to join in an aggressive march against her.[3]

Without such assurance of succor from Athens, it is highly probable that the Thebans might have been afraid to face, single-handed, Lysander and the full force of Sparta. But they now prepared for a strenuous defence. The first approach of Lysander with his army of Herakleots, Phokians, and others, from the north, was truly menacing ; the more so, as Orchomenus, the second city next to Thebes in the Bœotian confederacy, broke off its allegiance and joined him. The supremacy of Thebes over the cities composing the Bœotian confederacy appears to have been often harsh and oppressive, though probably not equally oppressive towards all, and certainly not equally odious to all. To Platæa on the extreme south of Bœotia, it had been long

---

[1] Demosthen. de Coronâ, c. 28, p. 258 ; also Philipp. i, c. 7, p. 44. Compare also Lysias, Orat. xvi, (pro Mantitheo, s. 15).

[2] Xen. Hellen. iii, 5, 16. Τῶν δ' Ἀθηναίων παμπολλοὶ μὲν ξυνηγόρευον, παντες δ' ἐψηφίσαντο βοηθεῖν αὐτοῖς.

[3] Xen. Hellen. *ut sup.*

Pausanias (iii, 9, 6) says that the Athenians sent envoys to the Spartans to entreat them not to act aggressively against Thebes, but to submit their complaint to equitable adjustment. This seems to me improbable. Diodorus (xiv, 81) briefly states the general fact in conformity with Xenophon

intolerable, and the unhappy fate of that little town has sad-dened many pages of my preceding volumes; to Orchomenus, on the extreme north, it was also unpalatable, — partly because that town stood next in power and importance to Thebes, — partly because it had an imposing legendary antiquity, and claimed to have been once the ascendant city receiving tribute from Thebes. The Orchomenians now joined Lysander, threw open to him the way into Bœotia, and conducted him with his army, after first ravaging the fields of Lebadeia, into the district belonging to Haliartus.[1]

Before Lysander quitted Sparta, the plan of operations con-certed between him and Pausanias, was that they should meet on a given day in the territory of Haliartus. And in execution of this plan Pausanias had already advanced with his Peloponne-sian army as far as Platæa in Bœotia. Whether the day fixed between them had yet arrived, when Lysander reached Haliartus, we cannot determine with certainty. In the imperfection of the Grecian calendar, a mistake on this point would be very conceiva-ble, — as had happened between the Athenian generals Hippokra-tes and Demosthenes in those measures which preceded the battle of Delium in 424 B. C.[2] But the engagement must have been taken by both parties, subject to obstructions in the way, — since each would have to march through a hostile country to reach the place of meeting. The words of Xenophon, however, rather in-dicate that the day fixed had not arrived; nevertheless, Lysander resolved at once to act against Haliartus, without waiting for Pau-sanias. There were as yet only a few Thebans in the town, and he, probably, had good reasons for judging that he would better succeed by rapid measures, before any more Thebans could arrive, than by delaying until the other Spartan army should join him; not to mention anxiety that the conquest should belong to himself exclusively, and confidence arising from his previous success at Orchomenus. Accordingly, he sent in an invitation to the Haliar-tians to follow the example of the Orchomenians, to revolt from Thebes, and to stand upon their autonomy under Lacedæmo-nian protection. Perhaps there may have been a party in the town disposed to comply. But the majority, encouraged too by

---

[1] Xen. Hellen. iii, 5, 17; Plutarch, Lysand. c. 28.

[2] Thucyd. iv, 89. γενομένης διαμαρτίας τῶν ἡμερῶν, etc.

the Thebans within, refused the proposition ; upon which Lysander marched up to the walls and assaulted the town. He was here engaged, close by the gates, in examining where he could best effect an entrance, when a fresh division of Thebans, apprised of his proceedings, was seen approaching from Thebes, at their fastest pace, — cavalry, as well as hoplites. They were probably seen from the watch-towers in the city earlier than they became visible to the assailants without; so that the Haliartians, encouraged by the sight, threw open their gates, and made a sudden sally. Lysander, seemingly taken by surprise, was himself slain among the first, with his prophet by his side, by a Haliartian hoplite named Neochôrus. His troops stood some time, against both the Haliartians from the town, and the fresh Thebans who now came up. But they were at length driven back with considerable loss, and compelled to retreat to rugged and difficult ground at some distance on their rear. Here, however, they made good their position, repelling their assailants with the loss of more than two hundred hoplites.[1]

The success here gained, though highly valuable as an encouragement to the Thebans, would have been counterbalanced by the speedy arrival of Pausanias, had not Lysander himself been among the slain. But the death of so eminent a man was an irreparable loss to Sparta. His army, composed of heterogeneous masses, both collected and held together by his personal ascendency, lost confidence and dispersed in the ensuing night.[2] When Pausanias arrived soon afterwards, he found no second army to join with him. Yet his own force was more than sufficient to impress terror on the Thebans, had not Thrasybulus, faithful to the recent promise, arrived with an imposing body of Athenian hoplites, together with cavalry under Orthobulus[3] — and imparted fresh courage as well as adequate strength to the Theban cause.

---

[1] Xen. Hellen. iii, 5, 18, 19, 20 ; Plutarch, Lysand. c. 28, 29 ; Pausan. iii, 5, 4.

The two last differ in various matters from Xenophon, whose account however, though brief, seems to me to deserve the preference.

[2] Xen. Hellen. iii, 5, 21. ἀπεληλυθότας ἐν νυκτὶ τούς τε Φωκέας καὶ τοὺς ἴλλους ἅπαντας οἴκαδε ἑκάστους, etc.

[3] Lysias, Or. xvi, (pro Mantitheo) s. 15, 16.

Pausanias had first to consider what steps he would take to recover the bodies of the slain. — that of Lysander among them;
whether he would fight a battle and thus take his chance of becoming master of the field, — or send the usual petition for burial-
truce, which always implied confession of inferiority. On sub-
mitting the point to a council of officers and Spartan elders, their
decision as well as his own was against fighting; not, however,
without an indignant protest from some of the Spartan elders.
He considered that the whole original plan of operations was broken
up, since not only the great name and genius of Lysander had
perished, but his whole army had spontaneously disbanded; that
the Peloponnesian allies were generally lukewarm and reluctant,
not to be counted upon for energetic behavior in case of pressing
danger; that he had little or no cavalry,[1] while the Theban cavalry was numerous and excellent; lastly, that the dead body of
Lysander himself lay so close to the walls of Haliartus, that even
if the Lacedæmonians were victorious, they could not carry it off
without serious loss from the armed defenders in their towers.[2]
Such were the reasons which determined Pausanias and the major
part of the council to send and solicit a truce. But the Thebans
refused to grant it except on condition that they should immediately evacuate Bœotia. Though such a requisition was contrary
to the received practice of Greece,[3] which imposed on the victor
the duty of granting the burial-truce unconditionally, whenever it
was asked and inferiority thus publicly confessed, — nevertheless,
such was the reluctant temper of the army, that they heard not
merely with acquiescence, but with joy,[4] the proposition of depart
ing. The bodies were duly buried, — that of Lysander in the
territory of Panopê, immediately across the Phokian border, but

---

[1] Accordingly we learn from an oration of Lysias, that the service of the
Athenian horsemen in this expedition, who were commanded by Orthobulus, was judged to be extremely safe and easy; while that of the hoplites
was dangerous (Lysias, Orat. xvi, pro Mantith. s. 15).

[2] Xen. Hellen. iii, 5, 23. Κορίνθιοι μὲν παντάπασιν οὐκ ἠκολούθουν αὐ-
τι ἰς, οἱ δὲ παρόντες οὐ προθύμως στρατεύοιντο, etc.

[3] See the conduct of the Thebans on this very point (of giving up the
slain at the solicitation of the conquered Athenians for burial) after the
battle of Delium, and the discussion thereupon, — in this History, Vol VI
ch. iii, p. 393 seq.

[4] Xen. Hellen. iii, 5, 24. Ο δε ἁσμενοί τε ταῖτα ἤκουσαν, etc.

not far from Haliartus. And no sooner were these solemnities completed, than the Lacedæmonian army was led back to Peloponnesus; their dejection forming a mournful contrast to the triumphant insolence of the Thebans, who watched their march and restrained them, not without occasional blows, from straggling out of the road into the cultivated fields.[1]

The death of Lysander produced the most profound sorrow and resentment at Sparta. On returning thither, Pausanias found himself the subject of such virulent accusation, that he thought it prudent to make his escape, and take sanctuary in the temple of Athênê Alea, at Tegea. He was impeached, and put on trial during his absence, on two counts; first, for having been behind the time covenanted, in meeting Lysander at Haliartus; next for having submitted to ask a truce from the Thebans, instead of fighting a battle for the purpose of obtaining the bodies of the slain.

As far as there is evidence to form a judgment, it does not appear that Pausanias was guilty upon either of the two counts. The first is a question of fact; and it seems quite as likely that Lysander was before his time, as that Pausanias was behind his time, in arriving at Haliartus. Besides, Lysander, arriving there first, would have been quite safe, had he not resolved to attack without delay; in which the chances of war turned out against him; though the resolution in itself may have been well conceived. Next, as to the truce solicited for burying the dead bodies, — it does not appear that Pausanias could with any prudence have braved the chances of a battle. The facts of the case, — even as summed up by Xenophon, who always exaggerates everything in favor of the Spartans, — lead us to this conclusion. A few of the Spartan elders would doubtless prefer perishing on the field of battle, to the humiliation of sending in the herald to ask for a truce. But the mischief of fighting a battle under the influence of such a point of honor, to the exclusion of a rational estimate of consequences, will be seen when we come to the battle of Leuktra, where Kleombrotus, son of Pausanias was thus piqued into an imprudence (at least this is alleged as one of the motives) to which his own life and the dominion of Sparta became forfeit.[2] Moreover, the army of Pausanias, comprising very few Spartans, con

---

[1] Xen. Hellen. iii, 5, 24. [2] Xen. Hellen. vi 4, 5.

sisted chiefly of allies who had no heart in the cause, and who were glad to be required by the Thebans to depart. If he had fought a battle and lost it, the detriment to Sparta would have been most serious in every way; whereas, if he had gained a victory, no result would have followed except the acquisition of the bodies for burial; since the execution of the original plan had become impracticable through the dispersion of the army of Lysander.

Though a careful examination of the facts leads us (and seems also to have led Xenophon[1]) to the conclusion that Pausanias was innocent, he was nevertheless found guilty in his absence. He was in great part borne down by the grief felt at Sparta for the loss of Lysander, with whom he had been before in political rivalry, and for whose death he was made responsible. Moreover, the old accusation was now revived against him,[2] — for which he had been tried, and barely acquitted, eight years before, — of having tolerated the reëstablishment of the Athenian democracy at a time when he might have put it down. Without doubt this argument told prodigiously against him at the present juncture, when the Athenians had just now, for the first time since the surrender of their city, renounced their subjection to Sparta and sent an army to assist the Thebans in their defence. So violent was the sentiment against Pausanias, that he was condemned to death in his absence, and passed the remainder of his life as an exile in sanctuary at Tegea. His son, Agesipolis, was invested with the sceptre in his place.

A brief remark will not be here misplaced. On no topic have Grecian historians been more profuse in their reproaches, than upon the violence and injustice of democracy, at Athens and elsewhere, in condemning unsuccessful, but innocent generals. Out of the many cases in which this reproach is advanced, there are very few

---

[1] The traveller Pausanias justifies the prudence of his regal namesake in avoiding a battle, by saying that the Athenians were in his rear, and the Thebans in his front; and that he was afraid of being assailed on both sides at once, like Leonidas at Thermopylæ, and like the troops enclosed in Sphakteria (Paus. iii, 5, 5).

But the matter of fact, on which this justification rests, is contradicted by Xenophon, who says that the Athenians had actually joined the Thebans and were in the same ranks — ἐλθόντες ξυμπαρετάξαντο (Hellen. iii, 5, 22).

[2] Xen. Hellen. iii, 5, 2ᶠ. Καὶ ὅτι τὸν δῆμον τῶν Ἀθηναίων λαβὼν ἐν τῷ Πειραιεῖ ἀνῆκε, etc. Compare Pausanias, iii, 5, 3.

wherein it has been made good; but even if we grant it to be valid against Athens and her democracy, the fate of Pausanias will show us that the ephors and senate of anti-democratical Sparta were capable of the like unjust misjudgment. Hardly a single instance of Athenian condemnation occurs, which we can so clearly prove to be undeserved, as this of a Spartan king.

Turning from the banished king to Lysander, — the Spartans had indeed valid reasons for deploring the fall of the latter. He had procured for them their greatest and most decisive victories, and the time was coming when they needed his services to procure them more ; for he left behind him no man of equal warlike resource, cunning, and power of command. But if he possessed those abilities which powerfully helped Sparta to triumph over her enemies, he at the same time did more than any man to bring her empire into dishonor, and to render its tenure precarious. His decemviral governments or dekarchies, diffused through the subject cities, and each sustained by a Lacedæmonian harmost and garrison, were aggravations of local tyranny such as the Grecian world had never before undergone. And though the Spartan authorities presently saw that he was abusing the imperial name of the city for unmeasured personal aggrandizement of his own, and partially withdrew their countenance from his dekarchies, — yet the general character of their empire still continued to retain the impress of partisanship and subjugation which he had originally stamped upon it. Instead of that autonomy which Sparta had so repeatedly promised, it became subjection every way embittered. Such an empire was pretty sure to be short-lived ; but the loss to Sparta herself, when her empire fell away, is not the only fault which the historian of Greece has to impute to Lysander. His far deeper sin consists in his having thrown away an opportunity, — such as never occurred either before or afterwards, — for organizing some permanent, honorable, self-maintaining, Pan-hellenic combination under the headship of Sparta. This is (as I have before remarked) what a man like Kallikratidas would have attempted, if not with far-sighted wisdom, at least with generous sincerity, and by an appeal to the best veins of political sentiment in the chief city as well as in the subordinates. It is possible that with the best intentions even he might have failed; so strong was the centrifugal instinct in the Grecian political mind. But what we have to reproach in Lysander is, that he never tried : that he abused the critical moment of cure for the purpose of infusing new poison into the system ; that he not only sacrificed the interests of Greece to the narrow gains of Sparta, but even the interests of Sparta to the still narrower monopoly of dominion in his own hands. That his measures worked mischievously not merely for Greece, but for Sparta herself, aggravating all her bad tendencies, — has been already remarked in the preceding pages.

That Lysander, with unbounded opportunities of gain, both lived and died poor, exhibits the honorable side of his character. Yet his personal indifference to money seems only to have left the greater space in his bosom for that thirst of power which made him unscrupulous in satiating the rapacity, as well as in uphold- ing the oppressions, of coadjutors like the Thirty at Athens and the decemvirs in other cities. In spite of his great success and ability in closing the Peloponnesian war, we shall agree with Pau- sanias[1] that he was more mischievous than profitable even to Sparta, — even if we take no thought of Greece generally. What would have been the effect produced by his projects in regard to the regal succession, had he been able to bring them to bear, we have no means of measuring. We are told that the discourse composed and addressed to him by the Halicarnassian rhetor Kle on, was found after his death among his papers by Agesilaus ; who first learnt from it, with astonishment and alarm, the point to which the ambition of Lysander had tended, and was desirous of exposing his real character by making the discourse public, — but was deterred by dissuasive counsel of the ephor Lakratidas. But this story (attested by Ephorus[2]) looks more like an anecdote of the rhetorical schools than like a reality. Agesilaus was not the man to set much value on sophists or their compositions ; nor is it easy to believe that he remained so long ignorant of those projects which Lysander had once entertained but subsequently dropped. Moreover the probability is, that Kleon himself would make the discourse public as a sample of his own talents, even in the life- time of Lysander ; not only without shame, but as representing the feelings of a considerable section of readers throughout the Grecian world.

---

[1] Pausanias, ix 32, 6.

[2] Ephorus, Fr. 27, ed Didot ; Plutarch. Lysander, c 30.

Most important were the consequences which ensued from the death of Lysander and the retreat of Pausanias out of Bœotia. Fresh hope and spirits were infused into all the enemies of Sparta. An alliance was immediately concluded against her by Thebes, Athens, Corinth, and Argos. Deputies from these four cities were appointed to meet at Corinth, and to take active measures for inviting the coöperation of fresh allies; so that the war which had begun as a Bœotian war, now acquired the larger denomination of Corinthian war, under which it lasted until the peace of Antalkidas. The alliance was immediately strengthened by the junction of the Eubœans, — the Akarnanians, — the Ozolian Lokrians, — Ambrakia and Leukas (both particularly attached to Corinth), — and the Chalkidians of Thrace.[1]

We now enter upon the period when, for the first time, Thebes begins to step out of the rank of secondary powers, and gradually raises herself into a primary and ascendant city in Grecian politics. Throughout the Peloponnesian war, the Thebans had shown themselves excellent soldiers, both on horseback and on foot, as auxiliaries to Sparta. But now the city begins to have a policy of its own, and individual citizens of ability become conspicuous. While waiting for Pelopidas and Epaminondas, with whom we shall presently become acquainted, we have at the present moment Ismenias; a wealthy Theban, a sympathizer with Thrasybulus and the Athenian exiles eight years before, and one of the great organizers of the present anti-Spartan movement; a man, too, honored by his political enemies,[2] when they put him to death fourteen years afterwards, with the title of "a great wicked man," — the same combination of epithets which Clarendon applies to Oliver Cromwell.

It was Ismenias, who, at the head of a body of Bœotians and Argeians, undertook an expedition to put down the Spartan influence in the regions north of Bœotia. At Pharsalus in Thessaly, the Lacedæmonians had an harmost and garrison; at Pheræ,

---

[1] Diodor. xiv, 81, 82; Xen. Hellen. iv, 2, 17.

[2] Xen. Hellen. v, 2, 36. Ὁ δ' (Ismenias) ἀπελογεῖτο μὲν πρὸς πάντα ταῦτα, οὐ μέντοι ἐπειθέ γε τὸ μὴ οὐ μεγαλοπράγμων τε καὶ κακοπράγμων εἶναι.

It is difficult to make out anything from the two allusions in Plato, except that Ismenias was a wealthy and powerful man (Plato. Menon, p. 90 B.; Republ. i, p. 336 A.).

Lykophron the despot was their ally; while Larissa, with Medius the despot, was their principal enemy. By the aid of the Bœotians, Medius was now enabled to capture Pharsalus; Larissa, with Krannon and Skotusa, was received into the Theban alliance,[1] and Ismenias obtained also the more important advantage of expelling the Lacedæmonians from Herakleia. Some malcontents, left after the violent interference of the Spartan Herippidas two years before, opened the gates of Herakleia by night to the Bœotians and Argeians. The Lacedæmonians in the town were put to the sword, but the other Peloponnesian colonists were permitted to retire in safety; while the old Trachinian inhabitants, whom the Lacedæmonians had expelled to make room for their new settlers, together with the Œtæans, whom they had driven out of the districts in the neighborhood, — were now called back to repossess their original homes.[2] The loss of Herakleia was a serious blow to the Spartans in those regions, — protecting Eubœa in its recent revolt from them, and enabling Ismenias to draw into his alliance the neighboring Malians, Ænianes, and Athamanes, — tribes stretching along the valley of the Spercheius westward to the vicinity of Pindus. Assembling additional troops from these districts (which, only a few months before, had supplied an army to Lysander[3]), Ismenias marched against the Phokians, among whom the Spartan Lakisthenes had been left as harmost in command. After a severe battle, this officer with his Phokians was defeated near the Lokrian town of Naryx; and Ismenias came back victorious to the synod at Corinth.[4]

By such important advantages, accomplished during the winter of 395–394 B. C., the prospects of Grecian affairs as they stood in the ensuing spring became materially altered. The allies assembled at Corinth, full of hope, and resolved to levy a large combined force to act against Sparta; who on her side seemed to be threatened with the loss of all her extra-Peloponnesian land-empire. Accordingly, the ephors determined to recall without delay Agesilaus with his army from Asia, and sent Epikydidas with orders to that effect. But even before this reinforcement could arrive, they thought it expe-

---

[1] Diodor. xiv, 82; Xen. Hellen. iv, 3, 3; Xen. Agesil. ii, 2.
[2] Diodor. xiv, 38–82. [3] Xenoph. Hellen. iii, 5, 6.
[4] Diodor. xiv, 82.

dient to muster their full Peloponnesian force and to act with vigor against the allies at Corinth, who were now assembling in considerable numbers. Aristodemus, — guardian of the youthful king Agesipolis son of Pausanias, and himself of the Eurystheneid race, — marched at the head of a body of six thousand Lacedæmonian hoplites;[1] the Spartan xenâgi (or officers sent on purpose to conduct the contingents from the outlying allies), successively brought in three thousand hoplites from Elis, Triphylia, Akroreia, and Lasion, — fifteen hundred from Sikyon; — three thousand from Epidaurus, Trœzen, Hermionê, and Halieis. None were sent from Phlias, on the plea (true or false[2]) that in that city the moment was one of solemnity and holy truce. There were also hoplites from Tegea, Mantineia, and the Achæan towns, but their number is not given; so that we do not know the full muster-roll on the Lacedæmonian side. The cavalry, six hundred in number, were all Lacedæmonian; there were, moreover, three hundred Kretan bowmen, — and four hundred slingers from different rural districts of Triphylia.[3]

The allied force of the enemy was already mustered near Cor-

---

[1] Xen. Hellen. iv, 2, 16. Xenophon gives this total of six thousand as if it were of Lacedæmonians *alone*. But if we follow his narrative, we shall see that there were unquestionably in the army troops of Tegea, Mantineia, and the Achæan towns (probably also some of other Arcadian towns,) present in the battle (iv, 2, 13, 18, 20). Can we suppose that Xenophon meant to include *these* allies in the total of six thousand, along with the Lacedæ-monians, — which is doubtless a large total for Lacedæmonians alone? Unless this supposition be admitted, there is no resource except to assume an omission, either of Xenophon himself, or of the copyist; which omission in fact Gail and others do suppose. On the whole, I think they are right; for the number of hoplites on both sides would otherwise be prodigiously unequal; while Xenophon says nothing to imply that the Lacedæmonian victory was gained in spite of great inferiority of number, and something which even implies that it must have been nearly equal (iv, 2, 13),— though he is always disposed to compliment Sparta wherever he can.

[2] From a passage which occurs somewhat later (iv, 4, 15), we may suspect that this was an excuse, and that the Phliasians were not very well affected to Sparta. Compare a similar case of excuse ascribed to the Mantineians (v, 2, 2).

[3] Diodorus (xiv, 83) gives a total of twenty-three thousand foot and five hundred horse, on the Lacedæmonian side, but without enumerating items. On the side of the confederacy he states a total of more than fifteen thousand foot and five hundred horse (c. 82).

inth; six thousand Athenian hoplites, — seven thousand Argeian — five thousand Bœotian, those from Orchomenus being absent, — three thousand Corinthian, — three thousand from the different towns of Eubœa; making twenty-four thousand in all. The total of cavalry was fifteen hundred and fifty; composed of eight hundred Bœotian, six hundred Athenian, one hundred from Chalkis in Eubœa, and fifty from the Lokrians. The light troops also were numerous, — partly Corinthian, drawn probably from the serf-population which tilled the fields,[1] — partly Lokrians, Malians, and Akarnanians.

The allied leaders, holding a council of war to arrange their plans, came to a resolution that the hoplites should not be drawn up in deeper files than sixteen men,[2] in order that there might be no chance of their being surrounded; and that the right wing, carrying with it command for the time, should be alternated from day to day between the different cities. The confidence which the events of the last few months had infused into these leaders, now for the first time acting against their old leader Sparta, is surprising. "There is nothing like marching to Sparta (said the Corinthian Timolaus) and fighting the Lacedæmonians at or near their own home. We must burn out the wasps in their nest, without letting them come forth to sting us. The Lacedæmonian force is like that of a river; small at its source, and becoming formidable only by the affluents which it receives, in proportion to the length of its course."[3] The wisdom of this advice was remarkable; but its boldness was yet more remarkable, when viewed in conjunction with the established feeling of awe towards Sparta. It was adopted by the general council of the allies; but unfortunately the time for executing it had already passed; for the Lacedæmonians were already in march and had crossed their own border. They took the line of road by Tegea and Mantineia (whose troops joined the

---

[1] Xen. Hellen. iv, 2, 17. Καὶ ψιλὸν δὲ, ξὺν τοῖς τῶν Κορινθίων, πλέον ἦν, etc. Compare Hesychius, v, Κυνόφαλοι; Welcker, Præfat. ad. Theognidem, p. xxxv; K. O. Müller, History of the Dorians, iii, 4, 3.

[2] Xen. Hellen. iv, 2, 13; compare iv, 2, 18, — where he says of the Thebans — ἀμελήσαντες τοῦ ἐς ἑκκαίδεκα, βαθεῖαν παντελῶς ἐποιήσαντο τὴν φάλαγγα, etc., which implies and alludes to the resolution previously taken.

[3] Xen. Hellen. iv, 2, 11 12

march), and advanced as far as Sikyon, where probably all the Arcadian and Achæan contingents were ordered to rendezvous.

The troops of the confederacy had advanced as far as Nemea when they learnt that the Lacedæmonian army was at Sikyon; but they then altered their plan, and confined themselves to the defensive. The Lacedæmonians on their side crossed over the mountainous post called Epieikia, under considerable annoyance from the enemy's light troops, who poured missiles upon them from the high ground. But when they had reached the level country, on the other side, along the shore of the Saronic Gulf, where they probably received the contingents from Epidaurus, Trœzen, Hermionê, and Halieis, — the whole army thus reinforced marched forward without resistance, burning and ravaging the cultivated lands. The confederates retreated before them, and at length took up a position close to Corinth, amidst some rough ground with a ravine in their front.[1] The Lacedæmonians advanced forward until they were little more than a mile distant from this position, and there encamped.

---

[1] Xen. Hellen. iv, 2, 14, 15.

In the passage, — καὶ οἱ ἕτεροι μέντοι ἐλθόντες κατεστρατοπεδεύσαντο, ἔμπροσθεν ποιησάμενοι τὴν χαράδραν, — I apprehend that ἀπελθόντες (which is sanctioned by four MSS., and preferred by Leunclavius) is the proper reading, in place of ἐλθόντες. For it seems certain that the march of the confederates was one of retreat, and that the battle was fought very near to the walls of Corinth; since the defeated troops sought shelter within the town, and the Lacedæmonian pursuers were so close upon them, that the Corinthians within were afraid to keep open the gates. Hence we must reject the statement of Diodorus, — that the battle was fought on the banks of the river Nemea (xiv, 83) as erroneous.

There are some difficulties and obscurities in the description which Xenophon gives of the Lacedæmonian march. His words run — ἐν τούτῳ οἱ Λακεδαιμόνιοι, καὶ δὴ Τεγεάτας παρειληφότες καὶ Μαντινέας, ἐξῇεσαν τὴν ἀμφίαλον. These last three words are not satisfactorily explained. Weiske and Schneider construe τὴν ἀμφίαλον (very justly) as indicating the region lying immediately on the Peloponnesian side of the isthmus of Corinth and having the Saronic Gulf on one side, and the Corinthian Gulf on the other; in which was included Sikyon. But then it would not be correct to say, that "the Lacedæmonians had gone out by the bimarine way." On the contrary, the truth is, that "they had gone out into the bimarine road or region, — which meaning however would require a preposition — ἐξῇεσαν εἰς τὴν ἀμφίαλον. Sturz in his Lexicon (v. ἐξιέναι) renders τὴν ἀμφ᾽ ιλον — viam ad mare — which seems an extraordinary sense of

After an interval seemingly of a few days, the Bœotians, on the day when their turn came to occupy the right wing and to take the lead, gave the signal for battle.[1] The Lacedæmonians, prevented by the wooded ground from seeing clearly, were only made aware of the coming attack by hearing the hostile pæan. Taking order of battle immediately, they advanced forward to meet the assailants when within a furlong of their line. In each army, the right division took the lead, — slanting to the right, or keeping the left shoulder forward, according to the tendency habitual with Grecian hoplites, through anxiety to keep the right or unshielded side from

the word, unless instances were produced to support it; and even if instances were produced, we do not see why the way from Sparta to Sikyon should be called by that name; which would more properly belong to the road from Sparta down the Eurotas to Helos.

Again, we do not know distinctly the situation of the point or district called τὴν Ἐπιεικίαν (mentioned again, iv, 4, 13). But it is certain from the map, that when the confederates were at Nemea, and the Lacedæmonians at Sikyon, — the former must have been exactly placed so as to intercept the junction of the contingents from Epidaurus, Trœzen, and Hermionê, with the Lacedæmonian army. To secure this junction, the Lacedæmonians were obliged to force their way across that mountainous region which lies near Kleônæ and Nemea, and to march in a line pointing from Sikyon down to the Saronic Gulf. Having reached the other side of these mountains near the sea, they would be in communication with Epidaurus and the other towns of the Argolic peninsula.

The line of march which the Lacedæmonians would naturally take from Sparta to Sikyon and Lechæum, by Tegea, Mantineia, Orchomenus, etc., is described two years afterwards in the case of Agesilaus (iv, 5, 19).

[1] Xen. Hellen. iv, 2, 18. The coloring which Xenophon puts upon this step is hardly fair to the Thebans, as is so constantly the case throughout his history. He says that "they were in no hurry to fight" (οὐδέν τι κατή- πειγον τὴν μάχην ξυνάπτειν) so long as they were on the left, opposed to the Lacedæmonians on the opposite right; but that as soon as they were on the right (opposed to the Achæans on the opposite left), they forthwith gave the word. Now it does not appear that the Thebans had any greater privilege on the day when they were on the right, than the Argeians or Athenians had when each were on the right respectively. The command had been determined to reside in the right division, which post alternated from one to the other; why the Athenians or Argeians did not make use of this post to order the attack, we cannot explain.

So again, Xenophon says, that in spite of the resolution taken by the Council of War to have files sixteen deep, and no more, — the Thebans made their files much deeper. Yet it is plain, from his own account, that no mischievous consequences turned upon this greater depth.

being exposed to the enemy, and at the same time to be protected by the shield of a right-hand neighbor.[1] The Lacedæmonians in the one army, and the Thebans in the other, each inclined themselves, and caused their respective armies to incline also, in a direction slanting to the right, so that the Lacedæmonians on their side considerably outflanked the Athenians on the opposite left. Out of the ten tribes of Athenian hoplites, it was only the six on the extreme left who came into conflict with the Lacedæmonians; while the remaining four contended with the Tegeans who stood next to the Lacedæmonians on their own line. But the six extreme Athenian tribes were completely beaten, and severely handled, being taken in flank as well as in front by the Lacedæmonians. On the other hand, the remaining four Athenian tribes vanquished and drove before them the Tegeans; and generally, along all the rest of the line, the Thebans, Argeians, and Corinthians were victorious, — except where the troops of the Achæan Pellênê stood opposed to those of the Bœotian Thespiæ, where the battle was equal and the loss severe on both sides. The victorious confederates, however, were so ardent and incautious in pursuit, as to advance a considerable distance and return with disordered ranks; while the Lacedæmonians, who were habitually self-restraining in this particular, kept their order perfectly, attacking the Thebans, Argeians, and Corinthians to great advantage when returning to their camp. Several of the Athenian fugitives obtained shelter within the walls of Corinth; in spite of the opposition of the philo-Laconian Corinthians, who insisted upon shutting the gates against them, and opening negotiations with Sparta. The Lacedæmonians however came so near that it was at last thought impossible to keep the gates open longer. Many of the remaining confederates were therefore obliged to be satisfied with the protection of their ancient camp;[2] which seems, however, to have been situated in such defensible ground,[3] that the Lacedæmonians did not molest them in it.

---

[1] See the instructive description of the battle of Mantineia — in Thucyd v, 71.

[2] Xen. Hellen. iv, 2, 20–23.

The allusion to this incident in Demosthenes (adv. Leptinem, c. 13, p. 472) is interesting, though indistinct.

[3] Xen. Hellen. iv, 2, 19. καὶ γὰρ ἦν λάσιον τὸ χωρίον — which illustrates

So far as the Lacedæmonians separately were concerned, the battle of Corinth was an important victory, gained (as they affirmed) with the loss of only eight men, and inflicting heavy loss upon the Athenians in the battle, as well as upon the remaining confederates in their return from pursuit. Though the Athenian hoplites suffered thus severely, yet Thrasybulus their commander,[1] who kept the field until the last, with strenuous efforts to rally them, was not satisfied with their behavior. But on the other hand, all the allies of Sparta were worsted, and a considerable number of them slain. According to Diodorus, the total loss on the Lacedæmonian side was eleven hundred; on the side of the confederates twenty-eight hundred.[2] On the whole, the victory of the Lacedæmonians was not sufficiently decisive to lead to important results, though it completely secured their ascendency within Peloponnesus. We observe here, as we shall have occasion to observe elsewhere, that the Peloponnesian allies do not fight heartily in the cause of Sparta. They seem bound to her more by fear than by affection.

The battle of Corinth took place about July 394 B. C., seemingly about the same time as the naval battle near Knidus (or perhaps a little earlier), and while Agesilaus was on his homeward march after being recalled from Asia. Had the Lacedæmonians been able to defer the battle until Agesilaus had come up so as to threaten Bœotia on the northern side, their campaign would probably have been much more successful. As it is, their defeated allies doubtless went home in disgust from the field of Corinth, so that the confederates were now enabled to turn their whole attention to Agesilaus.

That prince had received in Asia his summons of recall from the ephors with profound vexation and disappointment, yet at the same time with patriotic submission. He had augmented his army,

---

the expression in Lysias, Orat. xvi, (pro Mantitheo) s. 20.   ἐν Κορίνθῳ χω-
ρίων ἰσχυρῶν κατειλημμένων.

[1] Lysias, Orat. xvi, (pro Mantitheo) s. 19.

Plato in his panegyrical discourse (Menexenus, c. 17, p. 245 E.) ascribes the defeat and loss of the Athenians to "bad ground"— χρησαμένων δυσ-χωρίᾳ.

[2] Diodor. xiv, 83.

The statement in Xenophon (Agesil. vii, 5) that near ten thousand men were slain on the side of the confederates, is a manifest exaggeration· if indeed the reading be correct

and was contemplating more extensive schemes of operations against the Persian satrapies in Asia Minor. He had established such a reputation for military force and skill, that numerous messages reached him from different inland districts, expressing their anxiety to be emancipated from Persian dominion; and inviting him to come to their aid. His ascendency was also established over the Grecian cities on the coast, whom he still kept under the government of partisan oligarchies and Spartan harmosts, — yet seemingly with greater practical moderation, and less license of oppression, than had marked the conduct of these men when they could count upon so unprincipled a chief as Lysander. He was thus just now not only at a high pitch of actual glory and ascendency, but nourishing yet brighter hopes of farther conquests for the future. And what filled up the measure of his aspirations, — all the conquests were to be made at the expense, not of Greeks, but of the Persians. He was treading in the footsteps of Agamemnon, as Pan-hellenic leader against a Pan-hellenic enemy.

All these glorious dreams were dissipated by Epikydidas, with his sad message, and peremptory summons, from the ephors. In the chagrin and disappointment of Agesilaus we can sincerely sympathize; but the panegyric which Xenophon and others pronounce upon him for his ready obedience is altogether unreasonable.[1] There was no merit in renouncing his projects of conquest at the bidding of the ephors; because, if any serious misfortune had befallen Sparta at home, none of those projects could have been executed. Nor is it out of place to remark, that even if Agesilaus had not been recalled, the extinction of the Lacedæmonian naval superiority by the defeat of Knidus, would have rendered all large plans of inland conquest impracticable. On receiving his orders of recall, he convened an assembly both of his allies and of his army, to make known the painful necessity of his departure; which was heard with open and sincere manifestations

---

[1] Xen. Agesil. i, 37; Plutarch, Agesil. c. 15. Cornelius Nepos (Agesilaus. c. 4) almost translates the Agesilaus of Xenophon; but we can better feel the force of *his* panegyric, when we recollect that he had had personal cognizance of the disobedience of Julius Cæsar in his province to the orders of the Senate, and that the omnipotence of Sylla and Pompey in their provinces were then matter of recent history. "Cujus exemplum (says Cornelius Nepos about Agesilaus) utinam imperatores nostri sequi voluissent!"

of sorrow. He assured them that as soon as he had dissipated the clouds which hung over Sparta at home, he should come back to Asia without delay, and resume his efforts against the Persian satraps; in the interim he left Euxenus, with a force of four thousand men for their protection. Such was the sympathy excited by his communication, combined with esteem for his character, that the cities passed a general vote to furnish him with contingents of troops for his march to Sparta. But this first burst of zeal abated, when they came to reflect that it was a service against Greeks; not merely unpopular in itself, but presenting a certainty of hard fighting with little plunder. Agesilaus tried every means to keep up their spirits, by proclaiming prizes both to the civic soldiers and to the mercenaries, to be distributed at Sestus in the Chersonesus, as soon as they should have crossed into Europe, — prizes for the best equipment, and best disciplined soldiers in every different arm.[1] By these means he prevailed upon the bravest and most effective soldiers in his army to undertake the march along with him; among them many of the Cyreians, with Xenophon himself at their head.

Though Agesilaus, in leaving Greece, had prided himself on hoisting the flag of Agamemnon, he was now destined against his will to tread in the footsteps of the Persian Xerxes in his march from the Thracian Chersonese through Thrace, Macedonia, and Thessaly, to Thermopylæ and Bœotia. Never, since the time of Xerxes, had any army undertaken this march; which now bore an Oriental impress, from the fact that Agesilaus brought with him some camels, taken in the battle of Sardis.[2] Overawing or defeating the various Thracian tribes, he reached Amphipolis on the Strymon where he was met by Derkyllidas, who had come fresh from the battle of Corinth and informed him of the victory. Full as his heart was of Pan-hellenic projects against Persia, he burst into exclamations of regret on hearing of the death of so many Greeks in battle, who could have sufficed, if united, to emancipate Asia Minor.[3] Sending Derkyllidas forward to Asia to make known the victory to the Grecian cities in his alliance, he pursued his march through Macedonia and Thessaly. In the latter comp

---

[1] Xen. Hellen. iv, 2, 2–5; Xen. Agesil. i, 38; Plutarch, Agesil. c. 16

[2] Xen. Hellen. iii, 4, 24.

[3] Xenoph. Agesil. vii, 5; Plutarch, Agesil. c. 16.

try, Larissa, Krannon, and other cities in alliance with Thebes, raised opposition to bar his passage. But in the disunited condi·tion of this country, no systematic resistance could be organized against him. Nothing more appeared than detached bodies of cavalry, whom he beat and dispersed, with the death of Polychar-mus, their leader. As the Thessalian cavalry, however, was the best in Greece, he took great pride in having defeated them with cavalry disciplined by himself in Asia ; backed, however, it must be observed, by skilful and effective support from his hoplites.[1] After having passed the Achæan mountains or the line of Mount Othrys, he marched the rest of the way without opposition, through the strait of Thermopylæ to the frontier of Phokis and Bœotia.

In this latter part of his march, Agesilaus was met by the ephor Diphridas in person, who urged him to hasten his march as much as possible, and attack the Bœotians. He was further joined by two Lacedæmonian regiments[2] from Corinth, and by fifty young Spartan volunteers as a body-guard, who crossed by sea from Si-kyon. He was reinforced also by the Phokians and the Orcho-menians, — in addition to the Peloponnesian troops who had accompanied him to Asia, the Asiatic hoplites, the Cyreians, the peltasts, and the cavalry, whom he had brought with him from the Hellespont, and some fresh troops collected in the march. His army was thus in imposing force when he reached the neighbor-hood of Chæroneia on the Bœotian border. It was here that they were alarmed by an eclipse of the sun, on the fourteenth of August, 394 B. C. ; a fatal presage, the meaning of which was soon inter-preted for them by the arrival of a messenger bearing news of the naval defeat of Knidus, with the death of Peisander, brother-in-law of Agesilaus. Deeply was the latter affected by this irrepara-ble blow. He foresaw that, when known, it would spread dismay and dejection among his soldiers, most of whom would remain at-tached to him only so long as they believed the cause of Sparta

---

[1] Xen. Hellen. iv, 2, 4–9 ; Diodor. xiv, 83.

[2] Plutarch (Agesil. c. 17; compare also Plutarch, Apophth. p. 795, as corrected by Morus ad Xen. Hellen. iv, 3, 15) states two moræ or regiments as having joined Agesilaus from Corinth ; Xenophon alludes only to one besides that mora which was in garrison at Orchomenus (Hellen iv. 3, 15 Agesil. ii, 6).

to be ascendant and profitable.[1] Accordingly, he resolved, being now within a day's march of his enemies, to hasten on a battle without making known the bad news. Proclaiming that intelligence had been received of a sea-fight having taken place, in which the Lacedæmonians had been victorious, though Peisander himself was slain,— he offered a sacrifice of thanksgiving and sent round presents of congratulation, — which produced an encouraging effect, and made the skirmishers especially both forward and victorious.

To his enemies, now assembled in force on the plain of Koroneia, the real issue of the battle of Knidus was doubtless made known, spreading hope and cheerfulness through their ranks; though we are not informed what interpretation they put upon the solar eclipse. The army was composed of nearly the same contingents as those who had recently fought at Corinth, except that we hear of the Ænianes in place of the Malians ; but probably each contingent was less numerous, since there was still a necessity for occupying and defending the camp near Corinth. Among the Athenian hoplites, who had just been so roughly handled in the preceding battle, and who were now drafted off by lot to march into Bœotia, against both a general and an army of high reputation, — there prevailed much apprehension and some reluctance; as we learn from one of them, Mantitheus, who stood forward to volunteer his services, and who afterwards makes just boast of it before an Athenian dikastery.[2] The Thebans an Bœotians were probably in full force, and more numerous than at Corinth, since it was their own country which was to be defended. The camp was established in the territory of Korôneia, not far from the great

---

[1] Xen. Hellen. iv, 3, 13.

Ὁ μὲν οὖν Ἀγησίλαος πυθόμενος ταῦτα, τὸ μὲν πρῶτον χαλεπῶς ἔφερεν· ἐπεὶ μέντοι ἐνεθυμήθη, ὅτι τοῦ στρατεύματος τὸ πλεῖστον εἴη αὐτῷ, οἶον ἀγαθῶν μὲν γιγνομένων ἡδέως μετέχειν, εἰ δέ τι χαλεπὸν ὀρῷεν, οὐκ ἀνάγκην εἶναι κοινωνεῖν αὐτοῖς, etc.

These indirect intimations of the real temper even of the philo-Spartan allies towards Sparta are very valuable when coming from Xenophon, as they contradict all his partialities, and are dropped here almost relunctantly, from the necessity of justifying the conduct of Agesilaus in publishing a false proclamation to his army.

[2] Lysias, Orat. xvi, (pro Mantitheo) s, 20.   φοβουμένων ἁπάντων εἰκότως etc.

:emple of Itonian Athênê, where the Pambœotia, or general Bœotian assemblies were held, and where there also stood the trophy
erected for the great victory over Tolmides and the Athenians,
about fifty years before.[1] Between the two armies there was no
great difference of numbers, except as to the peltasts, who were
more numerous in the army of Agesilaus, though they do not
seem to have taken much part in the battle.

Having marched from Chæroneia, Agesilaus approached the
plain of Koroneia from the river Kephissus, while the Thebans
met him from the direction of Mount Helikon. He occupied the
right wing of his army, the Orchomenians being on the left, and
the Cyreians with the Asiatic allies in the centre. In the opposite
line, the Thebans were on the right, and the Argeians on the left.
Both armies approached slowly and in silence until they were
separated only by an interval of a furlong, at which moment the
Thebans on the right began the war-shout, and accelerated their
march to a run, — the rest of the line following their example.
When they got within half a furlong of the Lacedæmonians, the
centre division of the latter, under the command of Herippidas
(comprising the Cyreians, with Xenophon himself, and the Asiatic
allies) started forward on their side, and advanced at a run to meet
them; seemingly, getting beyond their own line,[2] and coming first
to cross spears with the enemy's centre. After a sharp struggle,
the division of Herippidas was here victorious, and drove back its
opponents. Agesilaus, on his right, was yet more victorious, for
the Argeians opposed to him, fled without even crossing spears.
These fugitives found safety on the high ground of Mount Helikon. But on the other hand, the Thebans on their own right completely beat back the Orchomenians, and pursued them so far as
to get to the baggage in the rear of the army. Agesilaus, while
his friends around were congratulating him as conqueror, immediately wheeled round to complete his victory by attacking the Thebans; who, on their side also faced about, and prepared to fight
their way, in close and deep order, to rejoin their comrades on
Helikon. Though Agesilaus might have let them pass, and assailed them in the rear with greater safety and equal effect, he pre-

---

[1] Plutarch, Agesil. c. 19
[2] Xen. Hellen. iv, 3, 17. ἀντεξέδραμον ἀπὸ τῆς Ἀνησιλάου φάλαγγος, etc

ferred the more honorable victory of a conflict face to ace. Such is the coloring which his panegyrist, Xenophon,[1] puts upon his manœuvre. Yet we may remark that if he had let the Thebans pass, he could not have pursued them far, seeing that their own comrades were at hand to sustain them, — and also that having never yet fought against the Thebans, he had probably no adequate appreciation of their prowess.

The crash which now took place was something terrific beyond all Grecian military experience,[2] leaving an indelible impression upon Xenophon, who was personally engaged in it. The hoplites on both sides came to the fiercest and closest bodily struggle, pushing shields against each other, with all the weight of the incumbent mass behind impelling forward the foremost ranks, — especially in the deep order of the Thebans. The shields of the foremost combatants were thus stove in, their spears broken, and each man was engaged in such close embrace with his enemy, that the dagger was the only weapon which he could use. There was no systematic shout, such as usually marked the charge of a Grecian army; the silence was only broken by a medley of furious exclamations and murmurs.[3] Agesilaus himself, who was among the front ranks, and whose size and strength were by no means on a level with his personal courage, had his body covered with wounds from different weapons,[4] — was trodden down, — and only escaped by the devoted courage of those fifty Spartan volunteers who formed his body-guard. Partly from his wounds, partly from the irresistible courage and stronger pressure of the Thebans, the Spartans were at length compelled to give way, so far as to afford a free passage to the former, who were thus enabled to

---

[1] Xen. Hellen. iv, 3, 19; Xen. Agesil. ii, 12.

[2] Xen. Hellen. iv, 3, 16; Xen. Agesil. ii, 9.

Διηγήσομαι δὲ καὶ τὴν μάχην· καὶ γὰρ ἐγένετο οἷα οὐκ ἄλλη των γ᾽ ἐφ ἡμῶν.

[3] Xen. Hellen. iv, 3, 19; Xen. Agesil. ii, 12.

Καὶ συμβαλόντες τὰς ἀσπίδας ἐωθοῦντο, ἐμάχοντο, ἀπέκτεινον, ἀπέθνησκον Καὶ κραυγὴ μὲν οὐδεμία παρῆν, οὐ μὴν οὐδὲ σιγή φωνὴ δὲ τ ς ἦν τοιαύτη, οἷαν ὀργή τε καὶ μάχη παράσχοιτ᾽ ἄν.

[4] Xen. Agesil. ii, 13. Ὁ δὲ, καίπερ πολλὰ τραύματα ἔχων πάντοσι καὶ παντοίοις ὅπλοις, etc.

Plutarch, Agesil. c. 18.

march onward and rejoin their comrades ; not without sustaining
some loss by attacks on their rear.[1]

Agesilaus thus remained master of the field of battle, having
gained a victory over his opponents taken collectively. But so far
as concerns the Thebans separately, he had not only gained no
victory, but had failed in his purpose of stopping their progress,
and had had the worst of the combat. His wounds having been
dressed, he was brought back on men's shoulders to give his final
orders, and was then informed that a detachment of eighty Theban hoplites, left behind by the rest, had taken refuge in the
temple of Itonian Athênê as suppliants. From generosity mingled with respect to the sanctity of the spot, he commanded that
they should be dismissed unhurt, and then proceeded to give directions for the night-watch, as it was already late. The field of
battle presented a terrible spectacle ; Spartan and Theban dead
lying intermingled, some yet grasping their naked daggers, others
pierced with the daggers of their enemies ; around, on the blood-
stained ground, were seen broken spears, smashed shields, swords
and daggers scattered apart from their owners.[2] He directed
the Spartan and Theban dead to be collected in separate heaps,
and placed in safe custody for the night, in the interior of his
phalanx ; the troops then took their supper, and rested for the
night. On the next morning, Gylis the Polemarch was ordered
to draw up the army in battle-array, to erect a trophy, and to
offer sacrifices of cheerfulness and thanksgiving, with the pipers
solemnly playing, according to Spartan fashion. Agesilaus
was anxious to make these demonstrations of victory as ostentatious as possible, because he really doubted whether he had
gained a victory. It was very possible that the Thebans
might feel confidence enough to renew the attack, and try to
recover the field of battle, with their own dead upon it ; which
Agesilaus had, for that reason, caused to be collected in a sepa-

---

[1] Xen. Hellen. iv, 3, 19 ; Xen. Agesil. ii, 12.

[2] Xen Agesil. ii, 14. Ἐπεί γε μὴν ἔληξεν ἡ μάχη, παρῆν δὴ θεάσασθαι
ἔνθα συνέπεσον ἀλλήλοις, τὴν μὲν γῆν αἵματι πεφυρμένην, νεκροὺς δὲ κειμέ-
νους φιλίους καὶ πολεμίους μετ' ἀλλήλων, ἀσπίδας δὲ διατεθρυμμένας, δόρατα
συντεθραυσμένα, ἐγχειρίδια γυμνὰ κουλεῶν τὰ μὲν χαμαὶ, τὰ δ' ἐν σώμασι, τὰ
δ' ἔτι μετὰ χειρός

rate heap and placed within the Lacedæmonian line.[1] He was,
however, soon relieved from doubt by a herald coming from the
Thebans to solicit the customary truce for the burial of their
dead; the understood confession of defeat. The request was immediately granted; each party paid the last solemnities to its own
dead, and the Spartan force was then withdrawn from Bœotia.
Xenophon does not state the loss on either side, but Diodorus gives
it at six hundred on the side of the confederates, three hundred
and fifty on that of the Lacedæmonians.[2]

Disqualified as he was by his wounds for immediate action, Age-
silæus caused himself to be carried to Delphi, where the Pythian
games were at that moment going on. He here offered to Apollo
the tithe of the booty acquired during his two years' campaigns in
Asia; a tithe equal to one hundred talents.[3] Meanwhile the polemarch Gylis conducted the army first into Phokis, next on a predatory excursion into the Lokrian territory, where the nimble
attack of the Lokrian light troops, amidst hilly ground, inflicted
upon his troops a severe check, and cost him his life. After this
the contingents in the army were dismissed to their respective
homes, and Agesilaus himself, when tolerably recovered, sailed
with the Peloponnesians homeward from Delphi across the Corinthian Gulf.[4] He was received at Sparta with every demonstration of esteem and gratitude, which was still farther strengthened
by his exemplary simplicity and exact observance of the public
discipline; an exactness not diminished either by long absence or

---

[1] Xen. Agesil. ii, 15. Τότε μὲν οὖν (καὶ γὰρ ἦν ἤδη ὀψε) συνελκύσαντες
τοὺς τῶν πολεμίων νεκροὺς εἴσω φάλαγγος, ἐδειπνοποιήσαντο καὶ
ἐκοιμήθησαν.

Schneider in his note on this passage, as well as ad. Xen. Hellen. iv, 3,
21 — condemns the expression τῶν πολεμίων as spurious and unintelligible.
But in my judgment, these words bear a plain and appropriate meaning,
which I have endeavored to give in the text. Compare Plutarch, Agesil.
c. 19.

[2] Diodor. xiv, 84.

[3] Xen. Hellen. iv, 3, 21; Plutarch, Agesil. c. 19. The latter says — εἰς
Δελφοὺς ἀπεκομίσθε Πυθίων ἀγομένων, etc. Manso, Dr. Arnold, and
others, contest the accuracy of Plutarch in this assertion respecting the time
of year at which the Pythian games were celebrated, upon grounds which
seem to me very insufficient.

[4] Xen. Hellen. iv, 3, 22, 23; iv, 4,

enjoyment of uncontrolled ascendency.   From this time forward
he was the effective leader of Spartan policy, enjoying an influence
greater than had ever fallen to the lot of any king before.   His
colleague, Agesipolis, both young and of feeble character, was won
over by his judicious and conciliatory behavior, into the most respectful deference.[1]

Three great battles had thus been fought in the space of little
more than a month (July and August) — those of Corinth, Knidus,
and Korôneia ; the first and third on land, the second at sea, as
described in my last chapter.   In each of the two land-battles the
Lacedæmonians had gained a victory ; they remained masters of
the field, and were solicited by the enemy to grant the burial-truce.
But if we inquire what results these victories had produced, the
answer must be that both were totally barren.   The position of
Sparta in Greece as against her enemies had undergone no improvement.   In the battle of Corinth, her soldiers had indeed manifested signal superiority, and acquired much honor.   But at the
field of Korôneia, the honor of the day was rather on the side of
the Thebans, who broke through the most strenuous opposition,
and carried their point of joining their allies.   And the purpose
of Agesilaus (ordered by the ephor Diphridas) to invade Bœotia,
completely failed.[2]   Instead of advancing, he withdrew from Korôneia, and returned to Peloponnesus across the gulf from Delphi ;
which he might have done just as well without fighting this mur-
derous and hardly contested battle.   Even the narrative of Xenophon, deeply colored as it is both by his sympathies and his
antipathies, indicates to us that the predominant impression carried
off by every one from the field of Korôneia was that of the tremendous force and obstinacy of the Theban hoplites, — a foretaste
of what was to come at Leuktra !

If the two land-victories of Sparta were barren of results, the
case was far otherwise with her naval defeat at Knidus.   That
defeat was pregnant with consequences following in rapid succession, and of the most disastrous character.   As with Athens at
Ægospotami,— the loss of her fleet, serious as that was, served

---

[1] Plutarch, Agesil. c. 17, 20; Xen. Hellen. v, 3, 20.

[2] Plutarch, Agesil. c. 17.   Cornelius Nepos, Agesil. c. 4.   " Obsistere ei
conati sunt Athenienses et Bœoti," etc.   They *succeeded* in barring his way
and compelling him to retreat.

only as the signal for countless following losses.   Pharnabazus and
Konon, with their victorious fleet, sailed from island to island, and
from one continental seaport to another, in the Ægean, to expel
the Lacedæmonian harmosts, and terminate the empire of Sparta.
So universal was the odium which it had inspired, that the task
was found easy beyond expectation.   Conscious of their unpopularity, the harmosts in almost all the towns, on both sides of the
Hellespont, deserted their posts and fled, on the mere news of the
battle of Knidus.[1]   Everywhere Pharnabazus and Konon found
themselves received as liberators, and welcomed with presents of
hospitality.   They pledged themselves not to introduce any foreign
force or governor, nor to fortify any separate citadel, but to guarantee to each city its own genuine autonomy.   This policy was
adopted by Pharnabazus at the urgent representation of Konon,
who warned him that if he manifested any design of reducing the
cities to subjection, he would find them all his enemies; that each
of them severally would cost him a long siege ; and that a combination would ultimately be formed against him.   Such liberal and
judicious ideas, when seen to be sincerely acted upon, produced a
strong feeling of friendship and even of gratitude, so that the Lacedæmonian maritime empire was dissolved without a blow, by the
almost spontaneous movements of the cities themselves.   Though
the victorious fleet presented itself in many different places, it was
nowhere called upon to put down resistance, or to undertake a
single siege.   Kos, Nisyra, Teos, Chios, Erythræ, Ephesus, Mitylênê, Samos, all declared themselves independent, under the protection of the new conquerors.[2]   Pharnabazus presently disembarked at Ephesus and marched by land northward to his own
satrapy ; leaving a fleet of forty triremes under the command of
Konon.

To this general burst of anti-Spartan feeling, Abydos, on the
Asiatic side of the Hellespont, formed the solitary exception.   That
town, steady in hostility to Athens,[3] had been the great military

---

[1] Xenoph. Hellen. iv, 8, 1–5.

[2] Xen. Hellen. iv, 8, 1–3 ; Diodor. xiv, 84.   About Samos, xiv, 97.

Compare also the speech of Derkyllidas to the Abydenes (Xen. Hellen.
iv, 8, 4) — Ὅσῳ δὲ μᾶλλον αἱ ἄλλαι πόλεις ξὺν τῇ τύχῃ ἀπεστράφησαν ἡμῶν
τοσούτῳ ὄντως ἡ ὑμετέρα πιστότης μείζων φανείη, ἂν, etc.

[3] Ἐκ γὰρ Ἀβύδου. τῆς τὸν ἅπαντα χρόνον ὑμῖν ἐχθρᾶς — says Demos

station of Sparta for her northern Asiatic warfare, during the last twenty years. It was in the satrapy of Pharnabazus, and had been made the chief place of arms by Derkyllidas and Agesilaus, for their warfare against that satrap as well as for the command of the strait. Accordingly, while it was a main object with Pharnabazus to acquire possession of Abydos, — there was nothing which the Abydenes dreaded so much as to become subject to him. In this view they were decidedly disposed to cling to Lacedæmonian protection; and it happened by a fortunate accident for Sparta, that the able and experienced Derkyllidas was harmost in the town at the moment of the battle of Knidus. Having fought in the battle of Corinth, he had been sent to announce the news to Agesilaus, whom he had met on his march at Amphipolis, and who had sent him forward into Asia to communicate the victory to the allied cities ;[1] neither of them at that moment anticipating the great maritime defeat then impending. The presence in Abydos of such an officer, who had already acquired a high military reputation in that region, and was at marked enmity with Pharnabazus, — combined with the standing apprehensions of the Abydenes, —was now the means of saving a remnant at least of maritime ascendency to Sparta. During the general alarm which succeeded the battle of Knidus, when the harmosts were everywhere taking flight, and when anti-Spartan manifestations often combined with internal revolutions to overthrow the dekarchs or their substitutes, were spreading from city to city, — Derkyllidas assembled the Abydenes, heartened them up against the reigning contagion, and exhorted them to earn the gratitude of Sparta by remaining faithful to her while others were falling off; assuring them that she would still be found capable of giving them protection. His exhortations were listened to with favor. Abydos remained attached to Sparta, was put in a good state of defence, and became the only harbor of safety for the fugitive harmosts out of the other cities, Asiatic and European.

Having secured his hold upon Abydos, Derkyllidas crossed the strait to make sure also of the strong place of Sestos, on the Eu-

---

thenes in the Athenian assembly (cont. Aristokrat. c. 39, p. 672 ; compare c. 52, p. 688).

[1] Xen Hellen. iv, 3, 2.

ropean side, in the Thracian Chersonese.[1] In that fertile peninsula there had been many new settlers, who had come in and
acquired land under the Lacedæmonian supremacy, especially since
the building of the cross-wall by Derkyllidas to defend the isthmus
against Thracian invasion. By means of these settlers, dependent
on Sparta for the security of their tenures, — and of the refugees
from various cities all concentrated under his protection, — Derkyllidas maintained his position effectively both at Abydos and
at Sestos; defying the requisition of Pharnabazus that he should
forthwith evacuate them. The satrap threatend war, and actually
ravaged the lands around Abydos, — but without any result. His
wrath against the Lacedæmonians, already considerable, was so
aggravated by disappointment when he found that he could not
yet expel them from his satrapy, that he resolved to act against
them with increased energy, and even to strike a blow at them
near their own home. For this purpose he transmitted orders to
Konon to prepare a commanding naval force for the ensuing
spring, and in the mean time to keep both Abydos and Sestos
under blockade.[2]

As soon as spring arrived, Pharnabazus embarked on board a
powerful fleet equipped by Konon; directing his course to Melos
to various islands among the Cyclades, and lastly to the coast of
Peloponnesus. They here spent some time on the coast of Laconia and Messenia, disembarking at several points to ravage the
country. They next landed on the island of Kythêra, which they
captured, granting safe retirement to the Lacedæmonian garrison,
and leaving in the island a garrison under the Athenian Nikophê-
mus. Quitting then the harborless, dangerous, and ill-provided
coast of Laconia, they sailed up the Saronic gulf to the isthmus of
Corinth. Here they found the confederates, — Corinthian, Bœotian, Athenian, etc., carrying on war with Corinth as their central
post, against the Lacedæmonians at Sikyon. The line across the

---

[1] Lysander, after the victory of Ægospotami and the expulsion of the
Athenians from Sestos, had assigned the town and district as a settlement
for the pilots and Keleustæ aboard his fleet. But the ephors are said to
have reversed the assignment, and restored the town to the Sestians (Plutarch, Lysand. c. 14). Probably, however, the new settlers would remain
in part upon the lands vacated by the expelled Athenians.

[2] Xen. Hellen. iv, 8, 4–6

isthmus from Lechæum to Kenchreæ (the two ports of Corinth) was now made good by a defensive system of operations, so as to confine the Lacedæmonians within Peloponnesus; just as Athens, prior to her great losses in 446 B. C., while possessing both Megara and Pegæ, had been able to maintain the inland road midway between them, where it crosses the high and difficult crest of Mount Geraneia, thus occupying the only three roads by which a Lacedæmonian army could march from the isthmus of Corinth into Attica or Bœotia.¹ Pharnabazus communicated in the most friendly manner with the allies, assured them of his strenuous support against Sparta, and left with them a considerable sum of money.²

The appearance of a Persian satrap with a Persian fleet, as master of the Peloponnesian sea and the Saronic Gulf, was a phenomenon astounding to Grecian eyes. And if it was not equally offensive to Grecian sentiment, this was in itself a melancholy proof of the degree to which Pan-hellenic patriotism had been stifled by the Peloponnesian war and the Spartan empire. No Persian tiara had been seen near the Saronic Gulf since the battle of Salamis; nor could anything short of the intense personal wrath of Pharnabazus against the Lacedæmonians, and his desire to revenge upon them the damage inflicted by Derkyllidas and Agesilaus, have brought him now so far away from his own satrapy. It was this wrathful feeling of which Konon took advantage to procure from him a still more important boon.

Since 404 B. C., a space of eleven years, Athens had continued without any walls around her seaport town Peiræus, and without any Long Walls to connect her city with Peiræus. To this state she had been condemned by the sentence of her enemies, in the full knowledge that she could have little trade, — few ships either armed or mercantile, — poor defence even against pirates, and no defence at all against aggression from the mistress of the sea. Konon now entreated Pharnabazus, who was about to go home, to leave the fleet under his command, and to permit him to use it in rebuilding the fortifications of Peiræus as well as the Long Walls of Athens. While he engaged to maintain the fleet by contributions from the islands, he assured the satrap that no blow could be

---

¹ See Sir William Gell's Itinerary of Greece, p. 4.   Ernst Curtius — Peloponnesos — p. 25, 26, and Thucyd. i, 108.

² Xen. Hellen. iv, 8. 7, 8; Diodor. xiv, 84.

inflicted upon Sparta so destructive or so mortifying, as the renovation of Athens and Peiræus with their complete and connected
fortifications. Sparta would thus be deprived of the most important
harvest which she had reaped from the long struggle of the Peloponnesian war. Indignant as he now was against the Lacedæmonians, Pharnabazus sympathized cordially with these plans, and
on departing not only left the fleet under the command of Konon,
but also furnished him with a considerable sum of money towards
the expense of the fortifications.[1]

Konon betook himself to the work energetically and without
delay. He had quitted Athens in 407 B. C., as one of the joint
admirals nominated after the disgrace of Alkibiades. He had
parted with his countrymen finally at the catastrophe of Ægospotami in 405 B. C., preserving the miserable fraction of eight or nine
ships out of that noble fleet which otherwise would have passed
entire into the hands of Lysander. He now returned, in 393 B. C.,
as a second Themistoklês, the deliverer of his country, and the
restorer of her lost strength and independence. All hands were
set to work; carpenters and masons being hired with the funds
furnished by Pharnabazus, to complete the fortifications as quickly
as possible. The Bœotians and other neighbors lent their aid
zealously as volunteers,[2] — the same who eleven years before had
danced to the sound of joyful music when the former walls were
demolished; so completely had the feelings of Greece altered
since that period. By such hearty coöperation the work was finished during the course of the present summer and autumn without any opposition; and Athens enjoyed again her fortified Peiræus
und harbor, with a pair of Long Walls, straight and parallel, joining it securely to the city. The third, or Phalêric Wall (a single
wall stretching from Athens to Phalêrum), which had existed down
to the capture of the city by Lysander, was not restored; nor was
it indeed by any means necessary to the security either of the
city or of the port. Having thus given renewed life and security

---

[1] Xen. Hellen. iv, 8, 9, 10.

[2] Xen. Hellen. iv, 8, 10; Diodor. xiv, 85.

Cornelius Nepos (Conon, c. 4) mentions fifty talents as a sum received
by Konon from Pharnabazus as a present, and devoted by him to this public work. This is not improbable; but the total sum contributed by the satrap towards the fortifications must, probably, have been much greater.

Peiræus, Konon commemorated his great naval victory by a golden wreath in the acropolis, as well as by the erection of a temple in Peiræus to the honor of the Knidian Aphroditê, who was worshipped at Knidus with peculiar devotion by the local population.[1] He farther celebrated the completion of the walls by a splendid sacrifice and festival banquet. And the Athenian people not only inscribed on a pillar a public vote gratefully recording the exploits of Konon, but also erected a statue to his honor.[2]

The importance of this event in reference to the future history of Athens was unspeakable. Though it did not restore to her either her former navy, or her former empire, it reconstituted her as a city, not only self-determining, but even partially ascendant. It reanimated her, if not into the Athens of Perikles, at least into that of Isokrates and Demosthenes; it imparted to her a second fill of strength, dignity, and commercial importance, during the half century destined to elapse before she was finally overwhelmed by the superior military force of Macedon. Those who recollect the extraordinary stratagem whereby Themistokles had contrived (eighty-five years before) to accomplish the fortification of Athens, in spite of the base but formidable jealously of Sparta and her Peloponnesian allies, will be aware how much the consummation of the Themistoklean project had depended upon accident. Now, also, Konon in his restoration was favored by unusual combinations, such as no one could have predicted. That Pharnabazus should conceive the idea of coming over himself to Peloponnesus with a fleet of the largest force, was a most unexpected contingency. He was influenced neither by attachment to Athens, nor seemingly by considerations of policy, though the proceeding was one really conducive to the interests of Persian power, — but simply by his own violent personal wrath against the Lacedæmonians. And this wrath probably would have been satisfied, if, after the battle of Knidus, he could have cleared his own satrapy of them completely. It was his vehement impatience, when he found himself unable to expel his old enemy, Derkyllidas, from the important position of

---

[1] Demosthen. cont. Androtion. p. 616. c. 21. Pausanias (i, 1, 3) still saw this temple in Peiræus — very near to the sea; five hundred and fifty years afterwards.

[2] Demosthen. cont. Leptin. c. 16. p. 477, 478; Athenæus, i, 3; Cornelius Nepos, Conon, c. 4.

Abydos, which chiefly spurred him on to take revenge on Sparta in her own waters. Nothing less than the satrap's personal presence would have placed at the disposal of Konon either a sufficient naval force, or sufficient funds for the erection of the new walls, and the defiance of all impediment from Sparta. So strangely did events thus run, that the energy, by which Derkyllidas preserved Abydos brought upon Sparta, indirectly, the greater mischief of the new Kononian walls. It would have been better for Sparta that Pharnabazus should at once have recovered Abydos as well as the rest of his satrapy; in which case he would have had no wrongs remaining unavenged to incense him, and would have kept on his own side of the Ægean; feeding Konon with a modest squadron sufficient to keep the Lacedæmonian navy from again becoming formidable on the Asiatic side, but leaving the walls of Peiræus (if we may borrow an expression of Plato) "to continue asleep in the bosom of the earth." [1]

But the presence of Konon with his powerful fleet was not the only condition indispensable to the accomplishment of this work. It was requisite further, that the interposition of Sparta should be kept off, not merely by sea, but by land, and that, too, during all the number of months that the walls were in progress. Now the barrier against her on land was constituted by the fact, that the confederate force held the cross line within the isthmus from Lechæum to Kenchreæ, with Corinth as a centre.[2] But they were unable to sustain this line even through the ensuing year, — during which Sparta, aided by dissensions at Corinth, broke through it, as will appear in the next chapter. Had she been able to break through it while the fortifications of Athens were yet incomplete, she would have deemed no effort too great to effect an entrance into Attica and interrupt the work, in which she might very probably have succeeded. Here, then, was the second condition, which was realized during the summer and autumn of 393 B. C., but which did not continue to be realized longer. So fortunate was it for Athens, that the two conditions were fulfilled both together during this particular year!

---

[1] Plato, Legg. vi, p. 778; καθεύδειν ἐᾶν ἐν τῇ γῇ κατακείμενα τὰ τείχη, etc.

[2] The importance of maintaining these lines, as a protection to Athens against invasion from Sparta, is illustrated in Xen. Hellen. v, 4, 19, and Andokides, Or. iii, De Pace, s. 26.

CHAPTER LXXV.

FROM THE REBUILDING OF THE LONG WALLS OF ATHENS TO THE PEACE OF ANTALKIDAS.

THE presence of Pharnabazus and Konon with their command-ing force in the Saronic Gulf, and the liberality with which the former furnished pecuniary aid to the latter for rebuilding the full fortifications of Athens, as well as to the Corinthians for the pro-secution of the war, — seem to have given preponderance to the confederates over Sparta for that year. The plans of Konon[1] were extensive. He was the first to organize for the defence of Corinth, a mercenary force which was afterwards improved and conducted with greater efficiency by Iphikrates; and after he had finished the fortifications of Peiræus with the Long Walls, he employed himself in showing his force among the islands, for the purpose of laying the foundations of renewed maritime power for Athens. We even hear that he caused an Athenian envoy to be despatched to Dionysius at Syracuse, with the view of detaching that despot from Sparta, and bringing him into connection with Athens. Evagoras, despot of Salamis in Cyprus, the steady friend of Konon, was a party to this proposition, which he sought to strengthen by offering to Dionysius his sister in marriage.[2] There was a basis of sympathy between them arising from the fact that Evagoras was at variance with the Phenicians both in Phenicia and Cyprus, while Dionysius was in active hostilities with the Carthaginians (their kinsmen and Colonists) in Sicily. Never-theless, the proposition met with little or no success. We find Dionysius afterwards still continuing to act as an ally of Sparta.

Profiting by the aid received from Pharnabazus, the Corinthians strengthened their fleet at Lechæum (their harbor in the Corinth-ian Gulf) so considerably, as to become masters of the Gulf, and

---

[1] Harpokration, v. ξενικὸν ἐν Κορίνθῳ. Philochorus, Fragm. 15Ρ, ed. Di-dot.

[2] Lysias, Orat. xix, (De Bonis Aristophanis) s. 21.

to occupy Rhium, one of the two opposite capes which bound
its narrow entrance. To oppose them, the Lacedæmonians on
their side were driven to greater maritime effort. More than one
naval action seems to have taken place, in those waters where the
prowess and skill of the Athenian admiral Phormion had been so
signally displayed at the beginning of the Peloponnesian war.
At length the Lacedæmonian admiral Herippidas, who succeeded
to the command of the fleet after his predecessor Polemarchus
had been slain in battle, compelled the Corinthians to abandon
Rhium, and gradually recovered his ascendency in the Corinthian
Gulf; with his successor Teleutias, brother of Agesilaus, still far
ther completed.[1]

While these transactions were going on (seemingly during the
last half of 393 B. C. and the full year of 392 B. C.), so as to put
an end to the temporary naval preponderance of the Corinthians,
— the latter were at the same time bearing the brunt of a desultory, but continued, land-warfare against the garrison of Lacedæmonians and Peloponnesians established at Sikyon. Both Corinth
and Lechæum were partly defended by the presence of confederate troops, Bœotians, Argeians, Athenians, or mercenaries paid
by Athens. But this did not protect the Corinthians against suf
fering great damage, in their lands and outlying properties, from
the incursions of the enemy.

The plain between Corinth and Sikyon, — fertile and extensive
(speaking by comparison with Peloponnesus generally), and constituting a large part of the landed property of both cities, was
rendered uncultivable during 393 and 392 B. C.; so that the Corinthian proprietors were obliged to withdraw their servants and
cattle to Peiræum[2] (a portion of the Corinthian territory without
the Isthmus properly so called, north-east of the Akrokorinthus,
in a line between that eminence and the Megarian harbor of
Pegæ). Here the Sikyonian assailants could not reach them, because of the Long Walls of Corinth, which connected that city
by a continuous fortification of twelve stadia (somewhat less than
a mile and a half) with its harbor of Lechæum. Nevertheless,
the loss to the proprietors of the deserted plain was still so great,
that two successive seasons of it were quite enough to inspire them

---

[1] Xen Hellen. iv, 8, 11.   [2] Xen. Hellen. iv, 4, 1 ; iv, 5, 1

with a strong aversion to the war;[1] the more so, as the damage fell exclusively upon them — their allies in Bœotia, Athens, and

[1] I dissent from Mr. Fynes Clinton as well as from M. Rehdantz (Vitæ Iphicratis, etc., c. 4, who in the main agrees with Dodwell's Annales Xenophontei) in their chronological arrangement of these events.

They place the battle fought by Praxitas within the Long Walls of Corinth in 393 B.C., and the destruction of the Lacedæmonian *mora* or division by Iphikrates (the monthly date of which is marked by its having immediately succeeded the Isthmian games), in 392 B.C. I place the former event in 392 B.C.; the latter in 390 B.C., immediately after the Isthmian games of 390 B.C.

If we study the narrative of Xenophon, we shall find, that after describing (iv, 3) the battle of Koroneia (August 394 B.C.) with its immediate consequences, and the return of Agesilaus home, — he goes on in the next chapter to narrate the land-war about or near Corinth, which he carries down without interruption (through Chapters 3, 4, 5, 6, 7, of Book iv.) to 389 B.C.

But in Chapter 8 of Book iv, he leaves the land-war, and takes up the naval operations, from and after the battle of Knidus (Aug. 394 B.C) He recounts how Pharnabazus and Konon came across the Ægean with a powerful fleet in the spring of 393 B.C., and how after various proceedings, they brought the fleet to the Saronic Gulf and the Isthmus of Corinth, where they must have arrived at or near midsummer 393 B.C.

Now it appears to me certain, that these proceedings of Pharnabazus with the fleet, recounted in the eighth chapter, come, in point of date, *before* the seditious movements and the *coup d' état* at Corinth, which are recounted in the fourth chapter. At the time when Pharnabazus was at Corinth in midsummer 393 B.C., the narrative of Xenophon (iv, 8, 8–10) leads us to believe that the Corinthians were prosecuting the war zealously, and without discontent: the money and encouragement which Pharnabazus gave them was calculated to strengthen such ardor. It was by aid of this money that the Corinthians fitted out their fleet under Agathinus, and acquired for a time the maritime command of the Gulf.

The discontents against the war (recounted in chap. 4 *seq.*) could not have commenced until a considerable time after the departure of Pharnabazus. They arose out of causes which only took effect after a long continuance, — the hardships of the land-war, the losses of property and slaves, the jealousy towards Attica and Bœotia as being undisturbed, etc. The Lacedæmonian and Peloponnesian aggressive force at Sikyon cannot possibly have been established before the autumn of 494 B.C., and was most probably placed there early in the spring of 393 B.C. Its effects were brought about, not by one great blow, but by repetition of ravages and destructive annoyance; and all the effects which it produced previous to midsummer 393 B.C. would be more than compensated by the presence, the gifts, and the encouragement of Pharnabazus with his powerful fleet. Moreover, after his departure, too, the Corinthians were at first successful at sea, and ac

Argos, having as yet suffered nothing. Constant military service
for defence, with the conversion of the city into a sort of besieged
post, aggravated their discomfort. There was another circumstance also, doubtless not without influence. The consequences of
the battle of Knidus had been, first, to put down the maritime
empire of Sparta, and thus to diminish the fear which she inspired
to the Corinthians; next, to rebuild the fortifications, and renovate
the shipping, commercial as well as warlike, of Athens; — a revival well calculated to bring back a portion of that anti-Athenian
jealousy and apprehension which the Corinthians had felt so
strongly a few years before. Perhaps some of the trade at Corinth may have been actually driven away by the disturbance of
the war, to the renewed fortifications and greater security of Peiræus.

Fostered by this pressure of circumstances, the discontented
philo-Laconian or peace-party which had always existed at Corinth, presently acquired sufficient strength, and manifested itself
with sufficient publicity to give much alarm to the government.
The Corinthian government had always been, and still was, oligarchical. In what manner the administrators or the council were
renovated, or how long individuals continued in office, indeed, we
do not know. But of democracy, with its legal, popular assemblies, open discussions and authoritative resolves, there was

---

quired the command of the Gulf, which, however, they did not retain for
more than a year, if so much. Hence, it is not likely that any strong discontent against the war began before the early part of 392 B. C.

Considering all these circumstances, I think it reasonable to believe that
the *coup d'état* and massacre at Corinth took place (not in 393 B. C., as Mr.
Clinton and M. Rehdantz place it, but) in 392 B. C.; and the battle within
the Long Walls rather later in the same year.

Next, the opinion of the same two authors, as well as of Dodwell, — that
the destruction of the Lacedæmonian *mora* by Iphicrates took place in the
spring of 392 B. C., — is also, in my view, erroneous. If this were true, it
would be necessary to pack all the events mentioned in Xenophon, iv, 4
into the year 393 B. C.; which I hold to be impossible. If the destruction
of the mora did not occur in the spring of 393 B. C., we know that it could
not have occurred until the spring of 390 B. C.; that is, the next ensuing
Isthmian games, two years afterwards. And this last will be found to be
its true date; thus leaving full time, but not too much time, for the antece-
dent occurrences.

nothing.[1] Now the oligarchical persons actually in power were vehemently anti-Laconian, consisting of men who had partaken of the Persian funds and contracted alliance with Persia, besides compromising themselves irrevocably (like Timolaus) by the most bitter manifestations of hostile sentiment towards Sparta. These men found themselves menaced by a powerful opposition party, which had no constitutional means for making its sentiments predominant, and for accomplishing peaceably either a change of administrators or a change of public policy. It was only by an appeal to arms and violence that such a consummation could be brought about; a fact notorious to both parties, — so that the oligarchical administrators, informed of the meetings and conversations going on, knew well that they had to expect nothing less than the breaking out of a conspiracy. That such anticipations were well-founded, we gather even from the partial recital of Xenophon; who states that Pasimêlus, the philo-Laconian leader, was on his guard and in preparation,[2] — and counts it to him as a virtue that shortly afterwards he opened the gates to the Lacedæmonians.

Anticipating such conspiracy, the government resolved to prevent it by a *coup d' état*. They threw themselves upon the assistance of their allies, invited in a body of Argeians, and made their blow the more sure by striking it on the last day of the festival called Eukleia, when it was least expected. Their proceeding, though dictated by precaution, was executed with the extreme of brutal ferocity aggravated by sacrilege; in a manner very different from the deep-laid artifices recently practised by the Spartan ephors when they were in like manner afraid of the conspiracy of Kinadon, — and more like the oligarchical conspirators at Korkyra (in the third year of the Peloponnesian war) when they broke into the assembled Senate, and massacred Peithias, with sixty

---

[1] Plutarch, Dion. c. 53

[2] Xen. Hellen. iv, 4, 2. Γνόντες δὲ οἱ ᾿Αργεῖοι καὶ Βοιωτοὶ καὶ ᾿Αθηναῖοι καὶ Κορινθίων οἵ τε τῶν παρὰ βασιλέως χρημάτων μετεσχηκότες, καὶ οἱ τοῦ πολέμου αἰτιώτατοι γεγενημένοι, ὡς, εἰ μὴ ἐκποδὼν ποιήσαιντο τοὺς ἐπὶ τὴν ειρήνην τετραμμένους, κινδυνεύσει πάλιν ἡ πόλις λακωνίσαι — οὕτω δὴ καὶ σφαγὰς ἐπεχείρουν ποιεῖσθαι.

iv, 4, 4 Οἱ δὲ νεώτεροι, ὑποπτεύσαντος Πασιμήλου τὸ μέλλον ἔσεσθαι, ἡσυχίαν ἔσχον ἐν τῷ Κρανίῳ· ὡς δὲ τῆς κραυγῆς ἤσθοντο, καὶ φεύγοντές τινες ἐκ τοῦ πράγματος ἀφίκοντο πρὸς αὐτοὺς, ἐκ τούτου ἀναδραμόντες κατὰ τὸν ᾿Ακροκόρινθον, προσβαλόντας μὲν ᾿Αργείους καὶ τοὶ; ἄλλους ἀπεκρούσαντο etc.

others in the senate-house.[1] While the choice performers at Co.
rinth were contending for the prize in the theatre, with judges
formally named to decide, — and while the market-place around
was crowded with festive spectators, — a number of armed men
were introduced, probably Argeians, with leaders designating the
victims whom they were to strike. Some of these select victims were massacred in the market-place, others in the theatre, and one even while sitting as a judge in the theatre. Others
again fled in terror to embrace the altars or statues in the
market-place, — which sanctuary, nevertheless, did not save their
lives. Nor was such sacrilege arrested, — repugnant as it was to
the feelings of the assembled spectators and to Grecian feelings
generally, — until one hundred and twenty persons had perished.[2]
But the persons slain were chiefly elderly men ; for the younger
portion of the philo-Laconian party, suspecting some mischief, had
declined attending the festival, and kept themselves separately assembled under their leader Pasimêlus in the gymnasium and
cyprus-grove called Kranium, just without the city-gates. We
find, too, that they were not only assembled, but actually in arms.
For the moment that they heard the clamor in the market-place,
and learned from some fugitives what was going on, they rushed up
at once to the Akrokorinthus (or eminence and acropolis overhanging the city) and got possession of the citadel, — which they maintained with such force and courage that the Argeians and the
Corinthians, who took part with the government, were repulsed in
the attempt to dislodge them. This circumstance, indirectly revealed in the one-sided narrative of Xenophon, lets us into the
real state of the city, and affords good ground for believing that
Pasimêlus and his friends were prepared beforehand for an armed
outbreak, but waited to execute it, until the festival was over, — a
scruple which the government, in their eagerness to forestall the plot,
disregarded, — employing the hands and weapons of Argeians who
were comparatively unimpressed by solemnities peculiar to Corinth.[3]

---

[1] Thucyd. iii, 70.

[2] Diodorus (xiv, 86) gives this number, which seems very credible. Xenophon (iv, 4, 4) only says πολλοί.

[3] In recounting this alternation of violence projected, violence perpetrated, recourse on the one side to a foreign ally, treason on the other by admitting an avowed enemy, — which formed the *modus operandi* of opposing

Though Pasimêlus and his friends were masters of the citadel.
and had repulsed the assault of their enemies, yet the *coup d' étai*

---

parties in the oligarchical Corinth, — I invite the reader to contrast it with
the democrati :al Athens.

At Athens, in the beginning of the Peloponnesian war, there were precisely the same causes at work, and precisely the same marked antithesis of
parties, as those which here disturbed Corinth. There was first, a considerable Athenian minority who opposed the war with Sparta from the first;
next, when the war began, the proprietors of Attica saw their lands ruined.
and were compelled either to carry away, or to lose, their servants and cat
tle, so that they obtained no returns. The intense discontent, the angry
complaints, the bitter conflict of parties, which these circumstances raised
among the Athenian citizens, — not to mention the aggravation of all these
symptoms by the terrible epidemic, — are marked out in Thucydides, and
have been recorded in the fifth volume of this history. Not only the positive loss and suffering, but all other causes of exasperation, stood at a higher pitch at Athens in the early part of the Peloponnesian war, than at Cor
inth in 392 B. C.

Yet what were the effects which they produced ? Did the minority resort
to a conspiracy, — or the majority to a *coup d' état* — or either of them to
invitation of foreign aid against the other? Nothing of the kind. The
minority had always open to them the road of pacific opposition, and the
chance of obtaining a majority in the Senate or in the public assembly,
which was practically identical with the totality of the citizens. Their opposition, though pacific as to acts, was sufficiently animated and violent in
words and propositions, to serve as a real discharge for imprisoned angry
passion. If they could not carry the adoption of their general policy, they
had the opportunity of gaining partial victories which took off the edge of
a fierce discontent; witness the fine imposed upon Perikles (Thucyd. ii, 65)
in the year before his death, which both gratified and mollified the antipa
thy against him, and brought about shortly afterwards a strong reaction in
his favor. The majority, on the other hand, knew that the predominance
of its policy depended upon its maintaining its hold on a fluctuating public assembly, against the utmost freedom of debate and attack, within certain forms and rules prescribed by the constitution; attachment to the
latter being the cardinal principle of political morality in both parties. It
was this system which excluded on both sides the thought of armed violence. It produced among the democratical citizens of Athens that characteristic insisted upon by Kleon in Thucydides, — " constant and fearless
security and absence of treacherous hostility among one another" (διὰ γὰρ
τὸ καθ' ἡμέραν ἀδεὲς καὶ ἀνεπιβούλευτον πρὸς ἀλλήλους, καὶ ἐς τοὺς ξυμμάχους τὸ αὐτὸ ἔχετε — Thuc. iii, 37), the entire absence of which stands so
prominently forward in these deplorable proceedings of the oligarchical
Corinth. Pasimêlus and his Corinthian minority had no assemblies, dikasteries, annual Senate, or constant habit of free debate and accusation, to

had been completely successful in overawing their party in the city, and depriving them of all means of communicating with the Lacedæmonians at Sikyon. Feeling unable to maintain themselves, they were besides frightened by menacing omens, when they came to offer sacrifice, in order that they might learn whether the gods encouraged them to fight or not. The victims were found so alarming, as to drive them to evacuate the post and prepare for voluntary exile. Many of them (according to Diodorus five hundred)[1] actually went into exile; while others, and among them Pasimêlus himself, were restrained by the entreaties of their friends and relatives, combined with solemn assurances of peace and security from the government; who now, probably, felt themselves victorious, and were anxious to mitigate the antipathies which their recent violence had inspired. These pacific assurances were faithfully kept, and no farther mischief was done to any citizen.

But the political condition of Corinth was materially altered, by an extreme intimacy of alliance and communion now formed with Argos; perhaps combined with reciprocal rights of intermarriage, and of purchase and sale. The boundary pillars or hedges which separated the two territories, were pulled up, and the city was entitled *Argos* instead of *Corinth* (says Xenophon); such was probably the invidious phrase in which the opposition party described the very close political union now formed between the two cities; upheld by a strong Argeian force in the city and acropolis, together with some Athenian mercenaries under Iphikrates, and some Bœotians as a garrison in the port of Lechæum. Most probably the government remained still Corinthian, and still oligarchical, as before. But it now rested upon Argeian aid, and was therefore dependent chiefly upon Argos, though partly also upon the other two allies.

To Pasimêlus and his friends such a state of things was intol-

---

appeal to; their only available weapon was armed violence, or treacherous correspondence with a foreign enemy. On the part of the Corinthian government, superior or more skilfully used force, or superior alliance abroad, was the only weapon of defence, in like manner.

I shall return to this subject in a future chapter, where I enter more at large into the character of the Athenians.

[1] Diodor. xiv, 86; Xen. Hellen. iv, 4, 5.

erable. Though personally they had no ill-usage to complain of, yet the complete predominance of their political enemies was quite sufficient to excite their most vehement antipathies. They entered into secret correspondence with Praxitas, the Lacedæmonian commander at Sikyon, engaging to betray to him one of the gates in the western Long Wall between Corinth and Lechæum. The scheme being concerted, Pasimêlus and his partisans got themselves placed,[1] partly by contrivance and partly by accident, on the night-watch at this gate ; an imprudence, which shows that the government not only did not maltreat them, but even admitted them to trust. At the moment fixed, Praxitas, — presenting himself with a Lacedæmonian *mora* or regiment, a Sikyonian force, and the Corinthian exiles, — found the treacherous sentinels prepared to open the gates. Having first sent in a trusty soldier to satisfy him that there was no deceit,[2] he then conducted all his force within the gates, into the mid-space between the two Long Walls. So broad was this space, and so inadequate did his numbers appear to maintain it, that he took the precaution of digging a cross-ditch with a palisade to defend himself on the side towards the city ; which he was enabled to do undisturbed, since the enemy (we are not told why) did not attack him all the next day. On the ensuing day, however, Argeians, Corinthians, and Athenian mercenaries under Iphikrates, all came down from the city in full force ; the latter stood on the right of the line, along the eastern wall, opposed to the Corinthian exiles on the Lacedæmonian left ; while the Lacedæmonians themselves were on their own right, opposed to the Corinthians from the city ; and the Argeians, opposed to the Sikyonians, in the centre.

It was here that the battle began ; the Argeians, bold from superior numbers, attacked and broke the Sikyonians, tearing up the palisade, and pursuing them down to the sea with much slaugh-

---

[1] Xen. Hellen. iv, 4, 8. καὶ κατὰ τύχην καὶ κατ᾽ ἐπιμέλειαν, etc.

[2] Xen. Hellen. iv, 4, 8. Nothing can show more forcibly the Laconian bias of Xenophon, than the credit which he gives to Pasimêlus for his good faith towards the Lacedæmonians whom he was letting in ; overlooking or approving his treacherous betrayal towards his own countrymen, in thus opening a gate which he had been trusted to watch. τὼ δ᾽ εἰσηγαγέτην, καὶ οὕτως ἁπλῶς ἀπεδε ξάτην, ὥστε ὁ εἰσελθὼν ἐξήγγειλε, πάντα εἶναι ἀδόλως, εἰά τερ ἐλεγέτην.

ter;[1] upon which Pasimachus the Lacedæmonian commander of cavalry, coming to their aid, caused his small body of horsemen to dismount and tie their horses to trees, and then armed them with shields taken from the Sikyonians, inscribed on the outside with the letter Sigma (Σ). With these he approached on foot to attack the Argeians, who, mistaking them for Sikyonians, rushed to the charge with alacrity; upon which Pasimachus exclaimed, — " By the two gods, Argeians, these Sigmas which you see here will deceive you ; " he then closed with them resolutely, but his number was so inferior that he was soon overpowered and slain. Meanwhile, the Corinthian exiles on the left had driven back Iphikrates with his mercenaries (doubtless chiefly light troops) and pursued them even to the city gates ; while the Lacedæmonians, easily repelling the Corinthians opposed to them, came out of their palisade, and planted themselves with their faces towards the eastern wall, but at a little distance from it, to intercept the Argeians on their return. The latter were forced to run back as they could, huddling close along the eastern wall, with their right or unshielded side exposed, as they passed, to the spears of the Lacedæmonians. Before they could get to the walls of Corinth, they were met and roughly handled by the victorious Corinthian exiles. And even when they came to the walls, those within, un willing to throw open the gates for fear of admitting the enemy, contented themselves with handing down ladders, over which the defeated Argeians clambered with distress and difficulty. Altogether, their loss in this disastrous retreat was frightful. Their dead (says Xenophon) lay piled up like heaps of stones or wood.[2]

This victory of Praxitas and the Lacedæmonians, though it did not yet make them masters of Lechæum,[3] was, nevertheless, of

---

[1] Xen. Hellen. iv, 4, 10. Καὶ τοὺς μὲν Σικυωνίους ἐκράτησαν καὶ διασπάσαντες τὸ σταύρωμα ἐδίωκον ἐπὶ θάλασσαν, καὶ ἐκεῖ πολλοὺς αὐτῶν ἀπέκτειναν.

It would appear from hence that there must have been an open portion of Lechæum, or a space apart from (but adjoining to) the wall which encircled Lechæum, yet still within the Long Walls. Otherwise the fugitive Sikyonians could hardly have got down to the sea.

[2] Xen. Hellen. iv, 4, 12. Οὕτως ἐν ὀλίγῳ πολλοὶ ἔπεσον, ὥστε εἰθισμένοι ὁρᾶν οἱ ἄνθρωποι σωροὺς σίτου, ξύλων, λίθου, τότε ἐθεάσαντο σωροὺς νεκρῶν.

A singular form of speech.

[3] Diodorus (xiv, 87) represents that the Lacedæmonians on this occasion

considerable importance. Shortly afterwards they received rein
forcements which enabled them to turn it to still better account.
The first measure of Praxitas was to pull down a considerable
breadth of the two walls, leaving a breach which opened a free
passage for any Lacedæmonian army from Sikyon to reach and
pass the isthmus. He then marched his troops through the breach,
forward on the road to Megara, capturing the two Corinthian dependencies of Krommyon and Sidus on the Saronic gulf, in which
he placed garrisons. Returning back by the road south of Corinth,
he occupied Epieikia on the frontier of Epidaurus, as a protection
to the territory of the latter against incursions from Corinth,—
and then disbanded his army.

A desultory warfare was carried on during the ensuing winter
and spring between the opposite garrisons in Corinth and Sikyon.
It was now that the Athenian Iphikrates, in the former place, be
gan to distinguish himself at the head of his mercenary peltasts
whom, after their first organization by Konon, he had trained to
effective tactics under the strictest discipline, and whose movements
he conducted with consummate skill. His genius introduced improvements both in their armor and in their clothing. He lengthened by one half both the light javelin and the short sword, which
the Thracian peltasts habitually carried ; he devised a species of
leggings, known afterwards by the name of Iphikratides ; and he
thus combined, better than had ever been done before, rapid motion,— power of acting in difficult ground and open order,— effective attack, either by missiles or hand to hand, and dexterous
retreat in case of need.[1] As yet, he was but a young officer, in

---

surprised and held Lechæum, defeating the general body of the confederates who came out from Corinth to retake it. But his narrative of all
these circumstances differs materially from that of Xenophon ; whom I
here follow in preference, making allowance for great partiality, and for
much confusion and obscurity.

Xenophon gives us plainly to understand, that Lechæum was *not* captured
by the Lacedæmonians until the following year, by Agesilaus and Teleutias.

It is to be recollected that Xenophon had particular means of knowing
what was done by Agesilaus, and therefore deserves credit on that head, —
always allowing for partiality. Diodorus does not mention Agesilaus in
connection with the proceedings at Lechæum.

[1] Diodor. xv, 44 ; Cornelius Nepos, Vit. Iphicrat. c. 2 ; Polyæn. iii, 9, 10

Compare Rehdantz, Vitæ Iphicratis, Chabriæ, et Timothei, c. 2, 7 (Berlin, 1845) — a very useful and instructive publication.

In describing the improvements made by Iphikrates in the armature of his peltasts, I have not exactly copied either Nepos or Diodorus, who both appear to me confused in their statements. You would imagine, in reading their account (and so it has been stated by Weber, Prolegg. ad Demosth. cont. Aristokr. p. xxxv , that there were no peltasts in Greece prior to Iphikrates ; that he was the first to transform heavy-armed hoplites into light-armed peltasts, and to introduce from Thrace the light shield or *pelta*, not only smaller in size than the round ἀσπὶς carried by the hoplite, but also without the ἴτυς (or surrounding metallic rim of the ἀσπὶς,) seemingly connected by outside bars or spokes of metal with the exterior central knob or projection (*umbo*) which the hoplite pushed before him in close combat. The *pelta*, smaller and lighter than the ἀσπὶς, was seemingly square or oblong and not round ; though it had no ἴτυς, it often had thin plates of brass, as we may see by Xenophon, Anab. v, 2, 29, so that the explanation of it given in the Scholia ad Platon. Legg. vii, p. 813 must be taken with reserve.

But Grecian peltasts existed before the time of Iphikrates (Xen. Hellen. i, 2, 1 and elsewhere) ; he did not first introduce them ; he found them already there, and improved their armature. Both Diodorus and Nepos affirm that he lengthened the *spears* of the peltasts to a measure half as long again as those of the hoplites (or twice as long, if we believe Nepos), and the swords in proportion — "ηὔξησε μὲν τὰ δόρατα ἡμιολίῳ μεγέθει — hastæ modum duplicavit." Now this I apprehend to be not exact ; nor is it true (as Nepos asserts) that the Grecian hoplites carried " short spears " — " brevibus hastis." The spear of the Grecian hoplite was long (though not so long as that of the heavy and compact Macedonian phalanx afterwards became), and it appears to me incredible that Iphikrates should have given to his light and active peltast a spear twice as long, or half as long again, as that of the hoplite. Both Diodorus and Nepos have mistaken by making their comparison with the arms *of the hoplite*, to which the changes of Iphikrates had no reference. The peltast both before and after Iphikrates did not carry a spear, but a *javelin*, which he employed as a missile, to hurl, not to thrust ; he was essentially an ἀκοντιστὴς or javelin-shooter (See Xenoph. Hellen. iv, 5, 14 ; vi, 1, 9). Of course the javelin might, in case of need, serve to thrust, but this was not its appropriate employment ; *e converso*, the spear might be hurled (under advantageous circumstances, from the higher ground against an enemy below — Xen. Hellen. ii, 4, 15 ; v, 4, 52), but its proper employment was, to be held and thrust forward.

What Iphikrates really did, was, to lengthen both the two offensive weapons which the peltast carried, before his time, — the javelin, and the sword. He made the javelin a longer and heavier weapon, requiring a more practised hand to throw — but also competent to inflict more serious wounds, and capable of being used with more deadly effect if the peltasts saw an opportunity of coming to close fight or advantageous terms. Pos-

the beginning of his military career.[1] We must therefore presume that these improvements were chiefly of later date, the suggestions of his personal experience; but even now, the successes
of his light troops were remarkable. Attacking Phlius, he entrapped the Phliasians into an ambuscade, and inflicted on them a
defeat so destructive that they were obliged to invoke the aid of a
Lacedæmonian garrison for the protection of their city. He gained
a victory near Sikyon, and carried his incursions over all Arcadia,
to the very gates of the cities; damaging the Arcadian hoplites so
severely, that they became afraid to meet him in the field. His
own peltasts, however, though full of confidence against these Peloponnesian hoplites, still retained their awe and their reluctance to
fight against Lacedæmonians;[2] who, on their side, despised them,
but despised their own allies still more. " Our friends fear these
peltasts, as children fear hobgoblins,"—said the Lacedæmonians,
sarcastically, endeavoring to set the example of courage by ostentatious demonstrations of their own around the walls of Corinth.[3]

The breach made in the Long Walls of Corinth by Praxitas
had laid open the road for a Peloponnesian army to march either
into Attica or Bœotia.[4] Fortunately for the Athenians, they had

---

sibly Iphikrates not only lengthened the weapon, but also improved its
point and efficacy in other ways; making it more analogous to the formidable Roman *pilum*. Whether he made any alteration in the *pelta* itself,
we do not know.

The name *Iphikratides*, given to these new-fashioned leggings or boots,
proves to us that Wellington and Blucher are not the first eminent generals who have lent an honorable denomination to boots and shoes.

[1] Justin, vi, 5.

[2] Xen. Hellen. iv, 4, 16; Diodor. xiv, 91.

Τοὺς μέντοι Λακεδαιμονίους οὕτως αὖ οἱ πελτασταὶ ἐδέδισαν, ὡς ἐντὸς ἀκον-
τίσματος οὐ προσῄεσαν τοῖς ὁπλίταις, etc.

Compare the sentiment of the light troops in the attack of Sphakteria,
when they were awe-struck and afraid at first to approach the Lacedæmonian
hoplites — τῇ γνώμῃ δεδουλωμένοι ὡς ἐπὶ Λακεδαιμονίους, etc. (Thucyd. iv,
34).

[3] Xen. Hellen. iv, 4, 17. ὥστε οἱ μὲν Λακεδαιμόνιοι καὶ ἐπισκώπτειν ἐτόλ-
μων, ὡς οἱ σύμμαχοι φοβοῖντο τοὺς πελταστὰς, ὥσπερ μορμῶνας παιδάρια, etc.

This is a camp-jest of the time, which we have to thank Xenophon for
preserving.

[4] Xenoph. Agesil. ii, 17. ἀναπετάσας τῆς Πελοποννήσου τὰς πύλας, etc.
Respecting the Long Walls of Corinth, as part of a line of defence

already completed the rebuilding of their own Long Walls; but they were so much alarmed by the new danger, that they marched with their full force, and with masons and carpenters accompanying,[1] to Corinth. Here, with that celerity of work for which they were distinguished,[2] they in a few days reëstablished completely the western wall; the more important of the two, since it formed the barrier against the incursions of the Lacedæmonians from Sikyon. They had then a secure position, and could finish the eastern wall at their leisure; which they accordingly did, and then retired, leaving it to the confederate troops in Corinth to defend.

This advantage, however, — a very material one, — was again overthrown by the expedition of the Lacedæmonian king, Agesilaus, during the same summer. At the head of a full Lacedæmonian and Peloponnesian force, he first marched into the territory of Argos, and there spent some time in ravaging all the cultivated plain. From hence he passed over the mountain-road, by Tenea,[3]

---

which barred ingress to, or egress from, Peloponnesus, — Colonel Leake remarks, — "The narrative of Xenophon shows the great importance of the Corinthian Long Walls in time of war. They completed a line of fortification from the summit of the Acro-Corinthus to the sea, and thus intercepted the most direct and easy communication from the Isthmus into Peloponnesus. For the rugged mountain, which borders the southern side of the Isthmian plain, has only two passes, — one, by the opening on the eastern side of Acro-Corinthus, which obliged an enemy to pass under the eastern side of Corinth, and was, moreover, defended by a particular kind of fortification, as some remains of walls still testify, — the other, along the shore at Cenchreiæ, which was also a fortified place in the hands of the Corinthians. Hence the importance of the pass of Cenchreiæ, in all operations between the Peloponnesians, and an enemy without the Isthmus" (Leake, Travels in Morea, vol. iii, ch. xxviii, p. 254).

Compare Plutarch, Aratus, c. 16; and the operations of Epaminondas as described by Diodorus, xv, 68.

[1] Xen. Hellen. iv, 4, 18. ἐλθόντες πανδημεὶ μετὰ λιθολόγων καὶ τεκτόνων, etc. The word πανδημεὶ shows how much they were alarmed.

[2] Thucyd. vi, 98.

[3] The words stand in the text of Xenophon, — εὐθὺς ἐκεῖθεν ὑπερβαλὼν κατὰ Τεγέαν εἰς Κόρινθον. A straight march from the Argeian territory to Corinth could not possibly carry Agesilaus by Tegea; Kœppen proposes Γενέαν, which I accept, as geographically suitable. I am not certain, however, that it is right; the Agesilaus of Xenophon has the words κατὰ τὰ στενά.

About the probable situation of Tenea, see Colonel Leake, Travels in Morea, vol. iii, p. 321; also his Peloponnesiaca, p. 400.

into the plain of Corinth, to the foot of the newly-repaired Long Walls. Here his brother Teleutias, who had recently superseded Herippidas as admiral in the Corinthian Gulf, came to coöperate with him in a joint attack, by sea and land, on the new walls and on Lechæum.[1] The presence of this naval force rendered the Long Walls difficult to maintain, since troops could be disembarked in the interval between them, where the Sikyonians in the previous battle had been beaten and pursued down to the sea. Agesilaus and Teleutias were strong enough to defeat the joint force of the four confederated armies, and to master not only the Long Walls, but also the port of Lechæum,[2] with its docks, and the ships

---

[1] Xen. Hellen. iv, 4, 19—iv, 8, 10, 11.

It was rather late in the autumn of 393 B.C. that the Lacedæmonian maritime operations in the Corinthian Gulf began, against the fleet recently equipped by the Corinthians out of the funds lent by Pharnabazus. First, the Lacedæmonian Polemarchus was named admiral; he was slain, — and his secretary Pollis, who succeeded to his command, retired afterwards wounded. Next came Herippidas to the command, who was succeeded by Teleutias. Now if we allow to Herippidas a year of command (the ordinary duration of a Lacedæmonian admiral's appointment), and to the other two something less than a year, since their time was brought to an end by accidents, — we shall find that the appointment of Teleutias will fall in the spring or early summer of 391 B.C., the year of this expedition of Agesilaus

[2] Andokides de Pace, s. 18; Xen. Hellen. iv, 4, 19. Παρεγένετο δὲ αὐτῷ ('Αγησιλάῳ) καὶ ὁ ἀδελφὸς Τελευτίας κατὰ θάλασσαν, ἔχων τριήρεις περὶ δώδεκα· ὥστε μακαρίζεσθαι αὐτῶν τὴν μητέρα, ὅτι τῇ αὐτῇ ἡμέρᾳ ὧν ἔτεκεν ὁ μὲν κατὰ γῆν τὰ τείχη τῶν πολεμίων, ὁ δὲ κατὰ θάλασσαν τὰς ναῦς καὶ τὰ νεώρια ᾕρεκε.

This last passage indicates decidedly that Lechæum was not taken until this joint attack by Agesilaus and Teleutias. And the authority of Xenophon on the point is superior, in my judgment, to that of Diodorus (xiv, 86), who represents Lechæum to have been taken in the year before, on the occasion when the Lacedæmonians were first admitted by treachery within the Long Walls.

The passage from Aristeides the rhetor, referred to by Wesseling, Mr. Clinton, and others, only mentions the battle at Lechæum— not the capture of the port. Xenophon also mentions a battle as having taken place close to Lechæum, between the two long walls, on the occasion when Diodorus talks of the capture of Lechæum; so that Aristeides is more in harmony with Xenophon than with Diodorus.

A few months prior to this joint attack of Agesilaus and Teleutias, the Athenians had come with an army, and with masons and carpenters, for the

within them; thus breaking up the naval power of Corinth in the Krissæan Gulf. Lechæum now became a permanent post of hostility against Corinth, occupied by a Lacedæmonian garrison, and occasionally by the Corinthian exiles, while any second rebuilding of the Corinthian Long Walls by the Athenians became impossible. After this important success, Agesilaus returned to Sparta. Neither he nor his Lacedæmonian hoplites, especially the Amyklæans, were ever willingly absent from the festival of the Hyakinthia; nor did he now disdain to take his station in the chorus,[1] under the orders of the choric conductor, for the pæan in honor of Apollo.

It was thus that the Long Walls, though rebuilt by the Athenians in the preceding year, were again permanently overthrown, and the road for Lacedæmonian armies to march beyond the isthmus once more laid open. So much were the Athenians and the Bœotians alarmed at this new success, that both appear to have

---

express purpose of rebuilding the Long Walls which Praxitas had in part broken down. This step would have been both impracticable and useless, if the Lacedæmonians had stood then in possession of Lechæum.

There is one passage of Xenophon, indeed, which looks as if the Lacedæmonians had been in possession of Lechæum *before* this expedition of the Athenians to reëstablish the Long Walls, — Αὐτοὶ (the Lacedæmonians) δ᾽ ἐκ τοῦ Λεχαίου ὁρμώμενοι σὺν μόρᾳ καὶ τοῖς τῶν Κορινθίων ϕυγάσι, κύκλῳ περὶ τὸ ἄστυ τῶν Κορινθίων ἐστρατεύοντο (iv, 4, 17). But whoever reads attentively the sections from 15 to 19 inclusive, will see (I think) thas this affirmation may well refer to a period after, and not before, the capture of Lechæum by Agesilaus; for it has reference to the general contempt shown by the Lacedæmonians for the peltasts of Iphikrates, as contrasted with the terror displayed by the Mantineians and others, of these same peltasts. Even if this were otherwise, however, I should still say that the passages which I have produced above from Xenophon show plainly that *he* represents Lechæum to have been captured by Agesilaus and Teleutias; and that the other words, ἐκ τοῦ Λεχαίου ὁρμώμενοι, if they really implied anything inconsistent with this, must be regarded as an inaccuracy.

I will add that the chapter of Diodorus, xiv, 86, puts into one year events which cannot all be supposed to have taken place in that same year.

Had Lechæum been in possession and occupation by the Lacedæmonians in the year preceding the joint attack by Agesilaus and Teleutias, Xenophon would surely have mentioned it in iv, 4, 14; for it was a more important post than Sikyon, for acting against Corinth.

[1] Xen. Agesilaus, ii, 17.

become desirous of peace, and to have sent envoys to Sparta. The Thebans are said to have offered to recognize Orchomenus (which was now occupied by a Lacedæmonian garrison) as autonomous and disconnected from the Bœotian federation ; while the Athenian envoys seem to have been favorably received at Sparta, and to have found the Lacedæmonians disposed to make peace on better terms than those which had been proposed during the late discussions with Tiribazus (hereafter to be noticed ;) recognizing the newly built Athenian walls, restoring Lemnos, Imbros, and Skyros to Athens, and guaranteeing autonomy to each separate city in the Grecian world. The Athenian envoys at Sparta having provisionally accepted these terms, forty days were allowed for reference to the people of Athens ; to which place Lacedæmonian envoys were sent as formal bearers of the propositions. The Argeians and Corinthians, however, strenuously opposed the thoughts of peace, urging the Athenians to continue the war ; besides which, it appears that many Athenian citizens thought that large restitution ought to have been made of Athenian property forfeited at the end of the late war, and that the Thracian Chersonese ought to have been given back as well as the three islands. On these and other grounds, the Athenian people refused to sanction the recommendation of their envoys ; though Andokides, one of those envoys, in a discourse still extant, earnestly advised that they should accept the peace.[1]

---

[1] Our knowledge of the abortive negotiations adverted to in the text, is derived, partly from the third Oration of Andokides called de Pace, — partly from a statement contained in the Argument of that Oration, and purporting to be borrowed from Philochorus — Φιλόχορος μὲν οὖν λέγει καὶ ἐλθεῖν τοὺς πρέσβεις ἐκ Λακεδαίμονος, καὶ ἀπράκτους ἀνελθεῖν, μὴ πείσαντος τοῦ Ἀνδοκίδου.

Whether Philochorus had any additional grounds to rest upon, other than this very oration itself, may appear doubtful. But at any rate, this important fragment (which I do not see noticed among the fragments of Philochorus in M. Didot's collection) counts for some farther evidence as to the reality of the peace proposed and discussed, but not conc'uded.

Neither Xenophon nor Diodorus make any mention of such mission to Sparta, or discussion at Athens, as that which forms the subject of the Andokidean oration. But on the other hand, neither of them says anything which goes to contradict the reality of the event ; nor can we in this case found any strong negative inference on the mere silence of Xenophon, in the case of a pacific proposition which ultimately came to nothing.

If indeed we could be certain that the oration of Andokides was genuine

The war being thus continued, Corinth, though defended by a considerable confederate force, including Athenian hoplites under

---

it would of itself be sufficient to establish the reality of the mission to which it relates. It would be sufficient evidence, not only without corroboration from Xenophon, but even against any contradictory statement proceeding from Xenophon. But unfortunately, the rhetor Dionysius pronounced this oration to be spurious; which introduces a doubt and throws us upon the investigation of collateral probabilities. I have myself a decided opinion (already stated more than once), that another out of the four orations ascribed to Andokides (I mean the fourth oration, entitled against Alkibiades) is spurious; and I was inclined to the same suspicion with respect to this present oration De Pace; a suspicion which I expressed in a former volume (Vol. V, Ch. xlv, p. 334). But on studying over again with attention this oration De Pace, I find reason to retract my suspicion, and to believe that the oration may be genuine. It has plenty of erroneous allegations as to matter of fact, especially in reference to times prior to the battle of Ægospotami; but not one, so far as I can detect, which conflicts with *the situation* to which the orator addresses himself, — nor which requires us to pronounce it spurious.

Indeed, in considering *this situation* (which is the most important point to be studied when we are examining the genuineness of an oration), we find a partial coincidence in Xenophon, which goes to strengthen our affirmative confidence. One point much insisted upon in the oration is, that the Bœotians were anxious to make peace with Sparta, and were willing to relinquish Orchomenus (s. 13–20). Now Xenophon also mentions, three or four months afterwards, the Bœotians as being anxious for peace, and as sending envoys to Agesilaus to ask on what terms it would be granted to them (Xen. Hellen. iv, 5, 6). This coincidence is of some value in reference to the authenticity of the oration.

Assuming the oration to be genuine, its date is pretty clearly marked, and is rightly placed by Mr. Fynes Clinton in 391 B. C. It was in the autumn or winter of that year, four years after the commencement of the war in Bœotia which began in 395 B. C. (s. 20). It was *after* the capture of Lechæum, which took place in the summer of 391 B. C. — and *before* the destruction of the Lacedæmonian *mora* by Iphikrates, which took place in the spring of 390 B. C. For Andokides emphatically intimates, that at the moment when he spoke, *not one military success* had yet been obtained against the Lacedæmonians — καίτοι ποίας τινος ἂν ἐκεῖνοι παρ' ἡμῶν εἰρήνης ἔτυχον, εἰ μίαν μόνον μάχην ἡττήθησαν; (s. 19). This could never have been said *after* the destruction of the Lacedæmonian *mora*, which made so profound a sensation throughout Greece, and so greatly altered the temper of the contending parties. And it seems to me one proof (among others) that Mr. Fynes Clinton has not placed correctly the events subsequent to the battle of Corinth, when I observe that he assigns the destruction of the *mora* to the year 392 B. C., a year *before* the date which he rightly allots to

Kallias, and peltasts under Iphikrates, became much pressed by the hostile posts at Lechæum as well as at Krommyon and Sidus, — and by its own exiles as the most active of all enemies. Still, however, there remained the peninsula and the fortification of Peiræum as an undisturbed shelter for the Corinthian servants and cattle, and a source of subsistence for the city. Peiræum was an inland post north-east of Corinth, in the centre of that peninsula which separates the two innermost recesses of the Krissæan Gulf, — the bay of Lechæum on its south-west, the bay called Alkyonis, between Kreusis and Olmiæ (now Psatho Bay), on its north-east. Across this latter bay Corinth communicated easily, through Peiræum and the fortified port of Œnoê, with Kreusis the port of Thespiæ in Bœotia.[1] The Corinthian exiles now prevailed upon Agesilaus to repeat his invasion of the territory, partly in order that they might deprive the city of the benefits which it de rived from Peiræum, — partly in order that they might also appropriate to themselves the honor of celebrating the Isthmian games, which were just approaching. The Spartan king accordingly marched forth, at the head of a force composed of Lacedæmonians and of the Peloponnesian allies, first to Lechæum, and thence to the Isthmus, specially so called ; that is, the sacred precinct of Poseidon near Schœnus on the Saronic Gulf, at the narrowest breadth of the Isthmus, where the biennial Isthmian festival was celebrated.

It was the month of April, or beginning of May, and the festival had actually begun, under the presidency of the Corinthians from the city who were in alliance with Argos ; a body of Argeians being present as guards.[2] But on the approach of Agesi-

---

the Andokidean oration. I have placed (though upon other grounds) the destruction of the *mora* in the spring of 390 B. C., which receives additional confirmation from this passage of Andokides.

Both Valckenaer and Sluiter (Lect. Andocid. c. x,) consider the oration of Andokides de Pace as genuine ; Taylor and other critics hold the contrary opinion.

[1] Xen. Agesil. ii, 18.

[2] Xen. Hellen. iv, 5, 1 ; Plutarch, Agesil. c. 21.

Xenophon, who writes his history in the style and language of a partisan, says that " *the Argeians* celebrated the festival, Corinth having now become Argos.' But it seems plain that the truth was as I have stated in the text, — and that the Argeians stood by (with others of the confederates probably

laus, they immediately retired to the city by the road to Kenchreæ, leaving their sacrifices half-finished. Not thinking fit to disturb their retreat, Agesilaus proceeded first to offer sacrifice himself, and then took a position close at hand, in the sacred gr nd of Poseidon, while the Corinthian exiles went through the solemnities in due form, and distributed the parsley wreaths to the victors. After remaining three days, Agesilaus marched away to attack Peiræum. He had no sooner departed, than the Corinthians from the city came forth, celebrated the festival and distributed the wreaths a second time.

Peiræum was occupied by so numerous a guard, comprising Iphikrates and his peltasts, that Agesilaus, instead of directly attacking it, resorted to the stratagem of making a sudden retrograde march directly towards Corinth. Probably, many of the citizens were at that moment absent for the second celebration of the festival; so that those remaining within, on hearing of the approach of Agesilaus, apprehended a plot to betray the city to him, and sent in haste to Peiræum to summon back Iphikrates with his peltasts. Having learned that these troops had passed by in the

---

also) to protect the Corinthians of the city in the exercise of their usual privilege; just as Agesilaus, immediately afterwards, stood by to protect the Corinthian exiles while they were doing the same thing.

The Isthmian games were *trietêric*, that is, celebrated in every alternate year; in one of the spring months, about April or perhaps the beginning of May (the Greek months being lunar, no one of them would coincide regularly with any one of our calendar months, year after year); and in the *second* and *fourth* Olympic years. From Thucydides, viii, 9, 10, we know that this festival was celebrated in April 412 B. C.; that is, towards the end of the *fourth* year of Olympiad 91, about two or three months before the festival of Olympiad 92.

Dodwell (De Cyclis Diss. vi, 2, just cited), Corsini, (Diss. Agonistic. iv, 3), and Schneider in his note to this passage of Xenophon, — all state the Isthmian games to have been celebrated in the *first* and *third* Olympic years; which is, in my judgment, a mistake. Dodwell erroneously states the Isthmian games mentioned in Thucydides, viii, 9, to have been celebrated at the beginning of Olympiad 92, instead of the fourth quarter of the fourth year of Olympiad 91; a mistake pointed out by Krüger (*ad loc.*) as well as by Poppo and Dr. Arnold; although the argumentation of the latter, founded upon the time of the Lacedæmonian festival of the Hyakinthia, is extremely uncertain. It is a still more strange idea of Dodwell, that the Isthmian games were celebrated at the same time as the Olympic games (Annal Xenoph. ad ann. 392)

night, Agesilaus forthwith again turned his course and marched
back to Peiræum, which he himself approached by the ordinary
road, coasting round along the bay of Lechæum, near the Therma,
or warm springs, which are still discernible : [1] while he sent a
mora or division of troops to get round the place by a mountain-
road more in the interior, ascending some woody heights command
ing the town, and crowned by a temple of Poseidon.[2]   The
movement was quite effectual. The garrison and inhabitants of
Peiræum, seeing that the place had become indefensible, aban
doned it the next day with all their cattle and property, to take
refuge in the Heræum, or sacred ground of Hêrê Akræa near the
western cape of the peninsula. While Agesilaus marched thither
towards the coast in pursuit of them, the troops descending from
the heights attacked and captured Œnoê,[3] — the Corinthian town
of that name situated near the Alkyonian bay over against Kreusis in Bœotia. A large booty here fell into their hands, which
was still farther augmented by the speedy surrender of all in the
Heræum to Agesilaus, without conditions.   Called upon to determine the fate of the prisoners, among whom were included men,

---

[1] See Ulrichs, Reisen und Forschungen in Griechenland, chap. i, p. 3.
The modern village and port of Lutráki derives its name from these warm
springs, which are quite close to it and close to the sea, at the foot of the
mountain of Perachora or Peiræum ; on the side of the bay opposite to
Lechæum, but near the point where the level ground constituting the Isthmus (properly so-called), ends, — and where the rocky or mountainous
region, forming the westernmost portion of Geraneia (or the peninsula of
Peiræum), begins. The language of Xenophon, therefore, when he comes
to describe the back-march of Agesilaus is perfectly accurate, — $\eta\delta\eta$ δ' $\epsilon\kappa$
$\pi\epsilon\pi\epsilon\rho\alpha\kappa\acute{o}\tau\sigma\varsigma$ $\alpha\dot{v}\tau\sigma\tilde{v}$ $\tau\grave{a}$ $\vartheta\epsilon\rho\mu\grave{a}$ $\dot{\epsilon}\varsigma$ $\tau\grave{o}$ $\pi\lambda\alpha\tau\grave{v}$ $\tau\sigma\tilde{v}$ $\Lambda\epsilon\chi\alpha\acute{\iota}ov$, etc. (iv, 5, 8).

[2] Xen. Hellen. iv, 5. 4.
Xenophon here recounts how Agesilaus sent up ten men with fire in
pans, to enable those on the heights to make fires and warm themselves ;
the night being very cold and rainy, the situation very high, and the troops
not having come out with blankets or warm covering to protect them. They
kindled large fires, and the neighboring temple of Poseidon was accidentally burnt.

[3] Xen. Hellen. iv, 5, 5.
This Œnoê must not be confounded with the Athenian town of that
name, which lay on the frontiers of Attica towards Bœotia.
So also the town of Peiræum here noticed must not be confounded with
another Peiræum, which was also in the Corinthian territory, but on the
Saronic Gulf, and on the frontiers of Epidaurus (Thucyd. viii, 10).

women, and children, — freemen and slaves, — with cattle and other property, — Agesilaus ordered that all those who had taken part in the massacre at Corinth, in the market-place, should be handed over to the vengeance of the exiles; and that all the rest should be sold as slaves.[1] Though he did not here inflict any harder measure than was usual in Grecian warfare, the reader who reflects that this sentence, pronounced by one on the whole more generous than most contemporary commanders, condemned numbers of free Corinthian men and women to a life of degradation, if not of misery, — will understand by contrast the encomiums with which in my last volume I set forth the magnanimity of Kallikratidas after the capture of Methymna; when he refused, in spite of the importunity of his allies, to sell either the Methymnæan or the Athenian captives, — and when he proclaimed the exalted principle, that no free Greek should be sold into slavery by any permission of his.[2]

As the Lacedæmonians had been before masters of Lechæum, Krommyon, and Sidus, this last success shut up Corinth on its other side, and cut off its communication with Bœotia. The city not being in condition to hold out much longer, the exiles already began to lay their plans for surprising it by aid of friends within.[3] So triumphant was the position of Agesilaus, that his enemies were all in alarm, and the Thebans, as well as others, sent fresh envoys to him to solicit peace. His antipathy towards the Thebans was so vehement, that it was a great personal satisfaction to him to see them thus humiliated. He even treated their envoys with marked contempt, affecting not to notice them when they stood close by, though Pharax, the proxenus of Thebes at Sparta, was preparing to introduce them.

Absorbed in this overweening pride and exultation over conquered enemies, Agesilaus was sitting in a round pavilion, on the

---

[1] Xen. Hellen. iv, 5, 5–8.

[2] Xen. Hellen. i, 5, 14. See Vol. VIII, Ch. lxiv, p. 165 of this History The sale of prisoners here directed by Agesilaus belies the encomiums of his biographers (Xen. Agesil. vii, 6; Cornel. Nep. Agesil. c. 5).

[3] Xen. Agesil. vii, 6; Cornelius Nepos, Ages. c. 5.

The story of Polyænus (iii, 9, 45) may perhaps refer to this point of time. But it is rare that we can verify his anecdotes or those of the other Tactic writers. M. Rehdantz strives in vain to find proper places for the sixty three different stratagems which Polyænus ascribes to Iphikrates

banks of the lake adjoining the Heræum,[1] — with his eyes fixed on the long train of captives brought out under the guard of armed Lacedæmonian hoplites, themselves the object of admiration to a crowd of spectators,[2] — when news arrived, as if under the special intervention of retributive Nemesis, which changed unexpectedly the prospect of affairs.[3] A horseman was seen galloping up, his horse foaming with sweat. To the many inquiries addressed, he returned no answer, nor did he stop until he sprang from his horse at the feet of Agesilaus; to whom, with sorrowful tone and features, he made his communication. Immediately Agesilaus started up, seized his spear, and desired the herald to summon his principal officers. On their coming near, he directed them, together with the guards around, to accompany him without a moment's delay; leaving orders with the general body of the troops to follow as soon as they should have snatched some rapid refreshment. He then immediately put himself in march; but he had not gone far when three fresh horsemen met and informed him, that the task which he was hastening to perform had already been accomplished. Upon this he ordered a halt and returned to the Heræum; where on the ensuing day, to countervail the bad news, he sold all his captives by auction.[4]

This bad news, — the arrival of which has been so graphically

---

[1] This Lake is now called Lake Vuliasmeni. Considerable ruins were noticed by M. Dutroyat, in the recent French survey, near its western extremity; on which side it adjoins the temple of Hêrê Akræa, or the Heræum. See M. Boblaye, Recherches Géographiques sur les Ruines de la Morée, p. 36; and Colonel Leake's Peloponnesiaca, p. 399.

[2] Xen. Hellen. iv, 5, 6.

Τῶν δὲ Λακεδαιμονίων ἀπὸ τῶν ὅπλων σὺν τοῖς δόρασι παρηκολούθουν φύλακες τῶν αἰχμαλώτων, μάλα ὑπὸ τῶν παρόντων θεωρούμενοι· οἱ γὰρ εὐτυχοῦντες καὶ κρατοῦντες ἀεί πως ἀξιοθέατοι δοκοῦσιν εἶναι. Ἔτι δὲ καθημένου τοῦ Ἀγησιλάου, καὶ ἐοικότος ἀγαλλομένῳ τοῖς πεπραγμένοις, ἱππεύς τις προσήλαυνε, καὶ μάλα ἰσχυρῶς ἱδροῦν-ι τῷ ἵππῳ· ὑπὸ πολλῶν δὲ ἐρωτώμενος, ὅ,τι ἄγγελλοι, οὐδενὶ ἀπεκρίνατο, etc.

It is interesting to mark in Xenophon the mixture of Philo-Laconian complacency, — of philosophical reflection, — and of that care in bringing out the contrast of good fortune, with sudden reverse instantly following upon it, which forms so constant a point of effect with Grecian poets and historians.

[3] Plutarch, Agesil. c. 22. ἔπαθε δὲ πρᾶγμα νεμεσητὸν, etc.

[4] Xen. Hellen. iv, 5, 7–9.

described by Xenophon, himself probably among the bystanders
and companions of Agesilaus, — was nothing less than the defeat
and destruction of a Lacedæmonian *mora* or military division by
the light troops under Iphikrates. As it was an understood privilege of the Amyklæan hoplites in the Lacedæmonian army always
to go home, even when on actual service, to the festival of the
Hyakinthia, Agesilaus had left all of them at Lechæum. The festival day being now at hand, they set off to return. But the road
from Lechæum to Sikyon lay immediately under the walls of
Corinth, so that their march was not safe without an escort. Accordingly the polemarch commanding at Lechæum, leaving that
place for the time under watch by the Peloponnesian allies, put
himself at the head of the Lacedæmonian *mora* which formed the
habitual garrison, consisting of six hundred hoplites, and of a *mora*
of cavalry (number unknown) — to protect the Amyklæans until
they were out of danger from the enemy at Corinth. Having
passed by Corinth, and reached a point within about three miles
of the friendly town of Sikyon, he thought the danger over, and
turned back with his *mora* of hoplites to Lechæum ; still, however, leaving the officer of cavalry with orders to accompany the
Amyklæans as much farther as they might choose, and afterwards
to follow him on the return march.[1]

Though the Amyklæans (probably not very numerous) were
presumed to be in danger of attack from Corinth in their march,
and though the force in that town was known to be considerable,
it never occurred to the Lacedæmonian polemarch that there was
any similar danger for his own *mora* of six hundred hoplites ; so
contemptuous was his estimate of the peltasts, and so strong was
the apprehension which these peltasts were known to entertain of
the Lacedæmonians. But Iphikrates, who had let the whole body
march by undisturbed, when he now saw from the walls of Corinth
the six hundred hoplites returning separately, without either cavalry or light troops, conceived the idea, — perhaps, in the existing
state of men's minds, no one else would have conceived it, — of
attacking them with his peltasts as they repassed near the town.
Kallias, the general of the Athenian hoplites in Corinth, warmly
seconding the project, marched out his troops, and arrayed them

---

[1] Xen. Hellen. iv, 5, 11, 12.

ín battle order not far from the gates ; while Iphikrates with his peitasts began his attack upon the Lacedæmonian *mora* in flanks and rear. Approaching within missile distance, he poured upon them a shower of darts and arrows, which killed or wounded several, especially on the unshielded side. Upon this the polemarch ordered a halt, directed the youngest soldiers to drive off the assailants, and confided the wounded to the care of attendants to be carried forward tc Lechæum.[1] But even the youngest soldiers, encumbered by their heavy shields, could not reach their nimbler enemies, who were trained to recede before them. And when, after an unavailing pursuit, they sought to resume their places in the ranks, the attack was renewed, so that nine or ten of them were slain before they could get back. Again did the polemarch give orders to march forward ; again the peltasts renewed their attack, forcing him to halt ; again he ordered the younger soldiers (this time, all those between eighteen and thirty-three years of age, whereas on the former occasion, it had been those between eighteen and twenty-eight) to rush out and drive them off.[2] But the result was just the same : the pursuers accomplished nothing, and only suffered increased loss of their bravest and most forward

---

[1] Xen. Hellen. iv, 5, 14. Τούτους μὲν ἐκέλευον τοὺς ὑπασπιστὰς ἀραμένους ἀποφέρειν ἐς Λέχαιον· οὗτοι καὶ μόνοι τῆς μόρας τῇ ἀληθείᾳ ἐσώθησαν.

We have here a remarkable expression of Xenophon, — " These were the only men in the mora who were *really and truly saved.*" He means, I presume, that they were the only men who were saved without the smallest loss of honor; being carried off wounded from the field of battle, and not having fled or deserted their posts. The others who survived, preserved themselves by flight; and we know that the treatment of those Lacedæmonians who ran away from the field (οἱ τρέσαντες), on their return to Sparta, was insupportably humiliating. See Xenoph. Rep. Laced. ix, 4; Plutarch, Agesil. c. 30. We may gather from these words of Xenophon, that a distinction was really made at Sparta between the treatment of these wounded men here carried off, and that of the other survivors of the beaten mora.

The ὑπασπισταί, or shield-bearers, were, probably, a certain number of attendants, who habitually carried the shields of the officers (compare Xen. Hellen. iv, 8, 39 ; Anab. iv, 2, 20), persons of importance, and rich hoplites. It seems hardly to be presumed that every hoplite had an ὑπασπιστής, in spite of what we read about the attendant Helots at the battle of Platææ (Herod. ix, 10–29) and in other places.

[2] Xen. Hellen. iv, 5, 15, 16. τὰ δέκα ἀφ' ἥβης.— τὰ πεντεκαίδεκα ἀφ ἥβης

soldiers, when they tried to rejoin the main body. Whenever the Lacedæmonians attempted to make progress, these circumstances were again repeated, to their great loss and discouragement; while the peltasts became every moment more confident and vigorous.

Some relief was now afforded to the distressed *mora* by the coming up of their cavalry, which had finished the escort of the Amyklæans. Had this cavalry been with them at the beginning, the result might have been different; but it was now insufficient to repress the animated assaults of the peltasts. Moreover, the Lacedæmonian horsemen were at no time very good, nor did they on this occasion venture to push their pursuit to a greater range than the younger hoplites could keep up with them. At length, after much loss in killed and wounded, and great distress to all, the polemarch contrived to get his detachment as far as an eminence about a quarter of a mile from the sea and about two miles from Lechæum. Here, while Iphikrates still continued to harass them with his peltasts, Kallias also was marching up with his hoplites to charge them hand to hand, — when the Lacedæmonians, enfeebled in numbers, exhausted in strength, and too much dispirited for close fight with a new enemy, broke and fled in all directions. Some took the road to Lechæum, which place a few of them reached, along with the cavalry; the rest ran towards the sea at the nearest point, and observing that some of their friends were rowing in boats from Lechæum along the shore to rescue them, threw themselves into the sea, to wade or swim towards this new succor. But the active peltasts, irresistible in the pursuit of broken hoplites, put the last hand to the destruction of the unfortunate *mora*. Out of its full muster of six hundred, a very small proportion survived to reënter Lechæum.[1]

---

[1] Xen. Hellen. iv, 5, 17.

Xenophon affirms the number of slain to have been about two hundred and fifty — ἐν πάσαις δὲ ταῖς μάχαις καὶ τῇ φυγῇ ἀπέθανον περὶ πεντήκοντα καὶ διακοσίους. But he had before distinctly stated that the whole *mora* marching back to Lechæum under the polemarch, was six hundred in number — ὁ μὲν πολέμαρχος σὺν τοῖς ὁπλίταις, οὖσιν ὡς ἑξακοσίοις, ἀπῄει πάλιν ἐπὶ τὸ Λέχαιον (iv. 5, 12). And it is plain, from several different expressions, that all of them were slain, excepting a very few survivors.

I think it certain, therefore, that one or other of these two numbers is er

The horseman who first communicated the disaster to Agesilaus, had started off express immediately from Lechæum, even before the bodies of the slain had been picked up for burial. The hurried movement of Agesilaus had been dictated by the desire of reaching the field in time to contend for the possession of the bodies, and to escape the shame of soliciting the burial-truce. But the three horsemen who met him afterwards, arrested his course by informing him that the bodies had already been buried, under truce asked and obtained; which authorized Iphikrates to erect his well-earned trophy on the spot where he had first made the attack.[1]

Such a destruction of an entire division of Lacedæmonian hoplites, by light troops who stood in awe of them and whom they despised, was an incident, not indeed of great political importance, but striking in respect of military effect and impression upon the Grecian mind. Nothing at all like it had occurred since the memorable capture of Sphakteria, thirty-five years before; a disaster less considerable in one respect, that the number of hoplites beaten was inferior by one-third, — but far more important in another respect, that half the division had surrendered as prisoners; whereas in the battle near Corinth, though the whole mora (except a few fugitives) perished, it does not seem that a single prisoner was taken. Upon the Corinthians, Bœotians, and other enemies of Sparta, the event operated as a joyous encouragement, reviving them out of all their previous despondency. Even by the allies of Sparta, jealous of her superiority and bound to her by fear more than by attachment, it was welcomed with ill-suppressed satisfaction. But upon the army of Agesilaus (and doubtless upon the Lacedæmonians at home) it fell like a sudden thunderbolt, causing the strongest manifestations of sorrow and

---

roneous; either the original aggregate of six hundred is *above* the truth, — or the total of slain, two hundred and fifty, is *below* the truth. Now the latter supposition appears to me by far the more probable of the two. The Lacedæmonians, habitually secret and misleading in their returns of their own numbers (see Thucyd. v, 74), probably did not choose to admit publicly a greater total of slain than two hundred and fifty. Xenophon has inserted this in his history, forgetting that his own details of the battle refuted the numerical statement. The total of six hundred is more probable, than any smaller number, for the entire mora; and it is impossible to assign any reasons why Xenophon should overstate it.

Xen. Hellen. iv, 5, 8–10.

sympathy.   To these manifestations there was only one exception,
— the fathers, brothers, or sons of the slain warriors; who not
only showed no sorrow, but strutted about publicly with cheerful
and triumphant countenances, like victorious athletes.[1]   We shall
find the like phenomenon at Sparta a few years subsequently, after
the far more terrible defeat at Leuktra; the relatives of the slain
were joyous and elate, — those of the survivors, downcast and
mortified;[2]   a fact strikingly characteristic both of the intense
mental effect of the Spartan training, and of the peculiar associations which it generated.   We may understand how terrible was
the contempt which awaited a Spartan who survived defeat, when
we find fathers positively rejoicing that their sons had escaped
such treatment by death.

Sorely was Agesilaus requited for his supercilious insult towards
the Theban envoys.   When he at last consented to see them, after
the news of the battle, their tone was completely altered.   They
said not a word about peace, but merely asked permission to pass
through and communicate with their countrymen in Corinth.   " I
understand your purpose (said Agesilaus, smiling), — you want
to witness the triumph of your friends, and see what it is worth.
Come along with me, and I will teach you."   Accordingly, on the
next day, he caused them to accompany him while he marched his
army up to the very gates of Corinth, — defying those within to
come out and fight.   The lands had been so ravaged, that there
remained little to destroy.   But wherever there were any fruit-
trees yet standing, the Lacedæmonians now cut them down.   Iphikrates was too prudent to compromise his recent advantage by
hazarding a second battle; so that Agesilaus had only the satisfaction of showing that he was master of the field, and then
retired to encamp at Lechæum; from whence he sent back the
Theban envoys by sea to Kreusis.   Having then left a fresh mora
or division at Lechæum, in place of that which had been defeated,

---

[1] Xen. Hellen. iv, 5, 10. Ἅτε δὲ ἀήθους τοῖς Λακεδαιμονίοις γεγενημένης
τῆς τοιαύτης συμφορᾶς, πολὺ πένθος ἦν κατὰ τὸ Λακωνικὸν στράτευμα, πλὴν
ὅσων ἐτέθνασαν ἐν χώρᾳ ἢ υἱοὶ ἢ πατέρες ἢ ἀδελφοί· οὗτοι δὲ, ὥσπερ νι-
κηφόροι, λαμπροὶ καὶ ἀγαλλόμενοι τῷ οἰκείῳ πάθει περι-
ῄεσαν.

If any reader objects to the words which I have used in the text, I request
him to compare them with the Greek of Xenophon.

[2] Xen Hellen. vi, 4, 16

he marched back to Sparta. But the circumstances of the march
betrayed his real feelings, thinly disguised by the recent bravado
of marching up to the gates of Corinth. He feared to expose his
Lacedæmonian troops even to the view of those allies through
whose territory he was to pass; so well was he aware that the
latter (especially the Mantineians) would manifest their satisfaction at the recent defeat. Accordingly, he commenced his day's
march before dawn, and did not halt for the night till after dark;
at Mantineia, he not only did not halt at all, but passed by, outside
of the walls, before day had broken.[1] There cannot be a more
convincing proof of the real dispositions of the allies towards
Sparta, and of the sentiment of compulsion which dictated their
continued adherence; a fact which we shall see abundantly illustrated as we advance in the stream of the history.

The retirement of Agesilaus was the signal for renewed enterprise on the part of Iphikrates; who retook Sidus and Krommyon,
which had been garrisoned by Praxitas, — as well as Peiræum and
Œnoê, which had been left under occupation by Agesilaus. Corinth was thus cleared of enemies on its eastern and north-eastern
sides. And though the Lacedæmonians still carried on a desultory
warfare from Lechæum, yet such was the terror impressed by the
late destruction of their mora, that the Corinthian exiles at Sikyon did not venture to march by land from that place to Lechæum,
under the walls of Corinth, —but communicated with Lechæum
only by sea.[2] In truth, we hear of no farther serious military
operations undertaken by Sparta against Corinth, before the peace
of Antalkidas. And the place became so secure, that the Corinthian leaders and their Argeian allies were glad to dispense with
the presence of Iphikrates. That officer had gained so much
glory by his recent successes, which the Athenian orators[3] even in
the next generation never ceased to extol, that his temper, naturally haughty, became domineering; and he tried to procure, either
for Athens or for himself, the mastery of Corinth, — putting to
death some of the philo-Argeian leaders. We know these circumstances only by brief and meagre allusion; but they caused

---

[1] Xen. Hellen. iv, 5, 16.   [2] Xen. Hellen. iv, 5, 19
[3] Demosthenes — περὶ Συντάξεως — ?. 8, p. 172.

the Athenians to recall Iphikrates with a large portion of his peltasts, and to send Chabrias to Corinth in his place.[1]

It was either in the ensuing summer, — or perhaps immediately
afterwards during the same summer, — 390 B. C., that Agesilaus undertook an expedition into Akarnania ; at the instance of the Achæans, who threatened, if this were not done, to forsake the Lacedæmonian alliance.   They had acquired possession of the Ætolian district of Kalydon, had brought the neighboring villagers into a
city residence, and garrisoned it as a dependence of the Achæan
confederacy.   But the Akarnanians, — allies of Athens as well
as Thebes, and aided by an Athenian squadron at Œniadæ, —
attacked them there, probably at the invitation of a portion of
the inhabitants, and pressed them so hard, that they employed the
most urgent instances to obtain aid from Sparta.   Agesilaus crossed
the Gulf at Rhium with a considerable force of Spartans and allies, and the full muster of the Achæans.   On his arrival the Akarnanians all took refuge in their cities, sending their cattle up into
the interior highlands, to the borders of a remote lake.   Agesilaus,
having sent to Stratus to require them not merely to forbear hostilities against the Achæans, but to relinquish their alliance with
Athens and Thebes, and to become allies of Sparta, — found his
demands resisted, and began to lay waste the country.   Two or
three days of operations designedly slack, were employed to lull
the Akarnanians into security ; after which, by a rapid forced
march, Agesilaus suddenly surprised the remote spot in which
their cattle and slaves had been deposited for safety.   He spent a
day here to sell this booty ; merchants, probably, accompanying
his army.   But he had considerable difficulty in his return march,
from the narrow paths and high mountains through which he had
to thread his way.   By a series of brave and well-combined hill-
movements, — which, probably, reminded Xenophon of his own
operations against the Karduchians in the retreat of the Ten-
Thousand, — he defeated and dispersed the Akarnanians, though
not without suffering considerably from the excellence of their
light troops.   Yet he was not successful in his attack upon any

---

[1] Diodor. xiv, 92; Xen. Hellen. iv, 8, 34.

Aristeides (Panathen. p. 168) boasts that the Athenians were masters of
the Acro-Corinthus, and might have kept the city as their own, but that
they generously refused to do so.

one of d ir citie , nor would he consent to prolong the war until seed-time, notwithstanding earnest solicitation from the Achæans, whom he pacified by engaging to return the next spring. He was, indeed, in a difficult and dangerous country, had not his retreat been facilitated by the compliance of the Ætolians; who calculated (though vainly) on obtaining from him the recovery of Naupaktus, then held (as well as Kalydon) by the Achæans.[1] Partial as the success of this expedition had been, however, it inflicted sufficient damage on the Akarnanians to accomplish its purpose. On learning that it was about to be repeated in the ensuing spring, they sent envoys to Sparta to solicit peace; consenting to abstain from hostilities against the Achæans, and to enrol themselves as members of the Lacedæmonian confederacy.[2]

It was in this same year that the Spartan authorities resolved on an expedition against Argos, of which Agesipolis, the other king, took the command. Having found the border sacrifices favorable, and crossed the frontier, he sent forward his army to Phlius, where the Peloponnesian allies were ordered to assemble; but he himself first turned aside to Olympia, to consult the oracle of Zeus.

It had been the practice of the Argeians, seemingly on more than one previous occasion,[3] when an invading Lacedæmonian army was approaching their territory, to meet them by a solemn message, intimating that it was the time of some festival (the Karneian, or other) held sacred by both parties, and warning them not to violate the frontier during the holy truce. This was in point of fact nothing better than a fraud; for the notice was sent, not at the moment when the Karneian festival (or other, as the case might be) ought to come on according to the due course of seasons, but at any time when it might serve the purpose of arresting a Lacedæmonian invasion. But though the duplicity of the Argeians was thus manifest, so strong were the pious scruples of the Spartan king, that he could hardly make up his mind to disregard the warning. Moreover, in the existing confusion of the calendar, there was always room for some uncertainty as to the question,

---

[1] Diodor. xv, 73. [2] Xen. Hellen. iv, 6, 1–14; iv, 7, 1.

[3] Xen. Hellen. iv, 7, 3. Οἱ δ᾽ Ἀργεῖοι, ἐπεὶ ἐγνωσαν οὐ δυνησόμενοι κωλύειν, ἐπεμψαν, ὥσπερ εἰώθεσαν, ἐστεφανωμένους δύο κήρυκας. ὑποφέροντας σπονδάς.

which was the true Karneian moon; no Dorian state having any right to fix it imperatively for the others, as the Eleians fixed the Olympic truce, and the Corinthians the Isthmian. It was with a view to satisfy his conscience on this subject that Agesipolis now went to Olympia, and put the question to the oracle of Zeus, — whether he might with a safe religious conscience refuse to accept the holy truce, if the Argeians should now tender it. The oracle, habitually dexterous in meeting a specific question with a general reply, informed him, that he might with a safe conscience decline a truce demanded wrongfully and for underhand purposes.[1] This

---

[1] Xen. Hellen. iv, 7, 2. Ὁ δὲ Ἀγησίπολις — ἐλθὼν εἰς τὴν Ὀλυμπίαν καὶ χρηστηριαζόμενος, ἐπηρώτα τὸν θεὸν, εἰ ὁσίως ἂν ἔχοι αὐτῷ, μὴ δεχομένῳ τὰς σπονδὰς τῶν Ἀργείων· ὅτε οὐχ, ὁπότε κάθηκοι ὁ χρόνος ἀλλ' ὅποτε ἐμβάλλειν μέλλοιεν Λακεδαιμόνιοι, τότε ὑπέφερον τοὺς μῆνας. Ὁ δὲ θεὸς ἐπεσήμαινεν αὐτῷ, ὅσιον εἶναι μὴ δεχομένῳ σπονδὰς ἀδίκως ἐπιφερομένας. Ἐκεῖθεν δ' εὐθὺς πορευθεὶς εἰς Δελφοὺς, ἐπήρετο αὖ τὸν Ἀπόλλω, εἰ κἀκείνῳ δοκοίη περὶ τῶν σπονδῶν, καθάπερ τῷ πατρί. Ὁ δ' ἀπεκρίνατο, καὶ μάλα κατὰ ταὐτά.

I have given in the text what I believe to be the meaning of the words ὑποφέρειν τοὺς μῆνας, — upon which Schneider has a long and not very instructive note, adopting an untenable hypothesis of Dodwell, that the Argeians on this occasion appealed to the sanctity of the Isthmian truce; which is not countenanced by anything in Xenophon, and which it belonged to the Corinthians to announce, not to the Argeians. The plural τοὺς μῆνας indicates (as Weiske and Manso understand it) that the Argeians sometimes put forward the name of one festival, sometimes of another. We may be pretty sure that the Karneian festival was one of them; but what the others were, we cannot tell. It is very probable that there were several festivals of common obligation either among all the Dorians, or between Sparta and Argos — πατρῴους τινας σπονδὰς ἐκ παλαιοῦ καθεστώσας τοις Δωριεῦσι πρὸς ἀλλήλους, — to use the language of Pausanias (iii, 5, 6). The language of Xenophon implies that the demand made by the Argeians, for observance of the Holy Truce, was in itself rightful, or rather, that it would have been rightful at a different season; but that they put themselves in the wrong by making it at an improper season and for a fraudulent political purpose.

For some remarks on other fraudulent manœuvres of the Argeians, respecting the season of the Karneian truce, see Vol. VII. of this History Ch. lvi, p. 66. The compound verb ὑποφέρειν τοὺς μῆνας seems to imply the underhand purpose with which the Argeians preferred their demand of the truce. What were the previous occasions on which they had preferred a similar demand, we are not informed. Two years before, Agesilaus had invaded and laid waste Argos; perhaps they may have tried, but without success, to arrest his march by a similar pious fraud.

was accepted by Agesipolis as a satisfactory affirmative. Nevertheless, to make assurance doubly sure, he went directly forward to Delphi, to put the same question to Apollo. As it would have been truly embarrassing, however, if the two holy replies had turned out such as to contradict each other, he availed himself of the *præjudicium* which he had already received at Olympia, and submitted the question to Apollo at Delphi in this form : " Is thine opinion on the question of the holy truce, the same as that of thy father (Zeus) ? " " Most decidedly the same," replied the god. Such double warranty, though the appeal was so drawn up as scarcely to leave to Apollo freedom of speech,[1] enabled Agesipolis to return with full confidence to Phlius, where his army was already mustered ; and to march immediately into the Argeian territory by the road of Nemea. Being met on the frontier by two heralds with wreaths and in solemn attire, who warned him that it was a season of holy truce, he informed them that the gods authorized his disobedience to their summons, and marched on into the Argeian plain.

It happened that on the first evening after he had crossed the border, the supper and the consequent libation having been just concluded, an earthquake occurred ; or, to translate the Greek phrase, " the god (Poseidon) shook." To all Greeks, and to Lacedæmonians especially, this was a solemn event, and the personal companions of Agesipolis immediately began to sing the pæan in honor of Poseidon ; the general impression among the soldiers being, that he would give orders for quitting the territory immediately, as Agis had acted in the invasion of Elis a few years be-

---

It is to this proceeding, perhaps, that Andokides alludes (Or. iii, De Pace. s. 27), where he says that the Argeians,'though st⁓ · in insisting that Athens should help them to carry on the war for · ession of Corinth against the Lacedæmonians, had nevertheless m⁓ separate peace with the latter, covering their own Argeian territory from invasion — αὐτοὶ δ' ἰδίᾳ εἰρήνην ποιησάμενοι τὴν χώραν οὐ παρέχουσιν ἐμπολεμεῖν. Of this obscure passage I can give no better explanation.

[1] Aristotel. Rhetoric. ii, 23. Ἡγήσιππος ἐν Δελφοῖς ἐπηρώτα τὸν θεὸν, κεχρημένος πρότερον Ὀλυμπίασιν, εἰ αὐτῷ ταὐτὰ δοκεῖ, ἅπερ τῷ πατρὶ, ὡς αἰσχρὸν ὂν τἀνάντα εἰπεῖν.

A similar story about the manner of putting the question to Apollo at Delphi, after it had already been put to Zeus at Dôdôna, is told about Agesilaus on another occasion Plutarch. Apophth. Lacon. p. 208 F.).

fore. Perhaps Agesipolis would have done the same here, construing the earthquake as a warning that he had done wrong, in neglecting the summons of the heralds, — had he not been fortified by the recent oracles. He now replied, that if the earthquake had occurred before he crossed the frontier, he should have considered it as a prohibition; but as it came after his crossing, he looked upon it as an encouragement to go forward.

So fully had the Argeians counted on the success of their warning transmitted by the heralds, that they had made little preparation for defence. Their dismay and confusion were very great; their property was still outlying, not yet removed into secure places, so that Agesipolis found much both to destroy and to appropriate. He carried his ravages even to the gates of the city, piquing himself on advancing a little farther than Agesilaus had gone in his invasion two years before. He was at last driven to retreat by the terror of a flash of lightning in his camp, which killed several persons. And a project which he had formed, of erecting a permanent fort on the Argeian frontier, was abandoned in consequence of unfavorable sacrifices.[1]

Besides these transactions in and near the isthmus of Corinth, the war between Sparta and her enemies was prosecuted during the same years both in the islands and on the coast of Asia Minor; though our information is so imperfect that we can scarcely trace the thread of events. The defeat near Knidus (394 B. C.), — the triumphant maritime force of Pharnabazus and Konon at the Isthmus of Corinth in the ensuing year (393 B. C.), — the restoration of the Athenian Long Walls and fortified port, — and the activity of Konon with the fleet among the islands,[2] — so alarmed the

---

[1] Xen. Hellen. iv, 7, 7; Pausan. iii, 5, 6.

It rather seems, by the language of these two writers, that they look upon the menacing signs, by which Agesipolis was induced to depart, as marks of some displeasure of the gods against his expedition.

[2] Xen. Hellen. iv, 8, 12. Compare Isokrates, Or. vii, (Areopag.) s. 13. ἁπάσης γὰρ τῆς Ἑλλάδος ὑπὸ τὴν πόλιν ἡμῶν ὑποπεσούσης καὶ μετὰ τὴν Κόνωνος ναυμαχίαν καὶ μετὰ τὴν Τιμοθέου στρατηγίαν, etc. This oration, however, was composed a long while after the events (about B. C. 353 — see Mr. Clinton's Fast. H., in that year); and Isokrates exaggerates; mistaking the break-up of the Lacedæmonian empire for a resumption of the Athenian. Demosthenes also (cont. Leptin. c. 16, p. 477) confounds the same two ideas and even the Athenian vote of thanks to Konon, perpetuated on a comme

Spartans with the idea of a second Athenian maritime empire, that they made every effort to detach the Persian force from the side of their enemies.

The Spartan Antalkidas, a dexterous, winning and artful man,[1] not unlike Lysander, was sent as envoy to Tiribazus (392 B. C.); whom we now find as satrap of Ionia in the room of Tithraustes, after having been satrap of Armenia during the retreat of the Ten Thousand. As Tiribazus was newly arrived in Asia Minor, he had not acquired that personal enmity against the Spartans, which the active hostilities of Derkyllidas and Agesilaus had inspired to Pharnabazus and other Persians. Moreover, jealousy between neighboring satraps was an ordinary feeling, which Antalkidas now hoped to turn to the advantage of Sparta. To counteract his projects, envoys were also sent to Tiribazus, by the confederate enemies of Sparta, Athens, Thebes, Corinth, and Argos; and Konon, as the envoy of Athens, was incautiously despatched among the number. On the part of Sparta, Antalkidas offered, first, to abandon to the king of Persia all the Greeks on the continent of Asia; next, as to all the other Greeks, insular as well as continental, he required nothing more than absolute autonomy for each separate city, great and small.[2] The Persian king (he said) could neither desire anything more for himself, nor have any motive for continuing the war against Sparta, when he should once be placed in possession of all the towns on the Asiatic coast, and when he should find both Sparta and Athens rendered incapable of annoying him, through the autonomy and disunion of the Hellenic world. But to neither of the two propositions of Antalkidas would Athens, Thebes, or Argos, accede. As to the first, they repudiated the disgrace of thus formally abandoning the Asiatic Greeks;[3]

---

morative column, countenanced the same impression, — ἐπειδὴ Κόνων ἠλευθέρωσε τοὺς Ἀθηναίων συμμάχους, etc.

[1] Plutarch, Artaxerx. c. 22.   [2] Xen. Hellen. iv, 8, 12–14.

[3] Diodor. xiv, 110. He affirms that these cities strongly objected to this concession, five years afterwards, when the peace of Antalkidas was actually concluded; but that they were forced to give up their scruples and accept the peace including the concession. because they had not force to resist Persia and Sparta acting in hearty alliance.

Hence we may infer with certainty, that they also objected to it during the earlier discussions, when it was first broached by Antalkidas; and that their objections to it were in part the cause why the discussions reported in the text broke off without result.

as to the second proposition, guaranteeing autonomy to every distinct city of Greece, they would admit it only under special reserves, which it did not suit the purpose of Antalkidas to grant. In truth the proposition went to break up (and was framed with that view) both the Bœotian confederacy under the presidency of Thebes, and the union between Argos and Corinth; while it also deprived Athens of the chance of recovering Lemnos, Imbros, and Skyros,[1] — islands which had been possessed and recognized by her since the first commencement of the confederacy of Delos; indeed the two former, even from the time of Miltiades the conqueror of Marathon.

Here commences a new era in the policy of Sparta. That she should abnegate all pretension to maritime empire, is noway difficult to understand — seeing that it had already been irrevocably overthrown by the defeat of Knidus. Nor can we wonder that she should abandon the Greeks on the Asiatic continent to Persian sway; since this was nothing more than she had already consented to do in her conventions with Tissaphernes and Cyrus during the latter years of the Peloponnesian war,[2] — and consented, let us add, not under any of that stringent necessity which at the same time pressed upon Athens, but simply with a view to the maximum of victory over an enemy already enfeebled. The events which followed the close of that war (recounted in a former chapter) had indeed induced her to alter her determination, and again to espouse their

---

It is true that Athens, during her desperate struggles in the last years of the Peloponnesian war, had consented to this concession, and even to greater, without doing herself any good (Thucyd. viii, 56). But she was not now placed in circumstances so imperious as to force her to be equally yielding.

Plato, in the Menexenus (c. 17, p. 245), asserts that all the allies of Athens — Bœotians, Corinthians, Argeians, etc., were willing to surrender the Asiatic Greeks at the requisition of Artaxerxes; but that the Athenians alone resolutely stood out, and were in consequence left without any allies. The latter part of this assertion, as to the isolation of Athens from her allies, is certainly not true; nor do I believe that the allies took essentialiy different views from Athens on the point. The Menexenus, eloquent and complimentary to Athens, must be followed cautiously as to matters of fact. Plato goes the length of denying that the Athenians subscribed the convention of Antalkidas. Aristeides (Panathen. p. 172) says that they were forced to subscribe it, because all their allies abandoned them.

[1] Xen. Hellen. iv, 8, 15.

[2] See a striking passage in the Or. xii. (Panathen.) of Isokrates, s. 110

cause. But the real novelty now first exhibited in her policy, is, the full development of what had before existed in manifest tendency, — hostility against all the partial land-confederacies of Greece, disguised under the plausible demand of universal autonomy for every town, great or small. How this autonomy was construed and carried into act, we shall see hereafter ; at present, we have only to note the first proclamation of it by Antalkidas in the name of Sparta.

On this occasion, indeed, his mission came to nothing, from the peremptory opposition of Athens and the others. But he was fortunate enough to gain the approbation and confidence of Tiribazus ; who saw so clearly how much both propositions tended to promote the interests and power of Persia, that he resolved to go up in person to court, and prevail on Artaxerxes to act in concert with Sparta. Though not daring to support Antalkidas openly, Tiribazus secretly gave him money to reinforce the Spartan fleet. He at the same time rendered to Sparta the more signal service of arresting and detaining Konon, pretending that the latter was acting contrary to the interests of the king.[1] This arrest was a gross act of perfidy, since Konon not only commanded respect in his character of envoy, — but had been acting with the full confidence, and almost under the orders, of Pharnabazus. But the removal of an officer of so much ability, — the only man who possessed the confidence of Pharnabazus, — was the most fatal of all impediments to the naval renovation of Athens. It was fortunate that Konon had had time to rebuild the Long Walls, before his means of action were thus abruptly intercepted. Respecting his subsequent fate, there exist contradictory stories. According to one, he was put to death by the Persians in prison ; according to another, he found means to escape and again took refuge with Evagoras in Cyprus, in which island he afterwards died of sickness.[2] The latter story appears undoubtedly to be the true one. But it is certain that he never afterwards had the means of performing any public service, and that his career was cut short by this treacherous detention, just at the moment when its promise was the most splendid for his country.

---

[1] Xen. Hellen. iv, 8, 16 ; Diodor. xiv, 85.

[2] Lysias, Or. xix, (De Bon. Aristoph.) s. 41, 42, 44 ; Cornelius Nepos. Conon, c. 5 ; Isokrates Or. iv (Panegyr.) s. 180.

Tiribazus, on going up to the Persian court, seems to have been detained there for the purpose of concerting measures against Evagoras, prince of Salamis in Cyprus, whose revolt from Persia was now on the point of breaking out. But the Persian court could not yet be prevailed upon to show any countenance to the propositions of Sparta or of Antalkidas. On the contrary, Struthas, who was sent down to Ionia as temporary substitute for Tiribazus, full of anxiety to avenge the ravages of Agesilaus, acted with vigorous hostility against the Lacedæmonians, and manifested friendly dispositions towards Athens.

Thimbron (of whom we have before heard as first taking the command of the Cyreian army in Asia Minor, after their return from Thrace) received orders again to act as head of the Lacedæmonian forces in Asia against Struthas. The new commander, with an army estimated by Diodorus at eight thousand men,[1] marched from Ephesus into the interior, and began his devastation of the territory dependent on Persia. But his previous command, though he was personally amiable,[2] had been irregular and disorderly, and it was soon observed that the same defects were now yet more prominent, aggravated by too liberal indulgence in convivial pleasures. Aware of his rash, contemptuous, and improvident mode of attack, Struthas laid a snare for him by sending a detachment of cavalry to menace the camp, just when Thimbron had concluded his morning meal in company with the flute-player Thersander, — the latter not merely an excellent musician, but possessed of a full measure of Spartan courage. Starting from his tent at the news, Thimbron, with Thersander, waited only to collect the few troops immediately at hand, without even leaving any orders for the remainder, and hastened to repel the assailants; who gave way easily, and seduced him into a pursuit. Presently Struthas himself, appearing with a numerous and well-arrayed body of cavalry, charged with vigor the disorderly detachment of Thimbron. Both that general and Thersander, bravely fighting, fell among the first; while the army, deprived of their commander

---

[1] Diodor. xiv, 99.

[2] Xen. Hellen. iv, 8, 22. Ἦν δὲ οὗτος ἀνὴρ (Diphridas) εὔχαρις τι οὐχ ἧττον τοῦ Θίμβρωνος, μᾶλλόν τε συντεταγμένος, κιὰ ἐγχειρητι κώτερος, στρατηγός. οὐδὲ γὰρ ἐκράτουν αὐτοῦ αἱ τοῦ σώματος ἡδοναί, ἀλλ ἀεί, πρὸς ὦ εἴη ἔργῳ, τοῦτο ἔπραττεν.

as well as ill-prepared for a battle, made but an ineffective resistance. They were broken, warmly pursued, and the greater number slain. A few who contrived to escape the active Persian cavalry, found shelter in the neighboring cities.[1]

This victory of Struthas, gained by the Persian cavalry, displays a degree of vigor and ability which, fortunately for the Greeks, was rarely seen in Persian operations. Our scanty information does not enable us to trace its consequences. We find Diphridas sent out soon after by the Lacedæmonians, along with the admiral Ekdikus, as successor of Thimbron to bring together the remnant of the defeated army, and to protect those cities which had contributed to form it. Diphridas, — a man with all the popular qualities of his predecessor, but a better and more careful officer, — is said to have succeeded to some extent in this difficult mission. Being fortunate enough to take captive the son-in-law of Struthas, with his wife, (as Xenophon had captured Asidatês,) he obtained a sufficiently large ransom to enable him to pay his troops for some time.[2] But it is evident that his achievements were not considerable, and that the Ionian Greeks on the continent are now left to make good their position, as they can, against the satrap at Sardis.

The forces of Sparta were much required at Rhodes; which island (as has been mentioned already) had revolted from Sparta about five years before (a few months anterior to the battle of Knidus), dispossessed the Lysandrian oligarchy, and established a democratical government. But since that period, an opposition-party in the island had gradually risen up, acquired strength, and come into correspondence with the oligarchical exiles; who on their side warmly solicited aid from Sparta, representing that Rhodes would otherwise become thoroughly dependent on Athens. Accordingly, the Lacedæmonians sent eight triremes across the Ægean under the command of Ekdikus; the first of their ships of war which had crossed since the defeat of Knidus.[3] Though the Perso-Athenian naval force in the Ægean had been either dismissed or paralyzed since the seizure of Konon, yet the Rhodian governmer possessed a fleet of about twenty triremes, besides considerable force of other kinds; so that Ekdikus could not even land on the

---

[1] Xen. Hellen. iv, 8, 18, 19.   [2] Xen. Hellen. iv, 8, 21, 22.
[3] Xen. Hellen. iv, 8, 21.

island, but was compelled to halt at Knidus. Fortunately, Teleutias the Lacedæmonian was now in the Corinthian Gulf with a
fleet of twelve triremes, which were no longer required there;
since Agesilaus and he had captured Lechæum a few months
before, and destroyed the maritime force of the Corinthians in
those waters. He was now directed to sail with his squadron out
of the Corinthian Gulf across to Asia, to supersede Ekdikus, and
take the command of the whole fleet for operations off Rhodes.
On passing by Samos, he persuaded the inhabitants to embrace
the cause of Sparta, and to furnish him with a few ships; after
which he went onward to Knidus, where, superseding Ekdikus, he
found himself at the head of twenty-seven triremes.[1] In his way
from Knidus to Rhodes, he accidentally fell in with the Athenian
admiral Philokrates, conducting ten triremes to Cyprus to the aid
of Evagoras in his struggle against the Persians. He was fortunate enough to carry them all as prisoners into Knidus, where he
sold the whole booty, and then proceeded with his fleet, thus augmented to thirty-seven sail, to Rhodes. Here he established a
fortified post, enabling the oligarchical party to carry on an active
civil war. But he was defeated in a battle, — his enemies being
decidedly the stronger force in the island, and masters of all
the cities.[2]

---

[1] Xen. Hellen. iv, 8, 23.

Diodorus (xiv, 97) agrees in this number of twenty-seven triremes, and
n the fact of aid having been obtained from Samos, which island was per-
uaded to detach itself from Athens. But he recounts the circumstances
n a very different manner. He represents the oligarchical party in Rhodes
as having risen in insurrection, and become masters of the island; he does
not name Teleutias, but Eudokimus (Ekdikus?), Diphilus (Diphridas?),
and Philodikus, as commanders.

The statement of Xenophon deserves the greater credence, in my judg
ment. His means of information, as well as his interest, about Teleutias
(the brother of Agesilaus) were considerable.

[2] Xen. Hellen. iv, 8, 24–26.

Although the three ancient Rhodian cities (Lindus, Ialysus, and Kamei-
rus) had coalesced (see Diodor. xiii, 75) a few years before into the great
city of Rhodes, afterwards so powerful and celebrated, — yet they still continued to exist, and apparently as fortified places. For Xenophon speaks
of the democrats in Rhodes as τὰς τε πόλεις ἔχοντας, etc.

Whether the Philokrates here named as *Philokrates son of Ephialtes*, is
the same person as the Philokrates accused in the Thirtieth oration of Ly-

The alliance with Evagoras of Cyprus, in his contention against Artaxerxes, was at this moment an unfortunate and perplexing circumstance for Athens, since she was relying upon Persian aid against Sparta, and since Sparta was bidding against her for it. But the alliance was one which she could not lightly throw off. For Evagoras had not only harbored Konon with the remnant of the Athenian fleet after the disaster of Ægospotami, but had earned a grant of citizenship and the honor of a statue at Athens, as a strenuous auxiliary in procuring that Persian aid which gained the battle of Knidus, and as a personal combatant in that battle, before the commencement of his dissension with Artaxerxes.[1] It would have been every way advantageous to Athens at this moment to decline assisting Evagoras, since (not to mention the probability of offending the Persian court) she had more than enough to employ all her maritime force nearer home and for purposes more essential to herself. Yet in spite of these very serious considerations of prudence, the paramount feelings of prior obligation and gratitude, enforced by influential citizens who had formed connections in Cyprus, determined the Athenians to identify themselves with his gallant struggles[2] (of which I shall speak more fully presently). So little was fickleness, or instability, or the easy oblivion of past feelings, a part of their real nature, — though historians have commonly denounced it as among their prominent qualities.

The capture of their squadron under Philokrates, however, and the consequent increase of the Lacedæmonian naval force at Rhodes, compelled the Athenians to postpone further aid to Evagoras, and to arm forty triremes under Thrasybulus for the Asiatic coast; no inconsiderable effort, when we recollect that four years before there was scarcely a single trireme in Peiræus, and not even a wall of defence around the place. Though sent immediately for the assistance of Rhodes, Thrasybulus judged it expedient to go

---

sias — cannot be certainly made out. It is possible enough that there might be two contemporary Athenians bearing this name, which would explain the circumstance that Xenophon here names the father Ephialtes — a practice occasional with him, but not common.

[1] Isokrates, Or. ix. (Evagoras) s. 67, 68, 82; Epistola Philippi ap. Demosthen. Orot. p. 161, c. 4.

[2] Lysias, Orat. xix, (De Bonis Aristoph.) s. 27-44

first to the Hellespont ; probably from extreme want of money to pay his men. Derkyllidas was still in occupation of Abydos, yet there was no Lacedæmonian fleet in the strait ; so that Thrasybulus was enabled to extend the alliances of Athens both on the European and the Asiatic side, — the latter being under the friendly satrap, Pharnabazus. Reconciling the two Thracian princes, Seuthes and Amadokus, whom he found at war, he brought both of them into amicable relations with Athens, and then moved forward to Byzantium. That city was already in alliance with Athens ; but on the arrival of Thrasybulus, the alliance was still further cemented by the change of its government into a democracy. Having established friendship with the opposite city of Chalkedon, and being thus master of the Bosphorus, he sold the tithe of the commercial ships sailing out of the Euxine ; [1] leaving doubtless an adequate force to exact it. This was a striking evidence of revived Athenian maritime power, which seems also to have been now extended more or less to Samothrace, Thasus, and the coast of Thrace.[2]

From Byzantium, Thrasybulus sailed to Mitylênê, which was already in friendship with Athens, — though Methymna and the other cities in the island were still maintained by a force under the Lacedæmonian harmost, Therimachus. With the aid of the Mitylenæans, and of the exiles from other Lesbian cities, Thrasybulus marched to the borders of Methymna, where he was met by Therimachus ; who had also brought together his utmost force, but was now completely defeated and slain. The Athenians thus became masters of Antissa and Eresus, where they were enabled to levy a valuable contribution, as well as to plunder the refractory territory of Methymna. Nevertheless, Thrasybulus, in spite of farther help from Chios and Mitylênê, still thought himself not in a situation to go to Rhodes with advantage. Perhaps he was not sure of pay in advance, and the presence of unpaid troops in an

---

[1] Xen. Hellen. iv, 8, 25–27.

Polybius (iv, 38–47) gives instructive remarks and information about the importance of Byzantium and its very peculiar position, in the ancient world, — as well as about the dues charged on the merchant vessels going into, or coming out of, the Euxine, — and the manner in which these dues pressed upon general trade.

[2] Xen. Hellen. v, 1, 7.

exhausted island might be a doubtful benefit. Accordingly, he sailed from Lesbos along the western and southern coast of Asia Minor, levying contributions at Halikarnassus [1] and other places until he came to Aspendus in Pamphylia; where he also obtained money and was about to depart with it, when some misdeeds committed by his soldiers so exasperated the inhabitants, that they attacked him by night unprepared in his tent, and slew him.[2]

Thus perished the citizen to whom, more than to any one else, Athens owed not only her renovated democracy, but its wise, generous, and harmonious working, after renovation. Even the philo Laconian and oligarchical Xenophon bestows upon him a marked and unaffected eulogy.[3] His devoted patriotism in commencing and prosecuting the struggle against the Thirty, at a time when they not only were at the height of their power, but had plausible ground for calculating on the full auxiliary strength of Sparta, deserves high admiration. But the feature which stands yet more eminent in his character, — a feature infinitely rare in the Grecian character, generally, — is, that the energy of a successful leader was combined with complete absence both of vindictive antipathies for the past, and of overbearing ambition for himself. Content to live himself as a simple citizen under the restored democracy, he taught his countrymen to forgive an oligarchical party from whom they had suffered atrocious wrongs, and set the example himself of acquiescing, in the loss of his own large property. The generosity of such a proceeding ought not to count for less, because it was at the same time dictated by the highest political prudence. We find in an oration of Lysias against Ergokles (a citizen who served in the Athenian fleet on this last expedition), in which the latter is accused of gross peculation, — insinuations against Thrasybulus, of having countenanced the delinquency, though coupled with praise of his general character. Even the words as they now stand are so vague as to carry little evidence; but when we re-

---

[1] Lysias, Or. xxviii, cont. Erg. s. 1–20.

[2] Xen. Hellen. iv. 8, 28–30; Diodor. xiv, 94.

The latter states that Thrasybulus lost twenty-three triremes by a storm near Lesbos, — which Xenophon does not notice, and which seems improbable.

[3] Xen. Hellen. iv, 8, 31. Καὶ Θρασύβουλος μὲν δὴ, μάλα δοκῶν ἀνὴρ ἀγαθὸς εἶναι, οὕτως ἐτελεύτησεν.

reflect that the oration was spoken after the death of Thrasybulus, they are entitled to no weight at all.[1]

The Athenians sent Agyrrhius to succeed Thrasybulus. After the death of the latter, we may conclude that the fleet went to Rhodes, its original destination, — though Xenophon does not expressly say so, — the rather, as neither Teleutias nor any subsequent Lacedæmonian commander appears to have become master of the island, in spite of the considerable force which they had there assembled.[2] The Lacedæmonians, however, on their side, being also much in want of money, Teleutias was obliged (in the same manner as the Athenians), to move from island to island, levying contributions as he could.[3]

When the news of the successful proceedings of Thrasybulus at Byzantium and the Hellespont, again establishing a toll for the profit of Athens, reached Sparta, it excited so much anxiety, that Anaxibius, having great influence with the ephors of the time, prevailed on them to send him out as harmost to Abydos, in the room of Derkyllidas, who had now been in that post for several years. Having been the officer originally employed to procure the

---

[1] Lysias, cont. Ergo. Or. xxviii, s. 9.

Ergokles is charged in this oration with gross abuse of power, oppression towards allies and citizens of Athens, and peculation for his own profit, during the course of the expedition of Thrasybulus; who is indirectly accused of conniving at such misconduct. It appears that the Athenians, as soon as they were informed that Thrasybulus had established the toll in the Bosphorus, passed a decree that an account should be sent home of all moneys exacted from the various cities, and that the colleagues of Thrasybulus should come home to go through the audit (s. 5); implying (so far as we can understand what is thus briefly noticed) that Thrasybulus himself should *not* be obliged to come home, but might stay on his Hellespontine or Asiatic command. Ergokles, however, probably one of these colleagues, resented this degree as an insult, and advised Thrasybulus to seize Byzantium, to retain the fleet, and to marry the daughter of the Thracian prince Seuthês. It is also affirmed in the oration that the fleet had come home in very bad condition (s. 2-4), and that the money, levied with so much criminal abuse, had been either squandered or fraudulently appropriated.

We learn from another oration that Ergokles was condemned to death. His property was confiscated, and was said to amount to thirty talents, though he had been poor before the expedition; but nothing like that amount was discovered after the sentence of confiscation (Lysias, Or. xxx, cont. Philokrat. s. 3).

[2] Xen. Hellen. iv, 8, 31.   [3] Xen Hellen. v, 1, 2.

revolt of the place from Athens (in 411 B. C.),[1] Derkyllidas had since rendered service not less essential in preserving it to Sparta, during the extensive desertion which followed the battle of Knidus. But it was supposed that he ought to have checked the aggressive plans of Thrasybulus; moreover, Anaxibius promised, if a small force were entrusted to him, to put down effectually the newly-revived Athenian influence. He was supposed to know well, those regions in which he had once already been admiral, at the moment when Xenophon and the Cyreian army first returned; the harshness, treachery, and corruption, which he displayed in his dealing with that gallant body of men, have been already recounted in a former chapter.[2] With three triremes, and funds for the pay of a thousand mercenary troops, Anaxibius accordingly went to Abydos. He began his operations with considerable vigor, both against Athens and Pharnabazus. While he armed a land-force, which he employed in making incursions on the neighboring cities in the territory of that satrap, — he at the same time reinforced his little squadron by three triremes out of the harbor of Abydos, so that he became strong enough to seize the merchant vessels passing along the Hellespont to Athens or to her allies.[3] The force which Thrasybulus had left at Byzantium to secure the strait revenues, was thus inadequate to its object without farther addition.

Fortunately, Iphikrates was at this moment disengaged at Athens, having recently returnd from Corinth with his body of peltasts, for whom doubtless employment was wanted. He was accordingly sent with twelve hundred peltasts and eight triremes, to combat Anaxibius in the Hellespont; which now became again the scene of conflict, as it had been in the latter years of the Peloponnesian war; the Athenians from the European side, the Lacedæmonians from the Asiatic. At first the warfare consisted of desultory privateering, and money-levying excursions, on both sides.[4] But at length, the watchful genius of Iphikrates discov-

---

[1] Thucyd. viii, 61; compare Xenoph. Anab. v, 6, 24.

[2] See above, Chapter lxxi, p. 156 of the present volume

[3] Xen. Hellen. iv, 8, 32, 83.

[4] Xen. Hellen. iv, 8, 35, 36. τὸ μὲν πρῶτον λῃστὰς διαπέμποντες ἐπολέμουν ἀλλήλοις........ Ὅπως δοκοίη, ὥσπερ εἰώθει, ἐπ᾽ ἀργυρολογίαν ἐπαναπεπλευκέναι.

ʒred opportunity for a successful stratagem. Anaxibius, having jusı ʒrawn the town of Antandrus into his alliance, had marched thither for the purpose of leaving a garrison in it, with his Lacedæmonian and mercenary forces, as well as two hundred hoplites from Abydos ıtself. His way lay across the mountainous region of Ida, south-ward to the coast of the gulf of Adramyttium. Accordingly, Iphikrates, foreseeing that he would speedily return, crossed over in the night from the Chersonese, and planted himself in ambush on the line of return march; at a point where it traversed the desert and mountainous extremities of the Abydene territory, neaı the gold mines of Kremastê. The triremes which carried him across were ordered to sail up the strait on the next day, in order that Anaxibius must be apprised of it, and might suppose Iphi-krates to be employed on his ordinary money-levying excursion.

The stratagem was completely successful. Anaxibius returned on the next day, without the least suspicion of any enemy at hand, marching in careless order and with long-stretched files, as well from the narrowness of the mountain path as from the circum-stance that he was in the friendly territory of Abydos. Not ex-pecting to fight, he had unfortunately either omitted the morning sacrifice, or taken no pains to ascertain that the victims were favor-able; so Xenophon informs us,[1] with that constant regard to the divine judgments and divine warnings which pervades both the Hellenica and the Anabasis. Iphikrates having suffered the Abydenes who were in the van to pass, suddenly sprang from his ambush, to assault Anaxibius with the Lacedæmonians and the mercenaries, as they descended the mountain-pass into the plain of Kremastê. His appearance struck terror and confusion into the whole army; unprepared in its disorderly array for sted-fast resistance, — even if the minds of the soldiers had been ever so well strung, — against well-trained peltasts, who were sure to prevail over hoplites not in steady rank. To Anaxibius himself, the truth stood plain at once. Defeat was inevitable, and there remained no other resource for him except to die like a brave man.

---

[1] Xen. Hellen. iv, 8, 36. Ὁ Ἀναξίβιος ἀπεπορεύετο, ὡς μὲν ἐλέγετο, οὐδὲ τῶν ἱερῶν γεγενημένων αὐτῷ ἐκείνῃ τῇ ἡμέρᾳ, ἀλλὰ καταφ-ρονήσας, ὅτι διὰ φιλίας τε ἐπορεύετο καὶ ἐς πόλιν φιλίαν, καὶ ὅτι ἤκουε τῶι ἀπαντώντων, τὸν Ἰφικράτην ἀναπεπλευκέ αι τὴν ἐπὶ Προικοννήσου, ἀμελέστε ρον ἐπορεύετο.

Accordingly, desiring his shield-bearer to hand to him his shield, he said to those around him, — " Friends, my honor commands me to die here; but do you hasten away, and save yourselves, before the enemy close with us." Such order was hardly required to determine his panic-stricken troops, who fled with one accord towards Abydos; while Anaxibius himself awaited firmly the approach of the enemy, and fell gallantly fighting on the spot. No less than twelve Spartan harmosts, those who had been expelled from their various governments by the defeat of Knidus, and who had remained ever since under Derkyllidas at Abydos, stood with the like courage and shared his fate. Such disdain of life hardly surprises us in conspicuous Spartan citizens, to whom preservation by flight was " no true preservation" (in the language of Xenophon),[1] but simply prolongation of life under intolerable disgrace at home. But what deserves greater remark is, that the youth to whom Anaxibius was tenderly attached and who was his constant companion, could not endure to leave him, stayed fighting by his side, and perished by the same honorable death.[2] So strong was the mutual devotion which this relation between persons of the male sex inspired in the ancient Greek mind. With these exceptions, no one else made any attempt to stand. All fled, and were pursued by Iphikrates as far as the gates of Abydos, with the slaughter of fifty out of the two hundred Abydene hoplites, and two hundred of the remaining troops.

This well-planned and successful exploit, while it added to the reputation of Iphikrates, rendered the Athenians again masters of the Bosphorus and the Hellespont, ensuring both the levy of the dues and the transit of their trading vessels. But while the Athenians were thus carrying on naval war at Rhodes and the Hellespont, they began to experience annoyance nearer home, from Ægina.

That island (within sight as the eyesore of Peiræus, as Perikles was wont to call it) had been occupied fifty years before by a population eminently hostile to Athens, afterwards conquered and

---

[1] See the remarks a few pages back, upon the defeat and destruction of the Lacedæmonian mora by Iphikrates, near Lechæum, page 350.

[2] Xen. Hellen. iv, 8, 39. Καὶ τὰ παιδικὰ μέντοι αὐτῷ παρέμεινε, καὶ τῶν Λακεδαιμονίων δὲ τῶν συνεληλυθότων ἐκ τῶν πόλεων ἁρμοστήρων ὡς δώδεκα μαχόμενοι συναπέθανον· οἱ δ' ἄλλοι φεύγοντες ἔπιπτον

expelled by her, — at last again captured in the new abode which
they had obtained in Laconia, — and put to death by her order.
During the Peloponnesian war, Ægina had been tenanted by
Athenian citizens as outsettlers or kleruchs; all of whom had been
driven in after the battle of Ægospotami. The island was then
restored by Lysander to the remnant of the former population, —
as many of them at least as he could find.

These new Æginetans, though doubtless animated by associations highly unfavorable to Athens, had nevertheless remained not
only at peace, but also in reciprocal commerce, with her, until a
considerable time after the battle of Knidus and the rebuilding of
her Long Walls. And so they would have continued, of their own
accord, — since they could gain but little, and were likely to lose
all the security of their traffic, by her hostility, — had they not
been forced to commence the war by Eteonikus, the Lacedæmonian
harmost in the island; [1] one amidst many examples of the manner
in which the smaller Grecian states were dragged into war, without any motive of their own, by the ambition of the greater, —
by Sparta as well as by Athens. [2] With the concurrence of the
ephors, Eteonikus authorized and encouraged all Æginetans to fit
out privateers for depredation on Attica; which aggression the

---

[1] Xen. Hellen. v, 1, 1. ὧν δὲ πάλιν ὁ Ἐτεόνικος ἐν τῇ Αἰγίνῃ, καὶ
ἐπιμιξίᾳ χρωμένων τὸν πρόσθεν χρόνον τῶν Αἰγινητῶν πρὸς τοὺς Ἀθηναίους,
ἐπεὶ φανερῶς κατὰ θάλατταν ἐπολεμεῖτο ὁ πόλεμος, ξυνδόξαν καὶ τοῖς ἐφόροις,
ἐφίησι λῄζεσθαι τὸν βουλόμενον ἐκ τῆς Ἀττικῆς.

The meaning of the word πάλιν here is not easy to determine, since (as
Schneider remarks) not a word had been said before about the presence of
Eteonikus at Ægina. Perhaps we may explain it by supposing that Eteonikus found the Æginetans reluctant to engage in the war, and that he did
not like to involve them in it without first going to Sparta to consult the
ephors. It was on *coming back* to Ægina (πάλιν) from Sparta, after having
obtained the consent of the ephors (ξυνδόξαν καὶ τοῖς ἐφόροις), that he issued
the letters of ınarque.

Schneider's note explains τὸν πρόσθεν χρόνον incorrectly, in my judgment.

[2] Compare Xen. Hellen. vi, 3, 8; Thucyd. iii, 13. The old Æginetan
antipathy against Athens, when thus again instigated, continued for a considerable time. A year or two afterwards, when the philosopher Plato was
taken to Ægina to be sold as a slave, it was death to any Athenian to land
in the island (Aristides, Or. xlvi, p. 384; p. 306 Dindorf; Diogenes Laert
iii, 19. Plutarch. Dion. c. 5).

Athenians resented, after suffering considerable inconvenience by
sending a force of ten triremes to block up Ægina from the sea,
with a body of hoplites under Pamphilus to construct and occupy
a permanent fort in the island. This squadron, however, was soon
driven off (though Pamphilus still continued to occupy the fort) by
Teleutias, who came to Ægina on hearing of the blockade; having
been engaged, with the fleet which he commanded at Rhodes, in
an expedition among the Cyclades, for the purpose of levying
contributions. He seems to have been now at the term of his
year of command, and while he was at Ægina, his successor,
Hierax, arrived from Sparta, on his way to Rhodes, to supersede
him. The fleet was, accordingly, handed over to Hierax at Ægina, while Teleutias went directly home to Sparta. So remarkable
was his popularity among the seamen, that numbers of them accompanied him down to the water-edge, testifying their regret and
attachment by crowning him with wreaths, or pressing his hand
Some, who came down too late, when he was already under weigh,
cast their wreaths on the sea, uttering prayers for his health and
happiness.[1]

Hierax, while carrying back to Rhodes the remaining fleet which
Teleutias had brought from that island, left his subordinate Gorgôpas as harmost at Ægina with twelve triremes; a force which
protected the island completely, and caused the fortified post occu-

---

[1] Xen. Hellen. v, 1, 3. Ὁ δὲ Τελευτίας, μακαριώτατα δὴ ἀπέπλευσεν οἴκαδε, etc.

This description of the scene at the departure of Teleutias (for whom,
as well as for his brother Agesilaus, Xenophon always manifests a marked
sympathy) is extremely interesting. The reflection, too, with which Xenophon follows it up, deserves notice, — "I know well that in these incidents
I am not recounting any outlay of money, or danger incurred, or memorable
stratagem. But by Zeus, it *does* seem to me worth a man's while to reflect,
by what sort of conduct Teleutias created such dispositions in his soldiers.
This is a true man's achievement, more precious than any outlay or any
danger."

What Xenophon here glances at in the case of Teleutias, is the scheme
worked out in detail in the romance of the Cyropædia (τὸ ἐθελοντῶν ἄρχειν
— the exercising command in such manner as to have willing and obedient
subjects) — and touched upon indirectly in various of his other compositions, — the Hiero, the Œconomicus, and portions of the Memorabilia
The *idéal* of government, as it presented itself to Xenophon, was the pater
nal despotism, or something like it.

pied by the Athenians under Pamphilus to be itself blocked up, insomuch that after an interval of four months, a special decree was passed at Athens to send a numerous squadron and fetch away the garrison. As the Æginetan privateers, aided by the squadron of Gorgôpas, now recommenced their annoyances against Attica, thirteen Athenian triremes were put in equipment under Eunomus as a guard-squadron against Ægina. But Gorgôpas and his squadron were now for the time withdrawn, to escort Antalkidas, the new Lacedæmonian admiral sent to Asia chiefly for the purpose of again negotiating with Tiribazus. On returning back, after landing Antalkidas at Ephesus, Gorgôpas fell in with Eunomus, whose pursuit, however, he escaped, landing at Ægina just before sunset. The Athenian admiral, after watching for a short time until he saw the Lacedæmonian seamen out of their vessels and ashore, departed as it grew dark to Attica, carrying a light to prevent his ships from parting company. But Gorgôpas, causing his men to take a hasty meal, immediately reëmbarked and pursued; keeping on the track by means of the light, and taking care not to betray himself either in the noise of oars or by the chant of the Keleustês. Eunomus had no suspicion of the accompanying enemy. Just after he had touched land near cape Zostêr in Attica, when his men were in the act of disembarking, Gorgôpas gave signal by trumpet to attack. After a short action by moonlight, four of the Athenian squadrons were captured, and carried off to Ægina; with the remainder, Eunomus escaped to Peiræus.[1]

This victory, rendering both Gorgôpas and the Æginetans confident, laid them open to a stratagem skilfully planned by the Athenian Chabrias. That officer, who seems to have been dismissed from Corinth as Iphikrates had been before him, was now about to conduct a force of ten triremes and eight hundred peltasts to the aid of Evagoras; to whom the Athenians were thus paying their debt of gratitude, though they could ill-spare any of their forces from home. Chabrias, passing over from Peiræus at night, landed without being perceived in a desert place of the coast of Ægina, and planted himself in ambush with his peltasts at some little distance inland of the Herakleion or temple of Herakles, amidst hollow ground suitable for concealment. He had before

---

[1] Xen. Hellen. v, 1, 6-10.

made agreement with another squadron and a body of hoplites under Demænetus; who arrived at daybreak and landed at Ægina at a point called Tripyrgia, about two miles distant from the Herakleion, but farther removed from the city. As soon as their arrival became known, Gorgôpas hastened out of the city to repel them, with all the troops he could collect, Æginetans as well as marines out of the ships of war, — and eight Spartans who happened to be his companions in the island. In their march from the city to attack the new comers, they had to pass near the Herakleion, and therefore near the troops in ambush; who, as soon as Gorgôpas and those about him had gone by, rose up suddenly and attacked them in the rear. The stratagem succeeded not less completely than that of Iphikrates at Abydos against Anaxibius. Gorgôpas and the Spartans near him were slain, the rest were defeated, and compelled to flee with considerable loss back to the city.[1]

After this brilliant success, Chabrias pursued his voyage to Cyprus, and matters appeared so secure on the side of Ægina, that Demænetus also was sent to the Hellespont to reinforce Iphikrates. For some time indeed, the Lacedæmonian ships at Ægina did nothing. Eteonikus, who was sent as successor to Gorgôpas,[2] could neither persuade nor constrain the seamen to go aboard, since he had no funds, while their pay was in arrears; so that Athens with her coast and her trading-vessels remained altogether unmolested. At length the Lacedæmonians were obliged to send again to Ægina Teleutias, the most popular and best-beloved of all their commanders, whom the seamen welcomed with the utmost delight. Addressing them under the influence of this first impression, immediately after he had offered sacrifice, he told them plainly that he had brought with him no money, but that he had come to put them in the way of procuring it; that he should himself touch nothing until they were amply provided, and should require of them to bear no more hardship or fatigue than he went through himself; that the power and prosperity of Sparta had all been purchased by willingly braving danger, as well as toil, in the cause of duty; that it became valiant men to seek their pay, not by

[1] Xen. Hellen. v, 1, 12, 13.
[2] So we may conclude from Xen. Hellen. v, 1, 13; Demænetus is found at the Hellespont v, 1, 26.

cringing to any one, but by their own swords at the cost of enemies. And he engaged to find them the means of doing this,
provided they would now again manifest the excellent qualities
which he knew them by experience to possess.[1]

This address completely won over the seamen, who received it
with shouts of applause; desiring Teleutias to give his orders forthwith, and promising ready obedience. " Well, (said he), now go
and get your suppers, as you were intending to do; and then come
immediately on shipboard, bringing with you provisions for one
day. Advance me thus much out of your own means, that we may,
by the will of the gods, make an opportune voyage."[2]

In spite of the eminent popularity of Teleutias, the men would
probably have refused to go on board, had he told them beforehand his intention of sailing with his twelve triremes straight into
the harbor of Peiræus. At first sight, the enterprise seemed insane, for there were triremes in it more than sufficient to overwhelm him. But he calculated on finding them all unprepared, with
seamen as well as officers in their lodgings ashore, so that he could
not only strike terror and do damage, but even realize half an
hour's plunder before preparations could be made to resist him.
Such was the security which now reigned there, especially since
the death of Gorgôpas, that no one dreamt of an attack. The harbor was open, as it had been forty years before, when Brasidas (in
the third year of the Peloponnesian war) attempted the like enterprise from the port of Megara.[3] Even then, at the maximum of
the Athenian naval power, it was an enterprise possible, simply
because every one considered it to be impossible; and it only failed
because the assailants became terrified, and flinched in the execution.

---

[1] Xen. Hellen. v, 1, 14–17.

[2] Xen. Hellen. v, 1, 18. Ἄγετε, ὦ ἄνδρες, δειπνήσατε μὲν, ἅπερ καὶ ὡς
ἐμέλλετε· προπαράσχετε δέ μοι μιᾶς ἡμέρας σῖτον· ἔπειτα δὲ ἥκετε ἐπὶ τὰς
ναῦς αὐτίκα μάλα, ὅπως πλεύσωμεν, ἔνθα θεὸς ἐθέλει, ἐν καιρῷ ἀφιξόμενοι

Schneider doubts whether the words προπαράσχετε δέ μοι are correct.
But they seem to me to bear a very pertinent meaning. Teleutias had no
money; yet it was necessary for his purpose that the seamen should come
furnished with one day's provision beforehand. Accordingly he is obliged
to ask *them* to get provision for themselves, or to lend it, as it were, to him;
though they were already so dissatisfied from not having received their
pay.

[3] Thucyd. ii, 94.

A little after dark, Teleutias quitted the harbor of Ægina, without telling any one whither he was going. Rowing leisurely, and allowing his men alternate repose on their oars, he found himself before morning within half a mile of Peiræus, where he waited until day was just dawning, and then led his squadron straight into the harbor. Everything turned out as he expected; there was not the least idea of being attacked, nor the least preparation for defence. Not a single trireme was manned or in fighting condition, but several were moored without their crews, together with merchant-vessels, loaded as well as empty. Teleutias directed the captains of his squadron to drive against the triremes, and disable them; but by no means to damage the beaks of their own ships by trying to disable the merchant-ships. Even at that early hour, many Athenians were abroad, and the arrival of the unexpected assailants struck every one with surprise and consternation. Loud and vague cries transmitted the news through all Peiræus, and from Peiræus up to Athens, where it was believed that their harbor was actually taken. Every man having run home for his arms, the whole force of the city rushed impetuously down thither, with one accord, — hoplites as well as horsemen. But before such succors could arrive, Teleutias had full time to do considerable mischief. His seamen boarded the larger merchant-ships, seizing both the men and the portable goods which they found aboard. Some even jumped ashore on the quay (called the Deigma), laid hands on the tradesmen, ship-masters, and pilots, whom they saw near, and carried them away captive. Various smaller vessels with their entire cargoes were also towed away; and even three or four triremes. With all these Teleutias sailed safely out of Peiræus, sending some of his squadron to escort the prizes to Ægina, while he himself with the remainder sailed southward along the coast. As he was seen to come out of Peiræus, his triremes were mistaken for Athenian, and excited no alarm; so that he thus captured several fishing-boats, and passage-boats coming with passengers from the islands to Athens, — together with some merchantmen carrying corn and other goods, at Sunium. All were carried safely into Ægina.[1]

The enterprise of Teleutias, thus admirably concerted and

---

[1] Xen. Hellen. v, 1, 18-22.

executed without the loss of a man, procured for him a plentiful
booty, of which, probably not the least valuable portion consisted
in the men seized as captives. When sold at Ægina, it yielded so
large a return that he was enabled to pay down at once a month's
pay to his seamen; who became more attached to him than ever,
and kept the triremes in animated and active service under his
orders.[1] Admonished by painful experience, indeed, the Athenians
were now, doubtless, careful both in guarding and in closing Peiræus; as they had become forty years before after the unsuccessful attack of Brasidas. But in spite of the utmost vigilance, they
suffered an extent of damage from the indefatigable Teleutias,
and from the Æginetan privateers, quite sufficient to make them
weary of the war.[2]

We cannot doubt, indeed, that the prosecution of the war must
have been a heavy financial burthen upon the Athenians, from
395 B. C. downward to 387 B. C. How they made good the cost,
without any contributory allies, or any foreign support, except what
Konon obtained during one year from Pharnabazus, — we are not
informed. On the revival of the democracy in 403 B. C., the poverty of the city, both public and private, had been very great,
owing to the long previous war, ending with the loss of all Athenian property abroad. At a period about three years afterwards
it seems that the Athenians were in arrears, not merely for the
tribute-money which they then owed to Sparta as her subject allies,
but also for debts due to the Bœotians on account of damage done;
that they were too poor to perform in full the religious sacrifices
prescribed for the year, and were obliged to omit some even of the
more ancient; that the docks as well as the walls were in sad want
of repair.[3] Even the pay to those citizens who attended the pub-

---

[1] Xen Hellen. v, 1, 24.

[2] Xen. Hellen. v, 1, 29.

Even ten years after this, however, when the Lacedæmonian harmost
Sphodrias marched from Thespiæ by night to surprise Peiræus, it was without gates on the landside — ἀπύλωτος — or at least without any such gates
as would resist an assault (Xen. Hellen. v, 4, 20).

[3] Lysias, Orat. xxx, cont. Nikomachum, s. 21-30.

I trust this Oration so far as the matter of fact, that in the preceding
year, some ancient sacrifices had been omitted from state-poverty; but the
manner in which the speaker makes this fact tell against Nikomachus, may
or may not be just.

lic assemblies and sat as dikasts in the dikasteries, — pay essential
to the working of the democracy, — was restored only by degrees;
beginning first at one obolus, and not restored to three oboli, at
which it had stood before the capture, until after an interval of
some years.[1] It was at this time too that the Theôric Board, or
Paymasters for the general expenses of public worship and sacrifice, was first established; and when we read how much the Athenians were embarrassed for the means of celebrating the prescribed sacrifices, there was, probably, great necessity for the
formation of some such office. The disbursements connected with
this object had been effected, before 403 B. C., not by any special
Board, but by the Hellenotamiæ, or treasurers of the tribute collected from the allies, who were not renewed after 403 B. C. as the
Athenian empire had ceased to exist.[2] A portion of the money dis-
bursed by the Theôric Board for the religious festivals, was employed in the distribution of two oboli per head, called the diobely,
to all present citizens, and actually received by all, — not merely by
the poor, but by persons in easy circumstances also.[3] This distribution was made at several festivals, having originally begun at the
Dionysia, for the purpose of enabling the citizens to obtain places at
the theatrical representations in honor of Dionysus; but we do not
know either the number of the festivals, or the amount of the total
sum. It was, in principle, a natural corollary of the religious idea
connected with the festival; not simply because the comfort and
recreation of each citizen, individually taken, was promoted by his
being enabled to attend the festival, — but because the collective
effect of the ceremony, in honoring and propitiating the god, was
believed to depend in part upon a multitudinous attendance and
lively manifestations.[4] Gradually, however, this distribution of

---

[1] Aristophan. Ecclesias. 300–310.

[2] See the Inscription No. 147, in Boeckn's Corpus Inscriptt. Græcor. —
Boeckh, Public Economy of Athens, ii, 7, p. 179, 180, Eng. transl. — and
Schömann, Antiq. Jur. Publ. Græc. s. 77, p. 320.

[3] Demosthenes, Philippic. iv, p. 141, s. 43; Demosth. Orat. xliv, cont.
Leocharem, p. 1091, s. 48.

[4] It is common to represent the festivals at Athens as if they were so
many stratagems for feeding poor citizens at the public expense. But the
primitive idea and sentiment of the Grecian religious festival — the satisfaction to the god dependent upon multitudinous spectators sympathizing
and enjoying themselves together (ἄμμιγα πάντας) — is much anterior to

Theôric or festival-money came to be pushed to an abusive and mischievous excess, which is brought before our notice forty years afterwards, during the political career of Demosthenes. Until that time, we have no materials for speaking of it ; and what I here notice is simply the first creation of the Theôric Board.

The means of Athens for prosecuting the war, and for paying her troops sent as well to Bœotia as to Corinth, must have been derived mainly from direct assessments on property, called eis-phoræ. And some such assessments we find alluded to generally as having taken place during these years ; though we know no details either as to frequency or amount.[1]   But the restitution of

---

the development of democracy at Athens. See the old oracles in Demosthen. cont. Meidiam, p. 531, s. 66 ; Homer, Hymn. Apollin. 147 ; K. F. Herrmann, Gottesdienstlich. Alterthümer der Griechen, s. 8.

[1] See such direct assessments on property alluded to in various speeches of Lysias, Orat. xix. De Bonis Aristoph. s. 31, 45, 63 ; Orat. xxvii. cont. Epikratem, s. 11 ; Orat. xxix. cont. Philokrat. s. 14.

Boeckh (in his Public Econ. of Athens, iv, 4, p. 493, Engl. transl., which passage stands unaltered in the second edition of the German original recently published, p. 642) affirms that a proposition for the assessment of a direct property-tax of one-fortieth, or two and a half per cent., was made about this time by a citizen named Euripides, who announced it as intended to produce five hundred talents ; that the proposition was at first enthusiastically welcomed by the Athenians, and procured for its author unbounded popularity ; but that he was presently cried down and disgraced, because on farther examination the measure proved unsatisfactory and empty talk.

Sievers also (Geschichte von Griech. bis zur Schlacht von Mantineia, pp. 100, 101) adopts the same view as Boeckh, that this was a real proposition of a property tax of two and a half per cent., made by Euripides. After having alleged that the Athenians in these times supplied their treasury by the most unscrupulous injustice in confiscating the property of rich citizens, — referring as proof to passages in the orators, none of which establishes his conclusion, — Sievers goes on to say, — " But that these violences did not suffice, is shown by the fact that the people caught with greedy impatience at other measures. Thus a new scheme of finance, which however was presently discovered to be insufficient or inapplicable, excited at first the most extravagant joy." He adds in a note: " The scheme proceeded from Euripides ; it was a property-tax of two and a half per cent. See Aristoph. Ecclesiaz. 823 ; Boeckh, Staatshaush. ii, p. 27.

In my judgment, the assertion here made by Boeckh and Sievers rests upon no sufficient ground. The passage of Aristophanes does not warrant us in concluding anything at all about a proposition for a property-tax. It is as follows : —

the Long Walls and of the fortifications of Peiræus by Konon, was an assistance not less valuable to the finances of Athens than

Τὸ δ' ἔναγχος οὐχ ἅπαντες ἡμεῖς ὤμνυμεν
Τάλαντ' ἔσεσθαι πεντακόσια τῇ πόλει
Τῆς τεσσαρακοστῆς, ἣν ἐπόρισ' Εὐριπίδης;
Κεὐθὺς κατεχρύσου πᾶς ἀνὴρ Εὐριπίδην
'Ὅτε δὴ δ' ἀνασκοπουμένοις ἐφαίνετο
'Ὁ Διὸς Κόρινθος, καὶ τὸ πρᾶγμ' οὐκ ἤρκεσεν,
Πάλιν κατεπίττου πᾶς ἀνὴρ Εὐριπίδην.

What this "new financial scheme" (so Sievers properly calls it) was, which the poet here alludes to, — we have no means of determining. But I venture to express my decided conviction that it cannot have been a property-tax. The terms in which it is described forbid that supposition. It was a scheme which seemed at first sight exceedingly promising and gainful to the city, and procured for its author very great popularity; but which, on farther examination, proved to be mere empty boasting (ὁ Διὸς Κόρινθος) How can this be said about any motion for a property-tax? That any finan cier should ever have gained extraordinary popularity by proposing a property-tax, is altogether inconceivable. And a proposition to raise the immense sum of five hundred talents (which Schömann estimates as the probable aggregate charge of the whole peace-establishment of Athens, Antiq. Jur. Public. Græc. s. 73, p. 313) at one blow by an assessment upon property! It would be as much as any financier could do to bear up against the tremendous *unpopularity* of such a proposition; and to induce the assembly even to listen to him, were the necessity ever so pressing. How odious are propositions for direct taxation, we may know without recurring to the specific evidence respecting Athens; but if any man requires such specific evidence, he may find it abundantly in the Philippics and Olynthiacs of Demosthenes. On one occasion (De Symmoriis, Or. xiv. s. 33, p. 185) that orator alludes to a proposition for raising five hundred talents by direct property-tax as something extravagant, which the Athenians would not en dure to hear mentioned.

Moreover, — unpopularity apart, — the motion for a property-tax could scarcely procure credit for a financier, because it is of all ideas the most simple and obvious. Any man can suggest such a scheme. But to pass for an acceptable financier, you must propose some measure which promises gain to the state without such undisguised pressure upon individuals.

Lastly, there is nothing *delusive* in a property-tax, — nothing which looks gainful at first sight, and then turns out on farther examination (ἀνασκοπουμένοις) to be false or uncertain. It may, indeed, be more or less evaded; but this can only be known after it has been assessed, and when payment is actually called for.

Upon these grounds I maintain that the τεσσαρακοστὴ proposed by Euripides was not a property-tax. What it was I do not pretend to say; but τεσσαρακοστὴ may have many other meanings; it might mean a duty of two

to her political power.   That excellent harbor, commodious as a
mercantile centre, and now again safe for the residence of metics

---

and a half per cent. upon imports or exports, or upon the produce of the
mines of Laureion; or it might mean a cheap coinage or base money, something in the nature of the Chian τεσσαρακοσταί (Thucyd. viii, 100). All that
the passage really teaches us is, that some financial proposition was made
by Euripides which at first seemed likely to be lucrative, but would not stand
an attentive examination.   It is not even certain that Euripides promised a
receipt of five hundred talents; this sum is only given to us as a comic
exaggeration of that which foolish men at first fancied.   Boeckh in more
than one place reasons (erroneously, in my judgment) as if this five hundred
talents was a real and trustworthy estimate, and equal to two and a half
per cent. upon the taxable property of the Athenians.   He says (iv, 8, p. 520,
Engl. transl.) that " Euripides assumed as the basis of his proposal for levying a property-tax, a taxable capital of twenty thousand talents," — and
that "his proposition of one-fortieth was *calculated* to produce five hundred
talents."   No such conclusion can be fairly drawn from Aristophanes.

Again, Boeckh infers from another passage in the same play of the same
author, that a small direct property-tax of one five-hundredth part had been
recently imposed.   After a speech from one of the old women, calling upon
a young man to follow her, he replies (v. 1006) : —

'Αλλ' οὐκ ἀνάγκη μούστιν, εἰ μὴ τῶν ἐμῶν
Τὴν πεντακοσιόστην κατέθηκας τῇ πόλει.

Boeckh himself admits (iv, 8, p. 520) that this passage is very obscure, and
so I think every one will find it.   Tyrwhitt was so perplexed by it that he
altered ἐμῶν into ἐτῶν.   Without presuming to assign the meaning of the
passage, I merely contend that it cannot be held to justify the affirmation,
as a matter of historical fact, that a property tax of one-five-hundredth had
been levied at Athens, shortly before the representation of Ekklesiazusæ.

I cannot refrain here from noticing another inference drawn by Sievers
from a third passage in this same play, — the Ekklesiazusæ (Geschichte
Griechenlands vom Ende der Pelop. Kriegs bis zur Schlacht von Mantineia,
p. 101.)   He says, — " How melancholy is the picture of Athenian popular
life, which is presented to us by the Ekklesiazusæ and the second Plutus,
ten or twelve years after the restoration of the democracy !   What an *impressive seriousness* (welch ein erschütternder Ernst) is expressed in the speech
of Praxagora !" (v. 174 *seqq.*).

I confess that I find neither seriousness, nor genuine and trustworthy
coloring, in this speech of Praxagora.   It was a comic case made out for the
purpose of showing that the women were more fit to govern Athens than
the men, and setting forth the alleged follies of the men in terms of broad
and general disparagement.   The whole play is, throughout, thorough farce
and full of Aristophanic humor.   And it is surely preposterous to treat what
is put into the mouth of Praxagora, the leading feminine character, as if it
were historical evidence as to the actual condition or management of Ath

and the importations of merchants, became speedily a scen ? of animated commerce, as we have seen it when surprised by Teleutias.
The number of metics, or free resident non-citizens, became also
again large, as it had been before the time of her reverses, and
including a number of miscellaneous non-Hellenic persons, from
Lydia, Phrygia, and Syria.[1] Both the port-duties, and the value
of fixed property at Athens, was thus augmented so as in part to
countervail the costs of war. Nevertheless these costs, continued
from year to year, and combined with the damage done by Æginetan privateers, were seriously felt, and contributed to dispose
the Athenians to peace.

In the Hellespont also, their prospects were not only on the decline, but had become seriously menacing. After going from
Ægina to Ephesus in the preceding year, and sending back Gor-
gôpus with the Æginetan squadron, Antalkidas had placed the
remainder of his fleet under his secretary, Nikolochus, with orders
to proceed to the Hellespont for the relief of Abydos. He himself landed, and repaired to Tiribazus, by whom he was conducted
up to the court of Susa. Here he renewed the propositions for
the pacification of Greece, — on principles of universal autonomy,
abandoning all the Asiatic Greeks as subject absolutely to the Persian king, — which he had tried in vain to carry through two years
before. Though the Spartans generally were odious to Artaxerxes,
Antalkidas behaved with so much dexterity[2] as to gain the royal
favor personally, while all the influence of Tiribazus was employed
to second his political views. At length they succeeded in prevailing upon the king formally to adopt the peace, and to proclaim
war against any Greeks who should refuse to accede to it, em-
powering the Spartans to enforce it everywhere as his allies and
under his sanction. In order to remove one who would have

---

ens. Let any one follow the speech of Praxagora into the proposition of
reform which she is made to submit, and he will then see the absurdity of
citing her discourse as if it were an harangue in Thucydides. History is
indeed strangely transformed by thus turning comic wit into serious matter
of evidence; and no history has suffered so much from the proceeding as
that of Athens.

[1] Xenoph. Hellen. v. 1, 19–24; compare vii, 1, 3, 4; Xenoph. De Vecti
galibus, chapters i, ii, iii, etc.; Xenoph. De Repub. Athen. i, 17

[2] Plutarch, Artaxerx. c. 22.

proved a great impediment to this measure, the king was farther induced to invite the satrap Pharnabazus up to court, and to honor him with his daughter in marriage; leaving the satrapy of Das-kylium under the temporary administration of Ariobarzanes, a personal friend and guest of Antalkidas.[1]   Thus armed against all contingencies, Antalkidas and Tiribazus returned from Susa to the coast of Asia Minor in the spring of 387 B. C., not only bearing the formal diploma ratified by the king's seal, but commanding ample means to carry it into effect; since, in addition to the full forces of Persia, twenty additional triremes were on their way from Syracuse and the Greco-Italian towns, sent by the despot Diony-sius to the aid of the Lacedæmonians.[2]

On reaching the coast, Antalkidas found Nikolochus with his fleet of twenty-five sail blocked up in Abydos by the Athenians under Iphikrates; who with thirty-two sail were occupying the European side of the Hellespont. He immediately repaired to Abydos by land, and took an early opportunity of stealing out by night with his fleet up the strait towards the Propontis; spreading the rumor that he was about to attack Chalkêdon, in concert with a party in the town. But he stopped at Perkôtê, and lay hid in that harbor until he saw the Athenian fleet (which had gone in pursuit of him upon the false scent laid out) pass by towards Pro-konnêsus.   The strait being now clear, Antalkidas sailed down it again to meet the Syracusan and Italian ships, whom he safely joined. Such junction, with a view to which his recent manœuvre had been devised, rendered him more than a match for his enemies. He had further the good fortune to capture a detached Athenian squadron of eight triremes, which Thrasybulus (a second Athenian citizen of that name) was conducting from Thrace to join the main Athenian fleet in the Hellespont. Lastly, additional reinforce-ments also reached Antalkidas from the zealous aid of Tiribazus and Ariobarzanes, insomuch that he found himself at the head of no less than eighty triremes, besides a still greater number which were under preparation in the various ports of Ionia.[3]

Such a fleet, the greatest which had been seen in the Hellespont

---

[1] Xen. Hellen. v, 1, 28.   [2] Xen. Hellen. v, 1, 25–27.
[3] Diodor. xv, 2.   These triremes were employed in the ensuing year for the prosecution of the war against Evagoras.

since the battle of Ægospotami, was so much superior to anything which could be brought to meet it, and indicated so strongly the full force of Persia operating in the interests of Sparta, — that the Athenians began to fear a repetition of the same calamitous suffering which they had already undergone from Lysander. A portion of such hardship they at once began to taste. Not a single merchant-ship reached them from the Euxine, all being seized and detained by Antalkidas; so that their main supply of imported corn was thus cut off. Moreover, in the present encouraging state of affairs, the Æginetan privateers became doubly active in harassing the coasting trade of Attica; and this combination, of actual hardship with prospective alarm, created a paramount anxiety at Athens to terminate the war. Without Athens, the other allies would have no chance of success through their own forces; while the Argeians also, hitherto the most obstinate, had become on their own account desirous of peace, being afraid of repeated Lacedæmonian invasions of their territory. That Sparta should press for a peace, when the terms of it were suggested by herself, is not wonderful. Even to her, triumphant as her position now seemed, the war was a heavy burden.[1]

Such was the general state of feeling in the Grecian world, when Tiribazus summoned the contending parties into his presence, probably at Sardis, to hear the terms of the convention which had just come down from Susa. He prod   the original edict, and having first publicly exhibited the re   seal, read aloud as follows:—

" King Artaxerxes thinks it just that the cities in Asia, and the islands of Klazomenæ and Cyprus, shall belong to him. He thinks it just also, to leave all the other Hellenic cities autonomous, both small and great, — except Lemnos, Imbros, and Skyros, which are to belong to Athens, as they did originally. Should any parties refuse to accept this peace, I will make war upon them, along with those who are of the same mind, by land as well as by sea, with ships and with money."[2]

---

[1] Xen. Hellen. v, 1, 28, 29.

[2] Xen. Hellen. v, 1 31.

In this document there is the same introduction of the first person immediately following the third, as in the correspondence between Pausanias and Xerxes (Thucyd. i, 128, 129).

Instructions were given to all the deputies to report the terms of this edict to their respective cities, and to meet again at Sparta for acceptance or rejection. When the time of meeting arrived,[1] all the cities, in spite of their repugnance to the abandonment of the Asiatic Greeks, and partly also to the second condition, nevertheless felt themselves overruled by superior force, and gave a reluctant consent. On taking the oaths, however, the Thebans tried indirectly to make good an exception in their own case, by claiming to take the oath not only on behalf of themselves, but on behalf of the Bœotian cities generally; a demand which Agesilaus in the name of Sparta repudiated, as virtually cancelling that item in the pacification whereby the small cities were pronounced to be autonomous as well as the great. When the Theban deputy replied that he could not relinquish his claim without fresh instructions from home, Agesilaus desired him to go at once and consult his countrymen. "You may tell them (said he) that if they do not comply, they will be shut out from the treaty."

It was with much delight that Agesilaus pronounced this peremptory sentence, which placed Thebes in so humiliating a dilemma. Antipathy towards the Thebans was one of his strongest sentiments, and he exulted in the hope that they would persist in their refusal so that he would thus be enabled to bring an overwhelming force to crush their isolated city. So eagerly did he thirst for the expected triumph, that immediately on the departure of the Theban deputies, and before their answer could possibly have been obtained, he procured the consent of the ephors, offered the border-sacrifice, and led the Spartan force out as far as Tegea. From that city he not only despatched messengers in all directions to hasten the arrival of the Periœki, but also sent forth the officers called xenâgi to the cities of the Peloponnesian allies, to muster and bring together the respective contingents. But in spite of all injunctions to despatch, his wishes were disappointed. Before he started from Tegea, the Theban deputies returned with the intimation that they were prepared to take the oath for Thebes alone, recognizing the other Bœotian cities as autonomous. Agesilaus and the Spartans were thus obliged to be satisfied with the minor triumph, in itself very serious and considerable, of having degraded

---

[1] Diodor. xiv, 110

Thebes from her federal headship, and isolated her from the Bœotian cities.[1]

The unmeasured and impatient miso-Theban bitterness of Agesilaus, attested here by his friend and panegyrist, deserves especial notice; for it will be found to explain much of the misconduct of Sparta and her officers during the ensuing years.

There yet remained one compliance for Agesilaus to exact. The Argeian auxiliaries were not yet withdrawn from Corinth; and the Corinthian government might probably think that the terms of the peace, leaving their city autonomous, permitted them to retain or dismiss these auxiliaries at their own discretion. But it was not so that Agesilaus construed the peace; and his construction, right or wrong, was backed by the power of enforcement. He sent to inform both Argeians and Corinthians, that if the auxiliaries were not withdrawn, he would march his army forthwith into both territories. No resistance could be offered to his peremptory mandate. The Argeians retired from Corinth; and the vehement philo-Argeian Corinthians, — especially those who had been concerned in the massacre at the festival of the Eukleia, — retired at the same time into voluntary exile, thinking themselves no longer safe in the town. They found a home partly at Argos, partly at Athens,[2] where they were most hospitably received. Those Corinthians who had before been in exile, and who, in concert with the Lacedæmonian garrison at Lechæum and Sikyon, had been engaged in bitter hostility against their countrymen in Corinth, — were immediately readmitted into the city. According to Xenophon, their readmission was pronounced by the spontaneous voice of the Corinthian citizens.[3] But we shall be more correct in affirming, that it was procured by the same intimidating summons from Agesilaus which had extorted the dismissal of the Argeians.[4] The restoration of the exiles from Lechæum on the

---

[1] Xen. Hellen. v, 1, 32, 33.

[2] Xen. Hellen. v, 1, 34; Demosthen. adv. Leptin. c. 13, p. 473.

[3] Xen. Hellen. v, 1, 34. Οἱ δ᾽ ἄλλοι πολῖται ἕκοντες κατεδέχοντο τοὺς πρόσθεν φεύγοντας.

[4] Such is in fact the version of the story in Xenophon's Encomium upon Agesilaus (ii, 21), where it is made a matter of honor to the latter, that he would not consent to peace, except with a compulsory clause (ἠνάγκασε᾽ that the Corinthian and Theban exiles should be restored. The Corin__

present occasion was no more voluntary than that of the Athenian exiles had been eighteen years before, at the Peloponnesian
war,—or than that of the Phliasian exiles was, two or three
years afterwards.[1]

---

exiles had been actively coöperating with Agesilaus against Corinth. Of
Theban exiles we have heard nothing; but it is very probable that there
were several serving with Agesilaus,—and also pretty certain that he
would insist upon their restoration.

[1] Xen. Hellen. v, 2, 8.